The Bible in Pastoral Practice

Using the Bible in Pastoral Practice

Series Editors: Stephen Pattison and David Spriggs

This series aims to open up more critical opportunities for using the Bible in pastoral practice at all levels, by documenting the ways in which it has been used, historically and in the present, and suggesting new and creative ways of using it in the future.

Titles in the series:

The Bible in Pastoral Practice: Readings in the Place and Function of Scripture in the Church
Edited by Paul Ballard and Stephen R. Holmes

Holy Bible, Human Bible: Questions Pastoral Practice Must Ask
Gordon Oliver

Using the Bible in Christian Ministry: A Workbook
Stephen Pattison

The Bible in Pastoral Practice

Readings in the Place and Function of Scripture in the Church

Editors:
Paul Ballard and Stephen R. Holmes

Consultants:
William Elkins, Rodney Hunter, John Rogerson and Christopher Rowland

William B. Eerdmans Publishing Company
Grand Rapids, Michigan / Cambridge, U.K.

First published 2005 by
Darton, Longman and Todd Ltd
1 Spencer Court, 140–142 Wandsworth High Street
London, SW18 4JJ

This edition published 2006 in the United States of America by
Wm. B. Eerdmans Publishing Co.
255 Jefferson Ave. S.E., Grand Rapids, Michigan 49503 /
P.O. Box 163, Cambridge CB3 9PU U.K.
www.eerdmans.com

Printed in the United States of America

10 09 08 07 06 7 6 5 4 3 2 1

ISBN-10 0-8028-3115-X
ISBN-13 978-0-8028-3115-6

Designed by Sandie Boccacci

Contents

Series Preface

The book you have before you is part of a three-volume series on using the Bible in pastoral practice.

The series is the fruit of a partnership between Bible Society and the School of Religious and Theological Studies at Cardiff University. Bible Society wants to make the voice of the Bible heard everywhere; this project aims to develop critical awareness of the ways in which the Bible is, and might better be, used in pastoral practice.

We take pastoral practice to be the activity of Christians that nurtures flourishing in all areas of human life – individual, ecclesiastical and social. So it might include campaigning against world debt, managing health-care organisations, chairing congregational meetings, preaching, taking school assemblies, neighbourhood visiting, bereavement counselling and conducting weddings, amongst many other activities. Pastoral practice thus widely defined includes the activities of lay people and clergy.

The project group's working assumption is that the Bible pertains, or should pertain, directly and indirectly to all pastoral activities. However, there seems to be little specific knowledge of how the Bible is actually used, or systematic consideration as to how it might be used better. So one of our aims has been actually to document the ways in which the Bible is and might be used.

A summary report of this preliminary empirical investigation, carried out by a specially appointed Fellow of the University, can be found on the School of Religious Studies website at Cardiff University (www.cardiff.ac.uk). This has been supplemented by historical and theoretical explorations in the practical interpretation of the Bible. One outcome of the project is the production of three books which, severally and together, should enable those involved in pastoral practice to analyse their own present use of the Bible and to learn how to use it more creatively.

This collection of essays, *The Bible in Pastoral Practice*, is the first of the books to be published. It provides a comprehensive overview of the enormous variety of questions raised by the ways that the Bible has been used in pastoral practice both down the ages and, most importantly, in the present. By drawing on the current approaches to the Bible found among biblical scholars and practical theologians it attempts to provide a resource for those concerned to bring the Bible back into the centre of pastoral practice. This should add to the knowledge of practitioners and provide them with some critical and imaginative ideas for using the Bible today. The second book, entitled *Holy Bible, Human Bible: Questions Pastoral Practice Must Ask*, offers an engaging personal view of how pastoral workers might use and wrestle with the Bible. The final book, *Using the Bible in Christian Ministry: A Workbook*, draws upon the empirical research and the other two books to allow pastoral workers to audit, analyse and improve their daily practice. It thus earths the whole series in everyday pastoral reality and makes the series not just intellectually stimulating but also directly useful.

As series editors, we are grateful to the editors, authors and contributors to all the books and to our publishers. If this volume and its companions succeed in opening up more critical and creative opportunities for the Bible in pastoral practice at all levels, then all the work that has been done will have been well worthwhile.

David Spriggs, Bible Society
Stephen Pattison, Cardiff University
Series Editors

Acknowledgements

This volume has arisen out of the project, jointly sponsored by the School of Religious and Theological Studies, Cardiff University and the Bible Society, which was the follow-on from a joint symposium held in Cardiff in the summer of 2000. The editors have been grateful for the support, enthusiasm and freedom given by the Project Management Group, under the joint chairmanship of Professor Stephen Pattison and the Revd Dr David Spriggs. Various people have also been instrumental in helping the task along, especially Emma Fisher in the School's office. Virginia Hearn, Commissioning Editor at Darton, Longman and Todd, has been patient and encouraging and, with her team, has made the whole enterprise possible. The contributors, too, ably and creatively responded to what was a challenging task and have been patient and co-operative in the editorial process. To all these and the many others who have shown their care and practical interest our thanks are sincerely given.

Material appearing in Chapter 10, 'Contextual and advocacy readings of the Bible' (Christopher Rowland and Zoë Bennett), is based on material originally published in *Political Theology* 2 (2000) and is reprinted with permission of the publishers Equinox Publishing Ltd. © Equinox Publishing Ltd 2004. Permission is being sought from New City Press for use of material from I/1 and I/9 of the *Works of St Augustine: a translation for the 21st century*; and Cistercian Publications for the use of the translation by Benedicta Ward of *The Sayings of the Desert Fathers: the alphabetic collection*, used in Chapter 2; and from the Panel on Worship of the Church of Scotland for the quotation from the *Book of Common Order* (1994) in Chapter 13. Every effort has been made to ensure that copyright has been observed but should there be any oversight, apologies are offered and the error will be rectified.

Paul Ballard
Stephen R. Holmes

List of Contributors

Herbert Anderson: Emeritus Professor of Pastoral Theology, Catholic Theological Union, Chicago, currently Visiting Professor of Pastoral Care, Yale Divinity School, USA.

Lewis Ayres: Assistant Professor of Historical Theology, Candler School of Theology, Emory University, Atlanta, GA, USA.

Paul Ballard: formerly Professor and Head of Department (teaching Practical Theology) in the School of Religious and Theological Studies, Cardiff University, Wales, UK.

Craig Bartholomew: H. Evan Runner Professor of Philosophy and Professor of Theology and Religion, Redeemer University College, Ancaster, Ont., Canada, and Co-ordinator of the Scripture and Hermeneutics Seminar of the Bible Society, UK.

Demetrios Bathrellos: Priest in the Greek Cathedral of the Holy Wisdom (Hagia Sophia), London, UK.

Zoë Bennett: Lecturer in Anglia Polytechnic University and Director of Postgraduate Studies in Pastoral Theology, Cambridge Theological Federation, UK.

Walter Brueggemann: William Marcellus McPheeters Professor of the Old Testament Emeritus, Columba Theological Seminary, Decatur, GA, USA.

John Colwell: Tutor in Christian Doctrine and Ethics, Spurgeon's College, London, UK.

Pamela Couture: Vice-President of Academic Affairs and Dean, Saint Paul School of Theology, Kansas City, USA.

William Elkins: Associate Professor of Hermeneutics, the Casperon School of Graduate Studies, and Drew Fellow, the Theological School, Drew University, Madison, NJ, USA.

Roger Ellis: formerly Reader in Medieval English Literature, School of English, Criticism and Philosophy, Cardiff University, Wales, UK.

Philip Endean SJ: Tutor in Theology, Campion Hall, Oxford University, UK.

Hueston Finlay: Residentiary Canon, and on the staff of St George's House, Windsor, UK.

Stephen R. Holmes: Lecturer in Theology, Faculty of Divinity, St Mary's College, St Andrew's University, Scotland, and consultant to the Bible Society, UK.

Rodney Hunter: Professor of Pastoral Theology, Candler School of Theology, Emory University, Atlanta, GA, USA.

David Lyall: formerly Principal of New College and Senior Lecturer in Christian Ethics and Practical Theology, now Honorary Fellow, School of Divinity, Edinburgh University, Scotland, UK.

Michael Quicke: C. W. Koller Professor of Preaching, Northern Baptist Theological Seminary, Lombard, IL, USA.

Gail Ricciuti: Associate Professor of Homiletics, Colgate Rochester Crozer Divinity School, Rochester, NY, USA.

John Rogerson: formerly Professor and Head of Department in the Department of Biblical Studies, Sheffield University, UK.

Christopher Rowland: Dean Ireland Professor of Exegesis of Holy Scripture, Queen's College, Oxford University, UK.

Derek Tidball: Principal of the London School of Theology (formerly the London Bible College) teaching Sociology and Pastoral Theology, London, UK.

Christine Trevett: Professor, teaching early Christian literature, in the School of Religious and Theological Studies, Cardiff University, Wales, UK.

Carl Trueman: Associate Professor of Church History and Historical Theology, Westminster Theological Seminary, Philadelphia, USA.

General Introduction: the underlying issues, challenges and possibilities

PAUL BALLARD and STEPHEN R. HOLMES

The Bible is at the heart of Christian life and witness. All traditions see it as the primary record of the saving events of the Gospel and as embodying the normative, apostolic interpretation of the faith. Thus down the centuries the understanding and interpretation of the Bible has been formative for Christian belief and practice.

This can be seen, indeed, in the New Testament itself. Even as the Christian notion of Scripture was emerging around the inherited Jewish Scriptures (usually in the Greek version, known as the Septuagint, designated by LXX) and the earliest apostolic writings, there are accounts of the purpose of the biblical texts. John 20:31 suggests an evangelistic application and 2 Peter 3:16–17 suggests instruction against heresy. And, importantly for our present purpose, pastoral work is a core and proper function for the deployment of Scripture: 'Every scripture inspired by God is also useful for teaching, for reproof, for correction and for training in righteousness' (2 Tim. 3:16 NRSV margin). Setting aside the debate about the nature of inspiration, it would appear, as indicated by the alternative reading cited, that the main concern in the writer's mind is the pastoral use of the Bible. This is further reinforced in that the New Testament letters and even the gospels (according to modern biblical critical scholarship at least) were written to address issues found in the emerging Christian communities that we would now think of as pastoral, that is, exploring how to live faithfully as Christians in the world.

History teaches us the same lesson. Before the rise of distinctively modern disciplines such as pastoral psychology, Christian responses to questions of ethics and daily living were shaped largely, and sometimes almost entirely, by appeals to the biblical text. So, for example, despite his respect for pagan philosophy, including its ethical content (*Stromata* 1), Clement of Alexandria's language, when he turns to offering guidance for Christian living in *The Instructor*, is full of biblical allusions and quotations. St Thomas Aquinas, asking so practical a question as to whether alms should be given out of illicitly acquired wealth, refers both to Scripture and to Patristic sermons and commentaries. In the Reformed tradition the point is only intensified. Whereas the Catholic and Orthodox traditions both have a strong sense of the importance of the tradition as carrying the interpretation of the Bible, the Protestant emphasis is on *sola scriptura* (Scripture alone), as being sufficient in all matters of doctrine and morals. This can be seen in the biblically infused allegory of the Christian life in Bunyan's *Pilgrim's Progress* or in the discussion about whether to abstain from certain foods in the Augsburg Confession (art. 26).

And in a real sense it continues to be true. The Scriptures are invoked and meditated upon in corporate and private devotion, and the pastor draws on the Bible in some way or other, whether visiting the sick or distressed in home or hospital, or guiding people through the turning points and crises of life such as birth, marriage or death.

The estrangement

There is, however, a real and deep problem. This project on the pastoral use of the Bible, of which the present volume is a part, emerged out of a widespread recognition that there has been a chasm opened up between those engaged in Biblical Studies and those in Practical Theology, whose function is the teaching of the theory and skills in pastoral care. Both groups are responsible, as part of their task, for providing the community of faith with insights and resources for its day-to-day witness and service, if not directly, then as guardians and mentors: the former as providing the foundations and methodologies for the interpretation of Scripture; the latter to support the growth in faith and practice of individuals and communities. That such a hiatus exists can be widely confirmed. Despite the teaching given in university and seminary the actual use of the Bible in spiritual development, pastoral discussion and even sermon is often too simplistic and naive. Moreover it is often difficult to see how to link the biblical text into pastoral conversation, with the result that the Bible is simply set aside or used inappropriately. This is reflected and compounded in the training process and by the structures of theological teaching which often keep them strictly separate. This is clearly undesirable and undermines the coherence of the Christian faith. It certainly weakens the positive and creative use of the Bible that should be seen in pastoral practice. Here it is only possible to indicate briefly why and how such a situation has arisen.

First, there is indeed the emergence of different disciplines in the theological spectrum. This post-Enlightenment development has been one of the results of the 'academising' and expansion of theological studies so that each area of concern has become specialised and self-contained. Each has also, in the context of the growth of modern knowledge and its challenge to traditional wisdoms, taken on and been influenced by other but different partner disciplines. So, for example, Biblical Studies works with historical methodologies and literary criticism while pastoral care draws on the human sciences such as psychology and sociology. It appears that the sub-disciplines of theology often have more in common with their sparring partners than they do with each other.

For Practical Theology this has meant responding, over the past century, to the emergent social sciences. These have opened up radical new understandings of the human condition that have often challenged the inherited approaches to, for example, moral responsibility or education. Thus the new burgeoning caring professions questioned much traditional pastoral practice and attitudes to ethical issues; but they have also positively offered alternative insights and skills. It is no wonder that pastoral care and associated activities are sometimes accused of selling out to the new humanisms, only becoming pale reflections of the new professions, and detached from their own tradition and heritage.

Such a situation is bound to be confusing, calling forth many and often radically different reactions and pastoral methodologies. It has been inevitably a time of exploration and experimentation as practitioners and theoreticians follow different leads offered by different schools of psychiatry, psychology and counselling mixed in with varying theological traditions and perspectives. It has also taken time for the new and the old to blend, to sort out their relative strengths and weaknesses and to begin creatively to inform each other. Not surprisingly, in recent decades, there has been a reaction and a conscious awareness of the need for pastoral care to recover its theological roots, including the Scriptures. In this latter regard it has been helped by finding common ground with some of the approaches to literary criticism such as narrative theory and hermeneutics, which can illuminate the nature of interpersonal relations and the life of the individual and thereby our understanding of human truth and worth.

A similar shift has overtaken Biblical Studies. The specialised study of the Bible, historical and literary, has too frequently become detached from the use of the Bible as Scripture in the community of faith, and this despite the fact that most modern scholars were and are people of faith whose primary interest is to ensure the continuing relevance of the Bible to that faith. This, too, produced a multiplicity of reactions, from a rigorous 'fundamentalism' that requires a false and untraditional literalism, to forms of reductionist liberalisms which can emasculate any sense of the divine reality, looking only at human experience. Again, however, there has been, in recent years, a shift from an all-absorbing concern with the historical, the origins and context of the biblical text, to a greater concern with the Bible as a literary text and, therefore, with its use, interpretation and engagement with the reader. This hermeneutical concern, going back in modern times to Schleiermacher, focuses on the reception of the Bible and its contemporary effects, that is, as Scripture that has to be listened to.

There is here, therefore, a convergence of perspective and interest, a double recovery of the Bible as a primary but underrated, yet complex, resource for pastoral practice. Much of what has been summarised above is the background to and is described more fully in the chapters that constitute this book, especially Parts II and III. Moreover, if there is a conclusion that can be drawn from the process of assimilating, gathering and editing this material from a wide range of professional and scholarly sources, it is that, perhaps, alongside the awareness of the very real problems and challenges, it is also possible to see a growing mutuality in this emerging common ground that will enable a fresh and hopeful dialogue between the two fields and the development of common understandings and action. There are already signs of this mutual engagement; for example in courses on the use of the Bible and schemes of study that endeavour to integrate learning with practice and/or cross-disciplinary study, as well as collaborative research. But such a convergence is no simple process and will only come about over a long period of time. It is presently, as this volume will indicate, all very tentative and experimental.

There are, however, two further contemporary reasons that make it difficult to access the Bible in pastoral practice. First, intellectually, culturally, technologically and socially we live in a complex, shifting and pluralistic world. It is a world that is changing fast and that continually throws out more and bigger challenges to inherited assumptions and faiths. Any recovery of the Bible will have to take cognisance of these pressures and to recognise that there are more and more issues that we confront that are not posed and so not answered in the Scriptures. Finding a biblical way of responding to them is simply difficult, if not impossible. It is not enough simply to treat the Bible as an oracle from which the timeless and perfect answer to every pastoral problem may be extracted. But to wrestle with Scripture to find wisdom with which to enter into dialogue with the contemporary pressures and understanding is not easy and is bound to produce divergence, dialogue and even controversy. Second, there is the recognition, raised by modern scholarship and current cultural and historical changes, that the Bible itself is many-layered, often difficult to accept at face value, even repugnant in some of its seeming beliefs and diverse in its self-understanding. One has only to look at the Psalms to recognise this. Such a task calls for continual patience in exploration. There are, thus, issues of authority and credibility. How can a collection of ancient texts speak cogently to the twenty-first century? Yet the Church, as already indicated, finds them to be at the formative heart of its understanding of God and the world.

Yet another, but important, reason for the tension between the use of the Bible and pastoral practice arises from differences in perspective or approach, a division that to some extent runs through the whole of the theological enterprise. Much theology can be described as deductive in form; that is, prin-ciples of faith and consequences for action can be drawn from prior givens. At the heart of such fundamental assertions lies the Bible, as source of Christian understanding. So doctrine or the ordering of worship and liturgy or, to some extent, ethics have, at least traditionally, looked for some prior basis for guidance in the authoritative teaching. But in recent years, often under the influence of some kind of 'liberation theology', the focus has switched to the context, the particularity, within which it is necessary to seek the appropriate Christian response and which can indeed shape the very understanding of God and God's relation with the world. There is a greater sense of encountering 'new things' that are drawn out of the encounter with the truth discovered in the existential reality, and, therefore, the possibility of fresh insights into the Gospel that can challenge inherited views. Such a dichotomy, however, is not absolute, but there can be a tension between the two approaches. And, importantly, the pastoral is always contextual, starting with the concrete situation and giving primacy to the needs of the particular. Experience tells us that there is often a struggle with the mystery of grace, and it is out of this wrestling that, for individuals and communities, new perspectives are found and new depths plumbed. Practical theology always wants to give theological value to living experience. Yet this is not alien to the Bible or the tradition for, as with Jacob, God has been revealed in encounters, fresh challenges and new demands.

Timeliness

Given all this, it is perhaps almost inevitable that the relation of Biblical Studies to Practical/Pastoral Theology has been something of a neglected area. And yet, as we have suggested, there is currently something of a convergence that makes taking up these issues timely. We are very conscious, however, that this book represents no more than a beginning, a first foray, into almost virgin territory. One of the exciting aspects of putting these pages together was the repeated comment from many people that this was relatively unworked ground. Indeed in some cases, particularly in the historical section, we were told that the soil had never been worked for this purpose. Few had thought to ask how Christian pastors had used the Bible in their day-to-day work in this or that period.

In seeking to address these somewhat neglected issues, we present here a series of chapters by experts in various fields. They come out of a range of different backgrounds from the United Kingdom and the United States: women and men, lay and ordained, from Catholic, Orthodox, Reformed, Anglican and evangelical traditions and with a breadth of practical and pastoral engagement. For each the issues raised in scholarly analysis are also relevant to contemporary Christian concerns. We are, however, also very conscious of the limitations of the material. A decision had to be made as to the parameters of the enterprise. It would be impossible to offer comprehensive and complete coverage. The discussion has inevitably been dominated by the transatlantic English-speaking traditions; but those who write have been and are themselves, in varying degrees, very practically engaged on the world stage on which they stand. There is a very deep awareness of the contextual nature of their own theological culture and of the cultural diversity of the present time. Thus there are explicit discussions of liberationist and feminist perspectives and the African experience and significant reference to other approaches such as Black theology. Areas that should have, perhaps, been more strongly noted, but are not entirely neglected, are the Catholic and Protestant traditions elsewhere in modern Europe (but see the bibliography below for possible sources of information) and the ancient churches of the Middle East which are currently in the news. Similarly we recognise that there are theological issues, such as the Christian use of the Jewish Scriptures and inter-faith contexts, which are referred to in passing but which could have occupied a more prominent place.

These papers, however, are not definitive maps but reports from initial explorations, a solid starting point for further enquiry. The coverage of the topics taken up is not, nor could be in the space available, remotely comprehensive. In some cases a bird's-eye survey of the main territory is offered. In others a detailed description of two or three examples of particular interest serve to give a flavour and illuminate the wider scene. But there is a real consistency that gives the whole a strong coherence. There is continuity from one contribution to another and issues noted in one place are taken up and filled out and given a fresh perspective in another without repetition. We believe, therefore, that there is enough to whet the appetite of the reader who is invited to dip in where their interest lies, and from that point to discover other authors and interests and thus to be led through unexpected paths as new vistas are opened up. Indeed, while there is every reason to read through the whole book, as it is arranged to follow a logical sequence, the aim also is to provide a reference book that can be mined for differing purposes as the occasion demands. It should, therefore, prove itself to be of interest and a resource to a wide number of people.

For scholars, we hope that our explorations are interesting enough for them to want to map out the territory better, filling in the details, extending the boundaries, correcting the errors and taking up the practical issues further.

For students, who are currently beginning to form habits which, for good or ill, will define a lifetime's pastoral ministry, this book offers an overview of an important dimension of that practice. We have striven to create something that can be used in the process of reflecting on experience as they, through placements and other practical work, seek to develop a professional practice that will serve them and their people well.

For teachers in pastoral and practical theology in seminaries, theological colleges and training courses, the aim has been to provide a first text in a neglected area that can be used in relation to a wide variety of courses on the use of the Bible. It also has material that teachers in biblical and historical subjects can selectively draw on. As such, therefore, it should contribute to the integration of theological studies and stimulate cross-disciplinary discussion.

For practitioners, those who are engaged in pastoral work at any level, our aim is to offer help for them to reflect on what they do and how the Bible can and does impinge on their work. We do this by asking what perspectives, insights and challenges can and should inform practice. All the chapters are directly related to practice, however theoretical they may appear, but the aim is to look at some of the theological and pastoral issues that lie behind the need to take decisions and turn them into action. Thus the book can contribute to the process of professional reflection and development which is necessary if day-to-day activities are to be given new creativity and energy. As the material can be used selectively, the busy pastor may find certain chapters of greater immediate interest but that, it is hoped, will lead to seeking time and opportunity to explore further. This could be the book that is the basis for sabbatical study or working with teams or study groups.

To a wider public it is suggested that these chapters could be of real interest to those concerned for the use and understanding of the Bible, for the wider life of the Church or in what the minister gets up to during the week.

The reader should find here challenge and hope. Challenge because these essays reveal the uncertainties and difficulties associated with the study of the Bible and its use in and for Christian living. The Bible is an enigma and often an anachronism. It can speak with an uncertain voice and be used to reinforce unacceptable beliefs and deeds. Just the sheer variety of the approaches to its use can be bewildering. Yet there is hope. It would be easy, having looked at the problems, simply to accept the pluralism and to revert back to a familiar mode, whether inclusivist or exclusivist. But that would be to miss the opportunity which, for all its problems, seems to be here presented. Through such an encounter one can begin to enrich one's own experience and to set it into a wider context, while at the same time offering what is already precious to others. If these pages can be part of that process the task has been worthwhile.

Design and content

The papers that follow are divided into three sections. In the first (Part I) we have asked theologians and historians to examine particular periods or traditions, raising the question of how the Bible was used by pastors in those contexts. The real value of these contributions, often with revealing anecdotes and references, is to suggest how, in an age of transition, such approaches may indeed bring out new perspectives for our use in this postmodern, unformed and fluid context. The second (Part II) offers a series of essays beginning in different current traditions of biblical scholarship, asking in each case how the insights of that form of scholarship might profitably be applied to the use of the Bible in pastoral practice. The third (Part III) is more disparate: each essay begins in a particular context of pastoral care (preaching, worship), or a discipline that is intrinsically related to pastoral care (ethics), or a tradition of Christian spirituality (Ignatian; evangelical), and asks how the Bible has, and should, be used with integrity within that context. The juxtaposition of these two last sections poses the essential question that has been at the heart of the whole project and for which these contributions are perhaps the agenda for the next stage. Each section is also provided with a brief introduction setting the scene, providing additional linkage between the chapters and indicating issues that might be taken up either by the reader in their reflection or in subsequent scholarly or professional debate.

The bibliographies at the end of each chapter are an integral part of the text. The reader has to hand a ready resource for following up the points that any discussion may have stimulated. The bibliographies reflect the style and approach of each writer and do not pretend to be comprehensive. The details of the sources are as given by the writer. While this means that these refer to the edition to hand for each writer, they should be sufficient to enable readers to search for and find other editions of the title published in another place or language, where relevant. It was decided not to have a cumulative listing as this tends to obscure the relevance of the reference and puts it out of context. Surprisingly few references recur with any frequency and those that do will be recognised as important and usually foundational to the field in question.

Finally we should address the issue of definitions. 'The Bible' is perhaps obvious enough, but we have deliberately not sought to address the question of the disputed make-up of the canon. Whether that includes the books of the Maccabees, for example, is a question to which, for the purposes of this book at least, we are merely indifferent. We are assuming, however, that Christian pastors will choose to employ the canonical Scriptures of their tradition in ways that are different from their deployment of liturgical material, hymnody, classic or modern spiritual writings and so forth.

'Pastoral practice' is more slippery. First, 'pastoral practice' can be narrowly defined as working with individuals, families or small groups over their specific problems, issues, hopes and joys. But Christian pastoral practice happens at many levels. Its aim is the growth in faith and practical wisdom of all who find themselves drawn to God in and through Christ. It has, therefore, many facets. It can happen within and beyond the boundaries of the

Church. While its focus may be on the pastoral conversation or in pastoral counselling, pastoral care is also given through the informal encounters and exchanges that impinge on another's condition. There are, thus, formal structures but also the informality of the supportive Christian community and personal Christian neighbourliness. Pastoral care is personal but also part of the perspective of the corporate gathering of the Church in worship, sacrament, hearing the sermon and Bible study. The normative focus of this project's understanding of pastoral care has been on the personal faith and practice of the individual while recognising that 'no man is an island' (Donne), that each of us is embedded in community and we are formed by many layers of relationships and social existence, not least as Christians in the life of the Church. This is apparent in the historical material (Part I), especially in the resolution of ethical issues. Part III was deliberately designed to reflect this broad sweep. The effect is to set pastoral care as such in a broader context, thus taking it out of isolation and showing that the use of the Bible in the pastoral context is pluriform. This is an area to which more attention needs to be given: looking at the multi-level uses of the Bible, from its explicit use as, for example, the basis for proclamation, to those situations in which it lies quietly in the background as the familiar, implicit accompaniment to professional and daily living. The place of the Bible in the Church needs to be much more highly nuanced than often appears. Perhaps the task is to find ways whereby people become literate in the Scriptures so that these are an almost subliminal resource that can inform every part of life. This is clearly inherent in some of the hermeneutic and narrative approaches indicated.

Second, we have no intention of restricting this to the work of paid or ordained ministers/priests; we are, however, normally thinking of those who are acting in some way as representatives of a Christian church in their caring work. A probation officer might spend all day visiting prisoners professionally and regard it as a Christian vocation, but that passes into the realm of what we mean here by 'pastoral practice' when she visits a prison as part of her church's explicit ministry of care and outreach on her day off. Nor do we wish to circumscribe in advance the possible activities, beneficiaries or occasions of pastoral care. It will take place in the most unlikely places with the most unlikely people. Indeed, the examples in the historical section of this book will serve to expand the imagination of most people as to what pastoral care might look like, as we begin to glimpse what it meant to be Christian believers in very different cultures. All we insist on in our definition of pastoral care is that the care, advice, admonition or encouragement is offered as part of the ministry of a Christian church. Under this condition, we feel able to insist that the use of the Bible is relevant, important and appropriate, and so is a worthy subject for study and reflection, in the hope that practice might improve and that people might benefit more from the inestimable riches that are found in the wisdom of the Christian Bible.

Select bibliography

The following are offered as introductions to the relevant fields of study or as basic sources of reference.

Biblical studies

Barton, J. (ed.) (1998) *The Cambridge Companion to Biblical Interpretation*. Cambridge: Cambridge University Press.

Barton, J. and Muddiman, J. (eds) (2001) *The Oxford Bible Commentary*. Oxford: Oxford University Press.

Dunn, J. D. G. and Rogerson, J. W. (eds) (2003) *Commentary on the Bible*. Grand Rapids, MI: Eerdmans.

Freedman, D. N. (ed.) (2000) *Eerdmans Dictionary of the Bible*. Grand Rapids, MI: Eerdmans.

Rogerson, J. (1999) *Introduction to the Bible*. London: Penguin.

Soulen, R. (2002) *Handbook of Biblical Criticism*. Louisville, KY: Westminster John Knox Press.

History of interpretation

Ackroyd, P. R. and Evans, C. F. (eds) (1969) *The Cambridge History of the Bible*. Cambridge: Cambridge University Press.

Coggin, R. J. and Houlden, L. (eds) (2003) *Dictionary of Biblical Interpretation*. London: SCM Press.

Fowl, S. E. (ed.) (1997) *The Theological Interpretation of the Bible: classic and contemporary readings*. Oxford: Blackwell.

Harrisville, R. A. and Sundberg, W. (eds) (2002) *The Bible in Modern Culture*. Grand Rapids, MI: Eerdmans.

Rogerson, J. et al. (1988) *The Study and Use of the Bible*. Basingstoke: Marshall Pickering.

Pastoral practice: historical

Clebsch, W. and Jaekle, C. R. (1964) *Pastoral Care in Historical Perspective*. Englewood Cliffs, NJ: Prentice Hall.

Evans, G. R. (ed.) (2000) *A History of Pastoral Care*. London: Cassell.

McNeil, J. T. (1952) *A History of the Cure of Souls*. London: SCM Press.

Practical theology

Atkinson, D. J. and Field, D. H. (eds) (1995) *New Dictionary of Christian Ethics and Pastoral Theology*. Leicester: IVP.

Carr, W. (ed.) (2002) *The New Dictionary of Pastoral Studies*. London: SPCK.

Hunter, R. (ed.) (1990) *Dictionary of Pastoral Care and Counselling*. Nashville, TN: Abingdon Press.

Ramsay, N. (ed.) (2004) *Pastoral Care and Counselling: redefining the paradigms*. Nashville, TN: Abingdon Press.

Woodward, J. and Pattison, S. (eds) (2000) *Pastoral and Practical Theology: a reader*. Oxford: Blackwell.

Wider horizons

Hunter, R. (ed.) (1990) *Dictionary of Pastoral Care and Counselling*. Nashville, TN: Abingdon Press.

Heitink, G. (1999) *Practical Theology: history, action, domains*. Grand Rapids, MI: Eerdmans. (European Protestantism)

Viau, M. (2004) Practical theology in the northern hemisphere French-speaking countries. *International Journal of Practical Theology* 8:1, 122–37. (This journal has a regular series of feature articles covering national and regional practices in practical theology.)

PART I: Listening to the Tradition

This historical material sets a context and expands our imagination. Our age is (somewhat surprisingly) not so different from those that came before that we can afford to ignore what others have done. Indeed it could be argued that in a postmodern age we need all the more to recover the insights of those who lived in pre-modern times. And our practices are sufficiently shaped by our inheritance to mean that we will only understand what we are doing by understanding what they have done. However, the answers offered in the past often seem foreign to us; but if we are prepared to learn from them, rather than rejecting them out of hand, they can teach us a new perspective on our own questions and problems, and offer a resource for working out how we may rightly and faithfully use the Bible in our pastoral practice today.

Clearly the essays in this Part introduce us to different historical periods and regional variations. Moreover, one of the obvious problems encountered is our simple lack of knowledge, especially for the first millennium and a half of Christian history. We do not have detailed accounts of how pastors and priests counselled converts, encouraged the penitent, or consoled the dying. At best, we might have the advice of a bishop, abbot or theologian, such as Chrysostom, Augustine, Pope Gregory or Cassian. But always we must ask the obvious questions: is this advice a repetition of what was commonly regarded as best practice, or a call to do something radically new and different? If the latter, was the call heeded or ignored? How localised was the practice described? (If a bishop in Rome encouraged certain things, what was happening in Naples, or Paris, or Athens? Or in the little upland villages of Umbria?) How widely did common practice differ from best practice?

A second question, perhaps less obvious, concerns the nature of the 'Bible' that was deployed. Asked most sharply by Christine Trevett in looking at an age before the New Testament was fully recognised as Scripture, this question resonates throughout history. A medieval friar, forbidden (at least notionally) by vows of poverty to own a (rare and precious) handwritten copy of the Scriptures, might receive the Bible perhaps largely through the liturgical mediation of the lectionary, and, of course, normally in Latin (though vernacular texts were increasingly available from the twelfth century). The same would be true of the secondary literature: commentaries, treatises and devotional manuals. The Bible, therefore, would be largely accessible by hearing it read or discussed in sermons or instruction or through art and drama such as the paintings in the churches or the mystery plays at York or Coventry. Thus it was one of the tasks of the Church to safeguard the 'true teaching' in what was really a fluid and often volatile situation.

Even after the invention of the printing press, Bibles and other books remained expensive and sometimes elusive. The British and Foreign Bible Society, one of the partners in the present project, was founded in 1804 precisely to provide Bibles for those who could not obtain or afford them. It is really only from the rise of popular education and mass media in the nineteenth century that the Bible became an everyday object. This is a very different position from the modern pastor, with her choice of translations, the ready availability of concordances, commentaries and other study aids. Yet, in another sense, this still meant that the situation was fluid and changing and that the Bible, especially given its special place in Protestantism, could be and has been freely appealed to and endlessly interpreted.

There is a further issue that is more central to the discussion as set out. Modernity and the introduction of critical historical and literary analysis introduced a new and radical and often sceptical (in effect if not in intention) element in our understanding of the Bible. This, indeed, is the context in which this volume is set, the tension apparent between the scholarly study of the Bible and pastoral and practical use. Nevertheless it is important that we see this modern condition in relation to the tradition that preceded it, and perhaps, even more importantly, to discover that there are signs that we are moving out of the era of the Enlightenment into a so-called postmodernism that both poses new challenges and also allows us to reread the pre-modern world afresh.

Despite such problems and questions, and given the almost impossible task of introducing such broad historical periods, the pieces, in different ways, each provide a helpful, authoritative and occasionally surprising picture of the practices by which Christian pastors have used the Scriptures in their work throughout history, and of the theological commitments and social or cultural contexts that have determined those choices. This, corresponding to the original brief, has meant that writers have had to go behind what are often scarce resources to discern how common men and women, whose stories are often hidden from sight, actually experienced the biblical reality. Each writer has, therefore, approached a difficult task in a different way.

Christine Trevett's discussion of texts illustrating practices of pastoral care in the earliest Christian communities offers a fascinating analysis concerning *loci* of authority in the early Church and how these related to the work of pastors. Despite the strangeness of much of the material here, the pastoral situations described (a wife's struggles with her unbelieving husband; excessive worldliness amongst the clergy) sound familiar enough, providing a point of contact with the modern situation (although some of the consequences are rather more extreme than modern Western pastors are used to, as with the husband's arranging for his wife's Christian teachers to be exe-cuted). She is surely right, however, to indicate that there are close parallels with the fluidity and pluralism of our own time.

Lewis Ayres explores the later Patristic tradition of the fourth and fifth centuries, when Christianity had become dominant in the Graeco-Roman world. This formative period laid down the classical foundations for Christian doctrine and ecclesial structures which included the final definition of the biblical canon and laid down normative patterns of interpretation based on contemporary rhetoric. The factor that was to mould the pastoral perspective of the Church, both East and West, was the emergence of the ascetic and monastic traditions. These provided the norm for holy living and, for example, shaped the defining manual for pastoral care in the West, Gregory's *Liber Regulae Pastoralis*. The laity were encouraged to aspire but it was accepted that they were living in the necessary mess of the fallen world. Ayres, however, focuses on a particular and burning issue of the time for many lay people in this time of transition. Drawing on Augustine's correspondence he shows how an ethical discussion was conducted on the basis of the dominical and Pauline material in the New Testament. This illustrates that the interpretation of Scripture was based on its 'clear meaning'; but that was not in any sense understood as a literalistic fundamentalism but an invitation to tease out a coherent and reasonable interpretation that played fair with both the text and the guiding tradition. Such an approach, which was often elaborated into formal models, was to become normative for the next thousand years and is still to be found in contemporary devotional Bible study (see, for example, Tidball and Ricciuti).

Demetrios Bathrellos describes another context that will be unfamiliar to many modern Western readers, and might offer challenge or surprise to them: the particular ways in which the Bible is lived and experienced within Eastern Orthodoxy. This follows on immediately from the Patristic period, reflecting the strong sense of tradition and continuity that is to be found within Orthodoxy. But its primary importance here is to introduce a dimension of pastoral spirituality that has become increasingly influential in our own time. There are now, through migration, Orthodox communities across the world. Moreover, since 1961, the Orthodox have been a strong component of the Ecumenical Movement. Not least, however, is the appeal of Orthodox spirituality in this post-Enlightenment age.

Roger Ellis's account of the medieval West focuses on two particular moments: the life of Margery Kempe, and the aftermath of the Fourth Lateran Council – chosen partly because, in the former case, there is a rich source concerning something for which we have almost no other evidence, and because the Council was a pivotal formative moment in the formation of high medieval practice. Thereby he succeeds in giving a picture of the complexity, variety and fecundity of pastoral appeals to the Scriptures in the Middle Ages.

Carl Trueman offers a magisterial survey of the three centuries of the Reformation, the Counter-Reformation and later, using incisive readings of key documents to note the way the biblical commitments of the Reformers played out in pastoral practice, the developments into the period of 'high orthodoxy', and the decay of these traditions of pastoral care through the rise of the new religious traditions of the eighteenth century. Although he concentrates on the Reformed tradition he shows how close in many ways Protestants of various kinds and Catholics were in their treatment of the Bible. This leads directly, not only to the next essay but also to Tidball's discussion of evangelical spirituality and Endean's exposition of Ignatius Loyola.

Hueston Finlay, faced with making sense of the vagaries of biblical scholarship in the nineteenth century and its application, again turns to particularities: here how interpretative commitments informed the preaching of three modern theological giants, Schleiermacher, Newman and Barth, each reacting differently to the Enlightenment dilemma, thereby offering a broad typology of approaches in this complex and crucial period. By concentrating on preaching Finlay also shows how scholarly concerns played themselves out in one central pastoral activity. These issues are taken up in Parts II and III, where they are worked out in relation to contemporary biblical scholarship.

CHAPTER 1:

The Church before the Bible

CHRISTINE TREVETT

Introduction

My subject is pastoral practice and the Bible, but in the early Church of the time *before* 'the Bible', before even the third century, when we find signposts on the road to a finalised canon such as the (now much-debated in date and provenance) Muratorian canon and other lists of writings agreed in one region or another to be, or not to be, authorised reading. I am conscious of how little we know about early Christians, and that writers sometimes extrapolate from what are just a few snippets of information on a topic. In fact the sparse and scattered evidence has been gleaned from different settings and circumstances. As Frances Young once put it (1991, 139), 'Reconstructing exactly what was going on is not easy.' As a result this chapter is not rich in certainty and there will be caveats.

I shall highlight some concerns and responses from this time, when to be Christian was to be regarded by some as succumbing to the peculiarity of Judaism and by others as being part of a counter-cultural, potentially subversive, possibly child-abusing 'cult'. Pliny the Younger in 112 CE described Christians as engaged not in a 'proper' religion but a *superstitio* (*Letters* 10.96). This was a time of fluidity in Christian thought and practice. There were many writings (*graphai*), albeit neither an established canon of Christian 'Scripture' nor an established definition of orthodoxy and heresy (Williams 1989, 2001; Wisse; Frend; Wiles). Yet this was also the period when a catholic understanding of office, order and the content of appropriate teaching was growing and consolidating.

Ignatius of Antioch, writing probably before 112 CE, was the earliest writer known to us to use the phrase 'the catholic church' (*Smyrnaeans* 8) and commentators refer to the 'emergent proto-orthodox faith' of this period (Hurtado, 558). Polished insights and manuals of guidance about pastoral practice belong to later centuries, however. In Hermas' *The Shepherd* from

Rome, in the Syrian Ignatius' letters to Christian communities in Asia Minor and in Polycarp of Smyrna's letter to Macedonian Philippi we see only early staging posts on the route to the language of creeds, councils and manuals of pastoral practice.

Given that 'The Bible' as we now understand it did not yet exist, then summaries of theory of the Bible in approaches to pastoral care, e.g. fundamentalist/biblicist; tokenist; imagist/suggestive; informative; thematic and so on (Pattison, 115) do not apply. Analysis has to be of a different kind. There have been many studies of the development of the canon and the early use of Christian tradition (e.g. von Campenhausen; Gamble 1985; Metzger; MacDonald 1995; Barton; Derrett; Koester 2000; Young 2002). We can add to them examinations of the Bible within the Bible (Evans and Sanders 1993; 1997) or of the Bible as used by individual writers (e.g. Hagner 1973; Hartog 2002) and in collections of writings such as those of the Apostolic Fathers (Petersen 1989; Koester 1957). Clebsch and Jaekle, as well as Volz and others, have written of early Church pastoral practice more generally. Pressing dilemmas have emerged as key factors in some writings (Milavic; Slee on the *Didache*), while Elizabeth Clark's fine study of asceticism and Scripture in early Christianity illustrated at length how Christian practice might not only *inform* biblical interpretation on a topic but indeed *mould* it into something distinctive. In that case ascetic practice was promoted by pastors' inventive and selective use of biblical texts. What follows, however, is somewhat different. Here I shall be touching upon (a) 'The Bible'; (b) Christian diversity and the context for Christian care; and finally (c) specific examples of pastoral responses to problems. These last emerge throughout this study and such 'snapshots' illustrate some tendencies and concerns among pastors and the pastored.

The Bible and the pastor's work

'Regarding the basic questions of *when, where and how* does the Bible begin to be treated in culture *as a bible*, the wise cultural commentator will have to admit to a fair amount of ignorance' (Carroll, 46). 'Pastoral practice' is not hard to identify in the period in question. It involved promoting, practising and for some overseeing, care for the stranger, the vulnerable (widows and their children among them) and the poor, sustaining the imprisoned in spirit and in body, providing guidance on matters of family relations and dealings with the world beyond the churches, creating a community conducive to spiritual growth, maintaining good relations within a church and giving guidance to define and maintain (or discourage) relations between Christians of differing kinds. 'The Bible', however, is much harder to define.

The Bible

At first the writings that were read and expounded were those that Jesus had valued also – namely the Law, Prophets and Writings, known through the Septuagint (LXX), the Greek version of the Jewish Scriptures, along with the additional texts of that version (Hoffmann; Pearson). Both Clement in Rome and Polycarp in Smyrna knew that the audience for their letters (to Corinth and to Philippi) was familiar with those Scriptures (*in sacris literis*, Polycarp, *Philippians* 12.1) and knew 'the oracles of God' (*1 Clement* 53.1; 62.3). Quotation formulae such as 'it is written' or 'the Scripture says' frequently introduced such material. The imperfect echo and the free allusion were common. Isaiah, Psalms and Proverbs were most used in Christian writings and the New Testament itself is witness to the sophistication of early Christians' allusion to what is now called the 'Old Testament' (Moyise). It went beyond the mere 'proof text' to intertexture and the play of textuality and orality. Nevertheless 'the problem of the Old Testament is central to the controversies of the second century' (Danielou, 199), even though Marcion (who was opposed by Justin, Irenaeus and Tertullian, among others) and the many new churches loyal to his anti-Jewish, ditheistic stance, did not in the end prevail over Law, Prophets and Writings – i.e., the writings of 'the old covenant'/*hē palaia diathēkē*, as Melito of Sardis dubbed them (Eusebius, *Ecclesiastical History* 4.26.14). (See Hoffmann; Pearson; Hvlavic; May.)

For some early Christians 'the living voice' was paramount (Alexander; Young 2002, 15) and a distinctively Christian tradition was growing in status, whether enshrined in written sources or not. When Polycarp deplored the perversion of 'the oracles of the Lord' (*Philippians* 7.1) it was the Christians' Lord and Christian teachings he had in mind, namely such unspecified tradition as witnessed to the cross and resurrection of Jesus Christ and to judgement (cf. Ignatius, *Philadelphians* 7–8; 9.2; *Smyrnaeans* 5). Like Paul, Ignatius too presented the Christian *kerygma* as equivalent to the sacred texts of the Jews. In other words, 'Christ has become the hermeneutical key which relativises the texts, even as they confirm the Christian testimony' (Young 2002, 16).

Yet the truths about Jesus Christ were sometimes defended using tradition now deemed non-canonical. Thus in *Smyrnaeans* 3 Ignatius' account of a post-resurrection appearance asserted the physical reality of the risen Jesus Christ (against the incursion of docetism) but it did so in a dominical saying not known from canonical gospels. (For the use of gospel material see Koester 1957; Trevett 1984; Massaux; Brown; Hill 2001; Petersen.) Indeed, some of the *non*-canonical writings which I shall use for the present chapter were probably more widely read and influential than many documents now deemed canonical. Some writings we now take to be central for the canon were in fact disputed and even condemned in some Christian quarters (the Gospel of John and the Revelation, for example). Certainly what would be the Christian Bible was already evolving. Paul's letters and Matthew's Gospel were within it (Massaux). Material reminiscent of the Sermon on the Mount, for example, appears with regularity in advice to Christians. Irenaeus defended the four-fold Gospel and Justin Martyr told of 'the memoirs of the Apostles' being read at length in churches (von Campenhausen 1972, 147–63). Gospel 'harmonies' (such as Tatian's *Diatessaron*) are evidence of meeting the practicalities of evangelism and teaching. From the time of Irenaeus it is clearer that some works by Christian authors *were* being cited as 'Scripture'. Nevertheless the acceptable limits of diversity were not yet established in a body of canonical texts.

The pastor

For Christians the fundamental questions were 'How is a life of Christian integrity to be defined?' and 'How is it to be lived?' Some pastors were creative and prophetic (a word I use advisedly: Trevett 2001) in the use of written and oral Christian tradition, and of the language of the prevailing culture too. Ignatius was one, and in writing to Ephesus, the seat of the influential and economically powerful cult of the virgin goddess Artemis/Diana (and also of the imperial cult), he was declaring Christianity's participation in the power-broking and the claims (religious, economic, political) which underpinned life in such a city of the East.

In the letter to Ephesus he did more than offer assurance, theological teaching and guidance on survival for Christians in the place where the temple of the virgin goddess was international bank, place of asylum for criminals, important social centre, powerful political force and one of the wonders of the ancient world. He was also declaring what would be the ultimate triumph of God's plan in Christ, over the forces which troubled those beyond the churches (Trevett 2005, III), and in carefully selected language:

> Be gentle for their cruelty and don't try to retaliate ... You [Ephesus] are the passage-way for those being slain for God's sake ... Let us do all things as if he were indwelling in us so that we were his temples and he our God in us ... And Mary's virginity and her birth-giving were hidden from the prince of this world, as also was the death of the Lord ...
>
> (*Ephesians* 10.2;12.2;15.3)

These 'mysteries' as he called them (as distinct perhaps from the Mysteries familiar to devotees of Artemis and others in Ephesus?) had not been hidden but 'cried aloud', manifested clearly when 'a star shone in heaven', 'and its light was unspeakable, and its newness caused astonishment'.

Thereafter 'all magic (Greek *mageia,* cf. magi; see Powell for a history of interpretation of the Magi) was dissolved'. Wickedness lost its hold, ignorance was removed, and 'the old kingdom was destroyed'. God was manifest as man by means of Christianity's own Virgin. The ultimate enemy was in God's sights, for 'the abolition of death was being planned' (*Ephesians* 19).

It would have been just such claims and promises which made and retained Christians, in this setting where competition (not least from the social, economic and religious forces of Artemis) was strong. The tradition to which the Syrian bishop appealed may have owed something to what we find also in Matthew's (Syrian) nativity story, though he went beyond that. Ignatius had planned to write again, especially about Jesus Christ, but no such proposed 'booklet' is extant (*Ephesians* 20). It would probably have told us a lot about Ignatius' understanding of 'the Gospel' and the kinds of traditions familiar to him.

Here was a persecuted pastor who was powerfully placed to minister to the wavering. A prisoner under guard, he was a preacher even when at a distance, matching his language to the situation of the audience. John the Seer had done as much to the churches in the same province, perhaps little more than a decade previously (Revelation 2—3, Hemer). Yet John and Ignatius came of different stock. Ignatius' writing was not saturated with Scripture, saturated though it was with language which was in touch with the realities of life in Ephesus.

At the time of greatest expansion of that powerful *polis* (under the emperor Trajan), when public buildings were being hauled into shape, Ignatius turned an observation of the commonplace into food for rejoicing. He compared Ephesian Christians to a building. They had grown tall thanks to the action of the 'crane' (*mēchanē*), he said. That was the cross of Jesus Christ which had raised them from the lowest level with the support of the rope, which was the Holy Spirit (*Ephesians* 9.1). Most significantly, however, in his letters he made rhetorical and religious capital of his own situation, turning the defeat of arrest and death into a triumphal journey across Asia (cf. *Romans* 2; 9.3; *Polycarp* 8.1). The Ephesian letter offered a determinedly counter-cultural presentation of processing, image-bearing, temple-like Christians, party to the cultus for which Ignatius was to die: 'Ignatius who is also called Theophoros [i.e., God-bearer] ... you, then, are fellow-travellers, God-bearers, temple-carriers, Christ-bearers, bearers of holiness' (*Ephesians* 9.2; Brent 1998). Their reaction to his message is not recorded. The interplay of guidance and response between pastor and pastored is rarely apparent in the sources. The recipients/hearers are deeply in shadow, being neither creators of the text nor answering back. They lived, lacked, lamented and loved off the page in second-century writings, most of them unnamed or subsumed within groups addressed as 'wives', 'slaves', 'the young', 'widows' and so on.

From much the same period but in Rome Hermas is associated with the aptly named document *The Shepherd*. It is an apocalypse but also a significant pastoral document of this period, in which 'Bible' material has scarcely any place. Its one clear citation is from a writing no longer known to us, namely *The Book of Eldad and Modat* (Hermas, 'Visions' 2.3.4). Jewish influence is clear in it, however (Osiek 1998; 1999 Introduction), while some faint echoes suggest the epistle of James or portions of the Sermon on the Mount. Though not rich in clear allusions to the Bible it is to *The Shepherd* that we must look if we want teaching on repentance and reconciliation in the churches (Trevett 2004a) and on joy in disciplined Christian living. (On Hermas see Trevett 2005, II.)

Evidently, then, appeal to 'the Scriptures' was not every Christian's key to sound pastoral practice, though in the 90s CE *1 Clement* (which did make such appeals) was similarly a product of Rome. The use of the Bible in written pastoral guidance varied even in a single region, and according to the needs of an audience and the nature of a document being produced. Christians were diverse, as were the contexts in which they operated.

Christianities and context

The world of the early Christians was not a 'me'-centred world but one of groups and of stratification: from the *domus* and the *familia* (in which the *matrona* belonged in law to another family and not to that of her husband) to the *oikos* (household) with its extended relationships of household and other slaves and freed persons, its children and dependent relatives. Thus the Household Code material of 1 Peter and Colossians, Ephesians, 1 Timothy and Polycarp's *Letter to the Philippians* addressed husbands and wives, children and slaves in conventional, hierarchical fashion, albeit with Christian twists towards reciprocity and the imitation of Christ (Moxnes; Balch 1981; 1988; Balch and Osiek 1997). The general advice was familiar to Greeks and Romans as the stuff of philosophers' and moralists' utterances about how society should function.

Beyond the household the *polis* mattered, with its networks of a 'political' social kind, of trade-related societies and burial clubs, and with its many cults. As is still the case in parts of southern Europe and in developing countries where tribe and family, patronage and obligation are not to be ignored, the welfare and honour of the group mattered. So did the fear of shame, i.e., of socially diminishing criticism.

Moreover theirs was a slave-owning society, and some Christians were enslaved (Harrill; Glancy). Slaves were cogs in the wheels of the economy, non-persons, sexual property, whose feelings and moral scruples (which they were generally assumed not to have) counted for little. They were recorded as 'bodies' when gifted in wills. In the biblical and other Christian texts there is no critique of the institution of slavery. More remarkably still, there is no word of guidance or comfort to those, male and female, adult and child, who lived the reality of helpless, non-autonomous availability yet heard the Christian rhetoric of modesty and chastity alongside the threats of punishment for those who fell short (e.g. in *The Shepherd* and *The Apocalypse of Peter*).

Our twenty-first-century Christian scene is like that of Ignatius and Alke (*Smyrnaeans* 13.2; *Polycarp* 8.3, cf. *Martyrdom of Polycarp* 17.2), of Justin Martyr and of the New Prophet leader Maximilla (Eusebius *Ecclesiastical History* 5.14; 5.16.13–19; 5.17.4; 5.18.13) in that both involve Christian diversity. To have found one, or even a few, examples of something in early sources is not to have discovered 'the Christian view' on that matter. What now we see retrospectively as 'orthodoxy' was not the monopoly of one kind of congregation alone. Polycarp's congregation(s), that of Revelation 2:8–11, those of the *Epistula Apostolorum* and the *Acts of Paul and Thecla* were in the same region and 'orthodox', but not necessarily the same (see too Robbins). The spectrum of diversity was bigger still when we take into account the beliefs and practices of those who were docetic in Christology (found widely in Asia Minor), Marcionite, loyalists of Cerinthus, of Gnosticism, Encratism or the New Prophecy (Montanism), those who were in theology modalists of one kind or another, and more. This would have been especially true in cosmopolitan Rome (Jeffers; Lampe; Trevett 2005, I and II). Second-century Christianity is 'really rather obscure', Frances Young has remarked, because the identification of a 'mainstream' is problematic (Young 2002, 57; see too Robbins).

Christians, we should also remember, were a tiny minority as well as diverse. It has been reckoned that even in Rome by the year 200 CE they would have accounted for no more than 1 per cent of the population (Stark, 4–9, citing R. M. Grant). Pastoral practice had to be about steering that minority (with very few from the highest orders of society within it) in seas of pagan culture. There were no charts in the forms of specialist Christian manuals, the canons of Councils, textbooks on penitential discipline, not excepting Hermas, and no guidelines on 'inter-faith relations'. Pastoral practice had to be about promoting the very formation and preservation of the community of the Church itself. 'Developing a distinctive Christian identity' was the task. As some see it, it has become so again in our own day (Pattison, 64–5).

The rural poor flocked to the cities and lived a hand-to-mouth existence. The urban non-destitute poor teemed in the overcrowded *insulae* tenements, minus sanitation and often minus cooking facilities. When *The Shepherd* told of the delicacy of the Holy Spirit, easily overcome and choked by having to live in too close a proximity to evil, the stifling *insulae* and the poorly ventilated, over-full *tabernae* workshops may have come to the mind of his audience (Hermas, 'Mandates' 5.2.6–8; cf. 5.1.3–4. See Osiek 1999, 119 and cf. Tertullian, *Martyrs* 1). Such challenges exist still for pastors where there is poverty and alienation, immigration and the enslavement born of worker exploitation (and sexual exploitation); disempowered women and poor housing; even legal action by mistrustful non-Christians – and particularly in countries where political and religious factors make Christians vulnerable. Still the prophet and pastor (whether professionally so or not) are sometimes found in the same skin.

Wrestling and tightrope-walking: the athletic pastor

In an age before mass literacy and with mass poverty it might be the Christian cobblers, washerwomen and dyers who were as much in the front line of evangelism and engaged in pastoral practice as were the like of Timothy or Polycarp. Those were the very types complained of by pagan writers as typical of the 'lower orders' Christian teachers who corrupted youth (see, e.g., Origen, *Against Celsus* 3.4). Standing supportively alongside a co-religionist were not just the *episkopoi* (the solid *paterfamilias* types, sufficiently unimpoverished to provide hospitailty, sufficiently educated to teach and provide readings from the Scriptures, individuals respected in the world beyond the Church – all these being the ideals of 1 Timothy 3:1–7; 4:6, 11–13). Rather they might be such as the visionary Hermas, who was not a presbyter and who formerly had been a slave ('Visions' 1.1), or the woman with oversight, probably a patroness, who was literate and transmitted teaching to the widows, such as Grapte in 'Visions' 2.4.3. Some of these pastoral practitioners would have been better versed than others in 'the oracles of God'.

Different models of 'pastoring' figured in debates as views about authority, office and order developed. This is seen in the *Didache* and clearly in the second-century Christian (or Christian-revised) *Ascension of Isaiah* (Hurtado, 595–602). Its authors were critical of 'selling out', status-seeking and the marginalisation of cherished people and traditions. The fate of Christian prophets was particularly in mind:

> In those days there will be many who love office, although lacking wisdom … many wicked elders and shepherds who wrong their sheep … and many will exchange the glory of the robes of the saints for the robes of those who love money, and there will be much respect of persons in those days … there will not be many prophets nor those who speak reliable words, except one here and there … among the shepherds and elders there will be great hatred towards one another.
>
> (*Ascension of Isaiah* 3.23ff., translated in Charlesworth; cf. Hall)

Those who continued to value the prophets' place in the care and teaching of congregations were finding themselves marginalised as institutionalisation increased. Prophets, no less than 'shepherds' and 'elders' (some people might be both, as was Polycarp) previously had had an important pastoral role in some churches. They had been advocates and comforters, convictors of wrong, speakers of discomforting truths (Hill 1979; Aune; Boring 1978, 1991; Trevett 2004b). They had taught, and (in inspired fashion they would have claimed) created fresh meaning from ancient texts and traditions. It is in their work that we see Scripture being used especially creatively and daringly – woven intertexturally with other traditions so as to speak to a new generation. The book of Revelation is witness to such prophetic erudition and adventurousness, rich as it is in creative allusion to past writings. Rightly Christian prophets have been dubbed 'the first theologians' (Gillespie 1994), though only hints of what they did have survived. In the *Ascension of Isaiah,* and implied in other sources, there was regret at their demise.

The Chief Pastor was the pastors' model (1 Peter 5:4, cf. 2.25; John 10:14; Heb. 13:20). They required tact and ingenuity to deal with unmet needs and ill-tempered *sourness* (a term found only in *The Shepherd*), for congregations might be faction-riven. Recrimination destroyed 'peace' (Hermas, 'Visions' 3.9.9; cf. 3.6.3) and discontent might be triggered by something petty or matters of everyday 'business', or food, or (in churches in which the pattern of patronage reflected that in wider society) giving and receiving and 'friendship' (*philos*) (Osiek 1999, 117). One mode of worship or a certain understanding of office and order might please some but alienate others (*1 Clement*; *Didache*). Authority and its abuse were constant refrains (3 John; *1 Clement*; Ignatius' letters, *The Shepherd,* the *Ascension of Isaiah*, Polycarp's *Letter to the Philippians*).

At the same time it is clear that individual Christians supported and advised one another, just as whole churches and individual leaders did (e.g. in the Pastoral Epistles; in the Roman church's advice to Corinth in *1 Clement* and in its philanthropic provision both for needy churches and for Christians sentenced to the mines (see Eusebius, *Ecclesiastical History* 4.23.10). Ignatius' letter to Polycarp contained a fund of pastor-to-pastor advice, not least on how to deal with 'troublesome' and 'plausible' people in a church (*Polycarp* 2.1; 3.1).

It was offered using a series of imperatives which carried few echoes of the Bible but involved the encouraging commonplaces of the day. The templates were medical, athletic, maritime and of the workshop. Metaphors were mixed:

> Press forward on your course ... pilots require wind and the storm-tossed sailor seeks a harbour ... Not all wounds are healed by the same plaster. Relieve convulsions with fomentations ... bear the sicknesses of all as a perfect athlete ... be sober as God's athlete ... stand firm as an anvil which is smitten. The task of great athletes is to suffer punishment and yet conquer. (Lake's translation).

The 'athletic' pastor Polycarp had to 'stand firm' (Ignatius, *Polycarp* 3.1) because some had a mind to 'overthrow' him. The pastorate might be akin to a wrestling match in which the opponents were in the wholly un-sheep-like congregation. Ignatius was brisk in response to Polycarp's liking for 'good' disciples (Ignatius, *Polycarp* 2.1); however it was the difficult ones he had to relate to.

At the same time there was advice to pray, to ask for wisdom and for all the spiritual gifts (1.3; 2.2). Ignatius provided no fail-safe passages of Scripture to 'poultice' the troubled and troublesome but instead encouraged Polycarp to be centred on Jesus Christ, waiting for the one who was 'above seasons', and who 'in every way endured for our sakes'. There were echoes of tradition of New Testament type: 'be prudent as the serpent ... pure as the dove' (Ignatius, *Polycarp* 2.2; Matt. 10:16), 'bear the sicknesses' of all (cf. Matt. 8:17). Mostly, however, Ignatius' language derived from the rhetoric of his age and class as he encouraged Polycarp to a less selective, less stratified and formal view of his church (Ignatius, *Polycarp* 1–3). He was to speak to each individually and to know each by name (Ignatius, *Polycarp* 1.3; 4.2). Though sermon and liturgy can not be tailored to the individual (Stone, 64) Polycarp also needed to do more sermonising (Ignatius, *Polycarp* 1.2; 4.2; 5.1). He should not be overbearing to Christian slaves of either sex (4.3), Ignatius advised; for Polycarp was not a poor man. The language was not that of the Bible but the task was clearly a theological one. It was, Ignatius wrote, to speak in God-likeness to each (1.3).

Just as trying were relations with the world beyond the churches, as converts continued to live in tension with the milieu from which they had come. 'They are surprised that now you do not join with them', wrote the author of 1 Peter about Christians and the pagan associates of the past (4:4). Converts were at the interface of the Christian and pagan worlds and were exceedingly vulnerable. The pastoral advice given and taken (or not) might determine even life or death in some cases, as the following example indicates. It provides no comfortable outcome but helps to contextualise the dilemma of counsellor and counselled.

In the 150s an anxiously evangelising Christian woman in Rome was warning her pagan husband of the perils of hell (Justin, *2 Apology* 2). Perhaps she knew the warnings of the Roman work *The Shepherd* (e.g. Hermas, 'Similitudes' 4.4) or maybe the colourful descriptions of hell in *The Apocalypse of Peter*. Whatever her source, she was having no success and she was minded to leave her marriage. Other Christians were advising her to stay in it. The advice may have owed something to Paul's teaching in 1 Corinthians 7, or perhaps that of the Roman document 1 Peter (3:1–6; 5:13), but she was a person of means and with good contacts and she proceeded to divorce the man. Her situation felt intolerable, given his infidelities and his table tainted by meat which had passed through pagan temples (cf. Acts 15: 29; 1 Cor. 8;

Rev. 2:14, 20). He was outraged at this final insult to his honour and patriarchal power. In terms of the prevailing norms it was she who had abandoned proper wifely behaviour when she abandoned the religion of the family (children and slaves would have followed the head of household into a new religion, cf. Acts 16:15, 31; 1 Cor. 1:16). So he initiated action against the Christians. Her catechist was put to death. Her fate, however, was not stated (M. Y. MacDonald, 205–13).

Paul, like the author of 1 Peter, would have counselled less 'up-front' evangelising in such a mixed marriage. In dealing with those without 'the word' Peter called for women's 'wordless' exemplary behaviour. They should be like Sarah, he suggested (3:6; cf. Gen. 18:12). They should be fearless (see Balch 1981, 105, 109; and especially Kiley 1987). Appeal to biblical exemplars in this way promoted certain characteristics in Christians and discouraged others (Trevett 2005, I; Young, 2002, 226–7 on 'the collage and moral types'). The Roman woman had not been 'wordless', however. She may have known too much of Sarah to be willing to imitate her. Sarah had been an expendable sexual chattel for Abraham in maintaining his own social kudos and security (in Gen. 12 and 20) and as a mother she had been a near victim of the *patria potestas* right of life or death over a son. It is little wonder that while counselling women to be Sarah-like, 1 Peter allows us to infer that they might be afraid. The woman had chosen to be fearless in her fashion, but more than once (not least by her conversion) she had not conformed to the norms of wifely behaviour. Her co-religionists, at least, suffered as a result. Pastors and members of congregations were walking a tightrope over a determined non-integration/counter-culturalism on one side (which John the Seer seems to have advocated) and on the other degrees of accommodation with the world (the woman might have stayed in marriage and practised a subversive conformity with her husband's lifestyle). Counselling from fellow Christians might at times prove decisive in averting disaster.

The Valens problem and Dionysius of Corinth

The final part of this study brings us to Polycarp (in the 130s?) giving rather than receiving advice and to Dionysius of Corinth, whose writings may have spanned several decades after 160 CE. Dionysius' concerns highlight for us the directions in which some churches were moving and a particular problem with Scripture.

The Valens problem

Ignatius' advice to Polycarp might lead us to believe that he was lacking on the episcopal/managerial front. In the martyrology which bears his name, however, Polycarp was described as 'the teacher of Asia', apostolic, prophetic and catholic, and he was revered after his death as one who had known those who had known the Lord, one of the 'great luminaries' of Asia (*Ecclesiastical History* 3.31.3; cf. 5.24.9–18). Paul Hartog's recent work shows him to have been a pastor of sensitivity and dynamism.

In his letter to Philippi (cf. Hartog versus Harrison on the unity of this letter) erroneous teaching and 'pseudo-brethren' (Polycarp, *Philippians* 6.3) were important concerns, with christological truth and tradition at stake. Some writers have posited opposition to Marcion, for example (contrast Hartog, 95–101 and Hoffmann, 53):

> Everyone, then, who does not confess that Jesus Christ has come in the flesh is an anti-Christ; and whoever does not confess the evidence of the cross is of the devil. And whoever uses perversely the oracles (*logia*) of the Lord for his own desires and says there is neither resurrection nor judgement this one is Satan's first-born.
>
> (Polycarp, *Philippians* 7.1; cf. Irenaeus *Against Heresies* 3.3.4; Hurtado, 549–61; Hartog, 90–95)

The occasion of the letter had been an invitation to Polycarp to expound on 'righteousness' (3.1).

Polycarp responded with a patchwork of reminiscences of material we know from the Sermon on the Mount/Plain and from 1 Peter (which had been addressed to Polycarp's native province, among others). They advocated 'not returning evil for evil, reviling for reviling' (1 Peter 3:9; Polycarp, *Philippians* 2.2) and 'Judge not that you be not judged ... with what measure you mete it shall be measured again to you' (Polycarp, *Philippians* 2.3; Matt. 7:1–2). Evidently Polycarp's concept of teaching about righteousness equated it with teaching created under the Christian dispensation (3.1-3). Jesus Christ, he wrote, *was* 'our righteousness' (8.1).

The Philippian church had had difficulties due to the actions of a presbyter called Valens and his unnamed wife. They were probably a cause of the Philippians' request for Polycarp's comment and of the tone of Polycarp's reply (Maier 1991; 1993; Hartog; Trevett 2005, III). Valens had poorly understood the significance of his office, Polycarp observed (11.1) and questions about 'righteousness' were now thick in the air.

The Philippians were well versed in the 'sacred writings' (12.1), i.e., Old Testament, but Polycarp claimed not to have their breadth of knowledge (*mihi autem non est concessum*, 12.1). His response was made in terms of dominical sayings and a warning against sin in relation to anger. It should probably be seen as an attempt to temper one kind of Christian culture with insights from another one (Polycarp's) which was less dominated by appeal to the legacy of Judaism. The change would be from Philippian concerns about purity/ pollution to a pastoral response motivated by desire to recall (Latin *revocate* 11.4) and reconcile the strayed.

Valens had risen to the office of presbyter while in Philippi (*Polycarp, Philippians* 11.1) and with his wife he had been tempted and fallible (11.4). Avarice (Latin *avaritia*) of some kind had been in the frame – though we need not think of this simply in terms of purloining church funds. Social climbing, lack of generosity or patronage, hoarding of one's wealth (cf. Trevett 2005, III on Acts 5:1–12) or expending energy, money and influence on worldly affairs (cf. Maier 1993, 238), 'networking' for business, gain and social betterment might well be construed as avarice and might lead to diminished provision for the vulnerable. In Rome *The Shepherd* had expounded at length on such matters. Rather than sinning by giving access to errorists (Marcionites and bribery have been suggested) Valens would have been complicit with the values of pagan society. Twice Polycarp said he was 'deeply sorry' for him and his wife (11.1 and again in 11.4) and he may have been echoing the Philippians' concern for purity when he described the wrongdoing in terms of contamination, and the fate of 'Gentiles': 'If any man does not avoid avarice he will be defiled by idolatry and judged as one of the Gentiles' (11.2).

Polycarp did not want the guilty couple to be regarded as beyond the pale. The wholeness of the community of faith was what mattered. They were straying members of the Christian body and not enemies, whereas the Philippians' model of discipline (supported by Scripture and bolstered by events which had shaken the church) may indeed have taken the miscreants for 'enemies' (cf. 2 Thess. 3:15), contaminators of the Christian group (cf. Hartog, 137). While the Asian acknowledged that the Philippians were well versed in the Scriptures (Polycarp, *Philippians* 12.1) he did not exchange quotations of the same kind. He knew only (he claimed rhetorically) 'Be angry but sin not' (Psalm 4:5; Eph. 4:26), followed by 'Do not let the sun go down on your wrath' (Eph. 4:26).

Polycarp was counselling patience rather than wrath (12.2), work towards repentance rather than ostracism of the members. 'Therefore yourselves be temperate also in this matter' (11.4; Dallen, 5–28), for to presbyters in particular fell the task of bringing back the straying. In this case it was one of their own kind. There was special need to be forgiving and not hasty in judgement (6.1–2). Moderation, forgiveness and reintegration were what Polycarp had in mind.

In Polycarp's *Philippians*, as I read it, 'Scripture' was figuring in the second-century struggle about post-baptismal sin, repentance and possible reconciliation (Trevett 2004a). There was no single view in the churches on this matter. What Hermas had 'heard from some teachers' about there being no second repentance ('Mandates' 4.3.1; which may have derived from the kind of ideology found in Hebrews 6:4–6; cf. 10:26–27) might be countered by appeal to other norms. The Philippian church's line may have been tough, exclusivist and related to a sense of betrayal; yet in the Gospel, as Polycarp understood it, there was forgiveness. Consequently behind his *florilegium* of echoes of Jesus' sermon and his repeated emphasis on compassion, mercy, the recall of the wandering (especially *Philippians* 2; 6; 11.4; 12) there was probably response to a list of less irenic citations, penned with moral 'righteousness' in mind.

Dionysius of Corinth

My final example concerns what Eusebius says of Dionysius of Corinth. The second century had no hypertext or chat room of the air but it did have the likes of Dionysius of Corinth. He was an avid communicator at this time when the pastoral letter was of significant currency and one who found his own writings transformed into interactive sites. Guidance got around, just as sermons did in the centuries of printing and just as advice of all kinds does in our own age of mass publication and the Internet. Individuals with know-ledge and known communication skills were requested to write to Christian communities. Polycarp had been and so too was Dionysius. He wrote 'general epistles' (Eusebius, *Ecclesiastical History* 4.23.1; cf. 23.12), saying, 'When Christians asked me to write letters I wrote them.'

Copied and recopied, such letters were distributed beyond their original addressees, just as the authors had intended. Even the 'personal' letter on matters pastoral (such as Dionysius had written to a woman called Chrysophera) would have been an item of carefully crafted rhetoric, its quality dependent on the education and skill of the writer. Such letters might act as cement for catholicity, might express solidarity and concern or be testing the territory to discover how the land lay with churches elsewhere. They were part of the support and ammunition in the constant skirmishes of ideas and Christian ideologies. In turn such texts and/or the theology they contained might be distorted deliberately in copying and transmission. Texts were rhetorical implements of power, but once they were copied and distributed the writer lost any hope of control over what was made of them. That was true also of the texts incorporated into the New Testament. In the second and third centuries the approach to the written text was not rigid but fluid and it might be responsive to others' (disputed) use of it (Ehrman 1993; Young 2002, 11–14). Dionysius discovered this to his dismay (Eusebius, *Ecclesiastical History* 4.23.12).

From Corinth Dionysius corresponded with Greeks and Cretans and with Christians farther afield. He wrote to the Lacedaemonians on peace and unity, to the Athenians on post-persecution decline and revival (*Ecclesiastical History* 4.18.2–3; 4.23.3). Then there was the matter of the churches' pressing need for ammunition to counter the Marcionite treatment of Scripture. Dionysius was in contact with Philip of Gortyna in Crete, who composed treatises against Marcion (Eusebius, *Ecclesiastical History* 4.23.5 and 25.1) and he lent his own intellectual prowess to churches in several Asia Minor provinces who were in need of material on right doctrine. By request he sent letters to Amastris and also to neighbouring Pontus, which was Marcion's birthplace (4.23.6), providing for the exegetical struggle 'interpretations of the divine scriptures' (*graphōn te theiōn exegēseis paratetheitai*).

Eusebius mentioned his 'many exhortations' about marriage and chastity also, which point to the growing second-century debate about Christian sexual asceticism. (This was the period not just of Marcionite hostility to marriage but of Gnostic negativity about the flesh and the rise of Encratism.) Similarly his concern about churches' refusal to offer reconciliation after errors of belief or practice was part of a wider debate (*Ecclesiastical History* 4.23.6; Trevett 2004a). Dionysius was firmly *for* receiving and reconciling the repentant and against a rigorously imposed celibacy.

We may be glimpsing in this Corinthian's (sometimes invited) interventions into the pastoring of churches something of an empire-wide 'proto-orthodox' opposition to certain doctrines and trends. Even 'orthodox' pastors did not necessarily concur about the Christian life, however, and he got a less-than-fulsome response from bishop Pinytos in Cnossos (Crete). There (he thought) the 'weaknesses' of the mass of Christians were being disregarded, as burdens with regard to 'chastity' (*hagneia*) were being imposed. Pinytos respectfully noted his admiration for Dionysius, but encouraged him to provide something less 'milky' in future (cf. 1 Cor. 3:1–3).

Pinytos may have been echoing Paul, and in the way many were to do in decades to come, that is, with a view to excusing Paul's unfortunate lack of rigour. The Cretan was no uncaring rigorist, however. Eusebius had the correspondence and he praised Pinytos' orthodoxy, learning and pastoral care as evidenced in his reply. Such letters would surely have illuminated the spectrum of developing catholic Christianities and the care of Christians in the second century, and probably the use of Scripture too, but they are lost to us.

The problem of texts and of Scripture was raised in Dionysius' letter to the church in Rome. He explained that his letters were being falsified as they were copied and distributed. (Had Roman Christians complained of some things they had heard?) Unnamed 'apostles of the devil' were adding or omitting things, he claimed, thus filling them with tares (Matt. 13:25; cf. Origen, *Commentary on Matthew* 27.45). This complaint makes clear the propaganda value of pastoral letters in the battle for one Christian lifestyle or another, or for doctrine. Yet the writings 'of the Lord' were treated recklessly too and were conspired against, he claimed. The very sources to which he would have been appealing were disputed and disrupted currency also. That has its modern parallels and generates challenges in pastoral practice.

The last word about Dionysius should be about authority and canonicity. We should not think of him as some kind of fundamentalist because he appealed to the injunction about 'neither adding to nor subtracting from' written tradition (*Ecclesiastical History* 4.23.12). In Christian usage we know these words from the 'Two Ways' material of *Didache* 4.1 and *Epistle of Barnabas* 19.2,11, as well as from a number of other (mostly Asia Minor) sources. The repetition of this Deuteronomic injunction (4:2; 12:32) should not lead us to think that a universally agreed text existed, or body of texts, which Dionysius and all who used the warning similarly were anxious to defend. Evidently that was not so. Rather such language served the purpose of many a writer in battles about tradition, perversion of the Lord's words (cf. *Epistle of the Apostles* 7.2; 50.8; Polycarp, *Philippians* 7.1; Irenaeus, *Against Heresies* 1 *praef.*) and in defence of his own work (van Unnik). Yet a closed body of writings *was* becoming a faint speck on the horizon. Another comment on the danger of adding to and subtracting from illustrates this.

It came from the anti-Montanist 'Anonymous' (Eusebius, *Ecclesiastical History* 5.16.3, referring to his anonymous source commonly so designated), who had decided no longer to write, as requested, to guide other congregations against perceived error. At some point after the 170s CE in Ancyra in Galatia (modern Ankara) its church was divided between the loyalists of the New Prophecy and others. Writings were matters at issue at this time and in Eusebius *Ecclesiastical History* 5.18.5 (Apollonius) we learn that the New Prophet Themiso had penned a didactic, 'apostolic' type general epistle, an act that was now being likened to *hubris*. The danger as well as efficacy of such writings was now appreciated. 'Anonymous' decided not to write since he did not want his own words being taken, he said, as possible additions to the writings and injunctions of 'the new covenant of the Gospel'. This shows that unspecified Christian ('new covenant') writings were already sacrosanct for some, so that the concept of canonicity was evolving and being honed in struggle.

Final word

The prayerful, Spirit-gifted pastor (such as Ignatius) might pen his own materials to expound on what the Christian dispensation implied, using tradition known to us now from the canon, from extra-canonical sources and other tradition otherwise unknown to us (*Ephesians* 20.1). One congregation might solicit the help of a good communicator elsewhere, to provide material for combating error or to shed light on a matter of concern to it. Traditions from what we now know as 'The Bible' figured to varying degrees (frequently in *1 Clement*, for example) and it seems to have been the crisis following Marcion's rise to prominence and the challenges posed by the New Prophecy which led to more systematic consideration and defence of the content of 'the Lord's' literature.

Before the Christian Bible was, and before Christianity was mother to culture, pastoral practice engaged with Christians as a tiny minority in the Graeco-Roman world, in situations of fear and need, church-building and sustenance of community, for individuals and groups. In so doing it had to take account of the concerns, language and expectations of the age, variously promoting counter-culturalism or degrees of acceptable accommodation. The appeal to writings and traditions was to a wider range than the Church was later to countenance.

Those most engaged with it in the workrooms and tenements, the wash-houses and the slaves' quarters were not necessarily 'the clergy caste'; but those who wrote about it and whose writings were themselves provision by a pastor for a flock, tended to be. In present-day consideration of the place of the Bible in pastoral practice it may be as well to remember those times, when there was not the luxury, or as some might occasionally see it the curse, of the Christian Bible's long-established existence.

Bibliography

Alexander, L. (1990) The living voice: scepticism towards the written word in early Christianity and in Greco-Roman texts, in D. J. A. Clines and S. E. Porter (eds), *The Bible in Three Dimensions*. Sheffield: Sheffield Academic Press, 221–47.

Aune, D. E. (1983) *Prophecy in Early Christianity and the Ancient Mediterranean World*. Grand Rapids: Eerdmans.

Balch, D. L. (1981) *'Let Wives Be Submissive.' the domestic code in 1 Peter* (SBLMS 26). Chico, CA: Scholars Press.

Balch, D. L. (1988) Household codes, in D. E. Aune (ed.), *Greco-Roman Literature and the New Testament: selected forms and genres*. Atlanta, GA: Scholars Press, 25–50.

Barton, J. (1997) *The Canon in Early Christianity*. Louisville, KY: Westminster John Knox Press.

Batson, D. (2002) *The Treasure Chest of the Early Christians: faith, care, and community from the Apostolic Age to Constantine the Great*. Grand Rapids, MI: Eerdmans.

Boring, M. E. (1978) The influence of Christian prophecy on the Johannine portrayal of the Paraclete and Jesus. *New Testament Studies* 25, 113–23.

Boring, M. E. (1991) *The Continuing Voice of Jesus: Christian prophecy and the Gospel tradition*. Louisville, KY: Westminster John Knox Press.

Brent, A. (1998) Ignatius of Antioch and the imperial cult. *Vigiliae Christianae* 52, 30–58.

Brown, C. T. (2000) *The Gospel and Ignatius of Antioch*. New York: Peter Lang.

Carroll, R. P. (1998) Lower case Bibles: commodity, culture and the Bible, in J. C. Exum and S. D. Moore (eds), *Biblical Studies/Cultural Studies* (The Third Sheffield Colloquium, JSNTSS 266). Sheffield: Sheffield Academic Press, 46–59.

Charlesworth, J. H. (ed.) (1985) *The Old Testament Pseudepigrapha II*. London: Darton, Longman & Todd.

Clark, E. A. (1999) *Reading Renunciation: asceticism and Scripture in early Christianity*. Princeton: Princeton University Press.

Clebsch, W. A. and Jaekle, C. R. (1964) *Pastoral Care in Historical Perspective*. New York: Jason Aronson.

Dallen, J. (1992) *The Reconciling Community: the Rite of Penance*. Collegeville, MN: Pueblo Publishing.

Danielou, J. (1973) *Gospel Message and Hellenistic Culture*. London: Darton, Longman & Todd.

Dehandschutter, B. (1986) Polycarp's Epistle to the Philippians: an early example of

'Reception', in J.-M. Sevrin (ed.), *The New Testament in Early Christianity* (BETL 86). Leuven: Leuven University Press, 275–91.

Derrett, J. D. M. (1993) Scripture and norms in the Apostolic Fathers, in W. Hasse and H. Temporini (eds), *Aufstieg und Niedergang der römischen Welt* II.27.1. Berlin: de Gruyter, 649–99.

Duff, P. B. (2001) *Who Rides the Beast? prophetic rivalry and the rhetoric of crisis in the churches of the Apocalypse*. Oxford: Oxford University Press.

Ehrman, B. D. (1993) *The Orthodox Corruption of Scripture: the effect of christological controversies on the text of the New Testament*. Oxford: Oxford University Press.

Ehrman, B. D. (1996) The text of the gospels at the end of the second century, in D. C. Parker and C.-B. Amphaux (eds), *Codex Bezae: Studies from the Lund Colloquium*. Leiden: Brill, 95–122.

Evans, C. A. (1993) Listening for the echoes of interpreted Scripture, in C. A. Evans and J. A. Sanders (eds) *Paul and the Scriptures of Israel* (JSNTSS 83). Sheffield: Sheffield Academic Press, 47–51.

Evans, C. A. (ed.) (1997) *Early Christian Interpretation of the Scriptures of Israel* (JSNTSS 148). Sheffield: Sheffield Academic Press.

Frend, W. H. C. (1997) Christianity in the Second Century: orthodoxy and diversity. *Journal of Ecclesiastical History* 48, 302–13.

Gamble, H. Y. (1985) *The New Testament Canon: its making and meaning*. Philadelphia: Fortress Press.

Gamble, H. Y. (1995) *Books and Readers in the Early Church: a history of early Christian texts.* New Haven, CT: Yale University Press.

Gillespie, T. W. (1994) *The First Theologians: a study in early Christian prophecy*. Grand Rapids, MI: Eerdmans.

Glancy, J. A. (2002) *Slavery in Early Christianity*. Oxford: Oxford University Press.

Hagner, D. A. (1973) *The Use of the Old and New Testaments in Clement of Rome* (Suppl. Nov.Test. 34). Leiden: Brill.

Hall, R. G. (1990) The *Ascension of Isaiah*: community, situation, place and date in early Christianity. *Journal of Biblical Literature* 109, 289–306.

Harrill, J. A. (1995) *The Manumission of Slaves in Early Christianity*. Tübingen: Mohr-Siebeck.

Harrison, P. N. (1936) *Polycarp's Two Epistles to the Philippians*. Cambridge: Cambridge University Press.

Hartog, P. (2002) *Polycarp and the New Testament: the occasion, rhetoric, theme and unity of the Epistle to the Philippians* (WUNT 2.134). Tübingen: Mohr-Siebeck.

Hazlett, I. (ed.) (1991) *Early Christianity: origins and evolution to* AD *600: in honour of W. H. C. Frend*. London: SPCK.

Helleman, W. E. (ed.) (1994) *Hellenization Revisited: shaping a Christian response within the Greco-Roman world*. Lanham, MD: University Press of America.

Hemer, C. J. (1986) *The Letters to the Seven Churches of Asia in Their Local Setting* (SNTSS 11). Sheffield: Sheffield Academic Press.

Hill, C. E. (2001) Ignatius and the apostolate: the witness of Ignatius to the emergence of Christian Scripture, in M. F. Wiles and E. J. Yarnold (eds) *Studia Patristica* 36. Leuven: Peeters Press, 226–48.

Hill, D. (1979) *New Testament Prophecy*. Basingstoke: Marshall, Morgan & Scott.

Hoffmann, R. J. (1984) *Marcion: on the restitution of Christianity*. Chico, CA: American Academy of Religion; Scholars Press.

Hurtado, L. W. (2003), *Lord Jesus Christ: devotion to Jesus in earliest Christianity*. Cambridge: Eerdmans.

Hvlavic, R. (1996) *The Struggle for Scripture and Covenant: the purpose of the* Epistle of Barnabas *and Jewish–Christian competition in the second century* (WUNT 2.82). Tübingen: Mohr-Siebeck.

Jeffers, J. S. (1991) *Conflict at Rome: social order and hierarchy in early Christianity*. Minneapolis, MN: Augsburg Fortress Press.

Kiley, M. (1987) Like Sara: the tale of terror behind 1 Peter 3:6. *Journal of Biblical Literature* 106, 689–92.

Koester, H. (1957) *Synoptische Überlieferung bei den Apostolischen Vätern*, TU 65. Berlin: Akademie Verlag.

Koester, H (2000) *Ancient Christian Gospels: their history and development*. London: SCM Press.

Kreider, A. (ed.) (1991) *The Origins of Christendom in the West*. Edinburgh: Continuum/T&T Clark.

Lake, K. (1977) *The Apostolic Fathers* (LCL, 2 vols). London: Heinemann.

Lampe, P. (2003) *From Paul to Valentinus: Christians at Rome in the first two centuries*. London: Continuum.

MacDonald, L. M. (1995) *The Formation of the Christian Bible Canon* (rev. edn). Peabody, MA: Hendrickson.

MacDonald, M. Y. (1996) *Early Christian Women and Pagan Opinion: the power of the hysterical woman*. Cambridge: Cambridge University Press.

Maier, H. O. (1991) *The Social Setting of the Ministry as Reflected in the Writings of Hermas, Clement and Ignatius*. Waterloo, Ontario: Laurier.

Maier, H. O. (1993), Purity and danger in Polycarp's Epistle to the Philippians: the sin of Valens in social perspective. *Journal of Early Christian Studies* 1. 229–47.

Massaux, E. (1990) *The Influence of the Gospel of St. Matthew on Christian Literature before St. Irenaeus*. Leuven: Peeters Press.

May, G. (ed.) (2002) *Marcion und seine Kirchengeschichte/Marcion and his Input in Church History*. Berlin: de Gruyter.

Metzger, B. (1985) *The Canon of the New Testament, Its Origins, Development and Significance*. Oxford: Oxford University Press.

Milavec, A. (1989) The pastoral genius of the *Didache*: an analytical translation and commentary, in J. Neusner, E. S. Frerichs and A-J. Levine (eds), *Religious Writings and Religious Systems II (Christianity)*. Atlanta: Rowman & Littlefield, 89–125.

Moyise, S. (2001) *The Old Testament in the New Testament*. London: Continuum.

Moxnes, H. (ed.) (1997) *Constructing Early Christian Families: family as social reality and metaphor*. London: Routledge.

Osiek, C. (1983) *Rich and Poor in the* Shepherd of Hermas*: an exegetical-social investigation*. Washington, DC: Catholic Biblical Association of America.

Osiek, C. and Balch, D. L. (1997) *Families in the New Testament World: households and house churches*. Louisville, KY: Westminster John Knox Press.

Osiek, C. (1998) The oral world of early Christianity in Rome: the case of Hermas, in K. P. Donfried and P. Richardson (eds), *Judaism and Christianity in First Century Rome*. Grand Rapids, MI: Eerdmans, 151–72.

Osiek. C. (1999) *The Shepherd of Hermas: a commentary*. Minneapolis, MN: Augsburg Fortress Press.

Pattison, S. (2000) *A Critique of Pastoral Care*. London: SCM Press.

Pearson, B. (1990) *Gnosticism, Judaism and Egyptian Christianity*. Minneapolis, MN: Fortress Press.

Petersen, W. L. (ed.) (1989) *Gospel Traditions in the Second Century: origins, recensions, text and transmission*. London: University of Notre Dame Press.

Powell, M. A. (2000) The Magi as wise-men: re-examining a basic supposition. *New Testament Studies* 46, 1–20.

Robbins, V. K. (1996) *The Tapestry of Early Christian Discourse: rhetoric, society and ideology*. London: Routledge.

Rogerson, J., Rowland, C. and Lindars, B. (1988) *The Study and Use of the Bible II*. Basingstoke: Marshall, Morgan & Scott.

Slee, M. T. (2003) *The Church in Antioch in the First Century CE: communion and conflict*. Sheffield: Sheffield Academic Press.

Stark, R. (1996) *The Rise of Christianity: a sociologist considers history*. Princeton: Princeton University Press.

Stone, H. W. (1988) *The Word of God and Pastoral Care*. Nashville, TN: Abingdon.

Trevett, C. (1984) Approaching Matthew from the second century: the under-used Ignatian correspondence. *Journal for the Study of the New Testament* 20.59–67.

Trevett, C. (1996) *Montanism: gender, authority and the New Prophecy*. Cambridge: Cambridge University Press.

Trevett, C. (2001) Charisma and office in a changing church, in A. Kreider (ed.), *The Origins of Christendom in the West*, 181–205.

Trevett, C. (2004a) 'I have heard from some teachers': the second century struggle for forgiveness and reconciliation, in K. Cooper (ed.), *Retribution, Repentance, Reconciliation*. Woodbridge: Boydell & Brewer.

Trevett, C. (2004b) Early Christian prophets: wanderings, women and the course of change, in M. Riedl and T. Schabert (eds), *Propheten und Propheziehungen/Prophets and Prophecies* (ERANOS n.f.12). Wurzburg: Königshausen Neumann.

Trevett, C. (2005) *Christian Women and the Time of the Apostolic Fathers (pre 160 CE): Corinth, Rome and Asia Minor*. Cardiff: University of Wales Press.

van Unnik W. C. (1949) *Mete prostheinai mete aphelein*, dans l'histoire du canon. *Vigiliae Christianae* 3.1–6.

Volz, C. A. (1990) *Pastoral Life and Practice in the Early Church*. Minneapolis, MN: Augsburg Fortress Press.

von Campenhausen, H. (1969) *Ecclesiastical Authority and Spiritual Power in the Church of the First Three Centuries*. London: A. & C. Black.

von Campenhausen (1972) *The Formation of the Christian Bible*. Philadelphia: Fortress Press.

Wiles, M. (1991) Orthodoxy and Heresy, in I. Hazlett (ed.), *Early Christianity: origins and evolution to AD 600: in honuor of W. H. C. Frend*, 198–207.

Wilken, R. L. (2004) *The Church's Bible*. Grand Rapids, MI: Eerdmans.

Williams, R. (1989) Does it make sense to speak of pre-Nicene orthodoxy?, in R. Williams (ed.), *The Making of Orthodoxy: Essays in Honour of Henry Chadwick*. Cambridge: Cambridge University Press, 1–23.

Williams, R. (2001) Defining heresy, in A. Kreider (ed.), *The Origins of Christendom in the West*, 313–335.

Wisse, F. (1986) The use of early Christian literature as evidence for inner diversity and conflict, in C. W. Hedrick and R. Hodgson Jr (eds), *Nag Hammadi, Gnosticism and early Christianity*. Peabody, MA: Hendrickson, 177–90.

Young, F. M. (1991) The Greek Fathers, in I. Hazlett (ed.), *Early Christianity: Origins and evolution to AD 600*, 135–47.

Young, F. M. (2002) *Biblical Exegesis and the Formation of Christian Culture*, Peabody, MA: Hendrickson.

CHAPTER 2:
The Patristic hermeneutic heritage

LEWIS AYRES

Introduction

In order to understand the pastoral use of the Bible in early Christianity we must bear in mind two questions. First, we must ask ourselves how we characterise the boundaries of 'pastoral'. Second, we need to understand how early Christians saw the nature and function of Scripture.

Early Christians and early Christian ministers faced a range of pastoral situations that were no less complex than those faced today and in many cases they faced the same situations. From the sermons, letters, lives and theological treatises that survive, however, it is clear that at least those early Christians who could write understood their daily lives as Christians to be part of a process of purification and transformation, a training of the soul and body so that attention to the divine will and presence could be restored. Their concern with patterns of human behaviour and relationships was thus one of concern for those patterns that would aid in and reflect a soul being transformed. Although it is dangerous to try to summarise the attitude of thinkers over a period that covers many hundreds of years, especially one that involved so much development, we might say that for early Christians the effects of human sin were both noetic and ontological. On the one hand, sinful humanity was unable to discern the will of God for the world. Despite the omnipresence of God and the intended function of the creation as a revealing of the divine, sin had clouded the vision natural to humanity. On the other hand, the sinfulness of humanity resulted in human weakness before the corruption of fallen habits: the indwelling of God, the grace of God, was necessary for humanity to attend to God again. It is important to note that there were exceptions to this picture and that the universal effects of sin could be assumed in theologies with or without a strong account of original sin. Within this context the day-to-day lives of Christians were understood as part of an ongoing and slow process of purification of the mind, enabling it to attend to God and appropriately govern the body. The emergence of early Christian ascetic traditions witnesses to the development of a very widespread assumption that training the body was an inseparable part of training the soul (see Wilken 2003).

Within this picture understanding the function of Scripture is inseparable from the function of the incarnation. Just as the human Christ revealed the mystery of God, so too Scripture revealed that mystery, providing a language for humanity to understand God's dealing with Israel up to the coming of Christ, for understanding the significance of Christ and for understanding the transformation Christians undergo as they are transformed into his image and incorporated into his person. If we are to see how early Christians approached pastoral concerns we will need to begin by understanding something of their most basic categories for reading Scripture. For the purposes of this chapter I have focused on examples from the fourth and fifth centuries of the Christian era, a period of huge doctrinal significance and the period within which we begin to see more and more clearly the ways in which Christians approached complex pastoral problems. The categories that I sketch here are ones that were true for most Christian exegetes throughout the early Christian period, but they also reflect the deep engagement with Greek and Roman educational practices and reading techniques that was particularly important from the second century.

Categories for reading Scripture

Early Christian exegesis takes as its point of departure the 'plain' sense of the text of Scripture. I avoid the term 'literal sense' because it is frequently associated in modern discussion with the sense intended by the human author of a text or the sense that a text had for its initial readers. The plain sense is 'the way the words run' for a community in the light of that community's techniques for following the argument of texts. The plain sense is, then, the sense that a text had for a Christian of the period versed in ancient literary critical skills. The plain sense is pluralistic in a number of ways. A number of fourth- and fifth-century authors assume that one might understand 'the way the words run' in different ways. Augustine, for example, argues that one can read Revelation. 20:4 – which speaks of the saints reigning with Christ for a thousand years – as a prophecy of a literal thousand-year period *or* as a description of the Church's symbolic thousand-year existence. The reading one adopts depends largely on which figure of speech one takes to be used. Some writers explicitly state that God providentially ordered the words so that they could be taken in different ways. For some the flexibility of the plain sense results from its speaking about realities that are beyond comprehension.

Of course, early Christian readers do frequently equate the author's presumed intention with a text's plain sense. This equation needs, however, to be qualified. On the one hand, it is qualified by the frequent claim that the ultimate author of a text is God. By the shaping of events or the inspiration of human authors God may intend the words of a text to carry a multiple 'plain sense'. On the other hand, early Christian exegetes assume that the 'mind of the author' is to be discerned by a focus on elucidating the text, not by reconstructing the world within which the author wrote and by assuming that such a world was marked by a symbolic universe and by social structures distinct from those of the reader. This elision or lack of recognition of distinctions between the imaginative universe of reader and writer or text enables particular patterns in the text to serve as direct descriptors of the reader's world and community. The absence of modern historicist and social scientific concerns gives a different texture to interest in 'what the author intended'.

The plain sense was also pluralistic because early Christian exegetes assumed that many texts had a variety of functions in the education of the Christian mind. Almost all early Christian authors assume that one may also read the plain sense of many passages using different techniques as a 'figural' resource for the Christian seeking to grow in understanding of the mystery and process of purification in Christ (discussed in more detail below). When we seek to understand this variety of ways of reading the text, it is more helpful to speak of different reading practices than different 'levels' of the text. The plain sense is not abandoned as the reader moves to different 'levels' of the text, the plain sense itself *contains* different senses. As we shall see, the words and flow of the plain sense still shape and police figural readings. Having contended that early Christian exegesis focuses on the 'plain sense', I suggest we now divide early Christian exegetical/hermeneutical strategies into two categories, the 'grammatical' and the 'figural'. These categories are not mutually exclusive: 'grammatical' techniques are also used within 'figural' practices. Grammatical techniques are, however, the fundamental reading tools, essential for the good reading of Scripture.

Grammatical techniques have at their core skills learned at the hands of the *grammatikos* (in Greek) or *grammaticus* (in Latin). The *grammatikos* was broadly responsible for the education of children in their teenage years, but ancient education was highly flexible: grammatical studies were, however, the foundation of any later studies. They provided students not only with techniques and skills for reading, but also with a sense of the appropriate order to be followed in applying these techniques and of the ends of textual interpretation. A student was taught to begin with textual and manuscript criticism, especially important in an age when texts were hand copied. Then came practice in reading a text aloud. In an age without punctuation, this combination of literary-critical and oral techniques enabled students to identify who was speaking at a given point, and how to attribute passages to the characters speaking in the text. Next, students learned to identify historical and literary references and to apply appropriate medical, scientific or philosophical knowledge to understand the vocabulary or argument.

Faced with difficult passages, students would also learn to identify rhetorical techniques used and the plot and direction of a text: its *skopos* or *oikonomia* or *hypothesis*. When modern historical-critical scholars describe early Christian exegesis, they often identify an apparent lack of interest in interpreting terms within their immediate textual context. While this is by no means universally so, it is indeed true that Christian adaptation of ancient reading practices pushed Christians in certain directions. On the one hand, when Christians talk about the *skopos* of Scripture they usually refer to Scripture understood *as a unit*. The text of Scripture is taken to be a resource enabling a consistent, unitary vision of God and the order of creation. The function of Scripture for the Christian community pushes Christians to search for a canonical unity beyond that provided by the sense of any one discrete passage. On the other hand, perception of the unity of Scriptural teaching – as a necessary result of Scripture's function in the economy of salvation – makes Christians attentive to the individual terms used in Scripture. The function of Scripture as Scripture pushes Christians toward particular applications and adaptations of grammatical practice.

The final stage of textual analysis as taught by the *grammatikos* was judgement of a text, evaluating its moral content and drawing its lessons. This was both the capstone and the foundation of grammatical study. Greek and Roman children learned to treat this aspect of exegesis as its culmination *and*, from the very beginning of their education, to absorb moral maxims that they could find illustrated in classical texts. Understanding this moral aspect of education helps to clarify the ambiguous feelings of many intellectual Christians towards Roman education. Roman educators wanted students to learn the right lessons from the right texts. Education in reading technique, therefore, became a contested cultural area and Christians eventually sought to adapt these teaching techniques by focusing them on Scripture. This feature of Roman education also helps to explain why Christians so naturally read Scriptural texts as shaping a form of life, and it reminds modern readers to be clear about the distinction between figural practices – especially allegory – and moral readings.

Some readers will be puzzled by my lack of attention so far to parallels between Christian and Jewish exegesis. Such parallels can be found, for the origins of Christian exegesis lie within Second Temple Judaism, but by the fourth century very few Christians had the detailed knowledge of Judaism that would enable Jewish practices to be a continuing source. In any case, Jewish education itself drew on Roman and Greek models, although it continued to be centred on the study of Jewish texts.

Alongside 'grammatical' techniques early Christians used 'figural' reading practices (Dawson 2002). David Dawson has helped us see how Christian figural techniques describe relationships between one scriptural text (usually from the Old Testament) and an aspect of the incarnate Word's mission as described in the New Testament, using the former to inform a reading of the latter. Thus, for example, the relationship of the lovers in the Song of Songs could be used to explore the relationship between the soul and God; the details of the life of Moses could be used as an allegorical resource for describing the stages of the Christian life. The phrase 'an aspect of the incarnate Word's mission' used above requires further discussion. For early Christian readers the progress of purification or sanctification that constitutes Christian life is intrinsically connected to the life, activity and purpose of Christ, the incarnate Word. The 'mystery' of the incarnation includes the 'mystery' by which members of the Christian community are united to the person of Christ and purified towards the vision of God. Using a text from the Old Testament to illustrate the course and struggles of this mystery is of a piece with using Old Testament texts to illustrate Christ's actions and life. The figural reader seeks figures within the text both to understand the incarnate Word and to participate in the divine speech and action in creation.

For Dawson, these readings do not depend on a binary division between what texts literally say and what they non-literally 'mean'. In other words, they do not assert that (say) a given Old Testament text is 'really about' some event or experience that can be clearly stated apart from that text without loss. The assumption that this is the formal structure of figural practices has often prompted their rejection by post-Reformation scholars. Dawson argues, however, that for figural readers the relationship between the particularities of one text and the event or text conjoined with it is fundamental. Only by taking the two poles together can one engage in good exegesis: attention to the letter of the text read figurally illumines the event or text being illustrated and explored. As a number of modern scholars have shown (besides Dawson see also Young) the standard textbook categories that divide allegory from typology are modern categories and do not help us understand the nature of 'figural' reading practices. Similarly the idea that there is a fundamental division between 'Alexandrian' exegetes who favoured allegory and 'Antiochene' exegetes who were the precursors of modern historical-critical exegetes is also highly unhelpful.

This sketch of scriptural reading helps us understand the nature of theological practice in the period. Early Christians did not distinguish 'exegesis' and 'theology' in the way that modern scholars tend to do. At the same time, no one term designated the practice of talking and writing about the divine and about things in relationship to the divine among Christians in this period, certainly none that can helpfully be translated by the modern English 'theology'. Christians used a variety of terms – such as *philosophia, theologia* and *theōria* – all of which had long non-Christian histories. We can, however, make some progress in understanding how the reading of Scripture functioned for talking about God (and the world) by noting that the Christian adaptation of such words added distinct teleological and epistemological concerns to their sense.

The narrative structure of faith shaped Christian discussions of human nature and transformation in teleological directions: discussions of human transformation came to be seen as appropriately focused on shaping progress towards the goals of life with God and the (increasingly eschatological) contemplation of the divine being. At the same time those narratives also position talk about God and the world by offering perspectives on human capacity and incapacity and the role of Scripture in aiding and shaping human reflection: the structure of Christian narratives shape epistemological concerns. Despite their constant debate about human capacity, Christians insisted that the text of Scripture is, at this stage in the drama of redemption, the fundamental resource for knowledge of God and the world.

Reading the scriptural text to discern the goal and structure of Christian existence involves a constant discussion about which terminologies and philosophical resources are best suited to explicate the plain sense. Christian writers negotiated between the text and other resources that seemed attractive and persuasive. We can think of Scripture in the fourth century as 'the fundamental resource for the Christian imagination'. The phrase recognises the existence of a variety of other resources and the necessity of negotiating between competing attractions. To speak of the 'Christian imagination' is to indicate that Scripture provided a resource for thinking about the structure of the world and our perception and understanding of it. The better we understand the process of adapting (and transforming) technical terminologies and persuasive non-Christian ideas to read the resource of the plain sense, the better we understand early Christian 'theology'.

In an essay that takes Thomas Aquinas as its primary example, Bruce Marshall describes these negotiations in ways that are applicable to many early Christians:

> To say the plain sense is primary in the order of justification is to say that one does not take Scripture to be false, although what we identify as its plain sense may at any given point be false ... When the plain sense is thought of in this way, it is possible to retain the primacy of the plain sense in the order of justification, while still allowing that external arguments may lead to a change in the way the plain sense is construed. This is because, while it is always possible for external arguments to foster a reconsideration of the plain sense, no interpretation can count as an identification of the plain sense, no matter how well supported by external argument, which fails to agree with the way the words go ... Thus beliefs cannot be justified, as a criterion for the justification of other beliefs, which do not agree with the way the words go, that is, which cannot

> count as or cohere with the plain sense ... So, when confronted with evident conflict between ranges of internal and external beliefs both of which we would like to hold true, there are basically two courses of action consistent with the justificatory primacy of the plain sense – that is, with the requirement that beliefs held true be consistent with the way the words go: i) we can revise our identification of the plain sense in light of external beliefs; ii) we can revise our estimate of our external beliefs in light of the requirements of the plain sense.

Attention to Scripture

To understand early Christian use of Scripture we need not only to describe in the abstract Scripture's theological place and some common reading practices: we need to see something of the attitude towards Scripture evident throughout many early Christian writers. Here I want to concentrate on Augustine of Hippo. In the latter half of his *Confessions* he writes with great power of his emerging Christian view of creation, truth and the place of Scripture within his life. In Book 13 Augustine describes the place of Scripture in poetic terms that perfectly convey the centrality of Scripture in Christian reasoning for him:

> 15, 16. ... you alone, our God, have made for us a vault overhead in giving us your divine scripture. The sky will one day be rolled up like a book, but for the present it is stretched out above us like the skin of a tent, for your divine scripture has attained an even nobler authority now that the mortal writers through whom you provided it for us have died. And you know, Lord, you know how you clothed human beings in skins when they became mortal in consequence of their sin. That is why you are said to have stretched out the vault that is your book, stretched out like the skin of a tent those words of yours so free from discord, which you have canopied over us through the ministry of mortal men. The firm authority inherent in your revelation, which they have passed on to us, is by their very death spread more widely over all the world below, for in their lifetime it had not been raised so high or extended so far. At that time you had not yet stretched out the sky like a tent, nor had you caused their death to become resoundingly famous far and wide.
>
> 17. ... We know no other books with the like power to lay pride low and so surely to silence the obstinate contender who tries to thwart your reconciling work by defending his sins. Nowhere else, Lord, indeed nowhere else do I know such chaste words, words with such efficacy to persuade me to confession, to gentle my neck beneath your kindly yoke and invite me to worship you without thought of reward. Grant me understanding of your words, good Father, give me this gift, stationed as

I am below them, because it is for us earth-dwellers that you have fashioned that strong vault overhead.

18. Above this vault are other waters, and these, I believe, are immortal, immune to earthly decay. Let them praise your name, let them praise you, your angelic peoples above the heavens, who have no need to look up at the vault and learn by reading your word in it; for they behold your face unceasingly and there read without the aid of time-bound syllables the decree of your eternal will. They read it, they make it their choice, they love it; they read it always, and what they read never passes away, for in their act of choosing and loving they read the unchangeable constancy of your purpose. Their book is never closed, their scroll never rolled up, for you are their book and are so eternally, because you have assigned them their place above the vault you strongly framed over the weakness of your lower peoples. Into that vault we look up, there to recognize the mercy which manifests you in time, you who have created time; *for your mercy is heaven-high, O Lord, and your faithfulness reaches to the clouds*. Clouds are wafted away, but heaven abides. Preachers of your word are wafted away out of this life into another, but your scripture remains stretched above your people everywhere until the end of the world. ...

16, 19. As you exist in all fullness, so too do you alone possess the fullness of knowledge: you unchangeably exist, unchangeably know and unchangeably will ... This is why my soul is like an arid land before you, for as it cannot illumine itself from its own resources, neither can it slake its thirst from itself. So truly is the fount of life with you, that only in your light will we see light. These things you teach us with consummate wisdom in your book, which is the vault you provide for us, O our God, so that they may all become plain to us through contemplation of your wonders. Still, though, we must discern them through signs, and transient phases, and passing days and years.

19, 24. 'But first you must wash, get yourselves clean, purge the wickedness from your souls and take it out of my sight, that dry land may appear. Learn to do good, champion the orphan and defend the rights of the widow, that your earth may yield nourishing crops and fruit-bearing trees, and then come back and let us discuss matters,' says the Lord, 'so that there may be lights in the vault of heaven to shed their radiance on earth.'

Here the text of Scripture is the vault of heaven, and looking up to that vault enables us to order in importance and function all else we see. And yet that vault speaks of mysteries that are known fully only to God. Our progress towards understanding that vault comes not merely through greater and greater intellectual progress, but through a purification that enables the soul to shine on the earth. It is in this context that we can understand Augustine's acceptance of a principle of charity in interpretation, a principle set out clearly both in Book 12 of the *Confessions* and in his *On Christian Teaching*. The plain sense of a text may yield different meanings even to the most observant reader; all are acceptable that promote love and help to expunge vice.

Augustine here is mostly concerned with what I have termed grammatical exegesis of the plain sense. A generation before Gregory of Nyssa had offered a defence of figural reading that similarly reflects a sense of the mysteriousness of the scriptural text. A short extract will reveal the common themes:

> By an appropriate contemplation of the text, the philosophy hidden in its words [may] become manifest, once the literal meaning has been purified by a correct understanding. Paul somewhere calls the shift from the corporeal to the spiritual 'a turning to the Lord and the removal of a veil.' In all these different expressions and names of contemplation Paul is teaching us an important lesson: we must pass to a spiritual and intelligent investigation of Scripture so that consideration of the merely human element might be changed into something perceived by the mind ... We know that even the Word himself, who is adored by all the creation, passed on the divine mysteries when he had assumed the likeness of a man. He reveals to us the meaning of the law ... Christ trained his disciples' minds through sayings veiled and hidden in parables, images, obscure words, and terse sayings in riddles.

Gregory here writes about the Song of Songs and its significance if read figurally, but his sense of the scriptural text as a central resource for the Christian imagination and as pointing to the mysteries of God is parallel to Augustine's own sense of Scripture.

Pastoral reasoning

It is time now to turn to an example of pastoral reasoning in the early Church. I will stay with Augustine as we will then see very clearly his sense of the importance of the plain sense of Scripture. For this section of the chapter I will follow just one of his arguments about marriage and the place of women in the early Christian community. Augustine's works offer a number of discussions of pastoral problems that reveal both developing Christian views on marriage and the response of one bishop to complex pastoral situations. Augustine's *Letter* 262 to Ecdicia is frequently anthologised and commented on in this regard (see Clark). Ecdicia is a woman who has decided to adopt a celibate ascetic lifestyle, initially with some degree of support from her husband, but increasingly on her own. She finds herself with a husband who has begun an affair with another woman. Augustine writes to Ecdicia insisting that as a married woman she could no more adopt such a lifestyle on her own decision than could her husband decide unilaterally to do so. Indeed, even though he sins, his affair is Ecdicia's fault: she has created the context within which he is no longer able to find an outlet for his sexual desire within the marriage. Augustine sees the problem as also having a financial dimension. Ecdicia has at least one son who has been considerably disadvantaged by her decision to dispose of money that would otherwise have been his inheritance to some ascetics she favours. Augustine's response to Ecdicia has many sides: his view of the mutual obligations of a married couple is strong and, for some modern readers, insensitive to the problems inherent in a relationship that has perhaps failed. At the same time, Augustine analyses the situation in terms of the mutual consequences of decisions that are made and attempts to present the obligations of both parties to each other (and to their children). Despite his own preference for an ascetic lifestyle, he clearly sees the contract of marriage taking precedence over the desire of one party to adopt celibacy.

I have not, however, provided a reading from this letter, but from a short work written in 419–20 that deals with similar questions, *On Adulterous Marriages* (*De adulterinis coniugiis*). This text offers us a much more extended example of the use of Scripture in pastoral reasoning. We can follow some of the basic argument from a few short passages. The work is addressed to one Pollentius, who remains otherwise unknown. Pollentius has argued that a woman who has divorced because of adultery should be allowed to remarry. He has argued this position on the basis of Matthew 19:9: 'whoever divorces his wife, except for unchastity, and marries another, commits adultery.' Pollentius sees this verse as arguing that there are different reasons for divorce and that one divorced for adultery can remarry, but only in those circumstances. Augustine's refutation of this position places 1 Corinthians 7 alongside Matthew and argues that in fact there is only one reason for divorce and there should be no remarriage. He sees Pollentius' solution as logically flawed and as rendering Scripture incoherent. Let us begin by following some of his opening argument. Here we see an excellent example of grammatical techniques: Augustine argues for one particular hypothesis or plot that links together the various texts under consideration and he explores what he takes to be logical inconsistencies in and consequences of Pollentius' attempts to do the same. As we shall see a little later, he also considers a variety of pastoral consequences stemming from his reading:

> 1, 1. Dearest brother, Pollentius, the first question you presented for me to comment on, when you wrote to me, was about the words of the apostle: *To those, however, who are married, I give this command – not I, but the Lord – that a wife should not leave her husband; but if she does leave him, she should either remain unmarried or be reconciled to her husband; and a husband should not divorce his wife* (1 Cor. 7:10–11). Are these words to be under-

stood as forbidding the marriage of a woman who leaves her husband for some reason other than his adultery, which is the view you take; or do they command women to remain unmarried if they leave their husbands for the only reason allowed, namely the husband's adultery, which is the view I took in those books I wrote many years ago on the sermon the Saviour preached on the mountain, as Matthew relates it in the gospel? In your opinion, the woman who leaves her husband should not remarry, if she was not forced to leave because of her husband's adultery. You do not notice that, if her husband was not guilty of adultery, she was obliged not to leave him at all, rather than simply to remain unmarried if she left him. The woman who is being commanded to stay unmarried if she leaves her husband is not being denied the right to leave, but is being denied the right to remarry. If this is so, it follows that women who wish to be celibate are being given permission to do so without waiting for their husbands to consent, so that the words *a wife should not leave her husband* (1 Cor. 7:10) would appear to be a command addressed to those who might want a divorce with the right to remarry, not to those who might want to be celibate. Consequently those who wish to do without any sexual union, and not be burdened by marriage at all, will be allowed to leave their husbands, even when there is no adultery to justify it, and remain unmarried as the apostle says. Similarly, because the rules are the same for both, if husbands want to lead a life of celibacy, even without their wives' consent they will abandon them and stay unmarried. In your view, if the reason for the divorce was their partner's adultery, they would then be allowed to proceed to another marriage; but when there is not that justification, there is still the choice for the husband or wife either not to leave, or, if he or she does leave, either to remain unmarried or to go back to the original marriage. So when there is not the justification of the other's adultery, either spouse may choose one of three alternatives: either not to leave the other partner; or to leave and stay as they are; or, if they do not stay as they are, not to look for a second marriage but to go back to the first one.

2, 2. What has become of the fact that the same apostle does not want husbands and wives to avoid their marital duty to each other even for a short time, to be free for prayer, unless it is by mutual consent? How will his words be upheld: *To avoid adultery, however, each man should have his own wife, and each woman her own husband. The husband should do his duty to his wife, and the wife also her duty to her husband. The wife does not have authority over her own body, but her husband does; and likewise the husband does not have authority over his own body, but his wife does* (1 Cor. 7:2–5)? How can this be true, if it is not wrong for husband or wife to stay celibate without the other's consent? If a woman is allowed to divorce her husband provided she stays unmarried, she does not have a husband,

> but she herself has command over her own body; and the same applies for the husband too. Moreover in the text, *Anyone who divorces his wife, except in the case of adultery, causes her to commit adultery* (Matt. 5:32), how are we to interpret what is said here except as saying that a man is forbidden to divorce his wife, if there is no adultery to justify it?

Augustine here has followed a standard grammatical practice: asking his interlocutor to see if his interpretation is consonant with other things Paul says and with the overall plot of Scripture. He assumes a unity of teaching in the Scriptures and thus finds it appropriate to bring in Jesus' words in Matthew to reinforce his reading of Paul. He then continues:

> 3. Let us return to the actual words the apostle uses: *To those, however, who are married I give this command – not I, but the Lord – that a wife should not leave her husband; but if she does leave him, she should remain unmarried* (1 Cor. 7:10–11). Imagining him to be present, let us question him and ask his opinion. Why, apostle, did you say: *but if she does leave him, she should remain unmarried*? Is it right, or is it wrong, for her to leave him? If it is wrong, why do you command the one who leaves to stay unmarried? If, on the other hand, it is not wrong, there must surely be some justifying reason. When we look for this reason we find none, other than the only exception the Savior allowed, namely the case of adultery. Consequently, the only woman the apostle has commanded to remain unmarried, if she leaves her husband, is the one who leaves for the only reason for which it is not wrong to leave her husband. In the text, *I give this command ... that a wife should not leave her husband; but if she does leave, she should remain unmarried*, it is unthinkable that a woman who leaves in this way, with the intention of remaining unmarried, does anything against this commandment. It follows that unless it is understood to be someone who is allowed to leave (and it is not allowed unless the husband commits adultery), how can she be commanded to stay unmarried if she leaves? Would anyone say, 'If a woman leaves a husband who has not committed adultery, she should stay unmarried,' when it is wrong for her to leave at all when the husband has not committed adultery? When the Lord did not even desire celibacy to be adopted except by mutual agreement and consent, I think you will now see how much your interpretation is contrary to the marriage bond.

In this section Augustine has returned to Paul's words and tried to offer a new logic, one more closely attentive to his most basic intentions.

> 4, 4. ... Consider the case of a woman who wants to practice celibacy, but her husband does not. The wife leaves him, and starts to lead a life of

celibacy. She herself will stay chaste, but contrary to what the Lord wants, she will cause her husband to commit adultery; unable to stay celibate, he will look for someone else. What shall we say to the woman, other than what the saving teaching of the Church says? Do your duty to your husband, for fear that while you are looking for something to bring you greater honor, he will find something that will bring about his damnation. We would say the same to him too, if he wanted to practice celibacy without your consent. You do not have authority over your own body, but he does, just as he does not have authority over his own body, but you do. Do not withhold what you owe each other except by agreement. After we have said this, and other similar things relating to this matter, does it please you to have the woman use your reasoning to give us this answer: 'I hear the apostle saying, *I give this command ... that a wife should not leave her husband; but if she does leave him, she should either remain unmarried or be reconciled to her husband* (1 Cor. 7:10–11). See, I have left my husband, and I do not want to be reconciled to him, and I am staying celibate. He did not say, "If you leave your husband, you must stay unmarried until you are reconciled to him," but said, *Remain unmarried, or be reconciled to your husband.* "Do one or the other," he said. He allowed a choice between the two, and did not insist on the second of these things. I choose to remain unmarried and carry out what he commands in that way. You can criticize me, accuse me, blame me, and be as stern as you like, if I remarry.'

5, 5. How can I answer this other than by saying: You misunderstand the apostle? He would not have given the commandment to stay unmarried, if she leaves her husband, except to a woman who has the right to leave her husband, which is only in the case of adultery. This is not mentioned at that point, because it is so well known. When speaking about a man divorcing his wife, God our master made this reason the only exception. He left it to be understood that the same rule binds the husband too, since not only *does the wife not have authority over her own body, but her husband does, but likewise the husband does not have authority over his own body, but his wife does* (1 Cor. 7:4). Therefore, since you cannot claim that your husband has committed adultery, how can you think that by not remarrying you are excused for leaving him, when it is wrong for you to leave him at all?

Here Augustine follows another well-worn path in ancient exegesis: he shows how his interlocutor's logic would also lead to conclusions that he himself would reject. In order to make the point more dramatic Augustine composes a speech by one of Pollentius' pastoral charges. He ends by showing that the case can only be answered by following Augustine's interpretation. Only his reading, he argues, enables consistent attention to the basic thrust of Paul's words.

In the second book of the work Augustine turns to a number of related questions raised by Pollentius in another letter concerning the pastoral consequences of his teaching. Some of the most interesting material concerns Pollentius' attempts to argue that his teaching demonstrates a kindness in the face of the way that husbands may treat wives who have been adulterous. Pollentius is particularly concerned that such husbands may be driven to violence against their wives and may certainly be prone to resentment. Augustine's response shows that he recognises the force of Pollentius' concern but thinks it should be addressed by focusing on teaching Christian husbands the character of their roles. A Christian husband must bear in mind the general command to forgive. Augustine's approach shows some of the complexity of early Christian approaches to these problems. His attitude towards such pastoral problems demonstrates a close adherence to the 'plain' text of Scripture, and also a constant desire to place all such resulting commands and injunctions within the contexts of texts that teach the most basic attitudes of the Christian life.

> 14, 14. Let us reply also to that other point, where you think that, if it is wrong to marry again while they are still alive, husbands whose wives commit adultery will want them to be dead and will be driven to punish them relentlessly. To exaggerate that cruelty you said: 'Dearest father, this does not seem to me to be what God intends, when it leaves no room for kindness and religious duty.' You say this here, as though the reason why husbands should pardon wives who commit adultery is that it is right for them to marry again; and if this is not right they will not spare them, in order to make it right. On the contrary, the reason why they ought to show mercy to the sinful women is to obtain mercy themselves for their own sins. Those whose desire is to live a life of celibacy after divorcing their wives have even more reason to act in this way. The greater their desire to become holier, the more they ought to be more merciful, so that, by not taking human revenge themselves for their wives' violation of chastity, they will have divine assistance in preserving their own chastity. They should call to mind especially those words of the Lord: *Let the one who is without sin cast the first stone* (John 8:7). It does not say, 'the one who is without that sin,' as we are talking about men who are not unchaste, but *the one who is without sin*; and if they say they are like that, they delude themselves, and *the truth is not in them* (1 John 1:8). So, if they do not delude themselves, and the truth is in them, they will not be harsh and thirsting for blood. Knowing they themselves are not without sin they will pardon in order to obtain pardon for themselves, and they will leave room for kindness and religious duty. On the

contrary, there is no room for these considerations if it is sexual license, and not concern for religious duty, that wins their pardon for their wives' sins, that is to say, if they spare them because they are allowed to marry someone else, rather than because they themselves want to be spared by God.

15. How much better it is, and more honorable, and in short more worthy of the name of Christian, to get them not to insist on the blood of their adulterous wives by telling them what scripture says: Forgive the injustice of others, and when you pray your sins will be forgiven. Can someone maintain resentment toward a fellow human being, and then look for leniency from God? Can one have no compassion for a human being like oneself, and yet plead for one's own sins? Though flesh and blood oneself, one maintains the resentment; who will forgive that person's own sins (Sir. 28:2–5)? And tell them what the gospel says: Forgive and you will be forgiven (Luke 6:37); and this is to enable us to say, Forgive us our trespasses as we forgive those who trespass against us (Mt. 6:12). And quote the apostle: Not returning evil for evil to anyone (Rom. 12:17); and any similar texts of holy scripture, by whose influence a human spirit stirred by the desire for vengeance will relent because it is Christian.

Judgement and promise

The passages from Augustine discussed above provide an excellent example of the way in which Scripture guided pastoral thinking for early Christians. Even Augustine's interlocutor Pollentius, who has taken a very different view of these questions, seems to assume the same basic reading practices as determinative. One fundamental question raised by the discussion we have just overheard, however, concerns the nature of judgement in pastoral contexts. How, where and in what way should Christian leaders pass judgement on those who appear to have transgressed the plain sense of the text? Early Christians offer a wide variety of answers to such questions. Emerging sets of regulative canons from the fourth century indicate that a variety of scales of penance for different sins had begun to emerge. The railings of a John Chrysostom against sin of all kinds can be contrasted with the exhortations and pastoral sensitivity displayed in some of Augustine's letters.

One of the most striking traditions on judgement comes from the collections of 'sayings' of the desert fathers and mothers of fourth- and fifth-century Egypt. In these texts we see a strong focus on the avoidance of judgement, as a central part of the ascetic's growth in humility and awareness of the distinction between God and him or herself:

Abba Theodore also said 'If you are temperate, do not judge the

> fornicator, for you would then transgress the law just as much. And he who said "Do not commit fornication" also said, "Do not judge."'

In this saying Abba Theodore applies a standard principle of early Christian exegesis: arguing that one text functions as a hermeneutic key for reading others. He does not deny that God wishes people not to commit fornication, but he does not draw the inference that it is for human beings to judge the offenders. The reason is clear in the following saying:

> One day Abba Isaac went to a monastery. He saw a brother committing a sin and he condemned him. When he returned to the desert, an angel of the Lord came and stood in front of the door of his cell and said, 'I will not let you enter.' But he persisted and asked 'What is the matter?' and the angel replied, 'God has sent me to ask you where you want to throw the brother whom you have condemned.' Immediately he repented and said, 'I have sinned, forgive me.' Then the angel said, 'Get up, God has forgiven you. But from now on, be careful not to judge someone before God has done so.'

The refusal to usurp God's right to judge has here become a pastoral theology, one that teaches the other members of the community much about forbearance and the distinction between God and world, even while it also seems to subvert the idea of a community regulated by human judgement. Indeed, this theology must have caused much debate within large communities. In the same texts we can also trace an adaptation of this theology, such that it is only those external to the monastic community who should not be judged on the basis of 1 Corinthian 5:12–13:

> Abba Macarius went one day to Abba Pachomius of Tebennisi. Pachomius asked him, 'When brothers do not submit to the rule, is it right to correct them?' Abba Macarius said to him, 'Correct and judge justly those who are subject to you, but judge no-one else. For truly it is written: "Is it not those inside the Church whom you are to judge? God judges those outside."'

These perspectives on the nature of judgement evolved through exegetical reading practices very similar to those used by Augustine, a generation later and many hundreds of miles to the west. They similarly evolved in a context where Christians assumed that their actions towards each other had consequences for their own slow transformation and purification. Within a common exegetical tradition and a common account of the soul's transformation a range of positions had evolved. Early Christian use of Scripture in pastoral contexts thus both demonstrates continuity and great flexibility. In recent decades a number of people have begun to argue for a recovery of Patristic modes of exegesis, and it is exciting to see the range of ethical and pastoral positions that have been argued for on the basis of those reading practices (e.g. Fowl; Rogers). Those of us who have welcomed this recovery can perhaps begin to trace the re-emergence of a more fully theological discussion out of the discourses of modernity.

Bibliography

All translations of Augustine are taken from vols I/1 (*The Confessions*) and I/9 (*Marriage and Virginity*) of *The Works of Saint Augustine: a translation for the 21st century*, ed. J. Rotelle (Hyde Park, NY: New City Press, 1991–). All translations of Sayings of the Desert Fathers are from Benedicta Ward (trans.) *The Sayings of the Desert Fathers: the alphabetical collection* (Kalamazoo, MI: Cistercian Publications, 1975).

Ayres, Lewis (2004) *Nicaea and Its Legacy*. Oxford: Clarendon Press.

Clark, Elizabeth (1996) *St. Augustine on Marriage and Sexuality*. Washington, DC: Catholic University of America Press.

Dawson, David (2002) *Figural Reading, the Fashioning of Identity and the Suppression of Origen*. Berkeley, CA: University of California Press.

Fowl, Stephen E. (1999) *Engaging Scripture*. Oxford: Blackwell.

Marshall, Bruce D. (1990) Absorbing the world: Christianity and the universe of truths, in Bruce Marshall (ed.), *Theology and Dialogue: essays in conversation with George Lindbeck*. Notre Dame, IN: Notre Dame University Press, 69–102.

Reynolds, P. L. (1994) *Marriage in the Western Church*. Brill: Leiden.

Rogers, Eugene (1999) *Sexuality and the Christian Body: their way into the triune God*. Oxford: Blackwell.

Schlabach, Gerald (1998) 'Love is the Hand of the Soul': the grammar of continence in Augustine's doctrine of Christian love. *Journal of Early Christian Studies* 6, 59–92.

Wilken, R. L. (2003) *The Spirit of Early Christian Thought*. New Haven, CT: Yale University Press.

Young, Frances (1997) *Biblical Exegesis and the Formation of Christian Culture*. Cambridge: Cambridge University Press.

CHAPTER 3:
The Eastern Orthodox tradition for today

DEMETRIOS BATHRELLOS

The Bible in the Orthodox Church

For the Orthodox Church the Bible is of paramount importance. Bishop Kallistos Ware has put it as follows: 'the Christian Church is a Biblical Church: Orthodoxy believes this as firmly, if not more firmly, than Protestantism' (Ware, 1997). The whole life of the Orthodox Church, its doctrines, worship, sacraments, spirituality, ethics, and pastoral practice are shaped in accordance with the Scriptures.

The importance that the Orthodox Church attributes to the Bible, however, does not imply that the Bible stands over the Church. For one thing, Church and Scripture cannot and should not be juxtaposed. The Bible is not a book that came down from heaven. The Orthodox Church does not endorse a notion of divine inspiration according to which the authors of the scriptural books passively took down what the Holy Spirit dictated to them. Modern biblical scholarship has made us fully aware of the very complex procedures through which the Bible took shape, and we know that it took some time for this to be accomplished. We can now affirm more strongly than ever before that, as some of the early Church theologians were also keen on arguing, the Bible belongs to the Church (e.g. Tertullian, *De Praescriptione Haereticorum*). It is the Church that wrote, canonised, interpreted and interprets Scripture.

The fact, however, that Scripture does not stand over the Church does not give Christians the right to misinterpret or misuse it. The Bible is the Word of God, and has to be heard, understood and obeyed. The Orthodox Church's immense respect for the Bible makes it oppose liberal views that tend to accommodate Scripture to modern (or any other) ideas derived from secular sources or from the naively so-called 'common sense'. The Bible is the Word of God, and this Word is subject to neither judgement nor revision.

On the other hand, however, as Georges Florovsky has argued, the Bible is not only the Word of God, but also the word of human beings. It is a mistake to believe that human beings must be 'reduced to complete passivity' and be 'allowed only to listen and to hope' (Florovsky, 3). For Florovsky,

> human response is integrated into the mystery of the Word of God. It is not a divine monologue, it is rather a dialogue and both are speaking, God and man ... God wants, and expects, and demands this answer and response of man. It is for this that he reveals himself to man and speaks to him. He is, as it were, waiting for man to converse with him.
>
> (Florovsky, 3)

And, as he later writes, 'Scripture itself is at once both the Word of God and the human response – the Word of God mediated through the faithful response of man' (6). What all this points to is that our active human response to the Word of God, our response in terms of believing, praying, worshipping, interpreting, preaching and living it out, is not only legitimate but also necessary. It must, however, always be a response that remains faithful to the divine Word.

Moreover, the Bible is not only about God's Word, mediated through human words, but also about God's deeds. God saved us not only through the former but also through the latter. The Orthodox Church has kept a well-balanced combination of word and act, preaching and worship, Gospel and Sacraments. Its liturgical pattern has always reflected the core of the Emmaus story. Jesus Christ is made known as the risen Lord only when he breaks the bread. But his exposition and interpretation of the Scriptures along the way is an integral part in the process that leads to this recognition.

The Bible, of course, is also about Christ himself, the Son of God made man. At the centre of both the Bible and the Church stands the Triune God, God the Father who through God the Spirit sends God the Son to be Emmanuel, God with us. It is precisely the incarnate Son, one of the Holy Trinity, who gives the two Testaments, Old and New, their unity and makes them one narrative and one story. The trinitarian God allows for diversity in the expression of his revelation, but this is accomplished within a context of profound unity, which has Christ, the incarnate Word of God, at its centre. The many books (*biblia*, in Greek), are one book (*biblion*), one Bible (Florovsky, 19). A non-trinitarian and non-christological understanding of Scripture makes it into something different from what it actually is, because *Scriptura est non in legendo, sed in intelligendo* ('Scripture is not in the reading but in the understanding'), as Hilary of Poitiers famously put it (Florovsky, 17). But with this we reach the area of the interpretation of Scripture.

The indispensable need for correct interpretation

The word 'Orthodoxy' means both correct faith and correct worship (doxology). These two belong together and the Orthodox Church is sensitive to both. In the context of its worship the Church often expressed its faith through summarised doctrinal statements, to be used as confessions of faith, at baptism for instance. However, the faith encapsulated in the 'rule of faith', the Creed(s) and the definitions of the Ecumenical Councils, is a biblical faith.

The doctrinal statements are not self-standing. They presuppose the biblical story and the biblical message. As Florovsky has argued, the system (namely doctrine) presupposes the story and is not meant to supersede it (26–36). The doctrines of the Church were composed and have been used not in order to replace Scripture, even less to distort it, but in order to serve and protect the correct understanding of Scripture, and through this the correct understanding of God. The definition of the Council of Chalcedon, for instance, which states that Christ is one, but, at the same time, fully God and fully man, is faithfully derived from Scripture and reflects the living faith and experience of the Church. Its aim, however, is not to replace Scripture but to give us the key for a correct reading of it, without which Scripture does not even exist.

On the other hand, however, as George Bebawi and others have argued, in a certain way Scripture (as a concrete collection of books) also presupposes doctrine. The canonisation of the books of Scripture was made with the criterion of whether they were in conformity with the living faith of the Church, which was, and is, experienced in the Liturgy and encapsulated in the Church's 'rule of faith'. Chrysostom, a deeply biblical theologian and one of the greatest and more prolific commentators and interpreters of Scripture, is even more daring. In the opening verses of his commentary on the Gospel of Matthew, he argues that if the Spirit-inspired living memory and eschatological awareness of the presence of the Word of God in our midst had been strong enough, there would not be a need to have a written Scripture at all. If we had not put away from us the grace of the Spirit, God would speak to us in person, as he spoke to Noah, Abraham, Job, Moses and the Apostles, and his word would have been written in our hearts.

It was within the providence of God, however, to have a written Scripture. The Word of God is 'incarnate' in it, as another Father of the Church, St Maximus the Confessor, repeatedly claimed. It was also within God's providence for the Spirit to inspire not only those who wrote it but also those who canonised it, and interpreted it. It is noteworthy that the definitions of the Ecumenical Councils begin with the famous phrase, already used by the Apostolic Council, 'it has seemed good to the Holy Spirit and to us …' (Acts

15:28). The Conciliar interpretation of Scripture is for the Orthodox Church binding.

The Orthodox Church is not at one with the Protestant doctrine of *sola Scriptura*. Many Orthodox theologians, however, are not happy with the 'two-sources' (Scripture and tradition) theory either. We know that it was not the Christian Church but the Gnostics who claimed to derive knowledge from a secret tradition of allegedly apostolic origin. On the contrary, St Athanasius, for instance, claimed that the Scriptures are sufficient (*autarkeis*) (*Sermon against Greeks I).* According to this view, tradition is not a separate source of doctrinal truths alongside Scripture. As John Meyendorff, for instance, has argued, 'whatever value is attributed to tradition ... the Christian Church never added its own doctrinal definitions to Scripture ... The Church ... never believed in any "continuous revelation" ' (14). Tradition provides, however, the context within which Scripture is written, canonised, read, interpreted and preached. To have no tradition is perhaps as bad as to have false tradition. Without a proper context of tradition and Church life the authentic biblical message cannot be properly received and is bound to be distorted and eventually lost.

The Bible in the Orthodox Church is not an isolated reality but part and parcel of the Church's life. This guarantees the well-being of the Church, but it also guarantees the well-being of the Bible. The life of the Church protects the Bible from distortions, which it suffers when it is approached in improper and un-churchly ways. So, to give an example, contrary to some modern Western thinking, the Orthodox Church easily and unanimously has rejected as naive the view that Jesus' miracles or resurrection are no more than pious myths (with or without existential significance). This has been so not because the mind of the Orthodox Church is pre-critical or superstitious, but because the Orthodox Church interprets the Bible within the context of her own life, which is mysterious and miraculous. For instance, the historicity of the miracle of the multiplication of the loaves and the fish (which, by the way, tells us something about the Eucharist), can be accepted simply because the workings of similar miracles in churchly contexts is repeatedly reported. The reality of the temptations of Christ by the devil are not dis-puted, because Orthodox Christians themselves (clergy and monks in particular) experience demonic temptations, some of which happen in similarly dramatic ways. The transfiguration of Christ is also reflected in the life of the Orthodox, as (e.g.) many Orthodox Christians have seen their fellow Christians shining in the light of Christ as a result of their progress in spiritual life or of a recent participation in a sacrament. Moreover, many Orthodox have had the experience of encountering the risen Lord. In addition, the centuries-old relics (even of saints of the early Church), in many of which even the skin is preserved, relics through which God still works miracles and gives life, are a living sign of the eternal life which is to be fully realised in the eschatological kingdom. Thus a 'demythologised' understanding of Scripture amounts not only to theological heresy but also to the contradiction of the Orthodox Church's everyday experience. Heresies are not only about our beliefs but also about our lives. Liberal heresies like 'demythologisation' could only have been taken seriously in the Orthodox Church if the Bible were dissociated from her life. But, thankfully, by and large this has not happened. For the Orthodox the Bible is not simply a book; it is a living reality.

The problem of biblical criticism

Most Orthodox theologians do not object to proper historical research with regard to the emergence and formation of the Holy Scriptures. The Bible is not a book come down from heaven, as is the implicit presupposition of the fundamentalists, nor is it only the product of human mind, as is the implicit presupposition of the liberals. The Orthodox believe that the Bible is inspired but not dictated. It was human beings that were enabled to write down the Scriptures, and this not only allows us but also compels us to examine the ways in which this procedure took place by employing methods of historical (and other) criticism, as the Fathers themselves did to some extent.

`There are, however, two important reservations. The first is that the message of the scriptural books must not be fully defined on the exclusive basis of the (often difficult or impossible to reconstruct) historical context in which they appeared. The Bible is the Word of God, which goes beyond the local and historical context in which it first appeared and which is, properly understood and interpreted, valid for all places and times (in fact, this is often the implicit reason behind Patristic allegorical exegesis). Second, recognising that there can be no objective historical (or other) approach many Orthodox theologians demand that biblical criticism be exercised in a theologically proper way, knowing that it itself stands under the judgement of the Word of God and its authoritative interpretation by the Church (Kesich).

With regard to the biblical text, the Orthodox Church has the same New Testament as all other Christian Churches. Its authorised Old Testament text, however, is the Christian Old Testament, namely the Greek translation known as the Septuagint (LXX). Whenever this text differs from the original Hebrew, it is believed that the changes occurred under the guidance of the Holy Spirit. The Septuagint contains the so-called 'Deutero-Canonical Books', known in the West as 'The Apocrypha'. Some Orthodox theologians, however, consider them as not of the same importance as the rest of the Old Testament.

What is pastoral practice?

Florovsky points out that 'the "Apostolic preaching", therein [in the New Testament] embodied and recorded, had a double purpose: the edification of the faithful and the conversion of the world' (18). It is the former purpose that is served by what we would nowadays call 'pastoral practice'. For the Orthodox Church, under pastoral practice comes everything that is offered to the people of God in order to help them establish, maintain and develop their communion with the Triune God and their love towards their neighbour, and thereby to gain salvation. There are three elements on which the Orthodox Church places particular emphasis: acquaintance with the Word of God, the ascetic life and spirituality, and the sacraments (Jillions; Lazor).

These elements are interrelated. Fasting, prayer, obedience to God's will and spiritual life in general enable the Orthodox to participate in the sacraments, including the Eucharist, far more fully. In fact, to make a sincere effort to live the Christian life and to come to the Sacrament of Confession are prerequisites for receiving Holy Communion. And vice versa, worship gives Orthodox Christians the strength to continue their spiritual struggle with renewed force. Scripture is used in these cases as a basic component of both individual spiritual struggle and worship.

Many Orthodox priests advise their flock to read the Bible daily as part of their regular spiritual programme or 'canon'. This offers them spiritual nourishment and guidance. Orthodox worship, on the other hand, is impregnated with biblical material, which, once more, is used for the pastoral support of Orthodox Christians, as we will presently see.

Many other activities fall under the description of pastoral practice: visiting the sick, strengthening the weak, encouraging the broken-hearted, giving hope to those in despair, helping the confused to find their direction, supporting families, caring for the children, consoling the bereaved, rejoicing with those who rejoice and weeping with those who weep (Rom. 12:15). In the Orthodox Church, pastoral service is mainly offered by priests and bishops. Lay people, including monks and nuns, are also involved, but the main responsibility belongs to the clergy. It is, of course, a sign of healthy pastoral practice on the clergy's part to involve the right persons from their congregation in specific activities relating to the Church's pastoral practice.

The Bible as a pastoral book

> Now Jesus did many other signs in the presence of his disciples, which are not written in this book. But these are written so that you may come to believe that Jesus is the Messiah, the Son of God, and that through believing you may have life in his name. (John 20:30–31)

> 'I still have many things to say to you, but you cannot bear them now.'(John 16:12)

The Bible can be read from different and complementary perspectives. One of them is the pastoral perspective. In fact, the Bible, among other things, is a pastoral book. By using it in our pastoral work, we do something that corresponds to one of its essential characteristics, which, if denied or ignored, betrays the Bible itself. The New Testament in particular was written mostly (if not exclusively) by pastors, who addressed Christians of their time (albeit by no means only them), often having in mind their problems, questions and pastoral needs. Moreover, as St John Chrysostom has argued, Christ himself spoke and acted as a pastor (which offers, by the way, a helpful insight for the interpretation of the New Testament). When Jesus spoke to the Jews in general, or to the Pharisees, or to his own disciples, he did not only convey some 'eternal truths' in general and in the abstract. He both spoke and acted in certain ways, taking into account the concrete people who were around him, their dispositions, faith or unfaith, receptivity and willingness (or unwillingness) to understand him. His aim was to lead them to the knowledge of the truth (that is, to himself), which requires not simply didactic but, more broadly, pastoral skills. This is also what his disciples did. Paul fed the Corinthians with milk, because they were not mature enough to be fed with solid food (1 Cor. 3:2). He became all things to all people, that he might by all means save some (1 Cor. 9:22). This is what good pastors have always done and this is what we are asked to do in our pastoral work.

Worship

The most important 'pastoral activity' in the Orthodox Church is worship and the most valuable thing an Orthodox pastor can offer to his flock is the daily services and the frequent (daily, if possible) celebration of the Divine Liturgy in particular. The Orthodox Church is primarily a worshipping church. And nothing else besides the sacraments occupies such a central position in the worship of the Orthodox Church as the Bible. As Bishop Kallistos has put it:

> Orthodoxy regards the Bible as a verbal icon of Christ … In every Church, the Gospel Book has a place of honour on the altar; it is carried in procession at the Liturgy … ; the faithful kiss it and prostrate themselves before it. Such is the respect shown in the Orthodox Church for the Word of God. (Ware, 201)

These practices, of course, have obvious pastoral implications. They confer respect and awe for the written Word of God on those who participate in worship and are called to venerate, hear and then apply the Gospel in their lives. They evoke a sense of awe for a book which is the written Word of God. At the same time, its being placed on the altar reminds us that the Gospel belongs to the Church and that Gospel and Eucharist belong together. The incarnate Word of God comes to us through Scripture and the Eucharist. We need both in order to know Christ and attain salvation. The link between the Gospel and the Eucharist, however, tells us also that we cannot have the word without the sacrifice, either in our worship or in our pastoral practice. The sacrifice without the word cannot be fully understood. And the Word of God often becomes just words, if it is not accompanied by sacrifices – this is obviously important for pastors to remember.

Regarding the use of Scripture in worship, in the services of Matins and Vespers the whole Psalter is recited every week, and during Lent twice a week. Many psalms are said more than once in these services, whereas in all other services the Psalter occupies a prominent place. At Vespers on the eve of important feasts throughout the year, we have scriptural readings, usually from the Old Testament. And in the Liturgy there are always two New Testament readings, one from either the Acts or the Epistles of the Apostles and one from the Gospels. The whole New Testament (excluding the book of Revelation) is read throughout the year. Apart from this, biblical excerpts (e.g. from the psalms), vocabulary and concepts occur in many places within all services and give them a deeply biblical character. In fact many Orthodox services are mosaics of biblical quotations and allusions. As a result, the faithful in worship are exposed to biblical material presented in both direct and indirect ways. Moreover, all people come into some contact with the word of God in worship. Lay people chant and read the excerpts from the Old Testament and the Acts or the Epistles of the Apostles. The deacon or the priest or the bishop read the Gospel, and the priest or the bishop preaches.

However, the biblical character of a service is not guaranteed only by the presence of biblical excerpts. It has to be biblical also in essence, that is, it has to be rooted in and revolve around the creative and redemptive work of the Triune God as this is manifested in the Scriptures. The Orthodox services are biblical in this sense too. This cannot be easily changed, owing to the fact that the services of the Orthodox Church are fixed. It is not up to the priest or the bishop, or, even less, a lay person, to change them at will. No individual may interfere and add or detract anything from them. Only the Church can make changes. This removes the danger of arbitrarily changing the services and of accommodating them to other, non-biblical, patterns.

Furthermore, as Professor Stanley Harakas has argued, the profoundly scriptural Orthodox services have an immense emotive bearing upon the lives of the worshipping Christians. The services of the Holy Week, for instance, affect the ethical attitudes of the Orthodox in a very powerful way. In the service of Matins of Holy Monday Christ is characterised as a bridegroom (which is actually the key image for the first three days of Holy Week) for whose coming we should wait with eschatological watchfulness and alertness – this is of course an allusion to the Vespers Gospel reading, which is the parable of the ten virgins. In fact, the service refers to several stories from the Bible in different ways. Since on these days we read the last chapters of Genesis, the service includes hymns that refer to Joseph and his refusal to be seduced by the Egyptian woman. This story acts here as both a reminder and an exhortation for spiritual struggle to resist lust, a prerequisite for responding faithfully to the love of the bridegroom. The Gospel reading (Matthew 21:18–43) refers to the cursing and withering of the unfruitful fig tree and is focused mainly upon doing good and avoiding evil. The hymns are inspired by scriptural passages. They refer, for instance, to the Three Holy Young Men in the fiery furnace, to Christ's exhorting his disciples to keep his commandments, his calling for humble service instead of dominion, to his being the example of sacrificial love and to his oncoming passion. Finally a well-known and much-loved hymn (the *Exaposteilarion* of the day, which is also sung in the service of Matins of the two following days) reminds worshippers that virtue is not the outcome of human struggle but primarily a gift of God. The actual text is as follows: 'Your bridal chamber, O my Saviour, I see all adorned, but I have no garment so that I may enter it. Make bright the mantle of my soul, O Giver of light, and save me!' (Harakas). The pastoral implications of such a rich service are obvious. This is why during Holy Week a sermon is rarely delivered.

The Sacraments exhibit similarly significant biblical influence. Take for example a rather little-known sacrament, the Sacrament of the Blessing of Oil (*Euchelaion*), which is done for the cure of a sick person. The sacrament begins with a few prayers, including the Lord's Prayer and Psalms 142 and 50. Through them God is asked to grant us his mercy by forgiving our sins and curing both our souls and bodies, which reminds us of the biblical view that sin and illness are deeply linked. After this other prayers follow, some of which refer to healing miracles of Christ as well as to saints who were great healers.

Then follow fourteen New Testament readings and seven prayers. The pattern is as follows: first comes a reading from the Epistles of the Apostles, then a Gospel reading and finally a prayer, which has a deeply biblical content. The readings are: James 5:10–16 (which gives a clear biblical reference and foundation to the Sacrament); Luke 10:25–37 (the parable of the Good Samaritan, with its emphasis on unconditional love and the reference to 'wine and oil' for healing); Romans 15:1–7 (emphasis on love once more as well as on endurance and encouragement); Luke 19:1–11 (the story of Zacchaeus: the emphasis is on repentance and salvation; originally this was read when the sick person was back in his house, which was also anointed: 'today salvation has come to this house'); 1 Corinthians 12:27—13:7 (the well-known hymn to the virtue of love); Matthew 10:1 and 5–8 (Jesus gives his disciples the authority to 'cure the sick, raise the dead, cleanse the lepers, cast out demons' and instructs them 'freely you received; freely give'); 2 Corinthians 6:16—7:1 (Paul urges the Corinthians to cleanse themselves 'from every defilement of flesh and spirit'); Matthew 8:14–23 (Jesus heals the sick, fulfilling the relevant prophecy of Isaiah; he and his followers have nowhere to lay their heads; even the burial of parents cannot take precedence over following Jesus; 'and ... his disciples followed him': this Gospel story is probably used to remind us that the gift of healing is given to those who exhibit faithful discipleship); 2 Corinthians 1:8–11 (Paul's despair unto death is overcome by the power of God; the power of 'the prayers of many' is appreciated); Matthew 25:1–14 (the parable of the ten virgins: oil as a symbol and expression of love, mercy and good works; in Greek oil (*elaion*) and mercy (*eleos*) sound similar); Galatians 5:22—6:2 (reference to the fruits of the Spirit and to gentleness as the proper way to restore a sinner); Matthew 15:14–29 (the healing of the daughter of the Canaanite woman: the humility and faith of relatives is conducive to healing); 1 Thessalonians 5:14–23 (a call for sanctification of soul and body); Matthew 9:9–13 (the calling of Matthew: 'I desire mercy, not sacrifice'). After the fourteen New Testament readings and the seven prayers, the senior priest places the Gospel on the head of the sick person and prays for the forgiveness of his sins. The sick person is anointed with oil 'for the healing of soul and body'. The sacrament is extremely powerful in bringing about this healing. Through it many people have been (and are being) cured from incurable physical and spiritual diseases.

The liturgical sermon

To preach the Word is one of the main tasks of the presbyter and the bishop. A presbyter is ordained in order 'to proclaim the Gospel of Your [God's] kingdom' and 'to minister the word of Your [God's] truth', as the prayer for the ordination of a presbyter reads. The bishop is ordained by bishops holding the Gospel over his head, at the time just before the New Testament readings. He is ordained in order to become one who 'has contended valiantly for the preaching of Your [God's] Gospel' (Hopko). He is expected to be subject to the Gospel and to preach it to the folk entrusted to him.

According to the Orthodox traditional practice (not always nowadays followed) the sermon in the Liturgy should come immediately after the Gospel reading. This is an indication that the sermon must be based on and inspired by the biblical text, and revolve around either the apostolic or the Gospel reading. The sermon must be delivered by either a priest or a bishop, namely by the person who is, acts and speaks as Christ in our midst (Hopko; Clark).

In many Orthodox Churches in the past sermons were preached rather rarely for practical reasons. This was the case, for instance, in Greece in the centuries of Ottoman occupation. In those days many priests did not always have the necessary education and training to deliver a sermon. In some cases, instead of delivering new sermons, the practice of reading edited sermons by Fathers of the Church or distinguished preachers was followed (this still happens in some monasteries). In other countries, like Albania, for instance, the communist regime had banished not simply preaching, but every religious activity. Bishop Kallistos Ware writes that in communist Russia 'the only instruction that they [parish priests] could give to their flock was through sermons during church services'. And he reports that 'often they took full advantage of this: I can recall attending celebrations of the Liturgy in the 1970s at which four or five different sermons were preached; the congregation listened with rapt attention, and thanked the preacher at the end with a great cry of gratitude – an experience I do not usually have when preaching in the west!' (1997, 146). Nowadays the practice of delivering a sermon in the Liturgy has been, by and large, fully restored. However, in some provincial dioceses bishops distribute written sermons to be read on Sundays. Moreover, bishops usually distribute encyclicals to be read on big feast days.

Religious education, Sunday schools and Bible study groups

Some traditionally Orthodox countries have Orthodox Christianity taught in the primary and secondary school as part of the compulsory curriculum. In Greece, for instance, Christianity is taught as the only true religion. The study of the Bible occupies a prominent place. Often priests with a degree in theology teach this module and with good reason consider it part of their pastoral activity (partly because it often gives them the opportunity to extend their pastoral work in schools). Most teachers though are lay people, men and women. The role of lay people in the pastoral practice of the Orthodox Church in general is not insignificant.

In fact, however, lay people play an important role in Sunday schools and Bible study groups. Many parishes, at least in the big cities of many Orthodox countries, now have Sunday schools. Bible study groups are also widespread, and have been so for many decades, not least in Greek Cyprus and many countries of the Diaspora (that is where emigrant communities have now settled), meeting in parishes or in buildings of Christian organisations or in houses, usually on a weekly basis. They aim at enhancing not only their members' knowledge but also their faith and love for God and his Church. Christian fellowship is also considered important and promoted. Focus is usually placed upon a significant passage, usually of the New Testament. A trained facilitator offers an introductory analysis and encourages discussion. Very often Patristic or other Orthodox commentaries are used and taken as authoritative. Usually modern scholarship is not adequately taken into account and sometimes the Gospel is not sufficiently related to the data of the modern world.

Monasticism

Monasticism has been for centuries an important source of Orthodox spirituality and an inspiration for their fellow Christians. Especially in our times, when most people's faith has grown cold, monasteries are among the rather few places where authentic Christian life is still extant. What we read in the Acts (2:44–45; 4:32–35) about common property and communal life devoted to prayer, hearing the word, fellowship and worship, is still encountered in Orthodox monasteries. It is to these places that Christians often go to seek support, encouragement and spiritual guidance. Monks and nuns, immersed as they are in scriptural theology and spirituality, often have a very simple, direct and powerful way of making the biblical word come alive. Their simplicity of life and way of talking reflects the simplicity of the Bible, which is truer than the sophisticated naivety of this world. But perhaps the most significant of all is that, as has been implied, monasteries offer an experience of the living world of the Bible, helping us to inhabit for a while a world which is not 'of this world'.

The Sacrament of Confession and spiritual direction

One of the most powerful ways by which Orthodox priests fulfil their pastoral vocation is the Sacrament of Confession. It is the priest as confessor to whom the broken-hearted turn in order to confess their sins and seek spiritual guidance. The use of the Bible in the Sacrament is indispensable. The parable of the Prodigal Son is often used as a significant example of repentance and confession. The publican of the parable of the Publican and the Pharisee, Peter, and the prostitute of the Gospel also stand out as examples of sincere repentance. In fact, many prayers of absolution mention them not only as examples of true repentance but also as signs of Christ's forgiveness. Zacchaeus is mentioned as an example of humility and indifference to shame, in order to encourage penitents to overcome shame and open their hearts to Christ. The Sacrament of Confession (or any other) cannot be offered impersonally, to somebody whom we cannot see face to face. This would not fit well with the Bible and the tri-personal biblical God. In the Orthodox Church Confession is always addressed to Christ, but takes place in the context of a personal encounter between the penitent and the priest. Abraham is often mentioned as an example of living faith. The cross of Christ and the possibility of understanding it only in the light of the resurrection will be mentioned to people who suffer, bodily or psychologically. Job's story will be also used as a useful case in point. The Old Testament story of Joseph will be mentioned as an example of God's providence. Other biblical themes, such as the temptations of Christ, his forbearance, and of course aspects of his teaching are often used too. Finally, many priests advise the penitents to read parts of the Bible for their spiritual nourishment.

The importance of the Sacrament of Confession and of the spiritual direction that is thereby given is immense. It is traditional in the Orthodox Church for Christians to go regularly to the same priest for Confession. This fosters a personal relationship and enables the pastor to get to know and therefore help the penitent far more effectively. What the priest in fact tries to do with the person who comes to him for confession and spiritual advice is to help him apply the word of God to his own life. The priest does not simply present the penitent with general gospel claims but helps him understand the Word of God, his own self and the relation between the two in a spiritually expedient and beneficial way.

The Orthodox church (temple) and the icons

In his book *The Russians and their Church*, Nicolas Zernov points out that 'one of the characteristics of Russian Christians has been their reluctance to use the spoken or written word as a means of conveying their ideas. They have preferred to express themselves through painting, music, architecture and the ritual of daily life' (1964, 4). Zernov's remark reminds us that there are not only individuals but also peoples who are deeply affected by the biblical message not only in its written form but also in the form of a temple or an icon. Probably this is more or less true for all people and certainly goes some way in explaining the central place the Orthodox Church gives to its churches and icons. But the main reasons are theological. Georges Florovsky has put it in this way:

> The New Testament is obviously more than a book. We do belong to the New Testament ourselves. We are the People of the New Covenant. For that reason it is precisely in the Old Testament that we apprehend revelation primarily as the Word: we witness to the Spirit 'that spoke through the Prophets'. For in the New Testament God has spoken by his Son, and we are called upon not only to listen, but to look at. 'That which we have seen and heard declare we unto you' (1 John 1: 3). (Florovsky, 24)

The Orthodox temple is the material and visual representation of both the biblical universe and the biblical story. Usually the roof of the church, if seen from the outside downwards, has the scheme of a cross. The typical Orthodox church has a dome, which is a symbol of heaven. When we are in the church and we look at the dome, we see a painting of Jesus Christ *pantocrator*, namely, of the ascended Christ who is to come again to judge the living and the dead (Acts 1:9–11). Christ is looking downwards and blesses his Church. Around Christ we see the Apostles, the Gospel writers and the Prophets, namely the Old and New Testament figures who have borne witness to him either before or after his incarnation (this points, *inter alia*, to the unity of the two Testaments). Mary with Jesus on her lap is represented on the apse, as the one who united heaven and earth by giving birth to the Son of God. On lower levels we have paintings of the Saints of the triumphant Church, surrounding the Saints of the militant Church, that is, the members of the worshipping community. In various places of the Church we also see paintings of the main events and teachings of Jesus' life. We see, for instance, the so-called *dodekaorton*, that is, the twelve icons representing the main events of Christ's life together with Pentecost and the Dormition of the Virgin, which is usually placed on the upper part of the so-called iconostasis, the screen that separates the main church from the sanctuary. But there are many other biblical themes that are painted in various parts of the church.

The same goes for Jesus' teachings. We find, for instance, paintings of the parables. I saw recently a painting of the parable of the Good Samaritan, and was able to see the iconographer's effort to offer a theological interpretation of the parable. Thus the Good Samaritan was Jesus Christ himself (we can deduce this from the fact that the Good Samaritan's halo bears a cross). And when Christ takes the man, a symbol of humanity that has been attacked and tortured by the devil, to the inn, which in turn is a symbol of the Church, Christ gives the innkeeper not two *denarii* but two scrolls, the Old and the New Testaments!

Very often, when Orthodox priests need, as part of their pastoral work, to introduce people to Christianity or teach them more about the Bible and the Christian life, they offer them a tour of the church. The architecture and the icons prove extremely effective in this respect. They not only teach us but also make us realise and feel that we are part of the all-inclusive biblical story and world, created, sustained, redeemed and judged by the living God and his Son in the Spirit. This gives us an opportunity not only to hear but also to see the Word. Because 'the Word became flesh and dwelt among us, and we beheld his glory, the glory as of the only begotten of the Father, full of grace and truth' (John 1:14).

Using biblical 'techniques' in pastoral practice

Stories

The Bible is as much a story as it is anything else. It begins with God creating the world and finishes with the consummation of the divine economy in the eschatological kingdom. Within this all-inclusive story we find other, smaller stories. If we deprive the Bible of its story/stories we will turn it into something significantly different from what it is. It is noteworthy that the apocryphal *Gospel of Thomas* includes many of Jesus' alleged sayings, but is not placed within the context of a story. This is one of the reasons why this could not have been a canonical gospel.

Stories are different from theological treatises and tell us things in their own way, which can very effectively respond to pastoral needs. If pastoral ministry is to be exercised in a way faithful to the Bible, not only theoretical admonitions but also stories are to be related to people: to people who suffer, die, doubt, pray, but without seeming to get any response to their prayer, people who try to find their calling, or wonder how they could confront their temptations or develop their gifts in a Christian way. The stories, however, will be not only from the Bible, but also from the desert fathers as well as from the lives of holy men and women of more recent times. Collections of stories from the monastic world, which often include sayings as well, as in fact happens in the Bible, are well known and used frequently by pastors. When Starets Zosima addresses his flock in Dostoievsky's *The Brothers Karamazov*, he makes extensive use of stories from his own (secular and monastic) life as well as from the lives of others (353–407). Despite the objections that we have about some of his stories, interpretations and teachings, the way he combines these elements reflects to some extent the biblical pattern. It is well known that the literary figure of Starets Zosima was inspired by *startsy* that Dostoievsky himself had met. Many modern Orthodox priests speak in similar ways in their pastoral work, making extensive use of teachings combined with and illustrated by stories, biblical and other.

Biographies

Without persons, there are no stories. Without the incarnate Son of God there would be no Scripture. In fact there is a sense in which the gospels are Jesus' biographies (Burridge). It is to him, to the incarnate Word, to whom the gospels primarily refer, and his story, including his death and resurrection, is of unique and salvific significance because it is the story of the incarnate Son of God. In the Orthodox Church pastoral practice is oriented not only towards the imitation of Christ but also towards the imitation of the saints. This is so, however, because the saints are imitators of Christ. They are those who have loved Christ with all their hearts, souls, minds and strength (Mark 12:30). It is no longer they who live, but Christ who lives in them (Gal. 2:20). They are the Gospel lived out. They speak as having authority, as Jesus did (Mark 7:29). It is the Holy Spirit of God that speaks through their mouth, as we read in the *Pastor* of Hermas. They are Christ-like paragons of holiness and wisdom. Through them the Triune God is glorified. In fact, they help us see and experience Jesus' presence in various places and times and through different patterns of life.

We see the close link between Christ and the saints already in the earliest account of the life of a saint, the account of the martyrdom of St Polycarp. His martyrdom shows us what is 'the martyrdom in accordance with the Gospel'. The name of the Roman official responsible for Polycarp's arrest and execution is Herod and Jews are involved in his execution, as happened with Jesus. The text reports that the father of Herod did not want the body of Polycarp to be given to the Christians 'lest they leave the Crucified and start to venerate him [Polycarp]'. But the text adds that this is impossible, on account of the fact that we love the saints 'because they are disciples and imitators of the Lord'.

Orthodox priests make use of the biblical and the 'post-biblical' saints in their pastoral practice in different ways. They give Christians the name of a saint at their baptism and urge them to relate personally with this saint and imitate him or her. They celebrate the Liturgy on the saints' days. They speak to the Christians about the lives of the saints in order to encourage them in their spiritual strivings. Miracle-working icons and relics of saints are places for pilgrimage, and their sayings are sources of spiritual wisdom. In the Orthodox Church many people have a living experience of the presence of the saints in their lives, and this is something that the pastors make use of in order to ignite their flock's faith and love for God who is glorified in his saints.

Desiderata

There are ways in which the Bible could be used even more effectively in the Orthodox Church's pastoral practice. The Old Testament could be used more. Some theologians have argued that perhaps the lectionary of the Orthodox Church should be revised (with regard to the Sunday readings in particular) in order to help the worshipping community to be exposed to a wider selection of scriptural readings. Some also claim that we need more Old Testament readings, including those psalms that must be read in the services of Vespers and Matins, but are often omitted. It is also often pointed out that the liturgical sermon must be always related to the scriptural readings and that it must, if possible, be always delivered after the Gospel reading, in accordance with the ancient tradition. Some Orthodox pastors and theologians also think that perhaps the use of ancient languages in worship (Greek and Slavonic, for instance) makes the biblical readings (and not only them) difficult to comprehend and that, for this reason, the introduction of more modern forms of language, which is already happening to some extent, may be considered.

Some theologians also warn pastors of the danger of not always sufficiently relating the Orthodox tradition to the Holy Scripture. It is pointed out that the Fathers of the Church, for instance, must be always read, taught, preached, used for spiritual guidance and so on, against the backdrop of the Scriptures and not as isolated self-authenticating authorities. The practice of reading the Scriptures on a daily basis must be further encouraged. The great biblical saints are and must remain at a prominent place in the Church's calendar. Forms of sacramentalism or spirituality that consider acquaintance with the Word of God as of secondary importance must be forcefully combated. The pastors themselves should peruse the Word of God daily and ask Christ to guide them through his Spirit in finding ways to apply the Bible to their pastoral service for his glory and the salvation of his people.

Bibliography

For the texts of the early Greek Fathers, see the *Patrologia Graeca*.

Bebawi, George (2001) The Bible in Eastern Churches, in J. Rogerson (ed.) *The Oxford Illustrated History of the Bible*. Oxford: Oxford University Press, 242–55.

Burridge R. A. (1997) *What Are the Gospels? A comparison with Graeco-Roman biography*. Cambridge: Cambridge University Press.

Clark, Timothy (2001) The function and task of liturgical preaching. *St. Vladimir's Theological Quarterly* 45.25–54.

Dostoevsky, Fyodor (1995) *The Brothers Karamazov*. Oxford: Oxford University Press.

Florovsky, Georges (1972) *Bible, Church, Tradition: an Eastern Orthodox view*. Belmont: Norland.

Hall, Christopher (1998) *Reading the Scriptures with the Church Fathers*. Leicester: Inter-Varsity Press.

Harakas, Stanley (2002) Orthodox liturgy and ethics: a case study. *Studies in Christian Ethics* 15.1, 11–24.

Hopko, Thomas (1997) The liturgical sermon. *St. Vladimir's Theological Quarterly* 41, 175–82.

Jillions, J. (2003) Pastoral theology: reflections from an Orthodox perspective. *British Journal of Theological Education* 13.2, 161–74.

Kesich, Veselin (1992) *The Gospel Image of Christ*. New York: St. Vladimir's Seminary Press.

Lazor, P. (1996) Pastoral care today. *St. Vladimir's Theological Quarterly* 40,17–42.

Meyendorff, John (1978) *Living Tradition*. New York: St. Vladimir's Seminary Press.

Simonetti, Manlio (2001) *Biblical Interpretation in the Early Church: an historical introduction to patristic exegesis*. Edinburgh: T&T Clark.

Ware, Timothy (Kallistos) (1997) *The Orthodox Church*. Harmondsworth: Penguin.

Zernov, Nicolas (1964) *The Russians and Their Church*. London: SPCK.

CHAPTER 4:
The medieval experience

ROGER ELLIS

While formally considering a thousand years of history, this chapter concentrates, in the main, on two small periods of time: that covered by the adult life of Margery Kempe (1390–1440), a pious townswoman from King's Lynn in Norfolk; and, to a lesser extent, the immediate aftermath of the Fourth Lateran Council (1215), a period of enormous significance for subsequent developments in pastoral practice. It also confronts head on the fact that the Middle Ages have such very different understandings from our own of the Bible and of pastoral practice, to say nothing of the persons who engage in that practice, that we cannot apply their understandings in any straightforward way to our own times.

Margery Kempe

In about 1436–38 Margery Kempe, by then a widow in her sixties, completed the dictation to a priest of her life which, as she saw and presented it, clearly revealed God's miraculous dealings with her over the previous forty years. (Unlike her near contemporary Julian of Norwich, but in common with most women of her class and time, Margery was illiterate.) The narrative of God's dealings with her in her *Book* (Windeatt 1994, 2000) really begins about 1394–95, with the unconditional forgiveness of all her sins by Christ, who appeared to her in a vision to tell her so, and to promise that on her death she would pass immediately to heaven (ch. 5). Thereafter, she was in regular and direct communication with heavenly figures like Christ and the Virgin Mary. From them she sometimes received answers to questions that she was putting on her own behalf or on behalf of others. At other times her heavenly guides intervened to protect her from danger, or to confer upon her heightened spiritual sensations. Some of these she experienced only subjectively. Others, like tears and loud crying, to which she was prone, and which could be triggered by any reference to, or recollection of, the person of Christ (including, for example, the sight of a mother holding a baby, ch. 39), are embarrassingly public, and provoke strong reactions in the bystanders, for and against the brand of spirituality which they symbolise. Another marker of her changed state caused her almost as much trouble as her tears: God directed her to wear white, the colour reserved for virgins (ch. 15).

In engaging so directly with the spiritual, Margery sometimes seems to have bypassed the need for ordinary pastoral practice. Her heavenly mentors provide her with such immediate access to the spiritual realm that they regularly assume, or even displace, the pastoral functions by which the medieval Church sought to mediate God to the faithful. So, for example, Christ uses the words of the Bible to bring Margery reassurance, like any ordinary preacher: in ch. 14 he tells her that she is 'written upon [his] hands and … feet', so as to encourage her in times when he is apparently absent, since he is 'a hidden God' (Windeatt 1994, 65–6; cf. Isa. 49:26; 45:15).

A more telling example of divine intervention occurs (ch. 32) when Margery is in Rome and wants to go to communion, but cannot find an English-speaking priest to hear her confession and give her absolution, the necessary precondition of receiving the Eucharist. Notwithstanding the forgiveness she receives from Christ at the start of her spiritual life, Margery continues to use the sacrament of confession throughout her life. A German priest offers to hear her confession and, though understanding nothing of what she is saying, to give her absolution. This potentially irregular situation is resolved when Christ sends St John the Evangelist, in a vision, to hear her confession. She confesses to him, and he absolves her, 'highly strengthening her to trust in the mercy of our Lord' (Windeatt 1994, 117). Then, the text implies, she receives the Eucharist from the German priest. Heavenly speakers thus exercise those pastoral roles of counsel and encouragement and the provision of the sacraments that Margery routinely looks to the Church for.

This direct engagement with the spiritual realm carries the striking consequence that, though a lay woman and therefore near the bottom of the ecclesiastical heap, Margery is herself able to offer pastoral guidance to her contemporaries. Knowing her reputation as a holy woman, people regularly come to her for advice. Often, she owes her advice to direct divine inspiration; even when the text does not so describe its source, we generally learn after the event that her instincts were right. Margery regularly couches this advice in biblical terms. So, for instance, on a visit to Canterbury Cathedral (ch. 13) she is questioned about her knowledge of God by an old (Benedictine) monk. '"Sir", she said, "I will both hear of him and speak of him", repeating to the monk a story from Scripture' (Windeatt 1994, 63). A major tool of pastoral practice, a Bible story, is here enlisted in the defence of Margery's very distinctive take on spirituality.

The story fails to produce the desired result. It provokes the old monk to wish that she were 'enclosed in a house of stone' (Windeatt 1994, 63), and a younger co-religionist to declare that she is inspired either by the Holy Spirit or by the devil, since her words come from the Bible, which, in the nature of things, a lay woman might not be expected to know. Margery deftly turns to her advantage her presumed ignorance of the Bible by telling a non-biblical story with a sting in the tail, at her hearers' expense. This does not endear her to them. They have been aroused against her even before the old monk speaks, because she has spent nearly the whole day in their presence, weeping. They chase her out of the cathedral, shouting, 'You shall be burnt, you false Lollard!' (Windeatt 1994, 64).

This incident shows how ubiquitous, in some respects, was pastoral practice, and the use of the Bible as a tool of such practice, in the Middle Ages. Margery shows that she has completely internalised the religious understandings she has received from conventional ecclesiastical sources. At the same time, if in very different ways, the reactions of both Margery and her opponents witness to an anxiety about the adequacy of existing pastoral practice to articulate a person's spiritual instincts. The young monk is right about the difficulty, then as now, of discerning the origin of pretended spiritual gifts. The old monk seems to have a straightforward view of pastoral practice: it is something done by the clergy, and the laity are to be grateful for what they are given. More particularly, women are to be seen, if at all, and not heard. Even the saintly vicar of St Stephen's, Norwich, Richard of Caister, is startled enough, when first she asks to see him after lunch to talk to him 'for an hour or two' about the love of God, to exclaim, 'Bless us! How could a woman occupy one or two hours with the love of our Lord? I shan't eat a thing till I find out what you can say of the love of our Lord God in the space of an hour' (ch. 17; Windeatt 1994, 74).

Not that women were denied all right to engage in pastoral care. As wives they could instruct children and servants. Alternatively, they could undertake religious profession, as a nun or an anchoress, 'enclosed in a house of stone'. Or – though not much in evidence in England – there was the way of the beguines (or sisterhoods living in the wider community, mainly found in the Low Countries from the twelfth century: Stargardt; Bowie and Davies). As nuns, anchoresses or beguines, particularly if they were gently born, women had some scope for the exercise of their spiritual gifts. The anchoress Julian of Norwich (Colledge and Walsh; Spearing 1998) is, initially, anxious not to claim any authority for herself: as 'a woman, ignorant and frail', she cannot presume to teach her readers: Christ is the 'sovereign teacher' (Spearing 1998, 10–11). This comment comes from the Short Text of her work, possibly produced in 1373. Julian cut this expression of anxiety in the revised Long Text, produced some time after 1391 (Watson 1993 offers later dates for both). Her role as spiritual mentor is well evidenced in Margery's visiting her, some time after her conversion to the spiritual life, for counsel (ch. 18). Though Julian's writing is hugely more radical than Margery's in its probing of the relations between human sin and divine love, Julian was never, so far as we know, at risk of being burned as a heretic; it was easier for her precisely because she was 'enclosed in a house of stone'. The fate of the beguine Marguerite Porete (Babinsky) may warn, though, against any easy assumption that religious status conferred immunity from prosecution. Porete was burned at the stake in 1310 as a lapsed heretic for her religious understandings.

Margery goes to Julian, as to so many other religious leaders of her day in England – the list of those she visits reads like entries from a fifteenth-century religious *Who's Who* – for confirmation of the spiritual graces working in her, one of which, her tears, had caused such offence to the monks of Canterbury. Julian's advice to Margery is both general and liberally larded with scriptural proof-texts. Margery can be confident that the Spirit is at work in her tears because, Julian says, the Spirit 'moves never a thing against charity ... and ... makes a soul stable and steadfast in the right faith'. 'Tears of contrition, devotion or compassion' are marks of the Spirit:

> St Paul says that the Holy Ghost asks for us with mourning and weeping unspeakable ... he causes us to ... pray with mourning and weeping so plentifully that the tears may not be numbered. No evil spirit may give these tokens, because St Jerome says that tears torment the devil more than do the pains of hell. (Windeatt 1994, 78)

This advice may have been written up after the event, to record what Margery thinks Julian *ought* to have said to her; or maybe, like many who compensate for illiteracy with a highly developed verbal memory, Margery is remembering the very advice Julian gave her. Either way, the advice is striking in its literalisation of the Pauline message. In Romans 8:26, which Julian is quoting, Paul writes how the Spirit helps those who do not know how to pray properly by praying for them 'in groans that cannot be put into words'. I take it that she means that the very struggles of Christians to pray – their painfully inchoate and inarticulate longings for God – represent the direct action of the Spirit upon them. Margery goes further: it is the actual, numberless tears of the devout that prove the Spirit's activity. This detail shows that the Bible as a tool of pastoral practice depends crucially on the cultural context in and for which it is being interpreted. The later Middle Ages, as Huizinga remarked, was a time in which violent emotion was routinely expressed: readers, then as now, appropriated the Bible for their own purposes and needs.

The quotation has further relevance for us, in its ascribing to St Jerome the view that tears torment the devil. Scholars have so far failed to find a precise source in St Jerome's writing for this quotation (Windeatt 2000, 122), though

Margery is not alone among her contemporaries in so enlisting the saint, by way of this potentially misleading commonplace, in support of her practice. I note it now to remind readers that, in the Middle Ages, the Bible was not the only source of proof-texts for a spiritual director, and the historicity, or otherwise, of such a text mattered less than its capacity to offer a holy hook for a spiritual director (usually male) to hang his reflections on.

Margery's appeal to the authority of the Bible is immensely problematical at a time when the Wycliffites were mounting their challenge to the religious and political status quo (cf. Deanesly; McFarlane; Hudson 1978; 1988; McNiven; Ghosh). Though she remains, all her life, unshakeably orthodox, Margery proves extremely difficult for contemporaries to pigeonhole. A lay woman who travelled about the country unsupervised – though she was careful generally to get permission to do so from male authorities (McSheffrey, 53); a woman who claimed great spiritual graces, but had not embraced the cloistered life which would, by confining her movements, have provided a safe arena for their expression: what other pigeonhole remains to fit her into, if not that she is a Lollard? After all, the Lollards had a place in their movement for women preachers, and they were active in Margery's part of the country. In the super-heated atmosphere which prevailed up to and beyond the abortive Lollard rising of 1414, any religiously eccentric views were liable to be labelled heretical.

Hence, in 1417, Margery, at York, is interrogated by the Archbishop and other clerics (chs 50–52): an altogether more dangerous situation than she found herself in at Canterbury. The ill-informed and ill-intentioned accuse her, again, of being a Lollard; even the Archbishop, initially, thinks her wearing white a sign of heresy. She is asked why she travels about without written permission from her husband. She is quizzed about her understanding of the seemingly innocent Bible text, '*Crescite et multiplicamini*' ('Be fruitful and multiply') (Windeatt 1994, 159; Gen. 1:22), which some Continental heretics were using to justify sexual immorality (Windeatt 2000, 243). She answers in a way that not only demonstrates her orthodoxy, but attempts to carve out a space for her own way of life:

> These words are not only to be understood as applying to the begetting of children physically, but also to the gaining of virtue, which is spiritual fruit, such as by hearing the words of God, by giving a good example, by meekness and patience … and other such things – for patience is more worthy than miracle working. (Windeatt 1994, 159)

With these words, Margery positions herself strikingly in the ordinary currents of morality and piety. She is careful not to claim for herself the status of miracle-worker. Yet, at the same time, her words give her a role in the evangelisation of her neighbours 'by giving a good example', and spiritualise the physical blessings promised in Genesis 1:22 to make them refer to the sowing of the seed of the Gospel. The clerics at York find this intensely problematical: they cannot fault her understanding of the articles of the Faith, but they fear that because 'the people have great faith in her talk … she might lead some of them astray' (Windeatt 1994, 163). And when the Archbishop demands that she promise not to teach people in his diocese, she refuses point-blank.

Scripture, she claims, authorises her refusal. The woman who responded to Jesus' preaching with the words 'Blessed be the womb that bore you' earns from Jesus the reply 'So are they blessed who hear the word of God and keep it' (Windeatt 1994, 165; Luke 11:27–28). Christ's reply puts the onus on the hearers of the preached word to practise what it preaches, just as Margery has said she does. Margery is using the quotation so as to create a space for ordinary pious utterance, by women no less than men; and maybe, since the woman in the gospel addresses Christ with a fervent blessing, to create a place for the ecstatic utterance which routinely characterises her expressed religious understandings. There may also be a barely veiled criticism of those like her present opponents who, in failing to recognise her spiritual gift, may be hearing the word of God from her but are certainly not keeping it. In reaction, the clerics declare that she must be diabolically deluded, and one of them quotes against her the Pauline prohibition on women preaching (1 Cor. 14:34–35). Margery has to argue that she is not preaching, since she never goes into a pulpit (no more did the later Lollards!) and is only using 'conversation and good words' to speak of God.

Another cleric now says that she told him 'the worst tale about priests' that he ever heard (Windeatt 1994, 164). The Archbishop demands to hear it. Margery's exemplum tells of a priest who saw a bear devouring the blossoms of a pear tree and immediately discharging them at its rear end. A hermit explains to the priest that he is himself both the pear tree, 'flowering through … saying of the services and administering of the sacraments', and the bear, spending his time, in every other respect, like a man of the world (Windeatt 1994, 165). Such a story is part of the stock-in-trade of the medieval pulpit (Owst; Wenzel; Spencer). Notwithstanding its round condemnation of a member of the clerical elite, which it shares with Lollard writing, it offers no evidence of Lollard affiliations. Lollards were renowned for their dislike of fables and secular literature as tools of preaching, a dislike which, to be sure, some orthodox thinkers shared (Ellis 2001, 27). Moreover, Margery's allegorisation of her narrative contrasts with Lollard insistence on, and appeal to, the 'naked letter' of the biblical text in their preaching and writing (again, this approach was not in itself heterodox). Sermons to the people by orthodox preachers, like those in the collection edited by Ross, often have recourse, just like Margery, to allegorised stories. Margery's use of the story, then, shows her internalising one of the most important tools of pastoral practice, the sermon; it also shows how the Bible, as a tool of pastoral practice, has become a site of conflict between orthodox and heretical understandings.

The *locus classicus* for any understanding of the importance of the sermon in the Middle Ages is, of course, the *Regula Curae Pastoralis* (*Rule of the Pastoral Office*) (*c.* 591: Davis) of St Gregory the Great, a work accorded considerable authority throughout the Middle Ages. Regrettably, this work understands pastoral care very narrowly as the exercise of preaching by bishops, on whom historically the task of preaching devolved. Even as a preacher's manual, the *Regula* leaves much to be desired. It has no real interest in the dynamics of preaching, and it gives the hearers very little role beyond allowing them to utter 'free and sincere words' which show them 'capable of taking right views on some matters' (2.8; Davis, 76–7); indeed, it warns them against 'judging rashly the way of life of their superiors if, by chance, they observe anything reprehensible' (3.4; Davis, 99). Like St Paul, the preacher has to empathise with his hearers, 'transfer[ring] to himself the infirmities of others [and] … transfiguring the person of the unbeliever into himself' (2.5; Davis, 56–7), but only, it seems, to help him to preach with greater authority. In practice he may need to praise the hearers at the outset, in order to prepare them for the hard words that must follow: 'praise them for good qualities that could be present, *even though they actually may not be*' (my emphasis, 3.17; Davis, 143). Granted, the text occasionally admits to the difficulties of its own project. Virtue and vice, it tells us, can be confusingly alike: if allied with inactivity, humility is 'next door neighbour to laziness' (3.16; Davis, 137). Even here, though, it is characteristically the hearers who are likely to be agents of the confusion, miscalling miserliness frugality and prodigality open-handedness (2.9), and needing to be reminded that 'one virtue if not partnered by another is ineffective' (3.22; Davis, 163). Margery's clerical antagonists have the highest precedent for some of their illiberal attitudes.

Of course, bishops regularly delegated to others the authority to preach: especially, in the thirteenth century and after, to the newly created Mendicant Orders (Southern; McGinn and Meyendorff; Raitt et al.; Cross). The Dominicans were created for this very purpose. For all of them, preaching was a major weapon in the Church's arsenal for the combating of heresy and evangelising the faithful. Margery's devotion to the pulpit is considerable, though the preachers she hears sometimes find troublesome her noisy way of engaging with their message. One, a celebrated Franciscan, eventually bans her from his preaching because of her unruly behaviour when he talks about the passion of Christ (chs 61–2). He is not moved to change his mind even when Margery's priest-scribe offers him examples of other holy women and men who wept uncontrollably.

The priest-scribe learns of four of these holy weepers from books (ch. 62; cf. Ellis 1990). He reads one of them, and probably the others as well, in Latin, though all were available in English. The Latin text, a life by Jacques de Vitry of the beguine Marie of Oignies (d. 1213), he was told about by another priest. Possibly Margery herself drew the others to his attention. She tells us twice (chs 17, 58) that she was read to, almost certainly by a priest, from two of them: the anonymous thirteenth-century *Stimulus Amoris* (*Prick of Love*), often thought to have been written by the Franciscan St Bonaventura; and the *Incendium Amoris* (*Fire of Love*) by the Yorkshire hermit Richard Rolle (d. 1349). The informal and domestic context suggested by this picture, of one person reading to another, brings us tantalisingly close to what we might think of as a typical expression of modern spiritual direction. It also shows pastoral practice as a two-way flow between clerical and lay understandings: not simply a matter, as Margery's clerical contemporaries routinely thought it was, of (lay) ignorance being instructed by (clerical) knowledge. Religious instruction is more like an unbroken chain, whose individual members, clerical or lay, have a duty to teach others what they have themselves been taught.

The centrality of the Bible in these pastoral processes can be easily inferred from Margery's ready ability to quote from it: but we have a more direct way of demonstrating the point. In about 1413, we find Margery (ch. 58) complaining to Christ about her lack of a priest to 'fill [her] soul with [his] word and with reading of Holy Scripture' (Windeatt 1994, 181). Christ promises to send her someone to satisfy her desire; and, shortly after, a priest who has never seen her before arrives with his mother at Lynn. He is 'greatly moved to speak with her' (Windeatt 1994, 181). When she comes, he reads to her and his mother the episode in Luke where Jesus weeps over Jerusalem. Margery's tearful reaction, if startling, is the beginning of a prolonged period of collaboration: for nearly eight years he reads to her out of religious classics like the *Stimulus Amoris* and *Incendium Amoris*. He also reads to her a vernacular classic from the end of the fourteenth century by the Augustinian canon Walter Hilton, *The Scale of Perfection* (Clark and Dorward): or, just possibly, since she names it only as 'Hilton's book', another of Hilton's works specifically designed for lay readers, *Mixed Life* (Ogilvie-Thompson). Both parties profit from the exercise. Margery becomes religiously literate, though unable to read, and the priest has recognised that he has something to learn from her piety.

Pride of place in the reading list, though, goes to 'the Bible with doctors' commentaries on it' (Windeatt 1994, 182). This is almost certainly a copy of the Latin Vulgate Bible, and the commentaries are most probably the extensive marginal and interlinear glosses with which such Bibles were provided, and which quoted extensively from the Fathers and later authorities. Margery's prolonged exposure to such a Bible helps to account for her facility, later in life, with biblical Latin. How far such a glossed Bible is from the versions resulting from the Lollards' professed adherence to the 'naked letter' of the Bible hardly needs demonstrating, but it does remind us of the need for a generous understanding of what the Middle Ages understood by the Bible. The Bible needs to be seen in relation to the totality of its partnering commentaries and, indeed, of the whole literature which, directly and indirectly, it inspired (Lampe; Lawton). Margery may have derived her distinctive understanding of Genesis 1:22 from a moralised gloss on the verse. So, for example, the later printed *Biblia Latina* (1480–81) allegorised 'the fruits of the earth' as 'good thoughts'.

Unlike 'Hilton's book', however, which Margery could have read for herself if she had been able to read English, the Bible was unavailable to her except in Latin, the result of the banning in 1409, by the Archbishop of Canterbury, of all unlicensed Bible translations in the vernacular since the time of Wycliffe. Much has been written (e.g. Watson 1995) about this ban and its momentous, adverse consequences for the production of vernacular religious literature in the fifteenth century. One of the immediate consequences was the publication in 1410 by the Carthusian Nicholas Love, with the Archbishop's enthusiastic endorsement, of a work designed expressly for the laity, *The Mirror of the Blessed Life of Jesus Christ* (Sargent). This was an adaptation of the anonymous fourteenth-century work, *Meditationes Vitae Christi* (*Meditations on the Life of Christ*; Ragusa and Green), which was routinely ascribed, like the *Stimulus Amoris*, to St Bonaventura. This was probably another of the books read to Margery, either in the original or in Love's version, and it clearly colours her many imaginative re-creations (in her word, 'contemplations') of the life of Christ, and her emotional responses to any mention of that life.

Love, and pseudo-Bonaventura before him, provide the precedent: both versions include much material for which the Bible provides no direct warrant. Their texts thus fly in the face of the Wycliffite support for the 'naked text' of Scripture without fabulous accretion. Following pseudo-Bonaventura, Love back-handedly, in his prologue, acknowledges the force of the opposing argument, and allows the reader to read differently those parts of the work clearly biblical and those which may not be proved 'by holi writ or grondet [grounded] in expresse seyinges of holy doctours' (Sargent, 11). Non-canonical material is to be understood simply as 'a deuoute meditacion' on something that might have happened. Whatever assists the reader's devotion, that is, is to be encouraged. Yet, without access to a vernacular Bible, how are readers easily to know which parts of the work are canonical, and which not? While the Archbishop's ban remains in force they are unlikely, without clerical assistance, ever to be able to do so. For them, Love's entire text is not readily distinguishable from the gospel.

Moreover, the ideal readers of Love's work are not self-directing, but

> symple creatures ... whiche as childryn hauen nede to be fedde with

> mylke of lyhte doctryne [easy teaching] and not with sadde [serious] mete of grete clargye [learning] and of hye contemplacion
> (Sargent,10; cf. 1 Cor. 3:1–3).

There are two points to be noted here. First, which I find intensely ironic, is Love's use of the word *clargye*, referring both to a clerical caste and to its principal occupation. But, second, which I find depressing, is his use of the Pauline proof-text: clerics opposed to the production of vernacular Bible translations, who alleged that such translations caused, and/or were an effect of, heresy, routinely appealed to it (Deanesly, 96, 100, 417, 423; Ellis 2001, 21). Like Judaism, heresy is regularly castigated for failure to go beyond the literal senses of Scripture to the spiritual understandings which the orthodox clergy are empowered, by their grasp of Latin, to manipulate. Facing an appeal to the 'naked text', then, authority declares sacred all its additions to the text: glosses, allegorical interpretations, even the fraud of pious imaginations.

The legacy of the Fourth Lateran Council

The real irony, of course, is that both Margery and the Lollards, admittedly in very different ways, are the beneficiaries of two centuries of religious education, instituted by the Church, at the fourth Lateran Council, as a response to the spread of heretical movements, especially the Cathars (Deanesly; Leff; Moore). Recognising that the heretics were likely to appeal most immediately to the uneducated, the Council decreed that parish priests must have a minimum of religious instruction, which they should transmit to the laity in the vernacular (Pantin; Heffernan; McNeill and Gamer, 413–14). Throughout the thirteenth and fourteenth centuries, English bishops legislated accordingly. Thus in 1357 the chaplain of the Archbishop of York produced a vernacular metrical version of a Latin work by the Archbishop informing the priests of the archdiocese about the elements of the faith which they should be teaching their parishioners (Simmons and Nolloth). This translation was designed both for parish priests, who might have difficulty with the Archbishop's Latin, and pious lay folk. But, as a writer once said, give people translations and they end up wanting more translations. With hindsight, we can see that the Church was becoming the victim of its own successes.

Part of the problem lies in the way the Church evolved throughout the early Middle Ages in relation to the relatively undeveloped structures of the society to which it belonged (Southern). The Church was like the leaven in the lump, and the Benedictine monasteries, which were the real success story of the early Middle Ages, were the principal agent of the leaven. Founded and endowed by royalty and nobility, monasteries existed both to symbolise, by their commitment to a life of prayer and other religious observance, the salvation of the society to which they belonged, and to accomplish the salvation of individual members of that society: in the first instance, the monks themselves, then their benefactors. Any more direct involvement of the laity in the processes of salvation was unnecessary. Though never lost sight of, the person was routinely subordinated to a religious role in such structures. This same confusion of person and role persists throughout the Middle Ages, but becomes more acutely problematical at a time of rapid social change, which was what Europe witnessed from the eleventh century on with, in particular, the development of an urban proletariat and a flowering of education in cathedral schools and universities. Something like what we recognise as an individual, needing pastoral care tailored to his own situation, was beginning to emerge. These changes required changes in the organisation of the Church; but, if we except the already noted rise of the Mendicants, and the more limited rise, some forty years before, of the beguines, new structures were not generally forthcoming to address the new situations. After 1274, indeed, they were prohibited: new religious orders were required to adopt the rules of one of the older orders (Southern, 329). Monastic spirituality remained the main model (Leclercq; Bynum), and its articulation of the tension between individuals and their religious roles hardly met the needs of the new, lay electorate. Had Margery been 'enclosed in a house of stone', or content, with married women, to 'spin and card wool' (Windeatt 1994, 168), authority would have known what to make of her. As it was, they had only an ill-fitting monastic habit, so to say, to clothe her in (cf. Voaden, ch. 4).

And Margery herself had no option but to appeal to religious role models, most of which didn't fit her own experience. The texts adduced in support of her tears, as we have seen, were produced variously by a hermit, an Augustinian canon and Franciscan friars for recluses or Franciscan nuns; or they were about beguines, who, we have noted, made virtually no inroads into England. The one work Margery may have read that was expressly designed for seculars, *Mixed Life*, discourages them from attempting the contemplative heights of the spiritual life. Had Margery lived in Cologne in the early thirteenth century, she would have been exposed to the Dominican Eckhart, whose preaching, in the vernacular, had laid out before its hearers theological speculation of a dazzling and dizzying profundity (Southern, 301–4). But there was no Eckhart in fifteenth-century England. Hence, for example, the similarly dazzling speculations of the beguine Marguerite Porete, when translated into English in the fifteenth century, needed regular glossing by the anxious translator to make sure they squared with orthodox understandings (Doiron; Watson 1996).

Original writing in the vernacular faced similar challenges. In the 1380s, the spiritual classic, *The Cloud of Unknowing* (Hodgson; Spearing 2001), was produced, possibly by a Carthusian priest, for a young man, possibly also a Carthusian, who was about to be professed as a solitary. For the writer, there was a total and, in principle, unproblematical fit between person and religious profession: *this* profession enables *this* kind of contemplative to develop. Yet he is also uneasily aware that the contemplative experience may not fully match any monastic frame, and may be as available to seculars as to religious. Moreover, he cannot prevent his book from being read by people for whom he would judge it to be quite unsuitable. He obviously feels this problem acutely, and therefore produces a second work for the same reader on the same subject, *The Book of Privy Counselling*, whose circulation he tries yet more strenuously, but with not much more success, to restrict.

But even writing directed initially to a monastic readership was not immune from similar pressures. Consider, for instance, *The Twelve Patriarchs*, also known as *Benjamin Minor* (Zinn), a work written between 1153 and 1162 by the Augustinian canon Richard of St Victor. The Parisian convent of St Victor was, according to Richard's editor,

> in the forefront of the movement to renew the life of cloistered religious discipline under the aegis of the Rule of St Augustine. It also maintained a vigorous intellectual life, open to the new theological developments in the schools of Paris, developments that monastics, Benedictine and Cistercian alike, tended to shun. (Zinn, 3)

The Victorines had an influence out of all proportion to their size, and Richard was one of their most illustrious sons. *The Twelve Patriarchs* became a spiritual classic, using the most up-to-date faculty psychology to chart progress in the spiritual life under the allegory of the thirteen children, by his two wives and their servant girls, of the Old Testament patriarch Jacob (the 'twelve patriarchs' are his twelve sons). The chronological sequence of the children dictates their part in the allegory. Ruben, first born, is allegorised as the fear of God, representing the earliest stage of progress in the spiritual life; Benjamin, the last born, stands for the contemplative heights, since, according to Psalm 67:28, which Richard used, Benjamin is a young man '*in mentis excessu*' ('in an excess of spirit').

It looks, then, as if the individual religious is invited to apply the allegory personally to himself. If so, additional significance attaches to the number twelve: it is not only the number of Christ's first disciples, but also, often, the number of religious needed to make up a convent. A religious community, that is, is no more than the sum of its individual members. But religious may not all be at the same stage of spiritual development, and will hence need to read themselves differently in the allegory. In any case, one way and another, each reader contains *all* of Richard's possible spiritual states, at least as possibilities; no one progresses to the point where what has been left behind does not remain as a potential motive of future behaviour. Still more importantly, the individual exists in community not just as an individual, but as a religious role and office: cellarer, say, or sacristan. Hence the allegory relates not just to an individual but to his religious role as well. As I have noted elsewhere (Ellis 1992,196–7), Jacob's tenth child, Zabulon, or hatred of sin, speaks not just of hatred of one's own sin but speaks also of the abbot, the officer in the community to whom power of correction over the whole community is delegated, since the individual religious may need correction both for sins against the commandments and for less damaging breaches of convent regulations. That is, the pastoral practice for which monastic literature tries to legislate cannot be applied unproblematically to a modern situation, any more than can the religious literature produced for an explicitly lay readership in the Middle Ages.

For further proof of this claim we may turn, finally, to the *Dialogus Miraculorum* (*Dialogue of Miracles*) (Strange; Scott and Bland). This work was produced *c.* 1223 (Cross, 215) – in the immediate aftermath of the deliberations of the Lateran Council, and as a partial response to the continuing threat of heresy – by the Cistercian Caesarius of Heisterbach for members of his Order, especially the novices of his convent, for whom he was acting as novice master. The work functions explicitly as a tool of pastoral monastic practice, introducing the novices to the Order by way of exemplary narratives of Cistercian monks (the 'miracles' of the title) and detailed accounts of the requirements of religious life. It overlaps with much that would be produced for the laity in the next two hundred years.

Caesarius creates a lightly fictionalised account of contemporary pastoral practice by casting the work in the form of a dialogue (hence the other element of the work's title) between a monk and a novice. Dialogue is thus enshrined in the process of making a good monk, as it was in the evolution of Margery's own spirituality. It is not, of course, a dialogue of equals. The novice mostly gets to ask only about things he doesn't understand, and then, after he has heard the answers, to show that he now understands them. At the same time, the master, like any good teacher, gives instruction flexibly, and is willing, up to a point, to allow the novice's questions to shape the direction of his comments.

Overall, Caesarius operates a fairly clear-cut structure. He divides the work into two parts, each with six subdivisions (*distinctiones*). This time the number twelve refers not to Christ's disciples, but, the prologue tells us, to the twelve baskets of fragments collected by the disciples in John 6:12–13. In so activating the biblical emblem, Caesarius is acknowledging his work's dependence not only on the examples of his predecessors but also on the Bible itself. The *Dialogus*, that is, has to find some way of recuperating both elements of its own religious past for its immediate audience.

The two parts into which Caesarius divides the work have further significance for us. They correspond almost to what later writers will speak of as the purgative and illuminative ways. Caesarius calls the first 'merit'.

This part is largely taken up with cleaning the slate: 2–4 consider contrition, confession and temptation, and 5 the principal agents of temptation (the devils). Section 6 considers a distinctively Cistercian virtue, one prepared for, so to say, by the hard work required to complete the previous sections: simplicity. The second part, called 'reward', focuses on what God does for humans in return. This part stresses God's gifts to us, including visions (8) and miracles (10), and, what the Middle Ages saw as his greatest gifts, the Virgin Mary (7) and the Christ of the Eucharist (9). Framing this material is another structure, which deals with the conversion of the monk, meaning his entry into the Cistercian order (1), where he will end his days (11), before receiving his final reward from God (12).

This double articulation of the spiritual life as both individual and communal, the latter focused most clearly in the opening section, clearly parallels the double emphasis that characterised *The Twelve Patriarchs*. It differs from Richard in the flexibility of its operation. Thus, for example, in the section on contrition, Caesarius relates (2.20) the story of a monk who wishes to obtain the grace of tears. Having heard of a fellow Cistercian who had obtained this grace from a holy woman, he asks permission of his abbot to do the same. Notwithstanding his relatively recent profession, and notwithstanding the bad press which women routinely receive in the Middle Ages – as, indeed, in the pages of the *Dialogus* that deal with temptation – the abbot gives immediate permission. On his way, the young monk breaks his journey, and explains his quest to the lady of the house where he is spending the night. She jokingly asks him why he wants to visit '*istas beguinas*' ('those beguines') when she can bring to him a holy woman who can get whatever she wants from God. In the presence of this holy woman, the monk feels a stirring of grace, and is emboldened to ask for the grace to weep for his sins. The holy woman retorts that, as a monk, he ought to be already doing so; anyone unable to weep for his sins cannot be a monk.

In the event, she does obtain for him the grace he has requested. But more important things are at work in the story than this quasi-miracle. In the first place, there is the holy woman's definition of a monk as one who weeps for his sins. Her understanding can be seen as an ironic echo of older understandings, previously noted, of the monk as the religious representative of society. But a monk does not generally enter the Order fully fledged: he has to learn to become what he professes. (This was true even of those who joined the Cistercians from other Orders in which they found religious observance too lax.) Perhaps religious systems, now as then, would do well to remember this fact in the organisation of their pastoral practices.

More important still is the understanding of dialogue as a central tool of religious development. Everything happens in social contexts, whether in the convent or in a private house, with people swapping ideas in a form of holy gossip. Such dialogue witnesses tellingly to the flexibility and trust possessed by all the major figures in the story, and required of all who direct pastoral practice. The abbot thinks nothing of allowing the young monk to visit holy women for advice. The women are sufficiently at home with themselves even to be able to tease an earnest young man. Admittedly, the housewife is not sure what to make of those religious newcomers, the beguines, whose rise, late in the twelfth century, is probably contemporary with the events of the story, and witnesses to the same spirit of flexibility that characterised the first generations of Cistercians and would come to characterise the Mendicants. Two hundred years later, you will not find those to whom Margery Kempe goes making jokes about the religious newcomers in *their* midst; you will not find authority sending earnest young men to her for advice, though in fact several young men, like the priest mentioned who reads to her, do seek her out for advice. Women, that is, have a religious role at a tangent to the formal religious structures, which they can best exercise when those structures are not set hard like concrete.

Nothing so hardens a position, of course, as a sense of its heretical opposite. Heresy is no laughing matter: Caesarius shows the limits of his flexibility when confronting the errors of heretics. Even the novice attacks the Cathars for their belief that matter was created by the devil, and quotes a glossed Bible account of the creation story (Gen. 2:7) to prove his point: 'Moses makes it certain that God created both soul and body, when he says: "The Lord God formed man", i.e. the body, "of the dust of the ground, and breathed into his nostrils the breath of life" … i.e. the soul' (Scott and Bland, 1.344). But it is no simple matter to separate our truth from their lies. Witness the celebrated, and chilling, account, in that same chapter, of the recapture from the heretics of the city of Béziers. The victors ask the abbot how to distinguish the Cathars still in the city from the orthodox; the abbot, with no sense of irony, tells them to kill them all, because God will know his own.

A similar fate awaits heretics at the University of Paris, the subject of the next chapter (5.22), whose errors Caesarius lists for the novice. These neither simply echo Cathar, nor simply foreshadow Wycliffite, errors. Like the heretics who took Genesis 1:22 to sanction sexual immorality, these understand life in the Spirit to authorise fornication, since those joined to the Spirit, who is 'altogether separate from the flesh' (Scott and Bland, 1.348), cannot sin. On the other side, they resemble the orthodox preachers in their readiness to find God even in pagan literature: 'they said … that God had spoken through Ovid, just in the same way as through Augustine' (Scott and Bland, 1.348). Most present-day Christians would have no more time for the first error than Caesarius. Many, likewise, would share with Caesarius and other orthodox medieval thinkers – to say nothing of the Wycliffites – their disapproval of the heretics' understanding that God is to be found as directly in the erotic fables and metamorphic narratives of Ovid as in the writings of St Augustine. The heretics' error is, of course, easily intelligible in a medieval context, where

Latin was taught through the medium of classical authors like Ovid. Such material was routinely christianised by arguing that Ovid wrote to warn against the excesses he describes, or by reading his erotic narratives as spiritual allegories (Minnis, 5–6, 205–8). God spoke in such texts, if not directly, through the reader's overpainting them with a whitewash of Christian principles. I, however, do not share this view. I think we need an understanding of the presence and activity of God in the world sufficiently generous and flexible to allow us to trace that presence even in our religious negatives. At all events, that kind of flexibility is necessary for anyone who wants to exercise any form of pastoral practice.

Summary

The foregoing pages cannot do more than give a taste of the enormous range of texts and practices to be found in the Middle Ages. I have had no space, other than in passing, to talk of the major monastic development of the Middle Ages, the Benedictines, founded in 529; nor of an equally illustrious Order, the Carthusians, founded in 1084, who had an important role to play in the creation and dissemination of vernacular religious literature for the laity; nor, in the late fifteenth century, of the Dutch group known as *devotio moderna* (modern devotion), from which came the celebrated *Imitation of Christ* of Thomas à Kempis. I particularly regret not being able to talk about that most interesting religious experiment, the beguines, which seems to me a perfect – and, mostly, perfectly orthodox – antidote to the centralising ecclesiastical tendencies of the later Middle Ages. Nevertheless certain common characteristics and noteworthy features should have emerged.

- Omnipresent as a tool of pastoral direction, the Bible exists as the centre of a vast web of commentary and pious accretion, not all of it obviously religious, and all of it available for use, generally moralised, by the spiritual director. The Bible, so defined, exists to be accommodated to the interests and imperatives of the target audience: this last is clearly seen in the way opposing sides of a religious argument, like the Wycliffites and the orthodox, often appeal to the same texts to justify their own position and damn their opponents.
- Pastoral practice turns out to be similarly various. Formal and informal preaching, and what Margery Kempe calls 'giving a good example', provide arenas for its expression. So, too, written records of spiritual experiences, like Margery's *Book*, or maps and models of the spiritual life, like *The Twelve Patriarchs* and Love's *Mirror*. Some texts like the *Dialogus* mix instruction and spiritual experience – as, indeed, one way and another, all religious writing does.
- The individuals who used the Bible to minister to their fellows, and those

to whom they ministered, were also various, and were usually working with potentially confusing or conflicting models of pastoral practice. This is as true of texts produced for use in the convent as it is when spiritual direction migrates out of the cloister to engage with the confusions of the secular order. All of which seems to me a healthy sign. The roles of teacher and taught, which both parties have to accept for the pastoral situation to work, are provisional and temporary: the ultimate authority is God's. Great writers, like the author of the *Cloud*, freely admit that the pupil may outstrip the master. Flexibility in the exercise of these roles is therefore the *sine qua non* of good pastoral practice, since it draws attention to that unpredictable current of spiritual energy which passes between master and pupil, and points beyond both to its origin and its ending: to what John Taylor memorably called 'the go-between God'.

Bibliography

Babinsky, E. L. (trans.) (1993) *Marguerite Porete: The Mirror of Simple Souls*. New York and Mahwah, NJ: Paulist Press.

Biblia Latina cum Glossa Ordinaria (1992 [1480–1]). Facsimile. Turnhout: Brepols.

Bowie, F. (ed.) and Davies, O. (trans.) (1989) *Beguine Spirituality: an anthology*. London: SPCK.

Bynum, C. W. (1982) *Jesus as Mother: studies in the spirituality of the High Middle Ages*. Berkeley, CA: University of California Press.

Clark, J. P. H. and Dorward, R. (trans.) (1991) *Walter Hilton: The Scale of Perfection*. Mahwah, NJ: Paulist Press.

Colledge, E. and Walsh, J. (eds) (1978) *A Book of Showings to the Anchoress Julian of Norwich*, 2 vols. Toronto: Pontifical Institute of Mediaeval Studies.

Cross, F. L. (ed.) (1957) *The Oxford Dictionary of the Christian Church*. Oxford: Oxford University Press.

Davis, H. (trans.) (1950) *St Gregory the Great: Pastoral Care*. London: Longman, Green.

Deanesly, M. (1920) *The Lollard Bible and Other Medieval Biblical Versions*. Cambridge: Cambridge University Press.

Doiron, M. (ed.) (1968) '*The Mirror of Simple Souls*': a Middle English translation. *Archivio Italiano per la storia della Pietà* 5, 242–355.

Ellis, R. (1990) Margery Kempe's scribe and the miraculous books, in H. Phillips (ed.), *Langland, the Mystics and the Medieval English Religious Tradition*. Cambridge: D. S. Brewer, 161–75.

Ellis, R. (1992) Author(s), compilers, scribes and Bible texts: did the *Cloud*-author translate *The Twelve Patriarchs*? in M. Glasscoe (ed.) *The Medieval Mystical Tradition in England*. Cambridge: D. S. Brewer, 193–221.

Ellis, R. (2001) Figures of English ranslation, 1382-1407, in R. Ellis and E. Oakley-Brown (eds), *Translation and Nation: towards a cultural politics of Englishness*. Clevedon: Multilingual Matters, 7–47.

Ghosh, K. (2002) *The Wycliffite Heresy: authority and the interpretation of texts*. Cambridge: Cambridge University Press.

Heffernan, T. J. (ed.) (1985) *The Popular Literature of Medieval England*. Knoxville, TN: University of Tennessee Press.

Hodgson, P. (1982) *The Cloud of Unknowing and Related Treatises on Contemplative Prayer*. *Analecta Cartusiana* 3. Salzburg: Institut für Anglistik und Amerikanistik.

Hudson, A. (ed.) (1978) *Selections from English Wycliffite Writings*. Cambridge: Cambridge University Press.

Hudson, A. (1988) *The Premature Reformation: Wycliffite texts and Lollard history*. Oxford: Clarendon Press.

Huizinga, J. W. (1965) *The Waning of the Middle Ages*. Harmondsworth: Penguin.

Lampe, G. W. (ed.) (1969) *The Cambridge History of the Bible* vol. 2: *the West from the Fathers to the Reformation*. Cambridge: Cambridge University Press.

Lawton, D. (1999) Englishing the Bible, 1066–1549, in D. Wallace (ed.) *The Cambridge History of Medieval English Literature*. Cambridge: Cambridge University Press, 454–82.

Leclercq, J. (1961) *The Love of Learning and the Desire for God: a study of monastic culture*. New York: Mentor Omega Books.

Leff, G. (1967) *Heresy in the Later Middle Ages*. 2 vols. Manchester: Manchester University Press.

McFarlane, K. B. (1952) *John Wycliffe and the Beginnings of English Nonconformity*. London: Macmillan.

McGinn, B. and Meyendorff, J. (eds) (1986) *Christian Spirituality: origins to the twelfth century*. London: Routledge & Kegan Paul.

McNeill, J. T. and Ganer, H. M. (trans.) (1938) *Medieval Handbooks of Penance*. New York: Columbia University Press.

McNiven, P. (1987) *Heresy and Politics in the Reign of Henry IV: the burning of John Badby*. Woodbridge: The Boydell Press.

McSheffrey, S. (1995) *Gender and Heresy: women and men in Lollard communities, 1420–1530*. Philadelphia: University of Pennsylvania Press.

Minnis, A. J. (1988) *Medieval Theory of Authorship*. Aldershot: Wildwood.

Moore, R. I. (1975) *The Birth of Popular Heresy*: *documents of medieval history* vol. I. London: Edward Arnold.

Ogilvie-Thompson, S. J. (ed.) (1986) Walter Hilton's mixed life. *Elizabethan and Renaissance Studies* 92.15. Salzburg: Institut für Anglistik und Amerikanistik.

Owst, G. R. (1933) *Literature and Pulpit in Medieval England*. Cambridge: Cambridge University Press.

Pantin, W. A. (1962) *The English Church in the Fourteenth Century*. Notre Dame, IN: University of Notre Dame Press.

Ragusa, I. B. and Green, R.B. (trans.) (1961) *Meditations on the Life of Christ*. Princeton: Princeton University Press.

Raitt, J., McGinn B. and Meyendorff, J. (eds) (1988) *Christian Spirituality: High Middle Ages and Reformation*. New York: Crossroad.

Ross, W. O. (ed.) (1940) *Middle English Sermons*. London: Oxford University Press.

Sargent, M. G. (ed.) (1992) *Nicholas Love's Mirror of the Blessed Life of Jesus Christ*. New York: Garland.

Scott, H. von E. and Swinton Bland, C. C. (trans.) (1929) *The Dialogue on Miracles* 2 vols. London: George Routledge & Son.

Simmons, T. F. and Nolloth, H. E. (eds) (1901) *The Lay Folk's Catechism*. London: Kegan Paul, Trench, Trübner and Co.

Southern, R. W. (1970) *Western Society and the Church in the Middle Ages*. Harmondsworth: Penguin.

Spearing, E. C. (trans.) (1998) *Julian of Norwich: Revelations of Divine Love*. Harmondsworth: Penguin.

Spearing, A. C. (trans.) (2001) *The Cloud of Unknowing and Other Works*. Harmondsworth: Penguin.

Spencer, H. (1993) *English Preaching in the Late Middle Ages*. Oxford: Clarendon Press.

Stargardt, U. (1985) The Beguines of Belgium, the Dominican nuns of Germany, and Margery Kempe, in T. J. Heffernan (ed.), *The Popular Literature of Medieval England.* Knoxville, TN: University of Tennessee Press, 277–313.

Strange, J. (ed.) (1851) *Caesarius Heisterbachensis … Dialogus Miraculorum* 2 vols. Cologne: J. M. Heberle.

Voaden, R. (1999) *God's Words, Women's Voices: the discerning of spirits in the writing of late-medieval women visionaries.* York: York Medieval Press.

Watson, N. (1993) The composition of Julian of Norwich's *Revelation of Love. Speculum* 68, 637–83.

Watson, N. (1995) Censorship and cultural change in late-medieval England: vernacular heresy, the Oxford translation debate, and Arundel's Constitutions of 1409. *Speculum* 70, 822–64.

Watson, N. (1996). Melting into God the English way: deification in the Middle English version of Marguerite Porete's *Mirouer des simples ames anienties,* in R. Voaden (ed.), *Prophets Abroad: the reception of continental holy women in late-medieval England.* Cambridge: D. S. Brewer, 19–49.

Wenzel, S. (ed. and trans.) (1989) *Fasciculus Morum: a fourteenth-century preacher's handbook.* Pennsylvania: Pennsylvania State University Press.

Windeatt, B. (trans.) (1994) *The Book of Margery Kempe.* Harmondsworth: Penguin.

Windeatt, B. (ed.) (2000) *The Book of Margery Kempe.* Harlow: Longman.

Zinn, G. A. (trans.) (1979) *Richard of St Victor: The Twelve Patriarchs [etc.].* New York and Ramsey, NJ: Paulist Press).

CHAPTER 5:

The impact of the Reformation and emerging modernism

CARL TRUEMAN

Introduction

The period from 1500 to 1800 is without doubt one of the most traumatic in the history of the Western Church. In the sixteenth century, there is the rise of Protestantism in various ecclesiastical forms, and also the development of Tridentine Catholicism, both of which represent responses to the various problems relating to issues of authority and of pastoral care which had emerged within the late medieval Church. Then, in the latter part of the seventeenth century, the impact of Enlightenment patterns of thought, combined with the economic and social reshaping of European society, fuelled the development of various forms of pietism which manifested themselves in a number of ways, from a simple moralism to enthusiastic revivalism.

Common to all these phenomena was the centrality of the Bible both to theory and to practice; yet the status of the Bible in these various movements is perhaps not as simple or straightforward as has sometimes been thought. If Reformation Protestants prided themselves on placing the Bible in the hands of lay people, they were yet concerned that the interpretation and use of the Bible should not be reduced to an individual activity but should be grounded in the corporate activity of the Church where it could be guided by an established and educated church leadership. Reformation Catholics wished to retain the essentially sacerdotal approach to Scripture, yet they too made concessions to the rise of a more individually oriented piety and to the need to promote more theological literacy amongst lay people, as epitomised in the kinds of spirituality which proved so successful in the hands of the Society of Jesus. Then, in the later seventeenth and eighteenth centuries, pietism and revivalism helped to promote forms of Christianity that prioritised experience over learning and thus undermined the concern with ecclesiology and corporate interpretation that had been a hallmark of earlier Protestantism.

The Protestant Reformation

Before looking at some specific trends in the practical use of the Bible in the Reformation, it is worth making some general observations at the outset. First, it is important to realise that Protestant biblical exegesis in the sixteenth century did not simply stand in a position of radical discontinuity with the past. Scholars have long been aware of the importance of the Patristic authors, particularly Augustine and Chrysostom, fuelled both by a premodern respect for tradition and by the impact of the culture of Renaissance humanism on Reformation thinking. More recently, the positive connections between late medieval interpretation and Protestant exegesis have also been demonstrated. The latter represents, on one level, an extension and intensification of the concern for the literal sense which had characterised Western exegetes from the twelfth century; further, Protestants also showed great respect for the actual medieval commentary tradition, and the exegetical continuities with prior church traditions is now well established (Muller and Thompson; Steinmetz; Wengert 1987; Farmer; Thompson).

While there were these continuities, one point where Reformation Protestantism and medieval Catholicism diverged radically, and that had a significant pastoral impact, was in the emphasis upon individual assurance, which arose from the distinctive Protestant understanding of justification by grace through faith. For a medieval Catholic no one, other than a saint to whom a special revelation had been made, could know for certain that they were going to make it to heaven, and this basic issue stood at the centre of much pastoral practice in the Middle Ages, driving the penitential system, the Mass, indeed, the whole of the sacramental engine of the Church. For the Reformers, however, such assurance was basic to the believer's relationship with God, to self-understanding, and to practical, ethical behaviour towards others. It also profoundly affected the pastoral practices of the Church.

With the Reformation shift to the normativity of personal assurance of salvation and to an emphasis upon the individual, a whole new array of problems developed within the Church that required new pastoral responses. As the bar was raised so much higher in terms of personal knowledge of salvation, so the familiar pastoral structures of the Church, such as formal confession, were stripped away, catapulting people into a very strange, new world of Christian life and experience (Zachman; Beeke). It is difficult to imagine how traumatic this move was, but it must have generated considerable pastoral problems and appropriate pastoral responses at the level of method and practice, as witnessed, for example, by the debates within Lutheranism over the formal aspects of Christian worship and, perhaps most notably, the language to be used in the extensive development of catechisms and liturgy. Was the old language to be retained, but given new content? Or was the language itself to be changed in order to mark the radical break with the old? The need to promote the Reformation was to be balanced against the need to prevent too much pastoral chaos in the wake of the new personal piety that was emerging (Wengert 1997).

Central to all this, however, was the Protestant confidence in Scripture as the basic instrument in pastoral care: Scripture read, Scripture preached, Scripture applied. Even the sacraments took a logically subordinate position, in that they could only be performed within the context of the word preached (Luther 1520a, 43; Calvin, 4.17.39). Closely allied to this were the related notions of scriptural sufficiency and scriptural perspicuity. At the most basic level, scriptural sufficiency meant that all things necessary to salvation were contained in the Scriptures, and that there was no need for the Church to add a parallel stream of tradition to supplement what was lacking in Scripture itself. As we shall note later, this sphere of sufficiency did tend to expand as time went on and came, in the hands of some teachers, to embrace a whole lot more than just teaching about salvation and basic general principles for daily conduct. Perspicuity meant that Scripture's basic message was clear and comprehensible to all, that there was no need for the Church to interpret Scripture in a definitive sense for her members. Of course, perspicuity has to be qualified: many passages of Scripture were regarded as difficult to understand; and no passage was perspicuous in itself to those lacking Hebrew and Greek; but the central Protestant notion of perspicuity was that the basic message and application of Scripture in its broad outlines was clear and comprehensible to all who had it preached to them (Muller 2003). Nevertheless, we should also note that Protestantism was not a monolithic entity and a diversity both of understanding of Scripture and of pastoral practice in the light of Scripture can be noted in the sixteenth and seventeenth centuries.

The typical Protestant emphasis upon the word – read, spoken, preached – takes its cue from the life and theology of Martin Luther. For Luther, justification was by grace through faith, and faith came through grasping the Lord Jesus Christ, God manifested in the flesh, by trust in his word. Thus, Lutheran worship placed the word at the centre, and, although it retained a high view of the sacraments, made them logically subordinate to the word in that it was the promise attached to the sign that made the sacrament complete (Junghans). The emphasis on the word, however, became normative for all mainstream Protestants, Lutheran, Reformed and Anglican, and influenced church architecture, shifting the focus of church buildings from the altar to the pulpit.

Luther's understanding of the word, and its pastoral use, was shaped decisively by his understanding of the fallen human situation and of the means of redemption. If justification by faith determined the centrality of the word, it also determined the way in which the word was understood. Scripture for Luther was either Old Testament or New Testament, either law or gospel. The divisions are not primarily canonical but hermeneutical: all Scripture is both Old and New Testament, law and gospel, depending upon how the reader understands and responds to the text. If the response is to see Scripture as commanding good works whereby one might be made righteous, then such a reading is that of law; if the response is to see Scripture as promising righteousness in Christ reckoned to those who simply believe in him, then such a reading is that of gospel (Luther 1520b).

In addition to the hermeneutical distinction between law and gospel, there is also the issue of the nature of humanity itself. For Luther, all people need both the law and the gospel preached to them all the time: the law cuts down the human tendency to self-righteousness and to justification on the basis of autonomous effort and drives to despair; the gospel offers words of sweet comfort to build up and to encourage the believer. This constant turning from sin and self to Christ is something which continues throughout the whole of human life, and thus the principal pastoral function of Scripture in preaching is to drive the hearers from trust in their own efforts to trust in Christ. It should therefore be somewhat distinguished from the kind of conversionist preaching found later among the evangelical revivalists of the eighteenth century where particular patterns of experience were commended as normative for initiation into the Christian faith. Conversion, in a sense, is for Luther a constant, lifelong process, which begins at baptism; and the important sacramental context of Luther's theology, difficult though it can sometimes appear, should not be neglected or forgotten when dealing with the pastoral use of Scripture (Trueman 2003).

Underlying all of this was Luther's emphasis upon the centrality of Christ. It was only in Christ that God manifested himself to humanity as gracious; and only in Christ that the seriousness of the problem of sin could be dealt with in an effectual and decisive manner. It was this conviction that God's graciousness was only visible to the eyes of faith, and only available in the promise of God founded in Christ, that drove Luther to refashion much pastoral practice of his day. Most famously he opposed the selling of indulgences in 1517, not because at the time he rejected indulgences in themselves (though he was to move to such a position later) but because the way in which they were being peddled cheapened the grace of God and disembowelled the roles of Christ, faith and true forgiveness. Despairing consciences need consolation and indulgence, but of the kind provided by the promise in Christ, revealed by Scripture and grasped by faith, not by a simple financial transaction (Luther 1517).

It must be noted that this task is not restricted to those who are in some form of ordained full-time ministry. In his reconstruction of the notion of penance and confession, Luther sees it as the duty of any believer to minister the promises of the gospel to any other penitent believer who confesses their sins. In doing so, the individual speaking the promise is not acting in a merely declarative capacity of reminding the individual of what is the case; rather, they are performing a speech-act, a giving of a promise, which, as it is grasped by faith, performs the very thing that it promises. All believers, in union with Christ, are priests with Christ and are thus righteous before God but also bearers of the moral responsibility to be 'little Christs' to their neighbours. There is a very real sense, therefore, in which the speaker or preacher of the word of God is the herald of God, the one who brings the word of divine condemnation and then that of divine forgiveness to those who hear (Luther 1520a). This, of course, fuelled a need for pedagogical aids for educating all Christians above and beyond that which a weekly diet of sermons could achieve, a need that was met by the development of catechisms for giving lay people a much broader grasp of the overall shape of Christian truth. It also influenced Luther's approach to the liturgical context of the sermon. As Helmar Junghans usefully expresses it: 'In Christian freedom and out of pastoral concern for his flock, he took up into the new form [of the liturgy] what appeared to him would further faith and love in the Wittenberg of his time' (225). The pastoral, pedagogical, scriptural concerns are thus clear. Should one keep as closely as possible to the language of traditional Catholicism, changing the meaning of terms to a Protestant sense and only altering the language when absolutely necessary? Or should one engage in a wholesale reformation of the language as well? For Luther, the centrality, sufficiency and authority of Scripture did not mean that he had to engage in wholesale iconoclasm with regard to accepted practice. Such would have been pastorally counterproductive.

While the early Luther was happy to play somewhat fast and loose with the notion of a specifically ordained ministry, the crisis of the Peasants' War of 1525 precipitated something of a reaction against the language of universal priesthood and what might be called a 'higher' view of the Christian ministry, which tended to emphasise formal church structures and appointment to office with regard to the central act of preaching the word. Indeed, in John Calvin the language of universal priesthood is conspicuous only by its general absence. In fact, the work of Calvin, building on the insights of Melanchthon, represents a definite development of the application of Scripture in Protestant theology which moves it beyond the sharp law–gospel dichotomy so characteristic of Luther's preaching. Preaching, of course, remains central, and Calvin was absolutely clear in regarding the preacher of the Word as the herald of God to the congregation. Yet, while there is still a sharp opposition between law and gospel in the matter of justification, with the typical Lutheran antithesis between works and faith being maintained, there is also an increasing emphasis upon the law, specifically the principles of the Decalogue, as being a guide to behaviour for the regenerate. This so-called 'third use of the law' is not present in anything other than a very implicit sense in Luther's ethics but, in Melanchthon and then more so in Calvin, it became a significant ethical category, perhaps reflecting their background in Erasmian humanism, and inevitably influencing their preaching and application of Scripture. Of course, it must also be remembered that the context and agenda of Calvin's reform was very different from that of Luther. As a leading member of a city community, and one engaged in a struggle for the identity of the city itself, Calvin directly addressed many practical ethical and political questions that Luther was able on the whole either to avoid or to tackle only in a piecemeal, occasional manner. A similar situation had earlier marked the reforms of Huldrych Zwingli in Zurich, reforms which had subsequently been carried forward through the influential ministry of Heinrich Bullinger, who had used the covenant concept to articulate the ethical and moral obligations of Christianity, a theology that has occasioned considerable debate (Baker; McCoy and Baker; Bierma 1983, 1986; Lillback). For the Reformed, as opposed to the Lutherans, the transformation of society itself through the application of scriptural principles was part of the ecclesiastical programme of reform from its inception. Thus, in Geneva, Calvin worked to exert significant control over everyday life in terms of the maintenance of what he regarded as biblical standards, assisted by the Company of Pastors and the Consistory at Geneva; standards which, it has to be noted, could sometimes be applied with more rigour to his enemies than to his friends. It is therefore not surprising that we find in his sermons a much broader concern for specific application of biblical moral guidelines to areas of life that Luther would typically have left under the care of the civil authorities or the household (Naphy; Kingdon).

In this context, one should also remember that in a society dominated by the Church and with only slowly growing rates of literacy, the sermon without doubt played a central role in informing the listeners about events in the world around them and in interpreting how these events and their own position in relation to such were to be understood. Thus, for example, we find a concern for providence running as a thread through Protestant sermons from the Reformation onwards, an emphasis designed to highlight the special place of the times, and not infrequently the audience, to the grand flow of history as a whole (Walsham). At times, this could evidence itself in a strongly realistic eschatology, as in the case of Luther, who clearly thought of the times in which he lived as approaching the end of history and of himself as an immediate forerunner of the greater reformation which was to be inaugurated at the imminent return of Christ (Oberman, 668–9); but it could also show itself in the midweek sermons of the Pilgrim Fathers in America as they reminded their people of their God-given task to build the city on the hill (Stout 1988).

Post-Reformation developments

While the Reformation served to place preaching at the centre of the Church's practice, really elaborate reflection on the use of Scripture in pastoral practice became an increasingly significant issue in the generations after the initial work of the Reformers, as the impact of the reconfiguration of Christian life demanded by Reformation theology began to take effect. Despite the traditional scholarly neglect of this period, much work of great importance was done during this time.

The latter part of the sixteenth and the seventeenth century saw significant work in areas of biblical linguistics and exegesis (Farrar; Hall; Sykes; Muller 2003; Burnett). Within Protestant circles, the major motive for this scholarship was the conviction that the Scriptures, given in the original languages, were the uniquely authoritative word of God. At a pastoral level, this was reflected in the continued emphasis upon the preaching of the word as central to worship and piety. In this context, the writings of William Perkins (1558–1602) are particularly instructive, with his *The Arte of Prophecying; or a Treatise concerning the sacred and onely manner and methods of Preaching* (1607) becoming something of a classic text. In this work, Perkins elaborates on the task of the preacher by discussing the method of sermon construction, moving from selection of a biblical passage to identification of genre, dividing up of topics in order to make clear the structure and content of the text, and how then to move from this point to doctrinal synthesis and practical application. He also discusses the disposition of the preacher himself, outwardly in terms of physical mannerisms and the hiding of learning (to maintain the plain directness and comprehensibility of the sermon) and inwardly in terms of personal devotion to both God and to his people, a note which perhaps points towards the kind of experimental concerns which, in English nonconformist pietism and revivalism, will come to eclipse the more strictly doctrinal issues. Of particular interest is the advice which he gives on application, where Perkins identifies the various categories of listener one might find in any congregation: unbelievers who are ignorant and unteachable; those who are teachable but ignorant; those who have knowledge but are not yet humbled; those who are humbled; those who believe; some who are fallen or backslidden (Perkins 1607, 102–22). A number of comments are in order here. First, it is noteworthy that, like Luther, Perkins regards vigorous preaching of the law to be the appropriate response to those who are hard-hearted and impenitent. Only as they show signs of true repentance are such to be comforted with the gospel of justification.

Second, it is clear that Perkins sees the act of preaching as one part of a larger pastoral task where the application of Scripture is not simply undertaken in the somewhat indiscriminate setting of the public congregation but where the identification of individual needs, and the handling of those needs, if necessary, on an individual basis, is to take place. Thus, in the discussion of how Scripture is to be applied, he also introduces the ideas of catechising and confession. As to the latter, this is to be an individual thing, between offender and pastor, and is specifically designed to aid the restoration of the individual. As with the early approach of Luther, it is to involve individual application of the law and, when repentance is in evidence, a judicious application of the gospel.

As to catechising, here Perkins touches on one of the central means of scriptural education and application in the sixteenth and seventeenth centuries, and one which not only has a solid historical pedigree but also transcends typical party lines, being used by Lutherans, Reformed, Catholics and Socinians in order to promote their teachings and cultivate particular readings of the Bible within their different communities. For Perkins, the catechism is the way in which the very basic elements of biblical faith are taught to those who are humble yet unlearned, and its content covers repentance, faith, baptism (i.e., sacraments), imposition of hands (which Perkins interprets as the ministry of the word), the resurrection, and the last judgement (Perkins 1607, 107). The emphasis is upon simplicity, the 'milk' of the word as Perkins phrases it, rather than 'strong meat', and upon laying the doctrinal foundations, ignorance of which renders salvation impossible.

This emphasis upon catechism is a staple of English Puritan pastoral practice in the seventeenth century. Richard Baxter (1615–91) devoted considerable attention to it in his major exposition of the theory and practice of the pastoral ministry, *Gildas Salvianus, the Reformed Pastor* (1656). In this work, catechising is ranked second only to preaching in importance to the work of the minister, and every family and household in the parish is to be given a catechism in order to ensure that the work can go on (Baxter 1656, 420–1). In part, this is because Baxter regards catechising in itself as providing the kind of doctrinal knowledge and framework which goes to making the sermon itself more effective in the hearts of those who hear it (Baxter 1656, 316). It was also, however, an acknowledgement that congregations were made up of individuals with individual needs and capacities. Thus, Baxter also engaged in an extensive analysis of the different types of person who might be catechised, and also of how to deal with them: the unbeliever; the doubting believer; the disputatious schismatic; and those who are ignorant but teachable. This indicates the level of pastoral sophistication at which the Puritans operated, and their sensitivity to the necessity of accommodating their teaching to the needs of particular listeners (Baxter 1656, 423–82). John Owen (1616–83) has a similar view of the use of catechisms for encouraging individual growth in Christian knowledge and personal application of Christian truth, producing two catechisms, a lesser and a greater, specifically designed to take the believer from a knowledge of the rudiments of Christianity through to a more elaborate understanding of the faith: *The principles of the doctrine of Christ: unfolded in two short catechisms* (1645). For him, there was nothing more important, after preaching, than catechising (A3a). Such individual production of catechisms by ministers was typical of the age, and it was somewhat inevitable, therefore, that this culture of catechising would bear formal fruit in the official, Parliament-sanctioned, production of the Shorter and Larger Catechisms by the Westminster Assembly in the 1640s.

Several strands of sixteenth- and seventeenth-century concern flow together in the area of catechising. Given contemporary educational theory, concerned as it was with memory and the best way to memorise material, catechising commended itself as a pedagogical tool both for the way in which it broke complex matters down into relatively simple units, and for the way in which it used the drama of question and answer, and of the human voice, to impress upon the memory that which it intended to teach. As Perkins declared, 'The catechisme is the doctrine of the foundation of Christian religion, brieflie propounded for the helpe of the understanding and memorie in questions and answers made by the *lively voice*' (Perkins 1607, 106).

Underlying this, however, was a more theological motive: the need for believers to have a cognitive content for their faith that embodied knowledge as part of its very substance, and the need therefore for them to understand the Scriptures. Thus, Perkins could structure an exposition of a portion of Scripture as an elaborate catechism in order to teach his people Scripture and what Scripture meant, and to do this in a manner that impressed itself upon their memory. A good example of this is his 1593 tract, *An exposition of the Lords praier in the way of catechisme,* where exposition is reinforced by questions and answers and then driven home by lists of practical applications.

Behind this practice, of course, lay the implicit acknowledgement that preaching could usefully be supplemented by individual or household instruction. Baxter himself drew analogies with schoolmasters and physicians: as they required individual knowledge of their students and patients respectively, so the minister needed the same with regard to the needs of individual members of the congregation (Baxter 1656, 322). This, as we shall see below, fed into the Protestant development of casuistry as a pastoral tool. Interestingly, in this context, Baxter sees an overreaction to Rome's emphasis upon auricular confession as responsible for what he perceives to be the failure of Protestants to develop proper pastoral care for individuals (Baxter 1656, 323). In addition, of course, catechising covered a broad sweep of Christian doctrine in a way virtually impossible in an expository sermon anchored in only a small passage of biblical text. As such, catechising was both liberating, in that it gave the individual the larger picture by which individual biblical passages and sermons might be set in wider context; and, to the more cynically minded, allowed the ministers to control the interpretative framework within which the same might be understood. Indeed, Baxter hints at the use of catechism as a means of social control when he lists as one reason for the practice as being that of giving individuals and families something with which to keep themselves occupied not only on the Lord's Day but also at their workshops during the week, though, to be fair, he immediately follows these with reference to the fact that catechising also keeps ministers from being idle (Baxter 1656, 333–5).

Closely linked to the theory and practice of catechism was the rise of casuistry, the science of applying Scripture to particular cases of conscience. The practice was most effectively developed by the Jesuits, having its roots in the psychology of conscience that was developed by theologians in the Middle Ages; but in the sixteenth and seventeenth centuries it represented a response to pastoral issues which transcended denominations and thus manifested itself in Protestantism as well. The erosion of traditional, close-knit communities, the increasing mobility of sectors of the population, the slow but sure rise of literacy rates with the tendency towards social radicalism that often came in its wake, the problems of authority raised by the break-up of the Church at the Reformation, and the abolition (in Protestantism) or radical restructuring (in Tridentine Catholicism) of the patterns and mechanisms of pastoral care, raised questions of individual responsibility and the identification and application of biblical principles in a manner virtually unprecedented. In England, for example, both Catholics and Protestants produced books of casuistry to cater to their various constituencies, and within Protestantism this was not confined to any particular stream of church life (Wood; Rose).

Given its pastoral, experimental emphasis, influential streams of English Puritanism focused on the issue of assurance as one of the major forces shaping its own casuistical discussion (see Kendall and responses by Muller 1980; Helm; Beeke; Dever). There was also a very close pedagogical connection between catechism and casuistry, inevitable perhaps, given that both were focused on the theological and pastoral education of the individual or the household. A classic example of this is William Perkins' 1592 treatise, *A Case of Conscience*, subtitled, *The greatest that ever was: How a man may know, whether he be the childe of God or no.* While the latter part of the work is a translation of a tract by Zanchius, the first half is a most insightful example of Puritan pastoral application of Scripture. This consists of a discussion juxtaposing leading questions regarding Christian doctrine and the application of that doctrine to life with relevant biblical texts provided as answers. In fact, these texts represent a translation of 1 John in order, so what Perkins has effectively done is taken a book of the Bible, spliced it with pastoral questions, and thus produced a manual for dealing with lack of assurance. As such, it is a graphic example of the central importance of the actual text of the Bible to Puritan pastoral practice. Thus, the work represents a fusion of the Protestant emphasis on Scripture together with the catechetical practice of question and answer to the casuistical issue of addressing a particular pastoral need. Further, it uses this technique as a subtle means of interpreting the text of the Bible itself and constructing an argument in a manner of which the catechumen would be virtually unaware but by which he or she would be led to draw the correct Puritan conclusions. While the texts are apparently allowed to speak for themselves, their purpose is clearly shaped by the context provided by the question and, also, just as significantly, by the addition of brief glosses written by Perkins himself within the biblical texts themselves. These glosses effectively supply the theological substance of the catechism. Clearly, the Protestant notion of scriptural perspicuity was not to be misconstrued as something that precluded the need for the interpretative aid of teacher and church. For example:

> Christian: How then may we know that our sinnes are washed away by Christ? John 9: *If we confesses our sinnes* (namely, with an humbled heart, desiring pardon) *he is faithfull and just* (in keeping his promise) *to forgive us our sinnes and to cleanse us from al unrighteousness.* (Perkins 1592, 5)

The more complex the question relative to the point at issue, the more elaborate is the explanatory gloss built into the biblical text. Thus, when he addresses the issue of discerning true faith by its obedience to the commands, using 1 John 2:3, he feels obliged to indicate that the fulfilment of the commandments here spoken of is not a true and full one but simply a desire to fulfil them, a desire which God in his mercy will accept as the real thing (Perkins 1592, 7). This physical juxtaposition of the words of Scripture with Perkins's gloss on the printed page surely serves to blur the distinction between Scripture and interpretation. True, for the reader, the Perkinsian additions are italicised which perhaps goes a little way towards defusing the obvious problem; but if the book was used as an actual catechism, which would appear to be the intention, then surely the 'lively voice' would annihilate this distinction and give both biblical text and Perkinsian gloss equal authority in the mind of the catechumen, whose 'memory' as we know, according to Perkins's own understanding of pedagogy, is affected more by spoken words than by those merely written.

Behind Catholic casuistry lay elaborate discussions of the psychology of conscience. This was picked up by English Protestant theologians indicating that, whatever the differences on issues of authority and interpretation which may have existed between Rome and Protestantism, there was considerable similarity on matters of anthropology, and that this played into how Scripture and its teaching was to be applied to the individual, providing significant common ground in terms of theory and practice for both Catholics and Protestants. The need to provide more detailed pastoral guidance in a world where traditional patterns of life and structures of authority were being rapidly transformed was something common to the whole of Christendom. It also faced a world where economic and social changes were casting up a whole complex of issues and questions that individuals had never faced before, from relations to those of different religious persuasion through to issues surrounding international trade. In this context, it should not be a surprise that Protestants chose to emulate the Catholics in the production of manuals that purported to provide the principles for Christian behaviour and, not infrequently, straightforward answers to complicated questions.

For example, Perkins's 1596 treatise *A discourse of conscience wherein is set downe the nature, properties, and differences thereof: as also the way to get and keepe good conscience* commences with a discussion of the psychology of conscience, defining it as 'a part of the understanding in all reasonable creatures, determining of their particular actions either with them or against them', a definition which would scarcely have been objectionable to a Catholic theologian (Perkins 1596, 1). Similar discussion, with further elaboration and clear dependence upon medieval discussions, is to be found in his work, *The first part of the cases of conscience* (London 1604), and also in the highly influential book by the English Puritan and Professor at Franeker, William Ames, *Conscience with the power and cases thereof* (London and Leyden 1639). Nor was this type of discussion limited to the English-speaking Reformed world: on the Continent, for example, Gisbertus Voetius' great work of practical divinity, *Ta Ascetica, sive exercitia pietatis* contained similar discussion and application (1664); then, Jeremy Taylor, no friend of the Puritans, produced a major work, *Ductor dubitantium, or, The rule of conscience in all her generall measures serving as a great instrument for the determination of cases of conscience: in four books* (London 1660), dedicated to Charles II no less, which contained the typical discussion of pastoral psychology that was quite the match of any produced by the great Puritan casuists. While Catholics, however, would root their personal piety in the sacramental actions of the Church, for Protestants, this was much more closely connected to the scripture principle. Thus, for Perkins, the primary means by which this conscience may be kept in a healthy, upright and properly functioning condition is by the destruction of ignorance, something which is achieved by spending time learning the teachings of the word of God, thus connecting conscience and the moral psychology of casuistry with the Protestant scripture principle and the pedagogical tools of preaching and catechising (Perkins 1596, 167).

Nevertheless, even given the differing emphases on word and sacrament, there were profound continuities between Catholic and Protestant practices in the area of casuistry and personal piety. Perhaps the most striking example of this is the work of Edmund Bunny, *A book of Christian exercise appertaining to resolution, that is, shewing how that wee should resolue our selues to become Christians indeed. by R.P. Perused, and accompanied now with a tretise tending to pacification* (London 1585). This particular book is fascinating because Bunny was an Anglican of distinctly Reformed/Calvinistic sympathies while the R.P. whose treatise Bunny was editing and reprinting was none other than Robert Parsons, a leading Jesuit theologian. While Bunny, therefore, had no liking for Parsons as a man and no time for his ecclesiastical commitments, yet he saw in Parsons' work on personal piety and Christian life a useful source even for Protestants, albeit edited in a Protestant direction and containing essays by Bunny which served to act as a critical lens through which to read the Jesuit. Nonetheless, the work serves as evidence of the proximity, even self-conscious proximity, between the pastoral theories and practices of Rome and those of Protestants.

Perhaps the most extensive and comprehensive piece of Puritan casuistry was Richard Baxter's monumental *A Christian Directory*, published in 1673 and again in 1678. In this work, Baxter analysed the whole of life in all of its many spheres and gave clear scriptural guidance on everything from prayer and meditation to how to behave as a soldier. Divided into four sections on Christian ethics (general rules of Christian conduct), Christian economics (household management), Christian ecclesiastics (church life) and Christian politics (civic life), the *Directory* represents the apex of Puritan application of Scripture to all of life. One might perhaps describe Baxter's work as an attempt to take Protestant commitment to scriptural sufficiency as far as it can go, to the point where there is no aspect of life and no question which can be asked to which Scripture does not give a clear, practical answer, from choice of marriage partner and servants down to the appropriate amount of expenditure for raising children. Even the issue of how much money it is legitimate to expend upon children is raised and answered by Baxter as enough to keep them comfortable in a manner consistent with your own estate, but not so much that they become complacent; and, if they are ungodly, one should give them no more than their daily bread (Baxter 1678, Part IV, 224). In each question asked, the general ethical principles of Scripture are taken and applied in a way that, allowing for occasionally complex distinctions, provides a clear answer to how one should behave; and all of this leads to what is surely Protestant scriptural micro-management at its most extreme. In this context, the work must surely be linked to Baxter's own fear of social chaos, fostered by his experience of what he perceived as the sectarian anarchy of the New Model Army in the Civil War (Trueman 1999). Thus, the great burden of many of the applications in the second and third parts of the work is the creation of social stability built around each individual knowing their place in society and acting accordingly. For example, at one point Baxter asks the question of whether it is legitimate for merchants and traders to live among infidels. The answer is yes, for business promotes the good of all societies (Baxter 1678, Part IV, 211–13).

We see, therefore, in a work like *A Christian Directory*, Scripture being applied to every area of life, not simply in terms of broad principles but even down to very specific minutiae, outside of the immediate scope of congregational church life, such as the family and business. Now, it is certainly true that the original Reformers regarded Scripture as sufficient as a theological and ethical guide, but the elaboration and application of this basic conviction in later generations is quite remarkable and something that represents a significant development of the earlier approach. It would seem to indicate that, faced with the dissolution of the old forms of authority and control which the medieval Church had cultivated, partly as a result of the increasing mobility and fragmentation of the old social patterns, and partly through the shattering of the traditional institutional authority of the Church, Protestantism was forced to squeeze more and more micro-managing power out of an increasingly narrow basis.

Pietism, moralism, revivalism, and the undermining of Reformation pastoral care

While there was both continuity but also significant development in the use of Scripture in pastoral context in the generations after the initial Reformation, it must be clearly understood that all of this use of Scripture took place within a framework determined by the church authorities, whether the local church session or the wider context of broader church courts and control. This is a very important point to make in the present day because the appropriation of much Reformation and Puritan thinking on the Bible and pastoral practice by modern evangelicalism has often failed to appreciate this important ecclesiological dimension. The reason for this failure is not hard to find. The roots of evangelical thinking on the Church lie not in the classical trajectories of Protestant thinking but in the rather anti-ecclesiastical impulses of eighteenth-century revivalism and pietism.

So far the issue of the pastoral use of Scripture by Protestants can be seen as part of the larger issue of the interpretation and application of Scripture within the Protestant framework. On the one hand, there is a rejection of the absolute authority of the Church in such matters, with individuals having responsibility to understand Scripture for themselves; on the other hand, there is the need to avoid 'each doing (or understanding) what is right in their own eyes'. In theory, the Protestants overcame this by arguing that the subjective work of the Holy Spirit guaranteed, at least in the long run, that Christian individuals would arrive at positions marked by both orthodoxy and orthopraxy. In practice, they used pastoral authority, bolstered and applied by church courts and reinforced by catechetical and casuistical work, in order to make sure that the Holy Spirit's work was indeed effectively accomplished. In the latter part of the seventeenth and the eighteenth century, however, the rise of pietism and revivalism effectively bypassed, and thereby subverted, much of this original context for interpretation and application.

Pietism is notoriously difficult to define, but is perhaps best captured in the idea of the prioritisation of personal experience over doctrinal niceties, and a certain privatisation of the religious sphere (Stoeffler; Brecht; Lindberg). In England, this is perhaps best seen as the result of the collapse of Puritanism into nonconformity in the wake of the Act of Uniformity of 1662, which led to a decline of doctrinal knowledge (and concern) in subsequent generations who yet maintained the powerful experimental emphases of Puritan thought. Thus, for example, the influential work of Lewis Bayly, *The Practice of Piety* (*c.* 1612) continued to exert a profound influence, alongside other works which probed Christian experience and which were constantly being reprinted, such as Bunyan's *Pilgrim's Progress*, Baxter's *Practical Works* and Samuel Rutherford's *Letters*. In Bunyan's Christian, the reader was provided with a narrative which, through allegorisation of the biblical teaching on the Christian life, helped to formulate and make sense of Christian experience; indeed, in his *Grace Abounding to the Chief of Sinners*, Bunyan provided his readers with what is in many ways a testimony of personal religious experience shaped by Luther's law–gospel dialectic and driven at points by a morbid and terrifying introspection; the same experimental concern was true in a gentler and more engaging way in Rutherford's *Letters*, which, in a manner akin to Augustine's *Confessions*, drew on the Bible in order to make coherent sense of the various mood swings of the Christian life; and Baxter's voluminous practical works provided an effective way of understanding and micro-managing the Christian life in an unparalleled fashion. What is noteworthy, however, is that the doctrinal works of Rutherford and Baxter, with the exception perhaps of the former's political treatise, *Lex Rex*, enjoyed little or no further life beyond that of their authors. The taste for more doctrinal works of the Puritan era clearly abated in the late seventeenth and early eighteenth century, particularly as the institutions of higher learning which had fostered them were closed to nonconformists and were, in any case, having their curricula revised in terms of very different philosophical premises. This was paralleled by the dramatic collapse of large parts of English nonconformity into Unitarianism (Watts). The antidoctrinalism implicit in a strongly experiential reading and use of Scripture, combined with a ministry deprived of the classical, doctrinal education, proved a ready breeding ground for a Christianity that was in essence moralism and for the decay of traditional orthodoxy in its wake. This is perhaps most clearly seen in the various neonomian controversies which affected the British Isles of the time. In England, the republication of Tobias Crisp's *Christ Alone Exalted* in 1690, nearly fifty years after the author's death, brought the ageing Richard Baxter out of retirement to combat what he saw as a dangerously antinomian work. Instead, Baxter once again argued for a view of justification which was, to say the least, moralistic in tendency. Then, in Scotland, the controversy surrounding the republication in 1718 by James Hog of Edward Fisher's 1646 work, *The Marrow of Modern Divinity*. The book emphasised the centrality of assurance to the Christian life but was subsequently condemned by the Church of Scotland Assembly in 1720, a ruling upheld in 1722 (Lachman). Such a move indicated quite clearly that Protestantism was in many quarters taking on a more legalistic, moralistic hue and was increasingly uneasy with central aspects of Reformation teaching on faith and assurance. Such inevitably affected the use and application of Scripture in pastoral life.

The other powerful anti-ecclesiastical factor was the rise of revivalism. At base revivalism represented the culmination of certain trajectories within Christian life. As noted above, for a variety of reasons, religious, social and economic, a form of piety had developed in the seventeenth century that focused on the individual and his or her religious experience. This is evidenced by the popularity of Bunyan and Rutherford, and by the rising importance in some quarters of the personal conversion narrative as being that which validated individual Christian authenticity. Thus, when an experience of conversion became the hallmark of genuine Christianity, the traditional high view of the Church and the ministry as being the normal contexts for expounding and applying Scripture was placed under great strain; and the focus of preaching itself, the primary means of applying Scripture in the pastoral context, changed to that of wanting to cause this experience in the lives of hearers. The anti-institutional, anti-authoritarian, anti-sacramental implications of this position are obvious. Whereas, when the devil tempted Luther, Luther reminded him that he was baptised, one can imagine that when the devil tempted the product of an eighteenth-century revival, the response would have been to point him to a particular experience of conversion at a certain moment in time (Bebbington; Hatch on America).

It would certainly be wrong to cast revivalism as an anti-intellectual movement in terms of its leadership. While there was undoubtedly a lunatic fringe, the likes of John and Charles Wesley, George Whitefield, and the American theologian and pastor, Jonathan Edwards, were all well-educated men and theologically articulate (Rack; Stout 1991; Marsden). Indeed, Edwards' own theological writings are worthy of standing comparison with many of the intellectual productions of his day (Jenson; Holmes). The Wesleys and Whitefield both enjoyed considerable success on both sides of the Atlantic and – most significantly for understanding the declining place of doctrine – despite the fact that they fell out badly along classic Arminian–Calvinist grounds regarding predestination, nonetheless saw themselves as part of a single, larger movement, and divided from those with whom they had more theological common ground who yet opposed their conversionist style. Experience, not doctrine or understanding of Scripture beyond a mere Christian commitment to salvation by faith, was what bound them together.

What is significant in these men, therefore, is the change in emphasis that has taken place since the Reformation. The Reformation articulated on the whole a high view of the Church and pastoral ministry as the context for the pastoral application of Scripture, and stressed the importance of the sacraments, of preaching and of catechising for the growth of Christians. This was in large part because the importance of Scripture in the Church was in large part seen in non-negotiable doctrinal terms, with Christian experience being subordinate to this and conversion narratives playing little, if any, public role – a position modified somewhat by some of the Puritans. Scripture was therefore not first and foremost about a crisis experience of new birth. The revivalists, however, tended to be much more confident than their Reform-ation forebears about who was and who was not saved, partly because of the premium they placed on conversion experience over doctrine and daily walk; and thus they tended to see the validity of a person's ministry not so much in their institutional recognition but in their personal experience and effectiveness. Such ministers therefore looked to encouraging a crisis experience (genuine, not counterfeit) in their hearers as a way of growing the Church. Further, as in the case of the Wesleys and Whitefield, they were able to engage in itinerant ministries precisely because they saw their calling not as that of consistent Christian nurture but of calling lost souls into the Church. Thus, while preaching remained central to their project, sacraments and a high view of the church office fell by the wayside; and for all of the education of the leadership, the incipient experiential pragmatism of the movement raised obvious questions about the need for education over against the ability to produce the desired effect. It was, one might say, at root an anti-intellectual and therefore ultimately anti-doctrinal movement. The need for education in exegetical and theological skills which the Reformers and the Puritans would have regarded as crucial preparation for any kind of pastoral ministry was ultimately to prove unnecessary within a Christianity conceived of in terms of revivalism.

Bibliography (of modern references and historic texts discussed in detail)

Baker J. W. (1980) *Heinrich Bullinger and the Covenant: the other Reformed Tradition*. Athens, OH: Ohio University Press.

Baxter, Richard (1656) *Gildas Salvianus, the Reformed Pastor*. London.

Baxter, Richard (1678) *A Christian Directory*. London.

Bebbington, D. W. (1989) *Evangelicalism in Modern Britain: a history from the 1730s to the 1980s*. London: Unwin.

Beeke, J. R. (1991) *Assurance of Faith: Calvin, English Puristanism, and the Dutch second Reformation*. Zurich: Peter Lang.

Bierma, L. D. (1983) Federal theology in the sixteenth century: two traditions? *Westminster Theological Journal* 45, 304–21.

Bierma, L. D. (1996) *German Calvinism in the Confessional Age*. Grand Rapids, MI: Baker.

Brecht, M. B. (1993) *Geschichte des Pietismus* Band I. Göttingen: Vandenhoeck & Ruprecht.

Burnett, S. G. (1996) *From Christian Hebraism to Jewish Studies: Johannes Buxtorf (1564–1629) and Hebrew learning in the seventeenth century*. Leiden: Brill.
Calvin, John (1559) *Institutes of the Christian Religion*. Final edition, 1559.
Dever, M. E. (2000) *Richard Sibbes: Puritanism and Calvinism in late Elizabethan and early Stuart England*. Macon, GA: Mercer University Press.
Farmer, C. S. (1997) *The Gospel of John in the Sixteenth Century: the Johannine exegesis of Wolfgang Musculus*. Oxford: Oxford University Press.
Farrar, F. W. (1886) *History of Interpretation*. New York: Dutton.
Hall, Basil (1963) Biblical scholarship: editions and commentaries, in S. L. Greenslade (ed.), *The Cambridge History of the Bible* III. Cambridge: Cambridge University Press, 38–93.
Hatch, Nathan (1989) *The Democratization of American Christianity*. New Haven, CT: Yale University Press.
Helm, Paul (1982) *Calvin and the Calvinists*. Edinburgh: Banner of Truth.
Holmes, Stephen R. (2001) *God of Grace and God of Glory: an account of the theology of Jonathan Edwards*. Grand Rapids, MI: Eerdmans.
Jenson, R. W. (1988) *America's Theologian: a recommendation of Jonathan Edwards*. Oxford: Oxford University Press.
Junghans, Helmar (2004) Luther on the reform of worship, in Timothy J. Wengert (ed.), *Harvesting Martin Luther's Reflections on Theology, Ethics, and the Church*. Grand Rapids, MI: Eerdmans, 207–25.
Kendall, R. T. (1979) *Calvin and English Calvinism to 1649*. Oxford: Oxford University Press.
Kingdon, R. M. (1995) *Adultery and Divorce in Calvin's Geneva*. Cambridge, MA: Harvard University Press.
Lachman, D. C. (1988) *The Marrow Controversy*. Edinburgh: Rutherford House.
Lillback, P. A. (2001) *The Binding of God: Calvin's role in the development of covenant theology*. Grand Rapids, MI: Baker.
Lindberg, Carter (2005) *The Pietist Theologians*. Oxford: Blackwell.
Luther, Martin (1517) *Ninety-five Theses*, in H. T. Lehmann (ed.), *Luther's Works* 31. Philadelphia: Muhlenberg Press, 1957, 17–33.
Luther, Martin (1520a) *The Babylonian Captivity of the Church*, in H. T. Lehmann (ed.), *Luther's Works* 36. Philadelphia: Muhlenberg Press, 1959, 3–126.
Luther, Martin (1520b) *The Freedom of the Christian Man*, in H. T. Lehmann (ed.), *Luther's Works* 31. Philadelphia: Muhlenberg Press, 1957, 327–77.
Marsden, G. M. (2003) *Jonathan Edwards*. New Haven, CT: Yale University Press.
McCoy, C. S. and Baker J. W. (1991) *Fountainhead of Federalism: Heinrich Bullinger and the covenantal tradition*. Louisville, KY: Westminster John Knox.
Muller, R. A. (1980) Covenant and conscience in English Reformed theology: three variations on a 17th century theme. *Westminster Theological Journal* 62, 308–34.
Muller, R. A. (2003) *Post Reformation Reformed Dogmatics II: Holy Scripture*. Grand Rapids, MI: Baker.
Muller, R. A. and Thompson J. (eds) (1996) *Biblical Interpretation in the Era of the Reformation*. Grand Rapids, MI: Eerdmans.
Naphy, W. G. (1994) *Calvin and the Consolidation of the Genevan Reformation*. Manchester: Manchester University Press.
Oberman, H. A. (2003) Luther and the Via Moderna: the philosophical backdrop of the Reformation breakthrough. *Journal of Ecclesiastical History* 54, 641–70.
Owen, John (1645) *The principles of the doctrine of Christ: unfolded in two short catechisms*. London.

Perkins, William (1592) *A Case of Conscience. The greatest that ever was: how a man may know, whether he be the childe of God or no*. London.

Perkins, William (1593) *An exposition of the Lords praier in the way of catechisme*. London.

Perkins, William (1596) *A discourse of conscience wherein is set downe the nature, properties, and differences thereof: as also the way to get and keepe good conscience*. London.

Perkins, William (1607) *The Arte of Prophecying; or a treatise concerning the sacred and onely manner and methods of preaching*. London.

Rack, H. (1989) *Reasonable Enthusiast: John Wesley and the rise of Methodism*. Philadelphia: Trinity Press International.

Rose, E. (1975) *Cases of Conscience: alternatives open to Recusants and Puritans under Elizabeth I and James I*. Cambridge: Cambridge University Press.

Steinmetz, D. C. (ed.) (1990) *The Bible in the Sixteenth Century*. Durham, NC: Duke University Press.

Stoeffler, F. E. (1965) *The Rise of Evangelical Pietism*. Leiden: Brill.

Stout, H. S. (1988) *The New England Soul: preaching and religious culture in colonial New England*. Oxford: Oxford University Press.

Stout, H. S. (1991) *The Divine Dramatist: George Whitefield and the rise of modern Evangelicalism*. Grand Rapids, MI: Eerdmans.

Sykes, N. (1963) The religion of Protestants, in S. L. Greenslade (ed.), *The Cambridge History of the Bible* III. Cambridge: Cambridge University Press, 175–98.

Thompson, J. L. (2001) *Writing the Wrongs: women of the Old Testament among biblical commentators from Philo through the Reformation*. Oxford: Oxford University Press.

Trueman, C. R. (1999) Richard Baxter on Christian unity: a chapter in the enlightening of English Reformed orthodoxy. *Westminster Theological Journal* 61, 53–71.

Trueman, C. R. (2003) Was Luther an Evangelical? in Peter A Lillback (ed.), *The Practical Calvinist*. Fearn, Ross-shire: Mentor, 131–48.

Walsham, A. (2001) *Providence in Early Modern England*. Oxford: Clarendon Press.

Watts, Michael (1978) *The Dissenters: from the Reformation to the French Revolution*. Oxford: Clarendon Press.

Wengert, T. J. (1987) *Philip Melanchthon's Annotationes in Johannem in Relation to Its Predecessors and Contemporaries*. Geneva: Droz.

Wengert, T. J. (1997) *Law and Gospel: Philip Melanchthon's debate with John Agricola of Eisleben over* poenitentia. Carlisle: Paternoster Press.

Wood, Thomas (1952) *English Casuistical Divinity During the Seventeenth Century*. London: SPCK.

Zachman, R. C. (1993) *The Assurance of Faith: conscience in the theology of Martin Luther and John Calvin*. Minneapolis, MN: Fortress Press.

CHAPTER 6:

From Schleiermacher to Barth: meeting the challenge of critical scholarship

HUESTON FINLAY

Introduction

To attempt a comprehensive survey of the pastoral use of the Bible since 1800 is a task that could not be undertaken sensibly in the course of a short article. I have chosen instead, to focus on a much smaller field of inquiry and to see how that smaller field might shed light on the more general issues. This essay will, therefore, examine the work of three theologians who have written on the theory of biblical interpretation but have also been preachers of the highest order, Schleiermacher, Newman and Barth. I shall then conclude by looking briefly at the lessons that can be learnt from these three theologians, lessons that we might apply to preaching and pastoral work in the twenty-first century. First, however, it is necessary to outline the challenge facing these theologians; to understand what it was that prompted them to think as they did.

Interpreting the Bible in a strange new world

Prior to the eighteenth century the Bible had been read as a historical and literal document. This general standpoint gave rise to a number of beliefs. First, if the Bible was a genuine historical record then it was vital that it was read literally, for the truth it contained was expressed in a significant and purposeful manner. Second, if the Bible was to be read literally then the various biblical stories that make up the whole must describe a single temporal sequence; there must, in other words, be a single story running through the text. Third, that single story, or meta-narrative, could be maintained and described using other reading strategies such as allegory and typology. Nonetheless these other methods would always be secondary to the primary literal one. The conquest of literal over allegorical approaches was won back in the Patristic period, when the Antiochene and Alexandrian schools extolled one method over against the other. In the Middle Ages St Thomas Aquinas (1225–74) used the typical contemporary fourfold method but still insisted that theological argument could only be made on the basis of the literal sense. That same belief received renewed support in the Renaissance and the Reformation, and it came to a crescendo in the period usually referred to as 'Protestant Orthodoxy', a time when the doctrine of biblical infallibility came to light in conjunction with a doctrine of verbal inspiration. Such doctrines were to be found in men like Johannes Quenstedt (1617–88) and Abraham Calov (1612–86), who enjoyed the certainty of systems and whose work, as they saw it, was the arrangement of such dogmatic statements that could be directly derived from this infallible text.

Soon, however, that crescendo would sound less and less strident. It is difficult, and maybe even pointless, to try to identify the beginning of the decline. Perhaps one could look to a radical thinker like Benedict Spinoza (1632–77). Certainly his views on the Bible, and much else besides, resulted in his being reviled by the academic and ecclesiastical institutions in Germany until the late eighteenth century. Yet the decline might also have taken impetus from devout men who would now be regarded as part of the Pietist movement. Working at a specifically Pietistic university, Halle, academics like August Francke (1663–1727) and Johann Bengel (1687–1752) worked on the original biblical languages, and it is to the latter that we owe the basic modern Greek text of the New Testament. Even more importantly the Pietists understood the personal experience of Christians as the foundation for theological insight and scriptural study. This move has problems all of its own but it is, in any case, a long way from the dogmatic reading of infallible texts as promulgated by the orthodox theologians. Even more important is Johann Salomo Semler (1725–91). He too worked at Halle, but by this time the university had become a centre of Enlightenment research. He did not offer a detailed description of any method of interpretation, or record his thoughts in a brief and clear manner, yet he gave to the term 'literal' an alternative and fundamentally different meaning. Taking the work begun by his Pietistic forebears he argued that biblical interpretation should not be a mere verification of certain doctrines; instead the task of interpretation was to understand the text as their authors had. He proposed two essential rules: that the reader of the Bible be aware of the historical distance between themselves and the texts of the Bible, and that, although the reader should be aware of the nature of the texts of the Bible, they should still be interpreted in the same manner as any other book.

The strange new world had now come into existence. In former years to speak of a literal reading would have been to speak of a factual, a historical or, as Hans Frei (1974) would have it, a 'strongly realistic' reading. Now there was another possible meaning; a literal reading could refer to a reading that pursued grammatical accuracy and the sense originally intended by the author. The appearance of this alternative and new meaning brought a serious consequence: the Bible was scrutinised in a manner never previously contemplated. It was now possible to ask whether the stories in the Bible could really be regarded as factual accounts. Could the texts offer religious meaning outside of a factual basis? And if the texts are not infallible then what, if anything, is the role and purpose of typology and allegory? These were tough new questions.

How should one interpret the Bible?

Our three theologians and preachers would now have to deal with all these questions and more. Whether at the university podium or in the church pulpit, some response would have to be made. The next step is to examine how each of our theologians responded to life in this strange new world. What is presented below cannot be a comprehensive outline of the theories of interpretation advocated by these men, but a short overview.

Friedrich Schleiermacher (1768–1834)

Commonly recognised as the Father of hermeneutics, Schleiermacher's contribution to this field was immense. Much of the groundwork had already been done, but he was the first to draw everything together into a coherent and robust system, which he does in large measure in his posthumously published *Hermeneutics*. He placed hermeneutics alongside dialectics in his larger philosophical system. To imagine Schleiermacher as a philosopher is, to some minds, a little peculiar. However, alongside his more famous theological system stands another system constructed from the philosophical materials of his day. For our purposes it is interesting to note one of Schleiermacher's philosophical ideas, namely that thought and language are interdependent; it is impossible to think without language. It is for this reason that within his philosophical system Schleiermacher places dialectics and hermeneutics alongside each other. He understands dialectics as the art of thinking and hermeneutics as the art of interpretation. When it comes to interpretation these two arts might be regarded as the two sides of the same coin; dialectics produced the thought that is communicated in language, or specifically in a text, and hermeneutics attempts to retrieve that thought. This is a good example of how Schleiermacher reacted to the strange new world, embraced it and put it to work on his behalf, showing just how comfortable he was with the new understanding of what it meant to have a literal reading.

Not only was he at ease with this understanding, he was willing to take it some steps further. For the most part his predecessors were concerned with interpretation as it related either to the Bible or to the work of the classical Greek writers; Schleiermacher insisted that his theory of hermeneutics be applied to every text. This included contemporary texts and, perhaps strangely, it also included conversations. In fact he insists that 'wherever one encounters something strange in the way thoughts are being expressed in speech, one is faced with a task which can be solved only with the help of a theory' (1977, 181). That theory is driven by his belief that the ultimate aim of textual interpretation is to uncover the sense originally intended by the author. He writes:

> The task is to be formulated as follows: 'To understand the text at first as well as and then even better than its author'. Since we have no direct knowledge of what was in the author's mind, we must try to become aware of many things of which he himself may have been unconscious, except insofar as he reflects on his own work and becomes his own reader. Moreover, with respect to the objective aspects, the author had no data other than we have. (1977, 112)

Even the author of a text requires a theory to understand his own work. This sounds more modern than one might expect but it is a view that follows naturally from his famous – if not entirely original – catchphrase seen at the start of the quotation above. The quotation also indicates that the theory will comprise some difficult and comprehensive study.

The theory itself is made of two sides, the grammatical and the so-called psychological. The second side receives plenty of attention from a wide range of commentators, many of whom see it as the major part of Schleiermacher's theory and consequently consider that he overplays it. We should be careful from the outset to recognise that Schleiermacher often works with pairs of thoughts. Both sides, however, are equally important. The grammatical side concentrates on language and is described by means of two canons, one dealing with the way in which particular words are used in the particular language from which they are drawn, the other examining the sense of words as they stand in their particular context, that is, their use within a particular sentence. The explanation of his grammatical rules is complex; it involves a serious study of grammar, an inquiry into the nature and purpose of dictionaries, and discussions on how the interpreter might identify tautologies. Yet however complex they might be, one thing is clear: each discussion is motivated by his belief that the sense the interpreter is after is the sense originally laid down by the author of the text. To achieve this end an interpreter must know the language of the author, and know it as it was employed at the time of writing. Yet even such demanding grammatical analysis will not be sufficient for the task in hand.

The grammatical side of interpretation must be complemented by the psychological side. This second aspect is more interested in how the author made use of that language. Just as the grammatical side has two subdivisions, so too has the psychological. The first part is essentially an examination of style, the study of how the author may have structured and written his text; the second is about identifying the author's individual use of the linguistic sphere open to him. While the grammatical side of his theory is full of specific recommendations and tips, this second side is altogether less prescriptive. Nonetheless two procedures are repeatedly mentioned: the divinatory and the comparative. Actually both these procedures are also to be used in the first side of interpretation but one suspects it is in the second side that they come into their own. In ascertaining how an author wrote it is suggested that the interpreter should read other works by the same author or even other contemporary works; this is what Schleiermacher means by the comparative method. And lest hermeneutics begins to sound too much like an exact science, the divinatory method reminds us just how fragile the whole business is. We may study grammar and style for many hours but in the end we have to 'divine'– to make an educated guess at – the sense of a text. Some guesses will be better than others but none will ever reach the original goal.

The inability to come to a final and conclusive reading had not been seen by Semler but in other respects Schleiermacher remained faithful to him. His entire theory upheld Semler's first ground rule, that an interpreter ought to be aware of the historical distance between themselves and the text, but he also followed Semler's second rule when he insisted that his theory applied to all texts including the Bible. He argued against a 'special hermeneutics' for the Bible, although he was quite content to admit that 'in general a special hermeneutics is only an abbreviated procedure which must be governed by the general rules' (1977, 122). So, given his general theory, how did he suggest the Bible ought to be interpreted?

Clearly the Bible ought to be read in the language in which it was written; the interpreter, therefore, should be well versed in Hebrew and Greek. These linguistic studies should be accompanied by knowledge of Aramaic, the Septuagint, the Apocrypha, Macedonian Greek and those Jewish documents written in Greek. The second string of study is demanded because:

> The writers of the New Testament do not introduce any new words for their religious concepts, but speak from the linguistic sphere of the Bible and Apocrypha. Nevertheless, the question remains as to whether or not they have different religious ideas and so use words in distinctive ways. If they do not, there would be nothing new in Christian theology ... Since this question cannot be resolved immediately by means of hermeneutics, it seems to be a matter of judgement ... We would have to rely also on a judgement of feeling as to whether the New Testament seems to develop new ideas. But judgements of feeling can be accepted only if they are

> supported by philological and philosophical research. Only a person who has demonstrated his competence in similar investigations concerning other matters and bases his understanding on adequate study is worthy of our trust in this research. (1977, 125–6)

This long quotation brings a very interesting point to light. Schleiermacher appears to be most interested in the New Testament; this is certainly the case, although this preference is based not so much on hermeneutics as it is on dogmatics. He sees the New Testament as the record of a new and radically different story. Certainly the authors of this new story tried to convey their notions using the language of the common people but this language was actually inadequate to the task (see 1977, 82). They have used old words but given them new meanings; the result is a particularly difficult exercise in hermeneutics. He also tells his readers that there is a unity to the New Testament, that it is the product of one idea. For Schleiermacher this idea is encapsulated in one verse of Scripture: 'The Word became flesh and made his dwelling among us. We have seen his glory, the glory of the One and Only, who came from the Father, full of grace and truth (John 1:14).' Elsewhere Schleiermacher tells us that his entire theology is constructed with that one verse in mind (1981, 59). The incarnation is the bedrock of his theology and that to which the New Testament writers bear witness. Interpreting the New Testament according to his own theory is a matter, therefore, of finding a method by which to understand what the writers have to say about the incarnate Lord. It is a matter of understanding those original experiences and seeing in them something of our own religious experience.

Schleiermacher found the strange new world of historical criticism a positive contributor to his own theological enterprise. He took Semler's project to heart and brought it several steps forward. But this is not the only viable option.

John Henry Newman (1801–90)

In Newman we see the very opposite approach. This rather bold statement needs some qualification because it is evident that after his reception into the Catholic Church he felt less strongly about these matters than he did as an Anglican, when he utterly condemned the kind of German scholarship we saw in Semler and Schleiermacher. This kind of suspicion was not uncommon. Preaching a series of sermons before the University of Cambridge and published in 1825, H. B. Rose claimed that in Semler we meet 'some of the most brilliant specimens of that extraordinary talent for the construction of groundless hypotheses, which distinguishes the German Divinity'. Newman's *Lectures on Justification*, published in 1838, show that he too was opposed to the so-called benefits of modern biblical interpretation. Yet in his much later *Inspiration Papers* Newman respectfully analysed the work of various eminent theologians; he may not, in the end, have made their conclusions his own, but his tone is never hostile. These contrasting approaches highlight a difficulty. Newman wrote about interpretation in many of his works but often only by way of supporting or elucidating whatever he was then arguing. His sustained pieces, the *Inspiration Papers* of 1861–63, come to an abrupt stop and were never completed because Newman himself did not believe he held a clear view on the matter. It is understandable, therefore, that expert commentators hold differing views on what it is that Newman was saying, pointing to development in his thinking over the course of the years. Yet for all this uncertainty, there are significant themes in Newman's work that appear repeatedly and it might be reasonable to conclude that, even where emphasis may change, the core of what he had to say remains constant.

At the start of the nineteenth century, England, unlike Germany, had not yet ventured into our strange new world. Typically Anglicans believed that the Bible was literally inspired and infallible. When voices from the strange new world started to make the journey across the water there was a degree of consternation. Newman decided to meet the challenge by placing inspiration right at the centre of his thinking; in this regard, as in others, he was most unlike Schleiermacher. He outlined a number of possible explanatory models, all of which he considered acceptable, but some he thought better than others. The first and highest was that of dictation, although this model reduced the author to a mere instrument. The second was the principle of inerrancy, but it had to be admitted that there were other writings free from error that one might not wish to describe as inspired, at least in the same way. A third model was that which explained inspiration as a supernatural force, but this model depended on the effect of the text upon its readers and once again one could point to other writings that were influential without being inspired. The fourth model linked inspiration to supernatural teaching, that is, to divine instruction conveyed through human words. In the Bible, God had spoken. This view is similar to Barth's, as we shall see, but unlike Barth Newman claimed that deciding what God had actually said was a matter only for the Church. We hear him say this most conclusively when he speaks as a Catholic but even as an Anglican he was convinced that biblical interpretation was not a matter for the person in the pew. His appeal to the Church is, in any case, less final than it might first appear as the Church had never given an authoritative opinion on the entire contents of the Bible; much, if not most, of the text was left open and consequently still lay vulnerable to the criticisms of modern times. Newman explained, however, that inspiration did not extend to matters of chronology or science because the Bible was inspired in matters of faith and morals. Essentially his strategy was not to produce a method for positively describing the process of inspiration but to set out a means of negating much of the contemporary criticism being levelled against the Bible.

His view of inspiration enabled him to regard the Bible as both a religious work and a sacramental principle. The Bible is a religious work because it has its origin in God who made use of human writers as the instruments of his communication. Exactly because the Bible originated in God it cannot be read like any other book; the general hermeneutics of Schleiermacher are decidedly inappropriate. Moreover, no amount of theory or practice will unravel the mysteries contained within. Newman's doctrine bears the hallmarks of dogmatism. 'Religion', he once wrote, 'cannot be but dogmatic.' His sermons are full of dogmatism and they make reference to both the Old and the New Testament, the New because it records the words of Christ and the Old because it provides us with a collection of deep moral lessons.

Newman was greatly influenced by the Fathers of the Church of Alexandria, and it was to these Patristic figures that he turned when he developed his notion of the Bible as sacramental principle. He held that the Bible is a system of outward signs that contain hidden realities. Through his goodness God has taken ordinary human language, a thing that is itself weak and unfit, and made from it a means of divine communication. In much the same manner that bread and wine may satisfy the spiritual needs of the human soul, so too the Bible contains an invisible grace within its outward form. On the basis that the Bible is a religious book, Newman explained that it could not be interpreted as other books; this conclusion is only intensified when the Bible is regarded as a sacrament. But another important conclusion also follows from this principle: the text of Scripture is a manifestation of higher things, of supernatural truths and realities. These truths find their identity in Christ, who fills both the Old and New Testament. To understand these truths the interpreter must look beyond the plain text and learn to see with spiritual eyes.

Using this spiritual sight Newman felt able to use many ancient methods of interpretation. For example, following his beloved Alexandrian School, he was open to allegorical interpretation although he never took it to their extremes. Indeed allegorical interpretation generally was important if God was not to be confined to the plain sense of the text, if the text was to uphold its sacramental nature and point beyond itself to something greater. As an Anglican he went so far as to suggest that the mystical interpretation of Scripture was 'the characteristic principle' of doctrine, a 'most subtle and powerful method of proof'. Later he would come to value the literal sense, in the old understanding of the term, but he never lost sight of mystical interpretation, believing that it could be restricted from undue excess by paying attention to the christological character of the Bible as a whole.

He regarded the Bible as a unity even though he thought the New Testament was more excellent than the Old. The Old proclaimed the coming of Christ, the New, God incarnate. Continuity could be seen in several respects but chief among these is typology; once again we see an appeal to an older practice that had been condemned by the contemporary German theologians. In one of his sermons he said: 'The Old Testament is full of figures and tokens of the Gospel; types various, and, in their literal wording, contrary to each other, but all meeting and harmoniously fulfilled in Christ and the Church' (1868a, 203–4). Another means of conceiving continuity is in prophecy; what the Old Testament foretold about Christ found its fulfilment in the New. Newman was confident that there was a remarkable correspondence between the two Testaments, the kind of correspondence that could only come from God himself.

I began this section by baldly stating that Newman took the opposite course to Schleiermacher. His conclusions and his methods would certainly seem to suggest that this is in fact the case. Instead of embracing current scholarship, even in his later work, he sought to employ older methods, the kind of methods that had been used by the Church throughout history. So his two fundamental understandings of the Bible encouraged him to use allegorical interpretation and to appeal to typology as a means of holding the Testaments together. He was not unaware of current scholarship but he did not believe the private judgement of any individual capable of successfully interpreting the Bible; he preferred to stand initially under the authority of tradition and latterly, more specifically, of the Church. His approach is not a retreat from the debate of the day but a genuine attempt to deal with it. His views are instructive and might be seen as a bringing together of the two meanings of 'literal' as discussed above. On the one hand, he agrees that the Bible could be read in a strongly realist manner but, on the other, cognisance has to be taken of the original sense of the author. But – and it is a big but – the author is not the person who wrote down the words, but God himself. The strange new world finds in Newman a still newer possibility.

Karl Barth (1886–1968)

By the time Barth was writing, the strange new world was no longer new in the German intellectual and ecclesiastical institutions. Indeed Barth himself had been trained in exactly the kind of scholarship that saw literal interpretation as a searching after the original meaning of the author. For years he was a devout disciple of this tradition but his experience as a young minister in Safenwil caused him to rethink his position. His discomfort began in the pulpit; the historical-critical methods to which he had committed himself did not seem to solve the minister's specific problem, namely the sermon.

> I sought to find my way between the problem of human life on the one hand and the content of the Bible on the other. As a minister I wanted to

> speak to the *people* in the infinite contradiction of their life, but to speak the no less infinite message of the Bible. (1928, 100)

In an early essay he asks what it is that the Bible contains. Is it history? Is it morality? Is it religion? To all these questions he answers yes and no. The Bible is full of history, it contains plenty of good moral advice, it is a source book for godly living, it is all these things but it is much more besides: it is a new world, the world of God. We have been considering the new meaning of 'literal' as the advent of a strange new world; Barth now turns that concept on its head and suggests that it is within the Bible itself that we encounter the genuinely strange new world. In fact, in the Bible we encounter God; there, 'God stands before us as he really is.' 'God is *God*' (1928, 48).

One might be tempted to imagine that Barth was reacting to modern criticism in much the same way as Newman had before him. Newman, however, had held either an aggressive or largely passive stance towards historical criticism; Barth, by contrast, considered himself to be more critical than the historical critics themselves. In *Romans*, his commentary on the Epistle, he claims to have learnt much from the historical critics, for it is their scholarship that helped to establish 'what stands in the text'. This work is essential but it is not sufficient. Real understanding of the Bible begins where critics are content to stop. The first step in interpretation, the one performed by the historical critics, is to establish the text; the second is to penetrate through the text to the mystery that lies within; the third step is to seek to understand that mystery afresh. The hardest of these steps is the second: to penetrate to the real subject matter of the Bible is a human impossibility; whenever it does occur it does so only because God chooses to speak through the text. This appeal to a miraculous event signals just how far Barth wished to stand apart from Schleiermacher.

This understanding of the nature of the Bible needs some clarification. Barth is not suggesting that the Bible is infallible; he recognises that it is a human book and yet a book which witnesses to the transcending Word of God. In the first volume of his magisterial *Church Dogmatics* he speaks of this witness as 'contingent contemporaneity' (1975, 145f.). By this rather odd phrase he meant that the connection between the Word of God and the Bible is neither static nor necessary: it is instead a dynamic relationship. The Word of God is revealed *through* the human words of the text. This view gives a dynamic character to the notion of inspiration because the Bible only becomes what it really is – or can only be described as inspired – when God, in his graciousness, causes the ordinary human words of the Bible to become the Word of God. To those who have been given ears to hear, the Bible is, according to this understanding, an objective and reliable witness to God.

> The Word of God is God Himself in Holy Scripture. For God once spoke

> as Lord to Moses and the prophets, to the Evangelists and apostles. And now through their written word He speaks as the same Lord to His Church. Scripture is holy and the Word of God, because by the Holy Spirit it became and will become to the Church a witness to divine revelation. (1956, 457)

One might be forgiven for thinking that this view neatly avoids the question of interpretation, for if God speaks through the text the responsibility of communicating his Word becomes his and not that of an interpreter. Yet Barth does not actually say this. To his mind the Bible as Word of God needs no explanation because it is clear in itself, but because the Word in the Bible assumes the form of human words, these words are ambiguous and are consequently in need of interpretation. Such interpretation, however, must be 'responsibly undertaken and ... must consist in all circumstances in the freely performed act of subordinating all human concepts, ideas and convictions to the witness of revelation supplied to us in Scripture' (1956, 715).

There is only one response to the Word of God: subordination and obedience. It is impossible to hold together the autonomy of our own world of thought and the testimony of the Bible; instead we should 'concede to Scripture ... primacy and precedence' (1956, 721). This is essentially Barth's notion of the 'freedom of the Word', and latent within it is our 'freedom under the Word' which he describes thus:

> A member of the Church claims direct, absolute and material freedom not for himself, but only for Holy Scripture as the Word of God. But obedience to the free Word of God in Holy Scripture is subjectively conditioned by the fact that each individual who confesses his acceptance of the testimony of Scripture must be willing and prepared to undertake the responsibility for its interpretation and application. Freedom in the Church is limited as an indirect, relative and formal freedom by the freedom of Holy Scripture in which it is grounded. (1956, 661)

This claim of absolute freedom for Holy Scripture illustrates another important difference between Newman and Barth. For Newman the ultimate authority in matters of interpretation is the Church; for Barth, the Church must also stand in subordination to the Word of God.

> The Church does not claim direct and absolute and material freedom for itself but for Holy Scripture as the Word of God. But actual obedience to the authoritative Word of God in Holy Scripture is objectively determined by the fact that those who in the Church mutually confess an acceptance of the witness of Holy Scripture will be ready and willing to listen to one another in expounding and applying it. By the authority

> of Holy Scripture on which it is founded authority in the Church is restricted to an indirect and relative and formal authority. (1956, 538)

Barth closes off the option of appealing to the Church and yet insists that we must take responsibility for interpretation. As a consequence he must outline how such interpretation should be achieved.

An interpreter who is free under the Word should interpret according to three separate, although not necessarily temporally separate, phases. First there is the act of observation; the study of grammar, syntax, style and context. Then there is the act of reflection when the reader thinks along with the text. And the third phase is the act of appropriation, the act of assuming the witness into our own responsibility (1956, 736). In providing a description of these phases Barth did not intend to provide a manual of interpretation in the manner of Schleiermacher; these are theological rather than methodological descriptions. They are so because he wants to set interpretation within theology. Schleiermacher could consider hermeneutics as a precursor to this dogmatic system, for Barth it is the very heart of his work and must therefore take its place inside rather than outside his system. His eventual reaction to historical criticism and that strange new world of interpretation was one of disappointment and frustration; his solution was to rethink the doctrine of the Word of God, to see in the Bible an authority that had, he felt, been neglected in contemporary interpretation. The Word of God, he postulated, is a threefold entity. It is the revelation of God in Jesus Christ; it is the word of the prophets and apostles recorded in the written word; it is the preaching of the minister. Barth's understanding is deeply christological but above everything else it is urgent. Listening to, subordinating oneself to, and proclaiming the Word of God are urgent tasks. The hesitant preacher in the pulpit at Safenwil, the man who had experienced the sermon as the specific problem of the minister, had found a solution: the Word of God.

How is the theory put into practice?

We have looked at three contrasting ways of interpreting the Bible. Our next step is to see how the theory, the theological thinking, makes its way into practical expression and this we do by an investigation of the respective preaching styles. To this end there is no need to look at the entire corpus of sermons, which is just as well, given their extent; as a random sample, however, I shall use sermons preached at Christmas.

Friedrich Schleiermacher

The decision to look at Christmas sermons is particularly tough on Schleiermacher as he made it abundantly clear in his lectures on the life of Jesus that it was necessary to divide Jesus' life into three periods – before his baptism; baptism to arrest; arrest to ascension – but to concentrate on the second because it gave the purest picture of who Jesus really was. Indeed in these same lectures he wrote that 'a report of the birth of Christ has no essential place in the gospel narrative, or otherwise it would not be missing from John and Mark'. These conclusions were based on his extensive exegetical work and informed by his theory of interpretation. But despite this, Schleiermacher would be required to deliver Christmas sermons. On those occasions, did he simply ignore the Bible on the basis of what he must have regarded as an embarrassing lack of historicity, or did he find some other means of engaging with the text?

To answer that question it is necessary to understand something of Schleiermacher's Christology. In *The Christian Faith* he makes two key propositions, neither of which will be surprising given his predisposition for John 1:14:

1 The appearance of the Redeemer in history is, as divine revelation, neither an absolutely supernatural nor an absolutely supra-rational thing (1989, 62).
2 There is no other way of obtaining participation in the Christian communion than through faith in Jesus as the Redeemer (1989, 68).

His exegetical work may have cast suspicion on the historicity of the birth narratives but his insistence that neither Christ's divinity nor his humanity can be sacrificed, and that faith is exclusively grounded in that same Christ, is instructive in our understanding of his preaching. Even though he had decided, on the basis of his hermeneutics, that the birth narratives were historically inaccurate, he might preach instead about their theological witness, that is, what they have to say about Jesus. And in his sermon of 1821, 'Jesus Born the Son of God' (1890), this is exactly what he does. 'This, then,' he writes, 'is the central thought in all that stirs our hearts on these days of solemn festival; that the Saviour was born the Son of God' (280). His text is from Luke 1:31–32, 'Behold … thou shalt bring forth a Son, and shalt call his name Jesus. He shall be great, and shall be called the Son of the Most High.' He makes two chief points. First, Jesus was the Son of God from 'the moment of His appearing in this world', a fact intimated in the sermon text and attested to by Christ himself in the words 'I and my Father are one' and 'He that hath seen Me, hath seen the Father' (John 10:30 and 14:9). His second point builds on the first, as he proposes that it is the incarnation that gives meaning to the concept 'Christian love'. The sermon contains occasional biblical references but it is less a matter of picking out proof-texts than building on the picture of Jesus that is seen in the New Testament as a whole.

In another sermon, one preached in 1831 and entitled 'The Redeemer's First Appearance: A Proclamation of Joy that Awaits all People' (1835), he preaches on Luke 2:10–11. Here, he once again avoids historical questions and concentrates on the angelic announcement to the shepherds. He directs his congregation away from the narrative and towards the content of the message. The feast of Christmas is an invitation to move with confidence from the past to the future, in the sure knowledge that Christ was born for us, and that one day his light will overcome the darkness of this world. Our reaction at Christmas is, like that of the shepherds, one of great joy. Using the Bible in this way is typical of Schleiermacher: the characters of the narrative believe and we have the possibility of believing just as they did. The faith of the shepherds in Christ, still more the faith of the disciples, is not of a different character from our faith; if it were not so we would be members of a different religion. Of course, the witness of the apostles has a special place in the Church but our faith is as theirs. This theological decision is also seen in *The Christian Faith* where he argues that the 'feeling of absolute dependence' – the name he gives to religious affections – is a universal experience (1989, 30).

In his preaching, therefore, Schleiermacher makes very little, if any, explicit use of his hermeneutics. Instead the work of interpretation stands in the background, shaping and controlling his thinking on dogmatics, which in turn stands in the service of his sermons. For Schleiermacher, as for Barth after him, preaching was vital and he relegated dogmatics to its service stating that 'the dogmatic procedure has reference entirely to preaching, and only exists in the interests of preaching' (1989, 88). Elsewhere he famously described practical theology as the crown of theological study and nowhere does this ring more clearly than in his understanding of preaching. His progression of thought works something like this: from the study of the grammatical and psychological aspects of the various authors of the biblical text some general theological principles can be distilled; these principles, when put together in a systematic manner, provide a means of explaining the doctrines of the Church; it is these doctrines that are communicated in the sermon.

I began this section by suggesting that an examination of Christmas sermons was perhaps unfair to Schleiermacher but in another way it was advantageous because his interpretation of the Bible convinced him that the incarnation stands at the centre of the theological enterprise. When he preached he was attempting to evoke a contemporary encounter with Christ. In order to bring such an encounter about, various factors had to be present: first, the context of the encounter should be that of the community of believers; the sermon must be grounded firmly in the Bible; the sermon must arise out of the preacher's own intimate experience with the living Christ; and the sermon must be accepted in faith through the power of the Spirit (De Vries, 64–65). These are the conditions conducive to the evocation of an 'incarnational event'.

Schleiermacher was all too well aware of the challenges historical criticism posed to traditional Christian doctrine. He took those challenges seriously and made the study of the Bible one of his abiding concerns. He did not, however, think it necessary to provoke his congregation either with his methods or the historical doubts that arose from his methods; instead he averted attention away from questions of history towards a positive reception of revelation. In itself it is a perfectly reasonable strategy.

John Henry Newman

Newman was a fellow at Oriel College. When he was only twenty-seven years old the College made him Vicar of St Mary's, the University Church. The sermons he preached there, it has been commented, were 'the most important publication, not only of his Protestant days, but of his life' (Chadwick, 18). It is certainly true that in the course of his incumbency the congregation grew to a considerable size despite its small beginnings. In fact his sermons were so popular that some Oxford tutors devised obstructions to discourage their students from attending. From accounts of members of the congregation we know that attendance was not based on dramatic delivery or any kind of showmanship. Instead, at a time when there was considerable discontent about the gap that existed between what was preached on a Sunday and what was practised throughout the week, Newman articulated that frustration and sought to provide his congregation with a thorough grounding in the faith.

In part his sermons were purposefully directed against two fashions of the day: rationalism and evangelicalism. To his mind these fashions sooner or later arrived at the same conclusion: there is little need for doctrine. For the rationalist, doctrines are there to be weighed and measured, to be set against each other and to be systematically ordered, but not simply to be accepted as mysterious truths. For the evangelical, doctrines play second fiddle to a particular state of the heart. For Newman there was an obligation to preach the Gospel as it had been first given and to this end he would always pack his sermons full of doctrinal teaching. Schleiermacher's sermons were derived from his doctrinal explorations but Newman's were drawn from the tradition of the Church and from a reading of the Bible that ignored the historical-critical approaches of the day.

In his sermon 'The Incarnation' (1824) on the text 'The Word was made flesh and dwelt among us', there is an abundance of biblical quotation (1868b). It is a long sermon but there are at least twenty direct quotations from the Bible, with one-fifth of them drawn from the pages of the Old Testament. The purpose of the sermon, as the title might suggest, is to communicate the doctrine of the incarnation. With a cluster of biblical quotations Newman illustrates how briefly but clearly this doctrine was originally given; the Church has been compelled to lengthen these statements in order to protect the doctrine from heretics seeking to destroy it. With that introduction he launches into a detailed exposition of the traditional understanding of the incarnation and follows it with some instances recorded in Scripture where God manifested himself to humankind. In a transient manner God was in the Prophets, in John the Baptist and in St Paul; through the grace of Christ the Christian soul is renewed by a real presence of God; and Christ was present in the appearances of the Angels to the Patriarchs. In each of these ways God was, or is, present but each example is categorically different from 'that infinitely higher and mysterious union which is called the Incarnation'. To this doctrine we must hold fast and not be led astray by the various sceptical teachings of the heretics who reject the teaching of the Church and deny that 'Jesus Christ is come in the flesh'. Throughout this sermon the Bible is read very much according to the principles outlined in the earlier section: the Old Testament is interpreted christologically; the New Testament is read from a 'strongly realist' perspective; the teaching of the Church and the message of the Bible are considered to be two sides of the same coin.

In a sermon of 1825 he preached on the story of the angelic appearance to the Shepherds (1868c). Here also the ultimate point is the incarnation but instead of tackling the doctrine head on he pursues a more indirect line. Unlike his previous text this one is drawn from a piece of narrative and he makes use of that fact to great effect. He questions why the shepherds were chosen to receive this heavenly message and concludes that it is on account of their lowliness. 'Here', he writes, 'the highest and the lowest of God's rational creatures are brought together.' His first lesson, therefore, is that the Angel appeared 'to teach them not to be downcast and in bondage because they were low in the world'. His second lesson is based on the Angel exclaiming 'Fear not' and so putting the minds of the shepherds at rest, enabling them to rejoice. And rejoicing they made their way to Bethlehem to see the babe who, like themselves, dwelt in poverty. Of this condescension Newman says 'What an emptying of His glory to become man'. He has now reached the doctrine of the incarnation but this time instead of entering into a long explanation he describes it only as a mystery; a great mystery to be contemplated and accepted. The end point of this sermon is once again the Church's doctrine of the incarnation but before that point is reached Newman leads us in a meditation on the encounter between the Angel and the shepherds. He asks questions of the text that would only be reasonable to ask if the text was an accurate historical record, but so Newman believes it to be. It is a contrasting style to Schleiermacher's but it is no less reasonable.

Karl Barth

Barth's view on biblical interpretation, as we saw above, was grounded in the problem of preaching. It was a problem that he had experienced for himself and it was a problem that he specifically addressed in a little book entitled

Homiletics. In this book he outlines nine criteria for a sermon; one of these deals explicitly with Scripture, although many of the others do so implicitly. He writes:

> Preaching as exposition of scripture is in all circumstances under a constraint as regards both form and content. If *the* truth is really to be spoken in the church ... then all that is said in it must take place in the movement and discussion of the record of this truth. Preaching must not be a welling up out of our own speech. In both form and content it must be exposition of scripture. (1991, 88)

For Barth there could be no hope for the Church, or indeed any hope delivered from the Church, apart from the preaching of the Word of God. It is an urgent task, and one that should be taken just as seriously by the congregation as by the preacher; this is not a moment for entertainment – it is a time to listen to God speaking through his Word. Such is the importance of the task that Barth rarely had an introduction to his sermons, seldom made use of illustrations, never used theoretical language, and hardly ever tackled the latest sensational events on the basis that, in general, preachers 'should be good marksmen who aim their guns beyond the hill of relevance' (1991, 119).

His Christmas sermons preached to prisoners in Basel are good examples of both his homiletic style and his interpretation of the Bible. In 1962 his sermon, 'The Double Message of his Coming' (1967), took the text 'He has filled the hungry with good things; and the rich he has sent empty away' (Luke 1:53). On this occasion Barth did use a quotation from a local newspaper but only because it was directly about his congregation, the prisoners, suggesting that 'the festival of love and peace' is out of place in a prison. Barth repeated his scriptural text and proceeded to show just how untrue that statement was. He takes up key words in the text and expounds them; in turn he examines the 'he' in the text, what kinds of people are 'hungry' and what 'rich'. In truth the message of the sermon is simple: it is God who is in control; the rich are those who think they are in control of their own lives; and the hungry are those who need what they most want. There is no appeal to the rest of Scripture or to any theological jargon; it is a simple – but not simplistic – and effective sermon. Using a very similar technique he preached on the same passage that we examined in both Newman and Schleiermacher, the story of the shepherds. This time he concentrated on the angelic announcement 'For unto you is born this day in the city of David a Saviour' (1961). Some people, he tells his congregation, imagine this story to be a fairy tale but in reality it is more real than all stories in history, novels and news broadcasts put together. In this way he directs his listeners away from their normal expectations and towards that reality which is the strange new world of the Bible. In the body of his sermon he explains that 'you' includes all of us, that 'this day' is not Christmas day but every day of our life, and that the 'Saviour' is the one who brings salvation, God himself. The sermon is an invitation to see reality in a particular way; there is no browbeating – indeed we are especially told that the angel does not compel – but it is a statement of encouragement.

In a sermon of 1958 he used a different technique with respect to the Bible but achieves the same effect (1961). His text was from the Gospel of Luke, 'And she brought forth her firstborn son, and wrapped him in swaddling clothes, and laid him in a manger; because there was no room for them in the inn' (2:7). In this sermon he constructs a comparison between friends and family and the one who really stands by us, the one who is the son of God. Even in the depths of darkest being where we are all lost creatures, there, he will be with us. Not finding room in the inn did not stop the advent of the Saviour and neither will our sinfulness stop him standing by us.

> Down there Jesus Christ sets up quarters. Even better, he has already done so! Yes, praise be to God for this dark place, for this manger, for this stable of our lives! There we need him, and there he can use each one of us. There we are ready for him. (1961, 142)

This particular sermon has the tone of a forceful address. It has all the characteristics of the kind of Word event of which Barth speaks. There is the urgent air of expectation that awaits God's speech to the assembled faithful. God is present! God *is* present!

Conclusion

At first sight Schleiermacher, Newman and Barth appear to have little in common. Indeed, such is the diversity of their opinions that it might be thought impossible to draw them together. Perhaps that is indeed the case. Nonetheless, in representing diversity they indicate some of the ways in which the Bible is interpreted in our pastoral world today. To their methods we could also add methods of interpretation that have developed from political theology or from semiotic theories or from modern philosophical systems. Interpretation is now a multi-faceted activity and yet our three authors offer models that are worth taking note of despite the multiplicity of currently possible methodologies.

First, all three take the Bible seriously. All too often preaching ignores the seriousness of the text: on the one hand some preaching takes place without any direct reference to the text at all; on the other hand some preaching superimposes the same theological or doctrinal message on every passage of Scripture. Either extreme is a failure to take the Bible seriously. In the first instance the challenges of historical criticism – of the daunting strange new world – leave the preacher speechless; uncertain of the facts, the preacher presumes it is best to pass over the text in silence. In the second, the challenges of the historical-critical method are ignored and the Scripture is reduced to the role of proof-text. Every text is manipulated to fit a particular dogmatic stance and is not allowed space to speak for itself. Our three theologians, by contrast, are taking the text very seriously indeed. Certainly they treat the historical-critical problem in differing ways, but they nonetheless take the text very seriously indeed.

Second, for each there is an abiding connection between Scripture and doctrine. In different ways they speak against latitudinarianism: congregational members cannot believe just what they like. Of course the results of their deliberations will not fit easily together but they will all agree that doctrine stands in the service of preaching and that preaching is nothing other than an exposition of Scripture. This link between Scripture and doctrine is not always present in contemporary preaching. Indeed, the failings mentioned in the paragraph above are raised in this respect also.

Third, there is a sense in which all our theologians offer an exciting insight into the nature of Scripture and yet each could do well to listen more carefully to the others. In the final analysis Schleiermacher understands the preaching of Scripture as that which brings about an incarnational event; typically his emphasis is on experience. Newman wishes to safeguard Scripture from inappropriate interpretation by the individual; his emphasis is on tradition. Barth believes that Scripture contains a picture of reality, a strange new world, which when read can convey the Word of God, which, when heard, should be obediently followed; his emphasis is on revelation. These various emphases are appealing. And yet, at least in practical terms, they might be so much more striking if held in combination. Preaching that can expound Scripture through the avenues of experience, tradition and revelation will be strong stuff indeed. Schleiermacher, Newman and Barth offer us a renewed challenge in our practical use of the Bible in the modern world.

Bibliography

Barth, K. (1928) *The Word of God and the Word of Man*. London: Hodder & Stoughton.

Barth, K. (1956) *Church Dogmatics* I.2. Edinburgh: T&T Clark.

Barth, K. (1961) *Deliverance to the Captives*. London: SCM Press.

Barth, K. (1967) *Call for God*. London: SCM Press.

Barth, K. (1975) *Church Dogmatics* I.1. Edinburgh: T&T Clark.

Barth, K. (1991) *Homiletics*. Louisville, KY: Westminster/John Knox Press.

Chadwick, O. (1983) *Newman*. Oxford: Oxford University Press.

De Vries, D. (1996) *Jesus Christ in the Preaching of Calvin and Schleiermacher*. Louisville, KY: Westminster John Knox Press.

Frei, H. (1974) *The Eclipse of Biblical Narrative: a study in eighteenth and nineteenth century hermeneutics*. New Haven, CT: Yale University Press.

Newman, J. H. (1868a) *Parochial and Plain Sermons* vol. I. London: Rivingtons.

Newman, J. H. (1868b) *Parochial and Plain Sermons* vol. II. London: Rivingtons.

Newman, J. H. (1868c) *Parochial and Plain Sermons* vol. VIII. London: Rivingtons.

Newman, J. H. (1967) *On the Interpretation of Scripture*. Washington: Corpus.

Schleiermacher, F. (1835) *Sämmtliche Werke* II/3. Berlin: Reimer.

Schleiermacher, F. (1890) *Selected Sermons*. London.

Schleiermacher, F. (1981) *On the Glaubenslehre*. Atlanta, GA: Scholars Press.

Schleiermacher, F. (1987) *Servant of the Word: selected sermons of Friedrich Schleiermacher*. Philadelphia: Fortress Press.

Schleiermacher, F. (1989) *The Christian Faith*. Edinburgh: T&T Clark.

Schleiermacher, F. (1997) *Hermeneutics: the handwritten documents*. Atlanta, GA: Scholars Press.

PART II:
The Problems Posed by Contemporary Biblical Scholarship

One of the defining features of biblical scholarship at the turn of the twenty-first century is plurality. New interpretative methods have followed one another at increasingly short intervals throughout the previous two hundred years, leading to a situation where there is no agreement on the 'right' way to attempt to read a text, let alone the 'right reading' (if, indeed, such a thing exists). Instead a family of historical-critical methods jostle for position with fashionably postmodern hermeneutical theories (reader-response criticism, speech-act theory, and so on), liberative hermeneutics that focus on the context of the reading community as the key interpretative datum, a resurgence of avowedly theological readings, and a plethora of newer or minority approaches (reception history, for instance). Whether this situation is to be celebrated or decried, it is inescapable, and so this section of the book seeks to recognise the reality of it by asking five scholars to explore how different approaches to Biblical Studies might affect the way the Scriptures are used pastorally.

John Rogerson begins by noting the problems that historical and literary criticism raises, problems that are, perhaps, well enough known. He offers reasons why a better knowledge of biblical criticism might lead to an enhanced, rather than vitiated, discipleship. Echoing Samuel Taylor Coleridge, he argues that an appreciation of the humanity of the scriptural writers, and of the text they produced, will benefit us in our reading of it. Ultimately, however, the appeal is to the power of truth: if there are good reasons to believe that parts of the Old or New Testament's history does not correspond with the facts, then pastoral practice that assumes it does must be illegitimate.

Craig Bartholomew reflects on the rise of hermeneutics as a philosophical discipline, and suggests that behind different hermeneutical strategies are different visions of the world, and particularly of the Christ–world relationship. The effects of this in relation to pastoral practice are helpfully elucidated through discussions of two particular strands of modern biblical hermeneutics, narrative theology and the theological interpretation of the Bible.

Walter Brueggemann, picking up on the emergence of historical-critical method in the eighteenth century, discusses the trajectory that led through biblical theology to canonical approaches to Scripture, resulting in a post-liberal framework that finds meaning through the inhabitation of performed and performative texts. This leads him to consider contextual readings of Scripture, with special reference to Africa, a theme more fully taken up in the next chapter. As Brueggemann helpfully points out, post-liberal readings only make sense as readings based in practice, which must include pastoral practice.

Chris Rowland and Zoë Bennett focus on contextual readings of Scripture, such as liberation and feminist theologies. In an implicit rebuke to the notion that such readings are a feature of the latter half of the twentieth century only, lessons drawn from sixteenth-century Anabaptist martyrs and from William Blake's visionary poetry are traced into the experience of base communities in Brazil and groups of women struggling to understand their pastoral calling in the face of patriarchal institutions in Cambridge. This series of illuminating snapshots offers strong evidence for the way the Scriptures can equally oppress or liberate when deployed pastorally. This makes serious claims about the right and wrong use of the Bible in pastoral practice and raises, in acute form, the questions of interpretive norms. What does one do with texts or cultural assumptions that offend current enlightened common sense? What are the criteria of judgement and who arbitrates on that?

If the use of the Bible in pastoral care is to be considered faithful or professional, it needs to be responsible to biblical scholarship; not, it must be said, blown by every passing wind, eagerly embracing each faddish theory that enjoys fifteen minutes of fame in the academy, but honest enough to accept that those who study the Bible professionally have insights and knowledge that must be integrated with pastoral practice, and that intellectual honesty demands a serious wrestling with the interpretations and discoveries of current scholarship, a wrestling that will involve questioning of present patterns of practice and considerable uncertainty of outcome.

We have noted already, in the general introduction, and find echoed in some of the essays, the oft-heard complaint that the way the Bible is used in churches seems to indicate that this work has not been done, that uninformed and unreflective patterns of usage continue even in the pulpit, and that too often pastorally Bible use is found difficult and so either avoided, or reduced to a feeble cycling through a few favourite evocative texts. Clearly, this is inadequate, and the sort of reflection demonstrated by the authors in this section is the necessary scholarly precursor to more adequate practice being developed.

However, this is not a one-way street. If it is the case that 'all Scripture that is God-breathed is useful' then the pastoral usefulness of a method of reading the Bible is part of the valid test of that method's legitimacy. On this account, it is a part of the task of Biblical Studies both to demonstrate the usefulness of its various ways of handling the text to the work of 'teaching, reproof, correction and training in righteousness' and to listen to the critiques offered by those engaged in pastoral practice, whose experience is the form of that validation. These linked tasks of the creative integration of biblical perspectives into pastoral practice, and of demonstrating the pastoral outcomes of particular ways of reading Scripture, are no doubt difficult and complex, but they are also urgent. Our writers here demonstrate the exciting possibilities they present. Conversely, practical theologians, if they are to be a respected part of that academy, must be seen to take biblical scholarship seriously. Some of the challenges laid down are indeed taken up in the next Part. Anderson engages with narrative models and Quicke shows how it affects some types of preaching, while contextual issues are indicated in several places.

Two further points stand out from this group of essays. The first is that the postmodern interpretations of Scripture reach behind the Enlightenment enterprise and have affinities to the pre-critical approaches of the early Church and medieval and early Protestant times. But that cannot roll away or overlook the gains and losses of the past three hundred years. If there is to be a recovery of earlier traditions it must be through and beyond the critical processes that we have rehearsed. But it may be that there can be a new directness and immediacy in the use of the Bible that is akin to the traditional place of Scripture at the centre of the community of faith.

Second, this is reinforced by the new stress on the interpretive roll of the reader and the context. This too reflects a traditional, normative assumption about Scripture. The Bible is interpreted in and through the Spirit who is present both in the gift of revelation and in the wisdom of reception. The Spirit that 'breathed' into Scripture is also the Spirit that inspires the reader and the Church, drawing them closer to God. These two poles are both essential and one cannot be suppressed by the other. The interpretation is part of being Scripture. As George Fox argued, it is not so much what Scripture means as what it means to you personally. To be reminded of that does not solve all the problems of correct interpretation, which has produced a long history of controversy; but it, perhaps, commits us to a continual exploring, so that we all, scholar or (to pick up Wycliffe's image) ploughboy, can approach the text and hear the Word of the Lord.

CHAPTER 7:

The gifts and challenges of historical and literary criticism

JOHN ROGERSON

Introduction

'A reading from the book of the prophet Isaiah'; 'A reading from the second letter of Paul to Timothy'; 'Hear the gospel of our Lord Jesus Christ according to Luke.' These introductions to the reading of passages from the Bible in church services are taken at random from the *Revised Common Lectionary*. They illustrate the problems posed for worshippers by biblical scholarship.

The Isaiah passage that is introduced is 50:4–9a, and while the introduction quoted above does not directly claim that the person who wrote or spoke the passage was the eighth-century prophet commonly called Isaiah of Jerusalem, this is a conclusion that would reasonably be drawn by any one unfamiliar with biblical scholarship. In fact, scholarship dates the passage to an unnamed prophet who probably worked in Babylon two centuries later than Isaiah of Jerusalem. There is no ambiguity about the second introduction. The words plainly indicate that Paul is the author of 2 Timothy; yet biblical scholarship is largely unanimous in supposing otherwise and in attributing 2 Timothy to a member of a church founded by Paul, who perhaps used some material deriving from Paul. The introduction to the reading from Luke's gospel implies that Luke (whoever he was) was the author of that work, whereas biblical scholarship argues that this author made extensive use of Mark's gospel and a collection of sayings of Jesus known as Q (the 'Q' derives from its German name, *Quelle* meaning 'source'). Some scholars have maintained that Luke also drew much of his material from Matthew.

This chapter has begun my drawing attention to one of two major problems presented to pastoral practice by biblical scholarship, that of the nature and authorship of the Bible. The other major problem is that of the relation of the historical information contained in the Bible to history as reconstructed by modern historical research.

Who wrote the books of the Bible?

The Bible claims to have been written by people whose relation to God was such that what they wrote came from God or was in some way inspired by him. Moses is said to have spoken with God 'mouth to mouth' (Num. 12:8) and many of the commandments to the Israelites in the books of Exodus, Leviticus and Numbers are preceded by the words 'the LORD said to Moses'. When Jeremiah is called to be a prophet God says to him 'whatever I command you you shall speak' (Jer. 1:7). Ezekiel is given a scroll to eat (Ezek. 2:8—3:3), the implication being that it contains the words that Ezekiel will proclaim to the people. In the New Testament it is claimed in 2 Peter 1:21 that no [Old Testament] prophecy 'ever came by the impulse of man, but men moved by the Holy Spirit spoke from God'.

Given these claims in the Bible about its origins, it was natural for early interpreters to link the authorship of its books with the question of their authority and integrity. To the question 'why can we trust the Bible?' the answer could be given 'because it was written by people who were inspired by God'. This did not, however, prevent biblical interpreters from asking critical questions. For example, the closing verses of Deuteronomy (Deut. 34:5–12) describe the death and burial of Moses and his succession by Joshua; and while some ancient interpreters argued that Moses could have been inspired by God to write about his own death, others ascribed these verses to Joshua rather than to Moses. However, these and other critical matters did not prevent the establishment of a broad consensus within Christianity (some of which was shared with Judaism) that Moses had written the first five books of the Bible, that the prophets had written the books named after them, that David had composed the Psalms, that Solomon had written Proverbs, Song of Songs and Ecclesiastes, and that Joshua, Samuel and Jeremiah had been responsible for some of the other books. The case of the New Testament was simpler. A matter of dispute was whether or not Paul had written the Letter to the Hebrews.

This consensus about the authorship, a consensus closely linked to the question of the authority and integrity of the Bible, lasted until the seventeenth century; but it is arguable that, popularly, something like this consensus is still assumed and that any contact that many church members may have with biblical scholarship is likely to be disturbing. Some of the reasons for this are as follows. First, there are the liturgical introductions to readings from the Bible at church services, such as the ones cited at the beginning of this chapter. Second, the contents of some Bibles reinforce the consensus. The copy of the Revised Standard Version to which I am referring in writing this chapter heads page 1 with the title 'The First Book of Moses Commonly Called Genesis'. Exodus is described as 'The Second Book of Moses' and so on. To be fair, not all Bibles present their material in this way. The conservative New International Version omits 'The First Book of Moses' and the rest; but even translations that represent more critical biblical scholarship such as the Revised English Bible still have headings such as 'The First Letter of Paul to Timothy'. A third reason why the consensus prevails is that the findings of biblical scholarship about how the Bible was written contradict what most people instinctively think about the authorship of books. When they buy a book they assume that the person named on the title page is the author. It is therefore disturbing to be told that 'The First Letter of Paul to Timothy' was not written by Paul. There is also a fourth, and most important, factor. Theories of authorship were originally closely bound up with belief in the authority and integrity of the Bible, and when biblical scholarship began to question traditional views this questioning was often seen as an attack on the Bible's authority and inspiration. If Paul did not write 1 Timothy when the letter itself begins 'Paul ... to Timothy', where does that leave the claims of the churches that the Bible is inspired and in some sense the 'Word of God'? Unless biblical scholarship can demonstrate that it upholds or even enhances the possibility of belief in the Bible's authority, confronting churchgoers with the results of biblical criticism will cause, and has caused, much perturbation. A fifth factor that must be considered is that biblical scholarship not only questions traditional beliefs about who wrote the Bible; it questions whether sayings attributed to prophets in the Old Testament and to Jesus in the New Testament were actually spoken by them. The matter of the words of Jesus is especially acute. In many churches the reading of the gospel, usually containing words of Jesus, is a central act of worship. If Jesus is believed to have been the Son of God, his words must carry especial authority, yet biblical scholarship asserts that he did not say all of the words attributed to him. How can these matters be resolved?

Authorship and actual words

It goes without saying that committed Christian discipleship involves more than hearing the occasional sermon in church, and that the problems raised by biblical scholarship will only be dealt with by way of serious study, however that is organised in any given situation. On the other side, biblical scholarship is not simply an academic exercise. It stands in a long tradition of activity within the churches, whose aim has been to use all the resources of human knowledge in order to understand and proclaim the message of the Bible. A further point to be emphasised is that the questions posed by biblical scholars arise from the text of the Bible itself, and are not artificially invented difficulties designed to make life awkward.

Bearing in mind the point that biblical scholarship seeks to deal with questions that arise from the text of the Bible, an ideal starting point for introducing biblical scholarship is a comparison of events, and sayings of Jesus, as recorded in the first three gospels. The Beatitudes occur in Matthew 5:1–12 and Luke 6:20–26. They have close similarities but also differences. How are these to be explained? The main possibilities are that the versions in Matthew and Luke are different reports of what was said on one occasion. Alternatively, they may represent what was said on two different occasions. Initially, the question can be left unanswered. The important point is that there is a genuine question that arises from the biblical text itself. Another set of passages that can be considered is Matthew 20:29–34, Mark 10:46–52 and Luke 18:35–43. In Matthew, Jesus heals two blind men while leaving Jericho on his way to Jerusalem, in Mark he heals Bartimaeus on his way out of Jericho, while in Luke he heals an unnamed blind man on his way into Jericho. Do we have three different incidents? Did Jesus heal a blind man when entering Jericho and did he then heal Bartimaeus and two other blind men while leaving the city; or do the three gospel accounts refer to one and the same incident, while not agreeing on the exact details?

The next step to take is to compare the first three gospels with the fourth gospel. The well-known differences include the following: Jesus visits Jerusalem only once during his ministry according to the first three gospels but four times according to John. The money-changers are expelled by Jesus from the temple at the beginning of his ministry in John (John 2:13–22) but at the end of his ministry according to the other gospels (Mark 11:15–18). The first disciples are called by the river Jordan according to John (John 1:35–51) but by the Sea of Galilee according to the others (Mark 1:16–20). There is also the striking difference between the parables and short sayings of Jesus that are found in the first three gospels and the long discourses of Jesus found in the fourth gospel.

If readers can begin to appreciate that these features of the biblical text call for explanation and may even be matters of considerable interest in themselves, the next question that can be faced is whether Jesus actually said the words attributed to him in the gospels, a matter that becomes particularly acute in John's gospel. The obvious point must be made that Jesus spoke Aramaic and that the gospels exist in Greek. From that perspective the only actual words of Jesus that we are likely to have are *Talitha cumi* ('little girl, arise') in Mark 5:41, *Ephphatha* ('be opened') in Mark 7:34, *Abba* ('father') in Mark 14:36 and the cry from the cross in Mark 15:34. Otherwise, the sayings of Jesus are available to us only in Greek translation. This does not mean, however, that what is available fails to do justice to what Jesus said and taught. On the contrary, while a sober critical approach to the first three gospels must acknowledge that the processes of transmission, translation and interpretation of the words of Jesus have left them in a form that does not necessarily coincide with what he must have said, there is still sufficient correspondence between what he said and what is recorded to enable us to glimpse his person and overhear this voice. C. H. Dodd authoritatively described the process of the compilation of the gospels in the following words:

> The materials out of which they [the units of tradition] were formed were already in existence, as an unarticulated wealth of recollections and reminiscences of the words and deeds of Jesus – mixed, it may be, with the reflections and interpretations of his followers. It was out of this unformed or fluid tradition that the units of narrative and teaching crystallized into the forms we know. At the early, unformed, stage we have to think, not of distinct narratives, with their individual features sharply marked, as we have them in the gospels, but of a host of remembered traits and turns of expression, often disjointed and without context, but abounding in characteristic detail. It was remembered, for example, that Jesus was addressed by suppliants in the striking, and perhaps compromising, terms, *eleēson huie Daueid* [have mercy, son of David], that on occasion he 'passionately'... forbade his patients to make publicity for him, that he was asked such questions as 'Which is the first commandment?' and 'What shall I do to inherit eternal life?', and that he referred inquirers to the commandments of the Decalogue, but laid especial stress on the two commandments of love to God and neighbour. But the precise occasions with which these features of his Ministry were associated were perhaps not always remembered, or were remembered differently by different witnesses; for the association of ideas is a very individual thing, and it often affects our recollection of events.
>
> (Dodd 1963, 171–2)

This is a description of the likely processes by which the gospels came into being that can readily be appreciated by non-experts, and that can build confidence in their content. But it also does something else of importance, and that is to be a reminder that the content of the Bible is more important than the processes by which it came into being. One of the problems with theories of inspiration is that they focus attention on the process to the detriment of the content. In fact, historically, it was the content of the books of the Bible that led faith communities to accept them as Scripture and authoritative. It was only later that theories about their production were formulated in terms of how named authors had been inspired; but in the process the power of its content, appreciated as narrative and poetry, was often overlooked.

The main point, however, is that whatever were the processes by which what he said in Aramaic was recorded in the gospels in Greek, the gospels taken as a whole provide a credible picture of the kind of teacher who must have existed in order to bring into being the Christian mission and church that are described, especially in the letters of Paul. This introduces a further point. There is very little theology in the first three gospels. They are more concerned to say that Jesus was crucified and exalted than to explain the cosmic significance of these events. For such explanations it is necessary to turn to the letters of Paul, and to the gospel of John. If Paul's interpretation of the significance of Jesus' death and exaltation is accepted, it may be easier to come to terms with the idea that not all of the words attributed to Jesus in the first three gospels were spoken by him, and that very little of his teaching in John's gospel represents his exact words. The point is that the significance of words and events is almost always appreciated in hindsight. In the Second World War, for example, those who were evacuated from Dunkirk and who fought in the Battle of Britain could not at the time have appreciated the importance of these events as turning points in the war. This only became clear as the war progressed. Similarly, the significance of the words and actions of Jesus became apparent only after his exaltation, a point made several times in the gospels, for example in John 12:16, where it is said of Jesus' triumphal entry into Jerusalem that 'His disciples did not understand this at first; but when Jesus was glorified, then they remembered that this [Zech. 9:9] had been written of him and had been done to him.' What we have, then, in the gospels, is an account of the ministry, death and exaltation of Jesus based upon many reminiscences and recollections of what he said and did, but refracted through the deeper understanding by his followers of the significance of all this following his exaltation. The gospels indeed contain authentic teachings of Jesus; but in some cases, especially in the fourth gospel, his words have been added to or have been expanded into long discourses. This has been a process not of falsification or misrepresentation, but one of clarification, designed to help readers of the gospels to understand the full significance of who Jesus was and what he said and did. To make such an adjustment in how to think about the gospels and read them, will also affect an understanding of Christian discipleship. So, too, all that has been written above about the words of Jesus could also be said of the Old Testament prophets; that there is a complex but understandable relationship between their actual words and deeds and the writings that bear their names (see Mowvley).

Biblical history and modern historical reconstruction

A matter of concern inside the Church as well as among the general public is whether the Bible (in this case usually the Old Testament) is historically true. That there is a continuing interest in this subject is indicated by recent television programmes on Moses and the Egyptian background to the reign of

Solomon; and there are regular reports in newspapers of the possible discovery of the remains of Noah's ark on the tops of various mountains in Central Asia. A best-selling book for many years has been W. Keller's *The Bible as History*, which seeks to demonstrate the truth of the Bible with the help of archaeology.

Instinctively, most people would like to believe that the Bible is 'true'; that Abraham and Moses actually existed and that there was a flood that destroyed large parts of the world. The 'fundamentalist' argument, that you either have to accept the whole of the Bible as accurate, or reject it entirely, seems to have some validity. Picking and choosing what one accepts as accurate means putting one's trust in scholars, who are often in disagreement.

To the question, 'why doubt the historical accuracy of the Bible?' the first answer must be that this question arises in the first instance from the biblical text itself. In Genesis 12:10–20 and 20:1–18 there are accounts of how Abraham, on entering the territory of foreign rulers, says that his wife, Sarah, is his sister. His reason for doing this is his fear that the foreign ruler will kill him in order to take Sarah into his harem, because of Sarah's great beauty. The details of the two stories are different. In Genesis 12:10–20 the country is Egypt and the ruler an unnamed pharaoh; in Genesis 20:1–18 the country is Gerar and the ruler is Abimelech. The stories, however, contain the same plot. Sarah is taken into the harem of the ruler because, according to Abraham, she is his sister not his wife. In both cases, divine intervention rescues Sarah and restores her to her husband, who is then acknowledged as such by the ruler. The first question that these two accounts raises is whether they report two separate, but similar, incidents or are differing versions of a single incident or tradition. (The question is further complicated by the fact that the very same thing happens to Abraham's son Isaac in Genesis 26:6–11, in Gerar, whose king is Abimelech.) A second question arises from reading Genesis as a sequential narrative. In Genesis 17:17 Sarah is described as being ninety years old. It is not unreasonable to ask why the king of Gerar in Genesis 20:2 should have found a ninety-year-old woman so desirable as to want to take her into his harem.

Another passage that could be considered is 1 Samuel 16:14—17:58. At the end of 1 Samuel 16 the introduction of David to Saul's court is described. Saul, who is being tormented by 'an evil spirit from the LORD' is advised to employ a musician whose playing will soothe the king. This player turns out to be David; but he is also described as 'a man of valour, a man of war', and he becomes Saul's armour-bearer. 1 Samuel 17 is the story of David and Goliath, and presents a different David: a David who is present at the scene of battle not as Saul's armour-bearer but because he is taking provisions to his elder brothers who are fighting in Saul's army. Indeed, when David responds to Goliath's challenge for an Israelite to fight him he declares that he is not used to armour (1 Sam. 17:39). Following David's defeat of Goliath, Saul enquires of his commander, Abner, whose son David is, that is, who David is. Abner confesses ignorance. This is very strange, considering that David is Saul's armour-bearer and musician, according to 1 Samuel 16:14–23.

It is important to notice that the difficulties raised by these chapters have long been recognised. In the ancient Greek translation of 1 Samuel 17, verses 12–31, 41 and 50 are not found, and neither are 1 Samuel 17:55—18:5 present. These omissions (if that is what they are) enable a consistent story to emerge. When the Philistine issues his challenge, David, who is Saul's armour-bearer, accepts the challenge and prevails over Goliath. There is no incident in which Saul enquires after the identity of David following his triumph.

It is possible to argue that 17:12–31 were later inserted (Smith 1881, 125–6) or that they were omitted by the Greek translators in order to remove the contradictions. In Horne (1825, Vol. I, 545) it is maintained that 1 Samuel 16:14–23 is misplaced and that it should come between 18:9 and 18:10. Horne, it should be pointed out, was defending the view that the Bible contained no errors of fact, and as part of that defence he stated the principle: 'Things are not always recorded in the Scriptures exactly in the same method and order in which they were done' (545). The fact that this and other difficulties have long been recognised and that strategies to deal with them have included the admission that not everything in the Bible is

> necessarily in the correct order, should be reassuring. It is easy to think that biblical criticism is an essentially recent enterprise which overturns eighteen or nineteen hundred years of faithful acceptance of the Bible at face value. In fact, difficulties in the text at all sorts of levels have long been noticed and discussed. (Rogerson 1998, 6–24)

What is different about biblical scholarship from the end of the eighteenth century compared with what went before, is that the strategies for dealing with the difficulties changed. Before the second half of the eighteenth century (Horne's *Introduction* is a good example despite its nineteenth-century date) difficulties were dealt with on the assumption that the Bible was free from errors because its divine origin must necessarily preserve it from mistakes. From the second half of the eighteenth century biblical scholars increasingly accepted that there were mistakes in the Bible without this in any way diminishing their respect for its authority. The change came about because traditional theories about the process by which God had inspired the biblical writers could no longer be maintained in the face of a growing body of scientific and historical knowledge that contradicted the Bible at a number of points. The biblical authors were seen for what they were: people who had lived in a particular society at particular times and who had been subject to the limitations of the scientific and historical knowledge of those times. This acceptance did not call into question the status of the biblical writers as 'men of God', as people who had experienced a close relationship with the divine, and which had led them to become prophets or psalmists or apostles. Indeed, concentration upon the human side of the Bible's production served to enhance the appreciation of the profundity of its message and to enable believers to relate more readily to those responsible for writing it.

In medieval art, biblical authors are often depicted as seated or standing at writing desks, responding to the promptings of the Holy Spirit, who takes the form of a bird whispering into the ear of the writer. This idea of the composition and inspiration of the Bible sets its authors apart. The view of the composition of the Bible maintained by biblical scholarship brings the biblical authors closer to ordinary Christians. They can be seen as people who were engaged in the life of their nation, often at crucial times. In ancient Israel, some prophets spoke and wrote when the nation was being threatened with defeat and conquest at the hands of powerful neighbours such as Egypt, Assyria and Babylon. Other prophets worked in exile in Babylon, while others experienced the conditions of the Second Temple period (540 BCE onwards) in which a small Jewish community looked back nostalgically to a past Golden Age in which David and Solomon had reigned. In the New Testament parts of the country were under Roman occupation, and various Jewish groups advocated and practised violent resistance against the ruling power. It was in this situation that the Church came into being and proclaimed its dangerous message that 'Jesus is Lord'. This change in understanding the Bible can be described as the substitution of a dynamic for a static view of its origin and significance. The biblical authors ceased to be stained-glass figures isolated from everyday life, and became flesh and blood personages to whom ordinary believers could relate. A price for this shift, however, had to be paid.

What has just been written has probably given the false impression that pre-critical understanding simply used the Bible to produce 'proof-texts'. While this may have been true at the level of systematic theology, the preaching of the Bible could and did make characters in the biblical narratives alive to congregations. Preachers could talk about Moses or David as 'men of God' facing difficult situations and could relate their responses to the problems facing the preachers and their congregations. Pre-critical scholarship could then use such narratives as those about Abraham or Sarah as a true story on the basis of which Abraham's action could be characterised as faithless or prudent. Critical scholarship, however, was less certain about the 'truth' of the incidents. In the twentieth century such material was classified as 'family saga' whose function was to record the preservation of the 'ancestress in danger'. It has to be admitted that if, as a result, preachers no longer felt able to preach on such material, or to use it in Bible studies, this was a loss. A new paradigm had been accepted, one that broke with the increasingly untenable explanations of how difficulties in the biblical text could be reconciled.

However, from the 1970s onwards, it was increasingly accepted in biblical scholarship that biblical texts could and should be approached from a literary standpoint. Texts could be classified according to genre or literary type; so Genesis 20:1–18 could be classified as 'family saga'. This did not rule out two further possibilities, however; first, that the narrative had been shaped by the distinctive theological concerns of the biblical author/editor which could be studied with profit, and second, that it could be viewed as a sophisticated literary creation with profound features of plot and characterisation. The recent literary approaches to the Bible can, indeed, be seen as a necessary corrective within biblical scholarship, which has enabled it to overcome an understandably one-sided preoccupation with historical-critical matters, to the detriment of an appreciation of the literary qualities of the biblical text. For the Bible in pastoral practice the advent of the new literary approaches is of fundamental importance. It enables readers to deal once more with biblical characters, while also having much to gain by seeing biblical stories as pieces of literature that can be studied from the angles of plot, characterisation, and 'point of view' (Bar-Efrat 1989).

Biblical history

So far, we have discussed the effect of biblical scholarship's acceptance of inaccuracies in the Bible upon the truth and use of particular narratives. What follows will deal with the larger question of history as presented in the Bible compared with history as reconstructed by modern research. It will deal mainly with the Old Testament.

Biblical scholars have long been aware that history recorded in the Bible parallels history recorded in other sources, and in the early eighteenth century two British scholars, Humphrey Prideaux and Samuel Shukford published works entitled respectively *The Old and New Testament connected in the History of the Jews and Neighbouring Nations* (1716) and *The Sacred and Profane History Connected* (1728). Both authors displayed scholarly judgement and critical acumen when handling non-biblical, mostly classical, sources, but their attitude to the Bible was summed up by Prideaux in the following words: 'the profane writer must give place to the sacred … The sacred writ, as being dictated by the holy spirit of God, must ever be of infallible truth' (Prideauz 1716–18, vol. I, 337). This meant that where the Bible disagreed with other sources, the Bible's account was always preferred.

This view began to change in the second half of the eighteenth century, and in the following centuries the decipherment of Egyptian hieroglyphs and Babylonian and Assyrian cuneiform made vast amounts of material available to historians with which to reconstruct the history of the ancient Near East. In the twentieth century, additional material was provided by archaeological expeditions to Palestine, Israel and the West Bank. At the time of writing, Old

Testament scholarship is deeply divided between so-called 'minimalists' and so-called 'maximalists'. The former accept the view that is generally held among archaeologists, that written sources are often unreliable witnesses to the past, and that archaeological findings must take precedence over written sources. As applied to the Bible, this leads to the view that little can be known for sure about ancient Israel until the early ninth century BCE, when a kingdom called Israel was established by Omri with its capital in Samaria. In the eighth century the kingdom of Judah with its capital in Jerusalem came to dominate the hill country of Judah and to take over some of the beliefs and traditions of its northern neighbour, Israel, when the latter was destroyed by the Assyrians between 734 and 721 BCE. This account not only questions what can be known about the reigns of David and Solomon; it takes for granted that the stories of Abraham, Isaac and Jacob, the Exodus and the occupation of Canaan at best lie beyond the possibility of historical verification and at worst are reconstructions of the past made long after the events and based upon no reliable evidence.

The 'maximalists' argue that the Bible can be used in conjunction with archaeology to provide a picture that is broadly in line with that of the Bible. A people called 'Israel' in Egyptian sources of the late thirteenth century BCE is in occupation of Canaan around 1200 BCE; and a hundred and fifty years later, as a result of conflict with the Philistines (one of the 'Sea Peoples' mentioned in Egyptian sources, that had settled in the coastal regions of Canaan), an Israelite leader named Saul established a type of 'kingship' in Israel. Saul was followed by David, who defeated the Philistines, made Jerusalem his capital, and created a small empire. He was succeeded by Solomon who built not only the temple in Jerusalem, but public buildings and fortifications in cities such as Gezer, Hazor and Megiddo. On Solomon's death the kingdom split into Israel in the north and Judah in the south.

This is not the place to enter the debate between the two sides, except to say that they have more in common than might appear to be the case, and that both agree that at many points the account of Israel's history in the books of Kings is broadly confirmed by extra-biblical sources such as Assyrian and Babylonian records. The main observation is that ordinary churchgoers will probably instinctively incline to the 'maximalists', and, indeed, to any position that seems to support the historical truth of the Bible. This is an understandable reaction of loyalty to the Bible, which should not be disparaged. However, in pastoral practice the attempt should be made to help them to see where the real significance of biblical history lies, and how it relates to modern reconstructed history (Rogerson, 49–57).

Modern history writing uses narratives to reconstruct a past that is known from such things as documents, chronicles and archaeological remains. The aims of the narrative depend on the historian and when he or she is writing. Older history writing tended to concentrate upon the great, upon kings and rulers. More recently there has been an interest in 'ordinary people' and in the part played by women in the past. History can be, and is, written from ideological standpoints, such as Marxism. No history writing can ever be definitive. Subsequent discoveries in research, and new ways of interpreting evidence or events will lead to modification or refutation of even the most distinguished contributions to history.

All this is true of attempts to reconstruct the history of ancient Israel. Over forty years ago John Bright's *A History of Israel* began with the founding fathers (Abraham, Isaac and Jacob) and generally followed the historical outline presented in the Bible itself. *The History of Israel* by the German scholar Martin Noth began with the Israelite tribes settled in Canaan in the thirteenth century BCE and treated the accounts of the Patriarchs and the exodus as the sacred traditions of a thirteenth-century Israelite tribal confederacy, that is, as beyond the possibility of historical reconstruction. In subsequent writing, attention has been focused upon early Israel as an attempt to form an egalitarian society in opposition to oppressive Canaanite city states in the thirteenth to eleventh centuries (Gottwald). The economic implications of Josiah's reforms in 622 BCE have been studied, as has the whole phenomenon of the impact of exile upon the people in the sixth century.

All these, and many other studies, can be welcomed as shedding light upon the historical background to the Old Testament; and there have been similar studies on the social, historical and economic background to the New Testament. What none of these studies can do, however, is to replace the Old and New Testaments as witnesses to the faith that existed in ancient Israel and the early Church, which was expressed through the medium of history-like narratives, especially in the Old Testament. From the point of view of certain historical facts, the Bible may be incorrect in the light of modern research. The same will be true of scientifically researched histories. The mistakes arise because sources are inaccurate or incomplete. The biblical writers had limited resources available for their work compared with modern historians, and were largely indebted to accounts of wars and public works conducted by the kings of Judah and Israel (cf. 1 Kings 11:41, 12:19, 14:15). Although the biblical writers tried to present the past as accurately as their resources allowed, they were not concerned to write history merely for the sake of it. They wrote because they had a story to tell about how God, the creator of the universe, had chosen Israel to be the means of making the divine will known to all nations. God had formed the nation out of enslaved Hebrews in Egypt, and had guided their fortunes through the vicissitudes of war, defeat, exile and restoration, and had taught them to hope for a new creation from which the evils and injustices of the present world would be free (cf. Isa. 65:17–25). The main task of pastoral practice must be to acquaint people with this overall story with its claims and lessons. To remain in a position where so many are ignorant of this story, hear the Old Testament only rarely, and are mainly concerned that the Bible should somehow be shown to be historically 'true' is to misuse and to misunderstand the Bible and its message in a grotesque way.

Conclusion

Although it must be conceded that there has been, and still is, a type of biblical scholarship whose aim has been to discredit the Bible, it remains true that the main purpose of biblical scholarship is to enable the Bible to be better understood. Much of its work is highly technical and of little direct relevance to the average person. While its results may appear to be negative, calling into question traditional theories of the authorship and inspiration of the Bible, arguing that not all the words of prophets or of Jesus are authentic, or questioning the historical accuracy of the Bible, the religious significance of the Bible has been enhanced rather than diminished by biblical scholarship. No set of texts has been subjected to such rigorous, critical scrutiny, and the results have enabled attention to be concentrated upon the essentials of the biblical witness. If biblical scholarship has been a problem to pastoral practice, this is because of the failure of the churches to provide the kind of continuing instruction that would lead to informed congregations with an adult, articulate faith. It is grotesque that members of congregations can be highly trained and skilled in areas such as medicine, the natural sciences and computer technology, and remain in adolescence so far as their knowledge of the Bible and Christian faith is concerned. If biblical scholarship presents a challenge, it is not to faith nor to the integrity of the Bible. It is a challenge to pastoral practice to operate in the modern world, and not to cling to old and outdated opinions. Biblical scholarship can liberate modern people from the guilt of not being able to believe literally in everything that the Bible contains. It can enthuse them with the message of the Bible, and transform their conception and practice of Christian discipleship.

Bibliography

Bar-Efrat, S. (1989) *Narrative Art in the Bible*. Sheffield: Almond Press.

Bright, J. (1960) *A History of Israel*. London: SCM Press.

Dodd, C. H. (1963) *Historical Tradition in the Fourth Gospel*. Cambridge: Cambridge University Press.

Gottwold, N. K. (1978) *The Tribes of Yahweh: a sociology of the religion of liberated Israel 1250–1050 BCE*. London: SCM Press.

Horne, T. (1825) *An Introduction to the Critical Study and Knowledge of the Holy Scriptures*. London.

Keller, W. (1956) *The Bible as History*. London: Hodder & Stoughton.

Mowvley, H. (1979) *Guide to Old Testament Prophecy*. London: Lutterworth.

Noth, M. (1950) *Geschichte Israels*. Göttingen: Vandenhoeck & Ruprecht.

Noth, M. (1958) *The History of Israel*. London: Adam & Charles Black.

(1998) *Revised Common Lectionary in NRSV, Sundays and Festivals. Principal service lectionary of the Church of England*. London: Mowbray.

Prideaux, H. (1716–18) *The Old and New Testament connected in the History of the Jews and Neighbouring Nations*. London.

Rogerson, J. (1998) Old Testament history and the history of Israel, in J. Rogerson (ed.), *Beginning Old Testament Study*. London: SPCK, 49–57.

Shukford, S. (1728) *The Sacred and Profane History Connected*. London.

Smith, W. Robertson (1881) *The Old Testament in the Jewish Church*. London: A. & C. Black.

CHAPTER 8:

In front of the text: the quest of hermeneutics

CRAIG BARTHOLOMEW

Introduction

One would imagine that pastoral care would be an area of theology where the Bible is central. Surprisingly however, as Stephen Pattison points out, 'pastoral theologians seem to have almost completely avoided considering the Bible ... There is an almost absolute and embarrassing silence about the Bible in pastoral care' (Pattison, 106). Two reasons for this spring to mind: the well-documented subjection of pastoral care to psychotherapy rendering theology and Scripture marginal and irrelevant, and the difficulty of relating the results of historical-critical readings of the Bible to pastoral care. Until late in the twentieth century historical criticism dominated biblical studies and it is arguable that it tended to lock the Bible into the past rather than facilitate an encounter with it as Scripture in the present.

Recent decades have, however, witnessed a remarkable recovery of emphasis upon practical theology as primarily a *theological* discipline. Stone speaks for a growing number of practical theologians when he asserts that, 'In order for pastoral care and counseling to be more than just psychotherapy "with a twist", it must have a sound theological base that informs its theory and practice' (Stone, 9, 10). This widespread recovery of practical theology as theology has brought with it something of a renewed interest in the Bible; but a renewed interest in theology does not necessarily imply a renewed focus on the Bible. Theology and biblical studies have become separate in the modern academy and only recently have we seen determined efforts to break this wall down. There thus remains considerable work to be done on the relationship between the Bible and practical theology.

In this respect hermeneutics holds out great hope. Any recovery of the Bible in practical theology faces the crucial question of 'how' to hear the Bible and more particularly how to hear it in relation to the interests of practical theology. Hermeneutics concentrates on this 'how question' in terms of the different components involved in the ecology of 'understanding' (author, text, reader, historicity and so on) and is therefore well positioned to help in the use of the Bible in practical theology, with its emphasis on experience and particularity. Indeed, because of its sensitivity to the ecology of factors involved in understanding there is already a widespread emphasis on hermeneutics in contemporary practical theology, with practical theologians regularly appealing to the works of Gadamer, Ricoeur and Habermas as they develop models of pastoral care (Gerkin 1984; Capps 1984).

Hermeneutics and depth analysis of the use of Scripture in practical theology

Pattison helpfully discerns five ways in which Scripture is used in pastoral care:

1 Fundamentalist – e.g. Adams and Crabb
2 Tokenist – e.g. Clinebell
3 Imagist or Suggestive – e.g. A. Campbell
4 Informative – e.g. Capps
5 Thematic – e.g. Oglesby

As Pattison (115) notes, the hermeneutical principles in these diverse and not necessarily mutually exclusive appropriations of Scripture remain implicit rather than explicit. In our opinion an advantage of a hermeneutic approach to the use of Scripture in practical theology is that it foregrounds that which is implicit and aims at a depth analysis of the use of Scripture.

This chapter is headed 'In front of the text'. This is both helpful and confusing. Helpful, because it is true that an effect of hermeneutics upon biblical interpretation has been to make us aware of the biblical books as texts with a unified, literary character, which come alive in engagement with a reader/s. The phrase 'in front of the text' comes from Ricoeur and it refers to the world that opens up in front of the text as the reader engages with the text. It is to be distinguished from that which the text refers to, which Ricoeur describes as 'behind the text'. The primary concern of historical criticism has been with that which lies behind the text, and by contrast hermeneutics has generally shown a refreshing concern with the text in its present, final form and the world the text opens up. Gadamer, for example, starts off his *Truth and Method* with a discussion of how one encounters a painting. Comparable to this in his hermeneutics is one's understanding of a text whereby a fusion of horizons occurs. This does not mean that hermeneutics is uninterested in historical questions when it comes to textual interpretation, but it does mean that generally speaking hermeneutics has privileged the final form of the text as the focus of interpretation. This has redirected the attention of many biblical scholars to the biblical texts in their final form, whether it is under the guise of canonical criticism or a smorgasbord of other approaches, and thereby opened up exciting new possibilities for engagement with the Bible as Scripture.

On the other hand 'In front of the text' could be confusing, because it might suggest that hermeneutics is simply another in the smorgasbord of methods of interpreting biblical texts. This is not the case. Indeed it has been suggested that Gadamer's great work should be called *Truth* or *Method*, because of its critique of scientific method as the key to understanding. Historical criticism exudes this type of approach which seeks neutral objectivity and which hankers after the right method so that the results can be assuredly scientific. Thus, generations of biblical scholars were initiated into source, form, tradition and redaction criticism and taught how to apply these methods rigorously to the Bible. This fixation with method often prevented us from encountering the biblical texts in their givenness. Gadamer, and especially Ricoeur, do not deny the place of method but they loosen its stranglehold by placing it within the dialogical process in which understanding occurs, a process facilitated by the prejudices of the interpreter and one whose goal is a fusion of horizons.

It is this sense of the ecology of understanding that has made hermeneutics so very attractive to practical theology. Recent decades have witnessed a widening of the horizons of practical theology, and hermeneutics fits well with this enlarged understanding. Practical theology has moved from a focus on the functions of the pastor and pastoral counselling in the light of Scripture to a focus on the whole Christian community and the contemporary situation of the believer/s. In the process praxis itself has been recovered as an indispensable element of practical theology (Farley, 7). The consequent breadth of interest in current practical theology is evident in Pattison and Woodward's (1994, 9) definition of practical theology as 'a place where religious belief, tradition and practice meets contemporary experiences, questions and actions and conducts a dialogue that is mutually enriching, intellectually critical, and practically transforming'. The breadth of this definition aside, contemporary practical theology is rightly aware of the historicity of Scripture and the particularity of the contemporary situation, and the consequent variety of factors that practical theology must attend to. In this respect it is fully in line with hermeneutics, at the heart of which is an acute awareness of the embedded-ness of text and reader in the historical process. The inability of the reader to stand somewhere outside of the historical process is central to hermeneutics, which developed out of Heidegger's critique of Husserl's last-ditch attempt to secure the autonomy of humankind in the knowing process, that is, epistemologically.

It might be thought that once hermeneutics has helped us identify the ecology of understanding, its work is done. However, this is to misconstrue the complexity of such an ecology. As is well known, small alterations in an ecology can trigger major effects. Indeed, within the hermeneutic tradition a variety of views have developed as scholars have sought to configure the ecology of understanding. Caputo helpfully identifies the following main approaches to contemporary hermeneutics, or what he calls the interpretation of interpretation after Heidegger's *Being and Time*: the late Heidegger; Gadamer; and finally deconstruction (Derrida).

> Gadamer and Derrida are in a sense 'exemplary' figures of these three movements. In the broad strokes I am painting here, e.g. Ricoeur's position is a derivative of Gadamer's and his criticisms of Gadamer only move hermeneutics closer to metaphysics. Likewise Derrida is part of a broader group of recent French philosophers who have made much the same argument against hermeneutics (e.g. Deleuze, and especially, Foucault). (Caputo, 304)

A way of understanding the difference these positions make to interpretation is as follows. Biblical scholars are nowadays well informed about the different components in the interpretive process. Thus, for example, John Barton, at the end of his *Reading the Old Testament*, uses M. H. Abrams' well-known diagram of the four basic elements in 'the total situation' of the work of art to sum up his discussion of the variety of methods in Old Testament studies. Any contemporary interpretative approach to the Bible must take into account 'the work', the universe underlying it, the artist/author/community, and the audience/reader/s. In Abrams' and Barton's diagrams 'the work' is the fixed centre of their triangles. However, this model fails to note that shifting the emphasis from one component in the triangle to another can radically destabilise the triangle and thus undermine the centrality of the text. The triangle evokes a geometrical objectivity – however, in fact this conceals an ideology of objective interpretation, which underlies this model. As Freund perceptively notes,

> Abrams's implicit presupposition is that these terms are fixed and determinate points of reference in a universal and timeless 'total situation' ... But this latter qualification – the enfranchisement of the viewer's perspective – is precisely the feature which introduces the subversive possibility that each term in the 'total situation' is radically unstable or indeterminate, a product of the beholder's gaze ... The drift of the 'pragmatic' or, as it is nowadays called, reader-response orientation in critical theory challenges the privileged position of the work of art and seeks to undermine its priority and authority not only by displacing the work from the centre and substituting the reader in its place, but by putting in doubt the autonomy of the work and, in certain cases, even causing the work to 'vanish' altogether. (Freund, 2)

Derrida might say that Barton, with his mathematical model of the triangle with the text at the centre, has espoused a strong metaphysics of presence. Freund rightly alerts us to the fact that there is more to interpretation than the four elements identified by Abrams. The 'more' relates to the sense of historicity in all interpretation, and the point made by Freund that how one configures these elements in the process of understanding is highly significant.

Underlying these alternative approaches to hermeneutics is, I suggest, the question of how we understand 'world'. Tracy (146–52) rightly draws attention to the contemporary importance of the theme of cosmology for theology. There is, he asserts, a growing sense that the anthropocentric centre of much contemporary theology needs to be challenged. Redemption cannot be understood without creation, and history cannot be understood apart from nature. In Tracy's view (147) this nexus of questions is 'the new *status questionis* that must be understood before the new constructive theological work can be assessed'. Similarly Farley (25, n26) notes that a recovery of praxis involving the interpretation of situations is closely related to the sort of analysis we find in Niebuhr's *Christ and Culture*.

This, in my opinion, is quite correct. Different perspectives on 'world' lead to different views of understanding, and there is a great need for theological attention to this question, and not least in practical theology. The question of how to understand 'world' is theological through and through, and there is no single answer to this question in the Christian tradition. Niebuhr argues that there are five basic ways in which Christians have understood the relationship between Christ and culture:

1 Christ *against* culture. This approach is intensely aware of how fallen cultures are and argues that Christians need to withdraw from secular cultures and witness to the world as an alternative group. Much anti-cultural Evangelicalism has been of this sort.
2 Christ *of* culture. In contrast to the above model this approach is so impressed with the cultures of our day that it thinks the Gospel can easily fit in with and develop all that is good in our cultures. This approach has little sense of the conflict between the Gospel and human culture and easily accommodates Christ to our culture.

Niebuhr recognises that few Christians nowadays would argue for either of these two extreme views. Most Christians try and understand the Christ–culture relationship in a more integrated way. Niebuhr calls these Christians 'Churches of the Centre'. Among them he discerns the following three approaches to the Christ–culture relationship.

3 Christ *above* culture. This approach thinks of nature as supplemented and fulfilled by grace. Aquinas and traditional Catholics represent this view.

4 Christ and culture *in paradox*. According to this view Christ and culture are a duality in which both have authority but in tension with each other. Luther is an example of this approach.
5 Christ *the transformer of culture* – this view argues that as a result of sin God's good creation has been corrupted by being misdirected, and that redemption leads to the healing/proper directing of culture.

Other categories that could be used to access this question are the relationship between nature and grace or the whole thorny problem of the relationship between faith and reason. The view we adopt of 'world' or of the Christ–culture relationship will deeply effect our understanding of the ecology involved in practical theology and thus of the role of Scripture in such an ecology. I will illustrate this, first, in relation to narrative theology and practical theology and, second, in relation to theological interpretation and practical theology.

Narrative, Scripture and practical theology

Recent decades have witnessed a renaissance of interest in narrative at a philosophical, biblical and theological level. Paul Ricoeur has written extensively on narrative and hermeneutics. For Ricoeur human beings are

> inherently narratively shaped, or story-shaped, with narrative offering a way of configuring a discordant concordance of time. As with metaphor, rather than seeing narrative as ornamental and dispensable ... narrative is necessary. Human identity and existence cannot be understood apart from the way in which we 'story' our lives. (Stiver 2001, 115)

Central to this narrative turn is the recognition that humans interpret and make sense of reality through story: 'all things human are in some way rooted in, or find their deepest structural framework in, a narrative or story of some kind' (Gerkin 1986, 26). Lesslie Newbigin, who worked as a missionary in India for many years and has written extensively about the significance of narratives to our thinking, draws the connection between world view and understanding when he writes, 'The way we understand human life depends on what conception we have of the human story. What is the real story of which my life story is part?' (1989, 15). Philosopher Alasdair MacIntyre agrees, affirming that our life decisions are shaped and ordered by our sense of how they fit within this larger context: 'I can only answer the question, "What am I to do?" if I can answer the prior question, "Of what story do I find myself a part?"'(MacIntyre, 216).

This type of emphasis on narrative has been appropriated in theology in different ways. The Yale, post-liberal school focuses on *the* biblical story as that which Christians should allow to absorb the world rather than the other way around. The California school, represented by James McClendon, attends to 'your story and my story', that is, to biographies and autobiographies, and stresses that theological concepts cannot be understood apart from their story shape in people's lives. Then there is the Chicago school of theology, of which Ricoeur and Tracy are major figures, which connects theology to the broader cultural narrative of which we are part.

Scripture as grand narrative

One way in which a narrative approach to Scripture has been appropriated in practical theology has been along the lines of the post-liberal emphasis on Scripture as providing the grand narrative that should function as such for Christians. Lesslie Newbigin speaks in this respect of the imperative for Christians to indwell the story of the Bible (1995, 88–92). Gerkin (1984, 1986) appropriates this approach in his practical theology, using the evocative alternative metaphor of 'to nest/le':

> This sense in which practical theological thinking is grounded in narrative is, of course, rooted in the faith that *the Bible provides us with an overarching narrative in which all other narratives of the world are nested*. The Bible is the story of God. The story of the world is first and foremost the story of God's activity in creating, sustaining, and redeeming the world to fulfil God's purposes for it. The story of the world is the story of God's promises for the world. It is also the story of the vicissitudes of God's gracious effort to fulfil those promises ... Most important of all, the Bible contains the story of God's disclosure and redemptive activity in the coming of Jesus. (1986, 48, italics mine)

Gerkin qualifies the statement above in terms of the pluralism of the stories of God's activity that we find in the Bible so that the themes of the Bible are often in tension to one another. Nevertheless, he insists that 'the stories of the Bible taken together disclose a way of seeing the world and human life in the world as always held within the "plot" of God's intentional purposes and direction. Life in the world is life nested within that overarching narrative' (1986, 49). Consequently, human experience today becomes 'the present experience of occasions for faithful adherence to the central metaphorical meanings of the grounding story of human identity' (1986, 50).

Several comments are pertinent at this point. First, is it possible to read Scripture as a (grand) narrative? This is a controversial matter among biblical scholars let alone postmodern philosophers and theologians. Considerable and productive attention has been given by biblical scholars to individual narratives within the Bible, but far less attention has been paid to the possibility of reading Scripture *as a whole* as a narrative. Indeed it is far more common for scholars from other theological disciplines such as missiology and practical theology to take such an approach seriously. Thus, Eugene Peterson, as a practical theologian, argues that the Bible is indeed a sprawling capacious narrative, and that a narrative or story approach to Scripture is illuminating because it helps us to see Scripture as the book which *tells us* about God and *invites us* to participate in his life. Within missiology Newbigin is well known for his story approach to the Bible (1995, 88–92).

A biblical scholar who has articulated a narrative approach to the Bible is Tom Wright (1991). Wright develops his narrative hermeneutic through reflection on his practice as a biblical scholar and through analysis of *how* – the hermeneutical question – the Bible is authoritative. Wright notes that Scripture is mostly narrative and he thus focuses the question of the authority of the Bible as follows:

> Somehow, the authority which God has invested in this book is an authority that is wielded and exercised *through* the people of God telling and retelling *their* story as the story of the world, telling the covenant story as the true story of creation. Somehow, this authority is also wielded through his people singing psalms. Somehow, it is wielded (it seems) in particular through God's people telling the story of Jesus. We must look then at the question of stories. What sort of authority might they possess? (18)

To respond adequately to the Bible as Scripture we have to take its storied shape seriously. For Wright this includes taking the Bible *as a whole* as a story. He invokes the analogy of an imaginary play by Shakespeare, whose fifth act has been lost. The first four acts provide such detail and such an intriguing plot that it is decided that the play must be staged. It is considered inappropriate to write up 'the fifth act'; rather the four acts are given to experienced Shakespearean actors who have to immerse themselves in the acts and then have to work out the fifth act for themselves. The first four acts are the authority for the fifth act; they constrain the variety possible in it. Wright suggests that we should think analogously of the Bible as a drama in five acts, namely: Creation, Fall, Israel, Jesus, the New Testament and the Church. The New Testament is the first scene in the fifth act, giving clues as to how the play is supposed to end. The Church would thus live under the authority of the story and be responsible for offering an improvisation and performance of the final act with sensitivity and creativity.

Wright argues that in all sorts of ways this dramatic narrative model is fertile hermeneutically. It helps us to see the relative authority of the Old Testament compared with the more immediate authority of the New Testament. It is Protestant in its insistence that the Bible is the real locus of authority, but Catholic in its recognition of the need for communal enactment of the story. We have to tell the story in our communities and allow it to challenge our traditions, to 'stretch our reason back into shape' and to reform our world views that are always in danger of becoming like the world's world views. In respect of this last point Wright is clear that we need to allow Scripture to norm our world view:

> When we tell the whole story of the Bible, and tell it … by articulating it in a thousand different ways, improvising our own faithful version, we are inevitably challenging more than just one aspect of the world's way of looking at things … We are undermining its entire view of what the world is … We are articulating a viewpoint according to which there is one God, the creator of all that is, who not only made the world but is living and active within it … who is also transcendent over it and deeply grieved by its fall away from goodness into sin … The story … will function as an invitation to participate in the story oneself, to make it one's own, and to do so by turning away from the idols which prevent the story becoming one's own … Evangelism and the summons to justice and mercy in society are thus one and the same, and both are effected by the telling of the story, the authoritative story … (1989, 28)

No doubt Christians of other traditions such as Yoder, Hauerwas and Hays, with their strong emphasis on story but in an Anabaptist, strongly pacifist context, would tell the scriptural story differently. Such differences remind us that we always access the biblical story in dialogue with our theological traditions. Wright's strength is his attempt in this article, and in his *The New Testament and the People of God*, to give sustained attention to how story and world view emerge from and relate to actual biblical interpretation. This is a much neglected area in biblical studies, but one of great consequence for the use of the Bible in practical theology.

Narrative reading and practical theology

Second, we do well to reflect on how such a narrative reading of the Bible would actually affect practical theology. As our references to Gerkin above indicate, it appears that such a reading of the Bible would yield the macro perspective or world view within which practical theology would operate. This is certainly Wright's primary emphasis. He rightly asserts that 'The Bible, clearly, is also to be used in a thousand different ways within the pastoral work of the church, the caring and building up of its members' (1989, 30), but his primary emphasis, as with Newbigin and Gerkin, is that Scripture provides the large story which we are to indwell. Thus, for example, within pastoral counselling, there may on occasion be no actual reference to the Bible, but the Bible would yield the story within which the understanding and practice of counselling operates. So, in effect, the main character in the counselling situation would be God and not just two or more autonomous human beings, and the counselee/s would be thought of as a creature in the *imago dei*, and so on and so forth.

However, once we press this issue of the relationship between the Christian/biblical story and praxis, the situation becomes more complex. A major issue in relating the Bible to practical theology is the Bible's historicity and diversity. Historical criticism has relentlessly drawn attention to the historical 'situated-ness' of the Bible and to the diversity within the Bible. Postmodernism has regularly focused on the ideology/ies of the Bible. Practical theology is concerned with contemporary experience and culture so that it is not surprising that its relationship to the Bible is not straightforward. We live in very different cultures from those of the Bible, and we cannot and should not avoid the significant effect that modern developments have brought to bear on pastoral care. The existential insights of experience and contemporary culture, the insights of psychology and other sciences, have to be taken on board. As Stone (37) rightly observes, in practical theology we need a 'trenches hermeneutic' which enables the practitioner to relate the different components in practical theology intuitively to the 'trenches' in which he or she works. How do the Bible and the Christian tradition function in the context of such an interpretative ecology?

The answer that keeps cropping up in the literature of practical theology is that of *correlation*. Thus Gerkin, having argued for a story approach to the use of the Bible in practical theology, elaborates on this in relation to the variety of contexts which practical theology has to take into account and, alluding to Gadamer, he says that

> Practical theology, seen from a narrative hermeneutical perspective, involves a process of the interpretive fusion of horizons of meaning embodied in the Christian narrative with other horizons that inform and shape perceptions in the various arenas of activity in which Christians participate. (1986, 61)

Gerkin speaks in this respect of the importance of 'a constant mutually critical correlation of perspectives' in an effort to fuse the horizon of a Christian perspective on the world and the other horizons in the pastoral activity. It is not easy to bring these different horizons into some kind of stable coherence but the task is essential:

> The desire for coherence and fusion is confronted by the pluralism and contradiction of interpretations. In the crucible of mutual criticism and search for a way of seeing that makes sense, a new and more comprehensive way of seeing the activity under consideration may

> emerge, though seldom are all the conflicts of differing perspectives resolved. (1986, 62)

Gerkin's articulation of correlation is helpful in alerting us to the sheer variety of horizons that intersect in the practice of pastoral care. What is less clear is just what he means by 'horizons' and exactly how critical dialogue might hope to solve the more fundamental horizon-al issues he has so clearly foregrounded. The potential tension in Gerkin's view (shared with Browning and Stone among others) is clear in Gerkin's *An Introduction to Pastoral Care* (1997), in which he affirms Lindbeck's post-liberal cultural-linguistic or narrative approach to theology, *but* then seeks to retain in balance with it an apologetic or correlational approach. This manifests the crucial question of whether or not a modern/postmodern perspective on the world in which human autonomy is central, and God non-existent, can be fused with the Christian/biblical story. Against this tendency is that fact that for scholars like Wright the whole point of a basic story or grand narrative is to make sense of life as a whole, and such grand narratives cannot easily be mixed up with each other: 'the whole point of Christianity is that it offers a story which is the story of the whole world. It is public truth.' Basic stories are in principle *normative* – they define starting points, ways of seeing, what is 'normal'– and *comprehensive*, giving an account of the whole.

One could ask therefore, is not the danger of correlation that it commits practical theology to being irretrievably *liberal*, in the sense that it ends up granting excessive authority to modernity and undermining the overarching narrative role that Gerkin and others want Scripture to play? For Tracy this is decidedly not the case:

> there is nothing in the 'revised correlational model' that demands a 'liberal' solution. There is only the demand ... that wherever and whoever the practical theologian is, she or he is bound by the very nature of the enterprise as theological to show how one interprets the tradition and how one interprets the present situation and how those two interpretations correlate: as either identities of meaning, analogies or radical nonidentities. (139, 140)

Once again this is helpful in alerting us to the challenges of practical theology, but the question remains as to whether or not the two interpretations can be kept as distinct as Tracy suggests. If the Christian/biblical story forms the grand story one indwells would it not be the context or paradigm within which one interprets the present situation? Such an approach, akin to what missiologists call contextualisation, would not remove tensions but it would ensure that the tensions are explored on a level playing field within the overarching framework of a single world view.

We noted earlier how the Christ–culture issue underlies the different ecologies of hermeneutics, and here, I suggest, is where we glimpse the truth of that statement again. According to Michalson (128–30) correlation derives from Kant's philosophy:

> Kant's own moral hermeneutics is in many ways the model for the correlative enterprise, which animates the powerful tradition linking Schleiermacher and Tillich and establishes such concepts as the 'experience of absolute dependence' and 'ultimate concern' at the centre of the dialogue between theology and modern culture. (129)

Kant's philosophy places theology under the tutelage of philosophy and it yields a Christ of culture or Christ in paradox with culture perspective. One gets at truth through the exercise of human autonomy via reason, with theology and Scripture strictly excluded or in a tense, paradoxical relationship to philosophy. If Michalson is right then the advocacy of correlation in practical theology buys into a Kantian conception of the world and epistemology. From a modern, liberal perspective in theology this will be a good thing. However, as Gerkin recognises, horizons often conflict head on in pastoral care. A question for correlation is that if horizons conflict at root in terms of fundamental perspective upon the world, then perhaps rather than thinking in terms of fusion through dialogue one should think of a choice between exclusive options. The route one chooses here could, I suggest, make a significant difference to the practice of pastoral care. A correlationist approach might encourage one to interpret the present situation apart from Scripture and tradition and then try and relate one's interpretation to Scripture and tradition, whereas a more post-liberal approach would use Scripture and tradition to inform and shape its analysis.

Correlation has not received much attention from biblical scholars. An exception is Francis Watson who advocates correlation in his proposal for a theological interpretation of the Bible. Watson rightly asserts that a theological hermeneutic will not be unhappy to draw on secular insights. Because the Church operates in the world, even though a theological hermeneutic will be ecclesial, 'It follows that any correct apprehension of Christian truth or the praxis that must accompany it will occur only through the mediation of a discourse that is not in itself distinctively Christian' (1). Watson justifies this drinking at the secular well through the doctrine of the Spirit at work in the world.

Watson connects his correlationist approach to theological interpretation to a feminist critique of Scripture. Indeed the ideological critique of the Bible of feminist, liberationist and other kinds is deeply indebted to a strategy of correlation. Such an approach is evident, for example, in Elaine Graham's *Transforming Practice*. Graham's work builds on that of Browning but with a stronger feminist agenda. Graham (2000, 108) articulates the hermeneutical challenge for practical theology succinctly when she says that her 'paramount concern is thus to remain true to the continuity of Christian witness whilst responding anew to the challenges of the present age'. The question is, how do we do this? Graham's strategy is very much that of correlation. She leans heavily on Habermas with his notion of ideal speech communities although she gives this a stronger gender orientation. Her proposal is that 'the key hermeneutical criterion for a reconstructed Christian practice is the "disclosure" of alterity' (2000, 106).

Watson refers to the way we understand 'world' as justification for his approach and as we noted earlier in relation to Tracy this is a central issue. Watson is right to invoke general revelation in this respect, but the crucial issue is how we read general revelation aright and whether or not such a reading operates independently of the Christian tradition as Watson suggests, particularly in our context of the pastoral situation. A theological epistemology such as that of O'Donovan's (1986) argues that although God's order in creation impinges on all, we can only read it aright in Christ. This would mean that practical theology needs a perspective shaped by Scripture and theology to provide the matrix within which the situation is interpreted rather than the situation being interpreted, as Tracy and Watson appear to suggest, apart from the tradition. At a practical level this will significantly affect the use of the Bible in practical theology. Thus, it is not surprising in my view that Scripture and Christian tradition play a negligible role in Graham's *Transforming Practice*. If Scripture and tradition are indispensable in interpreting situations then they will play a far more central role.

At stake in all of this is, of course, how we think about our culture today, which is generally labelled 'postmodern'. Most postmoderns would be deeply critical of a reading of the Bible along the lines of grand narrative as outlined above, because of their incredulity towards such narratives. How one reacts to this will depend largely upon one's analysis of postmodernism. Practical theologians such as Graham tend to be very sympathetic towards such a critique, albeit with a stronger feminist perspective, and this leads them away from a narrative approach such as that of Wright, or an approach with a strong biblical input. Tracy responds to contemporary pluralism by stressing the need to correlate a Christian perspective with that of other religions. An alternative approach to the pluralism of postmodernity would be to emphasise the need to allow particular traditions to flower more fully so that real comparison and dialogue can take place. Thus, for example, Wright's 'critical realism' opens him positively to some aspects of postmodernism but leaves him fiercely critical of other aspects, and he concentrates on allowing the Christian tradition to flower in his biblical interpretation.

Theological interpretation and practical theology

A development in biblical studies that may be most significant for the use of the Bible in practical theology is the minority renewal in so-called theological interpretation of the Bible. This renewal stems from a weariness of endless historical-critical endeavours which never seem to get on with reading the Bible as Scripture for the Church, and from the greater freedom in biblical studies that postmodernism has made possible. Theological interpretation is a broad church. It makes theology the immediate concern of exegesis and thereby opens up fruitful connections between biblical studies and the current concern in much practical theology to be theological. A particularly fertile example of theological interpretation and the way it may connect with contemporary praxis is O'Donovan's work in theological ethics and political theology. Ethics faces many of the same challenges as practical theology and it is illuminating to see how O'Donovan handles these challenges theologically.

O'Donovan's biblical, theological ethics and practical theology

We cannot here outline O'Donovan's approach to ethics and political theology in any detail. Suffice it to take note of the shape of the hermeneutical ecology in his work. O'Donovan respects historical criticism and draws on it in many different ways, but his work is driven by the possibility of a unified approach to Scripture. Particularly in *The Desire of the Nations* his commitment to the overarching narrative shape of the Bible is apparent. Scripture is like an iceberg, undergirding and informing in the most basic way all of O'Donovan's work.

However, his ethic is not only biblical but also theological; it recognises the need for concepts and models to mediate between Scripture and contemporary ethical issues:

> If we are to form and justify opinions on specific questions in ethics, we must do so theologically; which means bringing the formal questions of ethics to theological interpretation and criticism. This by no means implies, of course, that we shall accept the current understanding of these questions unhesitatingly from the lips of philosophers, for theology has something to say about how the questions are formulated as well as about how they are answered. (1996, 182)

The Desire of the Nations, which O'Donovan describes as a work in political theology, is precisely an exploration of that which comes between Scripture and political ethics. We do, according to O'Donovan, have to make the journey from what God said to Abraham to how to handle Iraq after September 11, but O'Donovan insists that while faith at an intuitive level may make that journey instantly, or the preacher in half an hour, it may take a lifetime of scholarship. What is fascinating about O'Donovan's work, and unusual nowadays, is the way Scripture is never left behind as his theological concepts take hold. Not only do the concepts come from Scripture, they are set in motion in tandem with a willingness to return to scriptural exegesis at myriad points. The result is the blossoming of a thousand exegetical flowers amidst the emerging structure of a theological ethic that is nothing if not conceptually robust. *Resurrection and Moral Order* and *The Desire of the Nations* contain nuggets of refined, exegetical studies throughout, often in O'Donovan's distinctive small print. It is gloriously assumed that the development of theological concepts and the exegesis of Scripture will complement each other in a rich, overflowing ecology.

O'Donovan's commitment to a theological ethic is apparent from the start. A Christian ethic must be evangelical: it must arise from the Gospel itself. And for O'Donovan this means not just that it must be biblical, but that its concepts must express the inner logic of the Gospel:

> We are not attempting to deny the richness of the New Testament's ethical appeal; but it is the task of theology to uncover the hidden relation of things that give the appeal force. We are driven to concentrate on the resurrection as our starting-point because it tells us of God's vindication of his creation, and so of our created life. (1986, 13)

Similarly in his quest for a political theology O'Donovan insists on the need for political concepts that will do the work of theory construction:

> Our search, then, is for true political concepts. But if the notion of 'political theology' is not to be a chimera, they must be authorised, as any datum of theology must be, from Holy Scripture. (1996, 15)

He thus argues that the kingdom of God embodied in Israel and fulfilled in Jesus is the appropriate theme from which to develop political concepts for a political theology.

All of which alerts us unequivocally to the fact that the recipe for O'Donovan's ethic contains many ingredients, notably biblical exegesis, theology, philosophy and history – a profound awareness of the tradition in all these areas. O'Donovan's work is comparable to Barth's *Church Dogmatics* in the extent to which it utilises Scripture in its theological analysis. O'Donovan's approach is, of course, particular and can be typed as broadly Evangelical with a strong kinship to Barth's theology. Inevitably, different theologies of Scripture would lead to different uses of the Bible. Pattison's

(2000) more liberal view of Scripture as one dialogue partner among several rather than as an authority over us probably leads to a very different type of practical theology compared with O'Donovan's ethics. However, even here there is no reason why the Bible should not play a much bigger role in practical theology as such a dialogue partner. For our purposes, O'Donovan's work is useful as an indicator of how the renewal of interest in theological interpretation may help us in relating the Bible to practical theology. Even if we disagree strongly with O'Donovan his agenda alerts us to the sort of issues that require attention if the use of the Bible in practical theology is to be renewed, issues such as:

1 Is it possible, and if so how, to read the Bible as a whole?
2 What kind of conceptual apparatus is required to relate the Bible to practical theology? Clearly the way the first question is answered will have implications for this question. O'Donovan's strong sense of the unity of Scripture will lead in a different direction to Pattison's insistence that there is no one view or theology in the Bible but a plurality.
3 From where do we get such an apparatus? Can we, like O'Donovan, derive concepts from Scripture or do we require a theological *discrimen* from the tradition in order to read Scripture for practical theology?
4 In this context what are the varieties of ways in which the Bible can function in practical theology? O'Donovan's rich use of Scripture alerts us to the fact that in practical theology several of Pattison's five categories of the use of the Bible may be legitimate in the right context. This is similar to what Louw (369) refers to as an 'organic' use of the Bible. A more directive use of Scripture will have its place provided it is used with a proper understanding of general revelation and the broad ecology of pastoral care. So too will Capps' use of the psalms of lament for grief counselling. At other points Scripture may be used informatively, suggestively and certainly thematically. The possibilities are endless.

Conclusion

In this chapter we have foregrounded ways in which attention to hermeneutics can help us in thinking through and promoting the use of the Bible in practical theology. What we have shown is that attention to the ecology of interpretation, which is at the heart of hermeneutics, enables us to discern the hermeneutical matrix implicit in such use. There is no doubt that the use of the Bible in practical theology is complex, but the clearer we can be about that complexity, the easier it will be for us to see a way forward for the creative, relevant use of the Bible, for which practical theology is now ripe.

Bibliography

Bartholomew, C. G. (2000) Uncharted waters: philosophy, theology and the crisis in biblical interpretation, in Bartholomew, C. G. et al. (eds), *Renewing Biblical Interpretation*. Grand Rapids, MI: Eerdmans; Carlisle: Paternoster, 1–39.

Bartholomew, C. G. et al. (eds) (2002) *A Royal Priesthood?: the use of the Bible ethically and politically. A dialogue with Oliver O'Donovan*. Grand Rapids, MI: Eerdmans; Carlisle: Paternoster.

Bartholomew, C. G. and Goheen, M. (2004/5) *The Drama of Scripture: finding our place in the biblical story*. Grand Rapids, MI: Baker Academic.

Bartholomew, C. G. (2004) Story and biblical theology, in C. G. Bartholomew et al. (eds), *Out of Egypt: biblical theology and biblical interpretation*. Grand Rapids, MI: Zondervan.

Barton, J. (1996) *Reading the Old Testament: method in biblical study*. London: Darton, Longman & Todd.

Browning, D. (1991) *A Fundamental Practical Theology: descriptive and strategic proposals*. Philadelphia: Fortress Press.

Capps, D. (1981) *Biblical Approaches to Pastoral Care*. Philadelphia: Westminster.

Capps, D. (1984) *Pastoral Care and Hermeneutics*. Philadelphia: Fortress Press.

Capps, D. (1993) *The Poet's Gift: toward the renewal of pastoral care*. Louisville, KY: Westminster/John Knox Press.

Caputo, J. D. (1987) *Radical Hermeneutics: repetition, deconstruction and the hermeneutic project*. Bloomington, IN: Indiana University Press.

Childs, B. S. (1992) *Biblical Theology of the Old and New Testaments: theological reflection on the Christian Bible*. Minneapolis: Fortress Press.

Farley, E. (1987) Interpreting situations: an inquiry into the nature of practical theology, in L. S. Mudge and J. N. Poling (eds), *Formation and Reflection*. Philadelphia: Fortress Press, 1–26.

Freund, E. (1987) *The Return of the Reader: reader-response criticism*. London: Methuen.

Gerkin, C. V. (1984) *The Living Human Document: re-visioning pastoral counseling in a hermeneutical mode*. Nashville, TN: Abingdon Press.

Gerkin, C. V. (1986) *Widening the Horizons: pastoral responses to a fragmented society*. Philadelphia: Westminster Press.

Gerkin, C. V. (1991) *Prophetic Pastoral Practice*. Nashville, TN: Abingdon Press.

Gerkin, C. V. (1997) *An Introduction to Pastoral Care*. Nashville, TN: Abingdon Press.

Graham, E. (1996) *Transforming Practice: pastoral theology in an age of uncertainty*. London: Mowbray.

Graham, E. (2000) Practical theology as transforming practice, in J. Woodward and S. Pattison (eds), *The Blackwell Reader in Pastoral and Practical Theology*. Oxford: Blackwell, 104–17.

Hurding, R. (1998) *Pathways to Wholeness: pastoral care in a postmodern age*. London: Hodder & Stoughton.

Lindbeck, G. A. (1984) *The Nature of Doctrine: religion and theology in a post-liberal age*. Philadelphia: Westminster Press.

Louw, D. J. (1998) *A Pastoral Hermeneutics of Care and Encounter*. Wellington, South Africa: Lux Verbi.

MacIntyre, A. (1981) *After Virtue*. Notre Dame, IN: University of Notre Dame Press.

Michalson, G. E. (1999) *Kant and the Problem of God*. Oxford: Blackwell.

Mudge, L. S. and Poling J. N. (eds) (1987) *Formation and Reflection: the promise of practical theology*. Philadelphia: Fortress Press.

Newbigin, L. (1989) *The Gospel in a Pluralist Society*. Grand Rapids, MI: Eerdmans.

Newbigin, L. (1995) *Proper Confidence: faith, doubt and certainty in Christian discipleship*. London: SPCK.

Oden, T. C. (1984) *Care of Souls in the Classic Tradition*. Philadelphia: Fortress Press.

O'Donovan, O. (1986) *Resurrection and Moral Order: an outline for evangelical ethics*. Leicester: Inter-Varsity Press.

O'Donovan, O (1996) *The Desire of the Nations: rediscovering the roots of political theology*. Cambridge: Cambridge University Press.

Pattison, S. (2000) *A Critique of Pastoral Care*. London: SCM Press.

Pattison, S. and Woodward, J. (1994) *Vision of Pastoral Theology: in search of words that resurrect the dead*. Edinburgh: Contact Pastoral Limited Trust.

Petersen, E. Living into God's story, in *The Ooze: conversation for a journey*. (www.theooze.com)

Stiver, D. R. (1996) *The Philosophy of Religious Language: sign, symbol, and story*. Oxford: Blackwell.

Stiver, D. R. (2001) *Theology after Ricoeur: new directions in hermeneutical theology*. Louisville, KY: Westminster John Knox Press.

Stone, H. W. (1988) *The Word of God and Pastoral Care*. Nashville, TN: Abingdon Press.

Tracy, D. (1987) Practical theology in the situation of global pluralism, in L. S. Mudge and J. N. Poling (eds), *Formation and Reflection*. Philadelphia: Fortress Press, 139–54.

Watson, F. (1994) *Church, Text and World: biblical interpretation in theological perspective*. Edinburgh: T&T Clark.

Woodward, J. and Pattison, S. (eds) (2000) *The Blackwell Reader in Pastoral and Practical Theology*. Oxford: Blackwell.

Wright, N. T. (1991) How can the Bible be authoritative? *Vox Evangelica* 21, 7–32.

Wright, N. T. (1992) *The New Testament and the People of God*. Minneapolis: Fortress Press.

CHAPTER 9:

The re-emergence of Scripture: post-liberalism

WALTER BRUEGGEMANN

In recent decades, important changes have occurred concerning the way the Bible is read in the academy and the way the Bible is heard in the Church. These immense changes hold important significance for the future of the Bible in the Church. For purposes of this discussion, we may characterise the change in recent decades as a move from 'liberal' to 'post-liberal' interpretation.

The historical-critical model of biblical interpretation

In this context, the term 'liberal' refers to a set of cultural, philosophical assumptions that arose in the seventeenth century and that have dominated biblical interpretation in the West for the past several centuries. That set of assumptions is frequently connected to the name of René Descartes, a French philosopher, who decisively established 'modern' ways of knowing and interpreting. The new perspective of Descartes placed unreserved confidence in the capacity of autonomous reason to read the Bible correctly and objectively. That is, such an interpreter is able to read, think and interpret without the support of or dependence upon interpretive communities rooted in tradition, and so to arrive at what the text 'meant' in its time of origin. The perspective of Descartes represented an immense break with traditional, church-dominated reading of the Bible and initiated a practice of reading the Bible in academic contexts that was undisciplined, unfunded and unfettered by church practice, faith or doctrine. The reason such a new mode of thought became attractive is that the European 'religious wars' rooted in the Reformation departure from Catholicism had placed great doubt upon the capacity of a divided church to offer authoritative reading of Scripture. Thus, as an alternative to church-dominated interpretation of Scripture, university-situated scripture study opted for Cartesian emancipation that came to treat the Bible primarily with regard to historical questions as a means of avoiding the theological questions of church interpretation that were felt to be heavy-handed and excessively authoritarian.

This newer approach, grounded in university epistemology and committed to 'objective' scholarship, eventually was reduced to 'historical criticism', the attempt to trace the 'history of the literature' and to situate each piece of scriptural literature in its assumed place of origin. Over time, Old Testament study in this perspective gelled into a consensus hypothesis about the development of the literature on the basis of a hypothesis of the religion of Israel. This latter hypothesis, articulated in nineteenth-century evolutionary categories, traced the religion of Israel from polytheistic and mythological assumptions to a religion of ethical monotheism, that is, faith in one God whose will and purpose was for justice and order in the earth. That *literary* and *religious* synthesis – that popularly goes under the name of Wellhausen, who late in the nineteenth century published the ultimate synthesis of the consensus hypothesis – is reflective of certain cultural conditions, methods and assumptions that prevailed in Old Testament interpretation well into the twentieth century and indeed continues with considerable force until today. It is fair to say that this *mode and hypothesis* have completely dominated the academic scene in Europe and North America; it has been taught, moreover, in theological schools that have educated pastors. As a result this hypothesis over time has had an enormous impact in the churches.

Only in retrospect are we able to see that along with the important gains of historical-critical readings, this 'liberal project' has been very costly for the Church and its missional self-understanding.

The evolutionary cast of the hypothesis concerning the development of Israelite religion has tilted toward supersessionism, so that later religious understandings are taken to be superior to earlier, culminating of course in Christian claims over against Judaism. More than that, an evolutionary hypothesis has meant that every religious claim is pertinent only to its particular time, place and circumstance; consequently, no claim has abiding normative status. The effect has been that such autonomous reading has proceeded without any capacity or interest in normative theological claims, so that the text simply becomes material for scholarly adventure.

The focus on historical-critical questions has made interpretation an elitist enterprise, for one needed elaborate learning and resources in order to delve into all of the data and complex issues related to the historical. As a result, biblical interpretation became largely the province of experts, with church-people only recipients of instruction.

The hegemonic force of Euro-American, elitist historical-critical interpretation has meant that the unrecognised cultural assumptions of the hegemonic West became intrinsic to the interpretive process. Consequently, hegemonic interpretation was, albeit unwittingly, a part of the larger threat of Western colonialism and imperialism. As a result, what was taken to be 'objective' was in fact the aggressive practice of privileged interpretations, mostly white, mostly male, mostly adherent to Enlightenment rationality.

The outcome of such interpretation, over time, was a Bible that was understood in thin, one-dimensional ways that 'explained' the text according to the criteria of Western rationalism. This approach could appreciate almost nothing of the wondrous 'thickness' of the text that has been decisive for the Bible's theological authority for communities of faith and practice. The outcome has been an enterprise of biblical interpretation that had, at best, an uneasy relationship to the Church and, at worst, an alienation from the Church; rationalistic and/or empirical modes of study in the long run could not fund the faith of the Church that is rooted in trust of the governing sovereignty of God over the life of the world, a deep conviction that is inimical to the categories prized in Enlightenment thought. Scripture study of this kind proceeds on the basis of *universal* epistemological assumptions that have little context within the deep faith of the Church that is avowedly rooted in the particularity of text claims, *particulars* related to the concreteness of Israel and the concreteness of Jesus of Nazareth. Thus in the long run, 'liberal interpretation' has accommodated the oddness of the Bible to the rationality of the Western intellect; through criticism a way was found to conform the Bible to Western reason. In recent time, however, such interpretive manoeuvres have been increasingly treated with suspicion, with a recognition that the 'thick' claims of the text are not thereby taken seriously, and with the derivative recognition that communities of faith must read in different modes if the Bible is to fund the daily life, faith and practice of the Church in normative ways.

The emergence of post-liberal biblical theology

Recent decades have witnessed the growing inadequacy of such 'liberal' interpretations with a variety of efforts to define, characterise and practise interpretation that is *after* the 'liberal project', that is, 'post-liberal'. It is widely affirmed that the pivotal moment in moving away from such 'liberal', historical-critical approaches came in 1919 when Karl Barth published his daring and explosive commentary on the Epistle to the Romans. In that book, Barth declared that his exposition and proclamation would no longer conform to the dominant assumptions of Western interpretive culture, but that he would read the text in an unfettered, 'naive' way as a person of faith who took at face value the deep and radical faith claims voiced by Paul. That is,

Barth would read as one who believed, trusted in and responded to the Gospel to which Paul bears witness.

Barth's affirmation is that there is within the Bible 'a strange new world' that does not conform to the categories or assumptions of modern Enlightenment thought (1928, 28–50). This remarkable claim for the Gospel has since that time been of profound importance. Barth's own statement was triggered by his sense that 'liberal theology' offered no standing ground to oppose Germany's policies in World War I. In the next decade, Barth's venture also served well the Confessing Church in Germany and its stand against National Socialism. Barth's non-foundationalism (that is, a refusal to appeal to 'universal' categories and a ready appeal to the particularities of faith) permitted a church stance and a church practice that needed no accommodation to regnant interpretive categories. In the 30s and 40s, still in the wake of Barth's spectacular breakthrough, there was nurtured a whole generation of acute and daring interpreters of the Old Testament who proceeded according to the assumptions of their evangelical faith. These scholars came to dominate the field at mid-century.

Through the middle of the twentieth century and into the 1970s, Barth's non-foundational, confessional approach to Scripture lived in an uneasy, not well-recognised tension with the older 'liberal' perspectives of historical criticism. This uneasy tension was reflected, for example, in George Ernest Wright's 'Theology of Recital' (1952) that he coupled with his appeal to the archaeological recovery of 'history'. In parallel fashion, Gerhard von Rad managed to equivocate enough to hold together 'ordinary history' and 'saving history':

> Thus there is a clear tension between the account actually given in the narrative and the intention of the narrator, whose aim was, with the help of this material, to describe the conquest of the land by all Israel, and who, in so doing, asked too much of it. In the end this conception was most succinctly given in the narrator's words that under Joshua Israel took possession of the whole land 'at one time' (*Hebrew* Josh. x.42). This was the rounding off of the construction of that magnificent picture made by later Israel of Jahweh's final saving act. Beyond it no further unification was really any longer possible. But our final comment on it should not be that it is obviously an 'unhistorical' picture, because what is in question here is a picture fashioned throughout by faith. Unlike any ordinary historical document, it does not have its centre in itself; it is intended to tell the beholder about Jahweh, that is, how Jahweh led his people and got himself glory. In Jahweh's eyes Israel is always a unity: his control of history was no improvisation made up of disconnected events: in the saving history he always deals with all Israel. This picture makes a formidable claim, and actually in the subsequent period it

> proved to have incalculable power to stamp affairs. How this came about is quite interesting. Israel made a picture of Jahweh's control of history on his people's behalf whose magnificence far surpasses anything that older and more realistic accounts offered. Faith had so mastered the material that the history could be seen from within, from the angle of faith. What supports and shapes this late picture of Israel's taking possession of the land is a mighty zeal for and glorification of the acts of Jahweh. (302)

For the most part, this odd tension went unrecognised; in varying styles more stress was given either to 'ordinary history' or to 'saving history', but in either case without any intentional decision or settlement about the relationship between the two. This state of affairs, however, could not eventually be sustained. In the 1960s, and more obviously in the 1970s, the grip of 'liberal' interpretive categories was broken, and interpretive scholarship was able to move to a 'post-critical' 'second naïveté' that fully comprehended critical matters but, at the same time, moved beyond them in a bold confessional posture (Wallace).

The proximate end of 'liberal' interpretive hegemony in the 1970s and the ensuing emergence of post-liberal interpretation is a complex matter. Within Old Testament studies, the dominant category of 'history' invited new suspicion (Perdue). Following John Van Seters and Thomas Thompson, confidence in archaeological recovery that had dominated the discipline eroded, as scholars no longer approached the data of archaeology in such trusting fashion (Van Seters; Thompson). It began to be clear, moreover, that the 'liberal' consensus had imposed upon the text an explanatory model that was inadequate and that failed to take into account either (a) the odd disjunctive character of the text itself or (b) the thick reading of faith communities that were not satisfied with 'modernist explanations' of the text.

This turn of affairs within the discipline, however, did not arise in a vacuum. It was indeed part of a larger emerging scepticism about the hegemonic authority of the Euro-American and governing, interpretive establishment. Indeed the 1970s became a period of immense distrust and rejection of established authority in the West, with an emerging sense that those outside of the hegemony could proceed on their own terms as interpreters without conforming to hegemonic categories that were never as 'objective' or 'universal' as imagined. The external events evoking such distrust and rejection included the Vietnam war that in the United States was conducted with enormous bureaucratic deception and self-deception, the subversion and corruption of the political processes by Watergate, the exposé of entrenched bias through the Civil Rights Movement, and the wave of violence evidenced in the assassinations of Martin Luther King Jr and Robert F. Kennedy, plus the Chicago Democratic Convention of 1968 when the police fired on protesting college students. On an international scale, broad subversion of established elitist authority was focused in the student demonstrations of Paris in 1968 that demanded and received an about-face in policy by the French government. All of these movements were, at the same time or in the wake of the remarkable opening process of Vatican II in Catholicism, with the Church being emblematic of the old authority that had to yield in costly ways to new cultural reality.

The new scepticism about old consensus assumptions within the field of Old Testament studies, coupled with the new subversion that occurred externally and broadly in culture, combined to create a readiness for new ventures in interpretation. In the 1970s, new methods, new voices, new advocacies and new journals emerged at a rapid rate. Interpretation was no longer committed to the 'liberal' categories of the historical criticism and no longer enthralled to the 'universal' assumptions of long-standing practice. It is as though the authority of 'the centre' had abruptly collapsed and many voices at the margin required a hearing. It is this collage of many voices at the edge, freed from long-standing hegemonic categories, which we may term 'post-liberal'. We may in particular identify two 'post-liberal' initiatives, *the canonical* and *the contextual*.

The canonical approach to Scripture

A canonical approach to scripture reading may be informed by the long history of modern historical criticism. In the end, however, the intent is to read not as a modern 'objective' reader, but to read as an assenting member of a faith community, that is, as a member of the Church that accepts Scripture as normative teaching, as the only rule for life and faith. We may identify four discussions of the canonical perspective that will make clear how deeply such reading departs from modernist, liberal reading habits. It is unmistakeable that in each case cited here the nerve of the Church in such reading – so as not to be controlled by modernist assumptions – is braced by and derivative from Karl Barth's initial proposal.

Brevard Childs

Within Old Testament studies themselves, it has been Brevard Childs more than any other scholar who has worked to re-situate the text of the Old Testament within the matrix of church conviction. (In lesser ways, James A. Sanders and Ronald Clements have also contributed to the discussion.) As early as 1970, Childs warned against an overinvestment in 'historical' questions that led to interpretation fragmentation and to a preoccupation with what was behind the text rather than in the text. In 1979, Childs considered the 'final form of the text' for each book of the Old Testament, and argued that the literary shape of the final form amounted to an intentional theological statement. (He attempted a like study of New Testament books (1984), though perhaps with less success.) In 1992, Childs moved even further in what he terms a 'canonical' approach with his thesis that the Old Testament and the New Testament constitute two witnesses to Jesus Christ. In this formidable study, Childs has gone well beyond a concern for 'final form', in order to insist that Scripture be read in the Church according to the 'Rule of Faith', by which he apparently means the Church's confession of the Trinity and the incarnation of Jesus Christ.

Among the examples of Childs's canonical reading that demonstrates his concern and the interpretive potential of his approach is his reading of Psalm 8. Childs focuses on verses 4–5:

> What are human beings that you are mindful of them,
> mortals that you care for them?
> Yet you have made them a little lower than God,
> and crowned them with glory and honor. (Ps. 8:4–5)

These verses clearly celebrate the human person as the pinnacle of creation, with a connection to Genesis 1:26–28. Childs, however, notices the reuse of these verses in the Old Testament in Matthew 21:16 (and parallels), 1 Corinthians 15:27 and Hebrews 2:6ff. In all these uses, the text is transposed to refer to Jesus as 'the man', so that human personhood is to be understood in and through and with reference to Jesus Christ. Such a christological re-reading of the text obviously stands at a distance from the first reading of the Old Testament text that is conventional in Old Testament historical criticism. Childs comments:

> If one wants to use the psalm in some broader fashion, if one is concerned to speak *theologically* about the content of the psalmist's faith, the simple descriptive task is not adequate. Certainly not for Christian theology! We are no longer in the community of Israel. We no longer have the temple in which to bring our praises to God. There is a break that separates, not only a Christian, but also any modern man from the world of the Old Testament ... From the point of view of Christian theology it seems highly dubious that one can speak meaningfully of man and his relationship to God and the creation without speaking Christologically. (1970, 158)

This presentation of Psalm 8 is a clear example of the way in which the canonical breaks free from and moves beyond the historical-critical. Childs's canonical approach characteristically offers a 'second reading' that would be readily rejected in modernist critical circles (cf. approach to Gen. 22:1–19 in 1992, 325–6).

George Lindbeck

Most influential in post-liberal interpretation has been the book by George Lindbeck, *The Nature of Doctrine*. It was he who made the phrase 'post-liberal' current as he championed a cultural-linguistic approach to the Bible and to theology as an urgent alternative both to an expressive-experiential perspective that championed the work of an autonomous, subjective interpreter, and to a propositional approach that froze faith into hardened formulae:

> Thus what propositionalists with their stress on unchanging truth and falsity regard as faithful, applicable, and intelligible is likely to be dismissed as dead orthodoxy by liberal experiential-expressivists. Conversely, the liberal claim that change and pluralism in religious expression are necessary for intelligibility, applicability, and faithfulness is attacked by the propositionally orthodox as an irrationally relativistic and practically self-defeating betrayal of the faith. A postliberal might propose to overcome this polarization between tradition and innovation by a distinction between abiding doctrinal grammar and variable theological vocabulary, but this proposal appears from other perspectives as the worst of two worlds rather than the best of both. In view of this situation, the most that can be done in this chapter is to comment on how faithfulness, applicability, and intelligibility might be understood in postliberal theologies, and then leave it to the readers to make their own assessments. (113)

Lindbeck's statement has become programmatic. We may identify six accent points in Lindbeck's proposal for post-liberal analysis that provide a large theological frame for the text work undertaken by Childs:

- Texts are *'thick'* and only a community of durability and sustained interpretation can sense and embrace the depth of meaning that is characteristically lost in conventional positivistic reading (115).
- The text is cast in and read in *communal language*, so that it does not emerge or survive because of the accomplishment of a venturesome individual. The texts are a long time being framed and require a community nurtured in thickness in order to read with discernment (120).
- The text is read and understood in terms of a rich *intertextuality* whereby the text is interpreted, illuminated or corrected by other texts (see below). Thus the text is not to be read *ad seriatim* or in a thin historical way, but as a part of a network of texts that form a coherent assertion (116).
- The text in its 'thickness' is pieced together into a coherence only by an act

of venturesome *imagination* whereby the coherence becomes more than the accumulation of the textual parts:

> There is, indeed, no more demanding exercise of the inventive and imaginative powers than to explore how a language, culture, or religion may be employed to give meaning to new domains of thought, reality, and action. Theological description can be a highly constructive enterprise. (115)

Thus the coherence is not a 'given' in the text itself, but results from the generative power of the interpreting community. That newly generated coherence of interpretation thus becomes the constitutive form of Scripture in that community.

- Everything thus depends upon the sustained, imaginative act of the community, whereby the text is *'practised'* or *'performed'* (123). It is evident, thus, that the text becomes what it is in a dialectical relationship with the reading community. Significant meaning for the community of faith arises and is given in this performing act of imagination.
- It is evident, finally, that this entire enterprise is to be understood as vigorously and determinedly *antifoundational*. That is, the community reads intuitively in terms of its own tradition and its circumstance and is thereby able to enact a venturesome faith claim that is not subjected to the measure of dominant rationality:

> It seems essential in our day to adopt an apologetic approach that seeks to discover a foundational scheme within which religions can be evaluated, and that makes it possible to translate traditional meanings into currently intelligible terms. The postliberal resistance to the foundational enterprise is from this perspective a fatal flaw. (129)

Thus post-liberal interpretation offers a rationality of its own that is rooted in the tradition of the community and not subject to veto by dominant rationality, including the rationality of Enlightenment culture or its derivative expression, historical criticism.

These characteristic markings of post-liberal interpretation, while enunciated distinctly one at a time, are of course profoundly interrelated. All of them together permit the reading practice of a faith community to proceed according to the reasonableness of its internal tradition and logic. I take it that that, in the end, is what Childs proposes and it is clear in every aspect how different such a project is from the conventional readings of 'liberal' historical criticism.

Garrett Green

Garrett Green, in his discussion, *Imagining God*, has contributed to a post-liberal canonical frame of reference for biblical interpretation. He has made a powerful case for the way in which a practical 'religious paradigm' functions as a 'narrative model' for the rendering of the text and the experiencing of the world:

> Religious language is not the expression of pre-linguistic religious experience but rather speech arising out of commitment to specific religious paradigms. People with different paradigmatic commitments characteristically have different experiences. What is *given* to the believer, and therefore to the theologian, is not a foundational experience but a religious paradigm: a normative model of 'what the world is like,' embodied in a canon of scripture and expressed in the life of a religious community. The way to recognize Christians – and, I am convinced, other religious people as well – is not by looking for experiences lying 'behind' their language but rather by observing how they imagine themselves in the world. Experience, in other words, is not the ground of religious imagination so much as its product. (133)

Green's emphasis on imagination as a rhetorical, interpretive act is a counter to an 'expressive-experiential approach' that claims that rhetoric simply 'reports' experience. Green has shown how such imaginative rhetoric 'produces' experience. Such normative imagination is prior to experience (134). In Green's purview, then, Christian interpretation, and consequently Christian experience, is rooted in acts of paradigmatic imagination. Green cites the familiar formulation of the Eucharist in 1 Corinthians 11:26 as an articulation of the 'melody of revelation in the polyphony of scripture' (151). He concludes: 'The most powerful way to change the world is precisely by interpreting it' (152).

Stephen Fowl

Stephen Fowl, in *Engaging Scripture,* has made a sustained argument that Scripture reading is only properly done in an ecclesial context, in a community that shares life as well as common faith. Fowl's test case concerns the Abraham narrative as read in the book of Galatians, a reading he understands as 'counter-conventional' (128–60). Fowl's judgement on Paul's reading of the Abraham narrative is boldly and daringly christocentric. Fowl is aware of the charge of supersessionism as he reads the Abraham narrative christologically (as does Paul). Fowl's judgement, however, is that this approach is not supersessionist, but is a proper reading in a particular community of interpretation among those who in friendship share a common life. Fowl of course is alert to the fact that Jewish reading communities will read differently. Such readings are equally legitimate in terms of a quite different reading community.

Jewish reading of biblical texts

Fowl's alertness to the distinctiveness of a Christian reading of texts in a christological way provides a transition to the reality of Jewish reading of biblical texts. Historical-critical readings have always been, as indicated above, allied with Protestant Christian scholarship. Thus reading in Judaism has always been an alternative reading and a self-conscious Jewish community of faith. Indeed, Jon Levenson (79–81) has welcomed Brevard Childs's exclusively Christian canonical reading. Levenson has vigorously noted that 'by universalizing the claims of historical-criticism', one denies the potential for pluralistic reading. Childs, however, has properly and acceptably 'relativized' historical criticism in order to make explicitly Christian reading possible (120–22). When readings can be accepted as specifically Christian (as Fowl proposes), then one can in principle take seriously specifically Jewish readings, thus giving up the supposed hegemony of historical criticism that is permeated with Western Christian assumptions. In his polemical and oft reprinted article, 'Exodus and Liberation', Levenson strongly insists that the Exodus narrative must receive a Jewish reading, whereas other readings in liberation hermeneutic distort the text by disregarding its Jewishness (127–59). In this particular case, Levenson is not at all inclined to accept particular readings other than the Jewish, given his judgement that the narrative text pertains primally, if not exclusively, to Jews. In any case, such a Jewish reading of the text is clearly distant from any liberal, universalising pretension.

A closer example of Jewish particularity in reading is that of David Weiss Halivni, whose work I know through the exposition of Peter Ochs. Halivni accepts that Jews must read according to the 'plain meaning' of the text that is everywhere recognised, but that after such a consensus recognition of meaning, one can then identify

> *the narrower range of meanings that he could consistently order into a narrative series that leads from beginning (Moses) to end (the present interpreter) in such a way that the series has narrative beauty and pragmatic power in his particular sub-community.* 'Pragmatic power' means the power to help the sub-community repair its current crisis in a way that is arguably consistent with the narrative. *If these conditions are met, then the narrative has 'pragmatic truth,'* which means, strictly *that it represents, a priori, a reasonable means of adopting the lessons of rabbinic/scriptural reading as conditions for reparative action today. The only remaining test of the narrative would be its relative success or failure in actually contributing to the repairs its author envisions.* (Ochs, 134)

Following Halivni, Ochs situates such 'pragmatic' reading in a 'particular sub-community', in this case, Judaism. The particularity of Jewish reading, moreover, is aimed at the particular need of the sub-community. In such a proposal, it is of course recognised that readings in other sub-communities are also legitimate, and also serve the acute need of such sub-communities. If we consider the *canonical, non-foundational, cultural-linguistic* advocacy of these scholars, it is clear how far we have come from universalising tendencies with attention to the canonical normative functions of texts in faith communities.

The contextual reading of the Bible

There is a second way in which post-liberal readings emerge, though this second mode of post-liberal readings is in some sense anticipated by the above canonical approaches. Whereas Childs, Lindbeck, Green and Fowl in particular stress the canonical, the second way is to read *contextually* in a local community of faith. In such local contexts it may happen that the reading is willy-nilly canonical. The concern and generative power of such reading, however, does not come from any canonical self-awareness, but from the particular and intense focus of immediate context. This approach tends to be an act of advocacy for the particular community and characteristically reads against a hegemonic propensity that may in its own way be canonical. In the above scholars named, Fowl, Ochs and Halivni move in the direction of the contextual but not as far or as specifically as others. There is now a panoply of such contextual biblical interpretations, largely drawn from church contexts outside the hegemonic culture of Euro-America. I will refer to four such studies that I think to be representative of this post-liberal trajectory of interpretation.

Elsa Tamez

In a study of Luke 2, Elsa Tamez (53–8) takes up the 'Peace of Augustus Caesar' that is contradicted by 'the Peace of Jesus of Nazareth'. She observes that by the use of the term 'Saviour' (*soter*), 'The figure of Augustus is deliberately evoked.' The figure of Jesus, moreover, is deliberately contrasted with that of Caesar. After establishing what might be seen as a contrast on historical-critical grounds, Tamez then draws the text immediately to the wrenching political reality of the contemporary world:

> Today we live Christmas as a truce, that is, a temporary suspension of hostilities, a passing 'cease fire.' As the days pass, the struggle for survival in the cities and the countryside continues, the violence of the street rises; in the places where there is armed conflict, the guerrillas and the army resume the war. (58)

By the time Tamez finishes her reading, it is clear that this text provides a crucial and vibrant offer of an alternative in the modern world. After Tamez, one has no wish to return the text to its ancient milieu, as the text is seen to matter decisively here and now. The interpretive move that Tamez makes from ancient Augustus Caesar to contemporary hegemony is, of course, not an uncommon one that is often made after historical-critical analysis. What makes her analysis 'post-liberal', however, is that we can be sure that in Tamez's own horizon the issue of contrasting the two modes of peace did not arise first of all from the text, but arose from her context among those who are on the down side of immense power in the world. It is the context that has enabled her to see the stark contrast that is then read from the text back to the context. It may well be that this is always the way the matter has worked but it was not acknowledged to work in that way in a 'liberal' milieu.

Musa Dube

Musa Dube of Botswana has written often and powerfully about colonial and post-colonial biblical interpretation. In the article to which I refer, she reports on her attendance at the US Society of Biblical Literature (SBL) meeting in Cape Town, 2002. It is important to recognise that the society, now given to international meetings far from the United States, is the elite guild of privileged US biblical scholars, including this author. It is traditionally committed to 'liberal', historical-critical study, though that is beginning to change. Dube's essay reports on the Cape Town meeting that had taken 'globalisation' as its theme. She comments specifically on a paper given by Justin Ukpong, a Nigerian scholar, who urged the conference to attend to 'African' interpretation.

Dube, however, rebukes not only the Society for its focus on globalisation, given her judgement that 'Globalization is the Grandson of Colonialization'; she also chides Ukpong for speaking generically of 'African' interpretation, for her insistence is that interpretation must be intensely local and knowing interpreters will recognise that 'African' interpretation is variegated and immensely complex:

> My response to his challenge begins by underlining the South African setting of Cape Town, by bringing those dusty shabby homes and roads of Khayelitsha, the lowest of the low places, to the perfectly paved grounds and tiled walls of Cape Sun Intercontinental, to the SBL 2000 International Meeting. (2002, 44–5)

Dube then makes a critical judgement that members of the Society visiting in Africa are likely to be scholars having insufficient interest who take insufficient trouble to find out about local reality; they likely remain tourists who are unaware and unconnected:

> But can the SBL come to South Africa, only six years after the end of the apartheid era, and leave without letting its practice be reconstituted by such a place, such a history, such a call to rededication to the struggle for justice? (2002, 45)

Her judgement is that the mindset of the members, as well as the perspective of Ukpong, are remote from the lived reality of South African townships, and that the globalisation championed in the conference is a new form of intellectual hegemony connected with Western, political-economic hegemony. She urges then that attention must be paid to the vast differences that globalisation tends to subsume under democratic capitalism to which many have no access, and to the race issues that are present in post-apartheid South Africa. Her urgent questions raise issues about the Society as a reading community, a questioning that drives to the heart of long-established 'liberal' reading practice. It is important that the guild should ask:

> 1. What colour is SBL, and why?
> 2. What routes does SBL travel in the global era, and why?
> 3. What spaces does SBL occupy: black, white, brown, yellow, or rainbow?
>
> As we begin consciously to do biblical studies in the 'global era' we know that some are globalizing and others are being globalized. Some, we presume, are standing in a space of resistance that seeks to counteract globalization and to sprinkle some village spirit on the globe. The alleys of globalization are not race, class, and gender neutral. SBL members should scrutinize the structures, conferences venues, theories, methods, and contents of their programs, as well as the various institutions that have allowed, and continue to allow, biblical studies to be a predominantly white discipline, while Christianity is notably growing among black people, especially in Africa more than on any other continent. The question to ask is: Does the Society of Biblical Literature and its members, in their various institutions of work, intend to take on the rainbow colors of our world or to continue 'whitening' the global village in biblical studies? (2002, 39)

In the end, Dube does not take up particular texts. She does, however, advocate a 'villagizing' of interpretation in place of 'globalizing'. Her critique is immensely poignant and demonstrates the way in which *context* is decisive for reading. Dube knows that any 'universal reading' is inescapably 'top down', and the *village context* as alternative provides a very different social environment for reading:

> The suppression of the village spirit in the global village became imme-

> diately apparent to me when I realized that while I could use the words 'globalizing' and 'globalization,' I did not have the equivalent words of 'villagizing' and 'villagization.' I have coined them here, to highlight the fact that part of counteracting globalization includes creating a multi-directional traffic. The village has something to offer in terms of community care, an economic system that strives to empower all its members and reverence for life. (2002, 62)

In another article Dube takes up the crucial role of women in the book of Acts (1999). She is, however, especially concerned with the movement of women in the African Independent Churches in South Africa and is able to trace the way in which the testimony of these churches and the testimony of the book of Acts are parallel. It is clear in her work, important for our purposes, to see that the point of reference for her is not in the book of Acts per se but in the 'African Independent Churches'. This is yet another example of her important work that is deeply rooted in concrete context.

R. S. Sugirtharajah

Dube's strong post-colonial advocacy is reinforced by the work of R. S. Sugirtharajah in his book, *Postcolonial Criticism and Biblical Interpretation*. In Chapter 2, Sugirtharajah traces a series of alternative reading methods that aim at 'redress, remuneration, and redemption', all readings that fall outside the epistemological scope of Western hegemonic practice that matched Enlightenment political and economic power. These alternative readings are characteristically designed to provide open space for oppressed communities to be nurtured in hope and freedom that in turn makes possible revolutionary interpretation and revolutionary action. Sugirtharajah cites examples of 'hegemonic' codes in the David narratives of 2 Samuel 7 and in Ecclesiastes (80). But following Mosala, Sugirtharajah observes that the book of Esther, by contrast, is an immense resource for the struggle for liberation among African women (81). Clearly, Esther is a model woman who refuses political and imperial values as a means of survival. It is clear, in a variety of examples cited by Sugirtharajah, that some texts (and particularly some readings) are preoccupied with *imposed power* with a chance for *alternative power* through alternative reading. It is easily noticed that the connection between *reading* and *power* is an interface nowhere on the horizon of the older historical criticism, for in that practice it was generally and uncritically assumed that the reader was an innocent and objective reporter on what the text itself yielded. In the contextual reading proposed here, it is clear that the context dictates issues that determine the nuance and accent in reading that is not noticed or appreciated in other contexts. In truth, of course, every reading is contextual. The older 'objective' scholarship, however, did not need to think that it was contextual, since the 'liberal' context cohered with Western hegemony and was thereby able to impose its reading and, consequently, its power on all other contexts.

African American perspective

Finally, some studies that grow out of African American context. On the one hand, Vincent Wimbush, from a critical social scientific perspective, considers the way in which biblical rhetoric may be an act of resistance. While Wimbush is an acute critical scholar, his own African American perspective, plus his beginning point, will mark his work as post-liberal and as intentional advocacy:

> We would in fact not even begin with 'the text'; we would instead privilege – we would begin and end with – 'world.' We would begin with some of the dynamics of human interaction, some of the perennial challenges and foibles of social formation: power relations, negotiations of difference(s), dominance, the hierarchialization and rehierarchialization of values, and so forth. These matters we assumed to be universal problematics and challenges – east, west, north, south; ancient, modern, postmodern. Texts, whether ancient or not, mythic or not, would then be understood to function variously as sources representing or masking some of these dynamics, as inspiration for, psychosocial trippers toward, the historical socio-cultural reifications of these dynamics. (2)

While the issues of power are generically universal as Wimbush claims, one of course must begin concretely and locally with a particular embodied form of power relationships. The simple fact of beginning with 'world', that is, the context in which the text has been generated or the context in which the text is read, indicates a break with any 'objective' reading that is an idealistic quest for 'meaning' that screens out the dimension of power in understanding the production and reception of text.

Wimbush's critical notion of resistance may be nicely twinned with Anthony Pinn's exposition of 'Black Religion'. Pinn understands Black Religion to be an artistic act of 'World Making' that is done through a 'hermeneutics of style' (133–41). Pinn himself is not interested in texts per se, but clearly Black Religion, via black preachers, characteristically has taken the biblical text as script for a 'world' that is alternative to the dominant white world of oppression and exploitation. It is clear that much of the African American church has not been excessively determined by 'liberal' historical criticism, even if its preachers have often studied such matters. It is clear that the context of oppression has been the propelling force in biblical interpretation in Black Religion and obviously, contextual study of the text can be made to serve the need of the context. In this regard, the use of the text in Black

Religion is not unlike the 'pragmatic' proposal of Halivni for reading in sub-communities whereby the text works at the needs of the sub-community.

These examples of contextual readings could be multiplied, as the break-up of 'liberal' hegemony has permitted a steady stream of textual expositions that are locally situated and informed. It remains for us to reflect upon the rather peculiar and ill-fitting interface between *canonical* perspectives and the *contextual* perspectives traced above, both of which are vigorously post-liberal. The *canonical* studies I have cited tend to be more erudite and well situated in Western academic milieus and perforce live close to the initial impetus of Karl Barth in his polemic against academic liberalism. By contrast, the *contextual* studies I have cited are more 'local' and emerge in cultural contexts largely remote from Western interpretive hegemony. Because they are local in their focus, such interpreters do not easily conform to the more rigorous notions of the canonical that are articulated by Childs, Lindbeck and Green.

Nonetheless, it seems to me that according to the criteria of Lindbeck that I have quoted above, the contextual studies do indeed conform to expectations of the canonical:

1 texts *thick* with durable meaning that is not exhausted by 'historical' study;
2 read in *communal language;*
3 read in a practice of *intertextuality;*
4 wrought through acts of venturesome *imagination* whereby connections are made between ancient text and contemporary reading;
5 *practised and performed concretely*, as acts of transformation and resistance;
6 vigorously and intentionally *anti-foundational.*

On all counts, such reading is post-liberal, even if it does not readily conform to the doctrinal content that is urgent for Childs, Lindbeck and Green. It is the process, perspective and situation of the reading that makes these contextual studies post-liberal. Thus I conclude that for all the difference in terms of the social location and subsequent accents in the more formal canonical and more immediately contextual, these perspectives do share a great deal. What they share is evident when these several readings are contrasted with the thin 'liberal' readings of historical criticism. Such a recognition of course still leaves open the question of the differing usefulness and importance of historical criticism when one moves beyond such critical categories to post-critical interpretation. Clearly as a tool (but not as a defining ideology), historical criticism is an important instrument for good reading that is characteristically employed by serious post-liberal readers. Such use of historical criticism, however, is done with full recognition that texts have no completed meaning that is intrinsic to them, but that meaning in text is evoked in an interactive dialogue with interpreters, each of whom is concretely located and situated.

The new characteristics of post-liberal exegesis

We may, finally, identify four aspects of interpretation that are characteristic of post-liberal work that were not on the horizon of 'liberal' historical criticism.

First, *post-liberal interpretation is an act of imagination*, that is, a capacity to 'image', host, and entertain an articulation of reality beyond the given, the conventional and the known (Brueggemann 1993). So long as 'liberal' interpreters understood the interpretive task in terms of 'historical' questions, the work of interpretation was seen to be the recovery of what was given in the past, wherein the text was taken to be only reportage on the given, 'happened' past. As interpretation moved away from such a preoccupation with the 'historical', it was able to consider 'the world in front of the text' as well as 'the world behind the text'; clearly the 'world in front of the text' is an imaginative construal. It is an imaginative construal undertaken by the text itself; beyond that, quite clearly it is also an act of imaginative construal by the reading community that takes up and dares to go beyond the imaginative construal of the text, now interpretation propelled by the needs of the interpreting community.

Richard Kearney has traced the way in which imagination as a valid mode of knowledge struggled against Enlightenment reductionism. Garrett Green, moreover, has shown the way in which 'canon' itself is an act of imagination that invites imagination in the reading community. Thus it is clear that post-liberal interpretation in an anti-foundationalist posture, will not let its venturesome way be tamed or contained in the categories of any conventional rationality. It is precisely by the nerve of imagination that interpretative communities have been able to receive and articulate the 'strange new world within the Bible' that does not conform to any of our known and more easily managed worlds.

Second, so long as liberal articulation had confidence in the reason and reasonableness of the interpreter and took such interpretation as 'objective', it could be accepted that interpretation was innocent and free of bias. As soon as the constructive dimension of interpretation was recognised and as soon as it was accepted that interpretation inescapably reads the text with reference to context, critical reflection necessarily recognised an ideological component in all texts and in all readings. Such an ideological bent – whether ideology is understood as 'distortion' (Marx) or as fundamental presupposition (Geertz), indicates that interpretation had lost its innocence and was in fact an act of negotiation between contexted advocacies for the right to interpret the text

(Ricoeur 1986). Thus *the critique of ideology*, so crucial in post-liberal reading, is able to acknowledge freely advocacy in reading and is further able to discern hidden advocacy in readings that claim objectivity. Thus in the exposé of 'colonial' readings and the impetus toward 'post-colonial' readings is both a ready recognition of advocacy and an effective discernment of hidden ideology. The acknowledgement of ideology and advocacy decisively rescues the text from any illusion of innocence and the interpreter from any self-deception about objectivity. It is of course more than a little ironic that some exponents of 'ideology critique' can still imagine themselves to be innocent and objective, so powerful is the continuing force of 'liberal' confidence (Carroll).

Third, we read texts as bodied interpreters fully situated in some body politic; *every reader and every reading is to some extent contextual*. We have seen how Dube, given the rubric of 'African interpretation', insists that the actual context of interpretation must be more local. We have seen, moreover, how Halivni moves beyond 'plain meaning' to 'pragmatic' interpretation that is a work of a sub-community, in his case Jewish. Reading in and for a sub-community of course vetoes any claim to be a detached, rational interpreter who proceeds by autonomous reason.

Fourth, post-liberal interpretation, unlike liberal interpretation, characteristically *has a practical urgency to it*. That is, reading is done with reference to the needs and possibilities of the sub-community; indeed a sub-community cannot afford to have interpretation that is a mere intellectual activity. In post-liberal reading, life-and-death matters are at stake for the interpreter and for the community of interpretation.

Thus post-liberal interpretation finally belongs to a concrete sub-community of practice. The ultimate characterisation of post-liberal interpretation, when given concreteness, is that the community (or sub-community) to which the text belongs is not just any 'sub-community'. It is, rather, a sub-community of faith, or in current discussion, a sub-community of faithful Christians or of faithful Jews. The text is read rightly only by a community that takes the text as a commanding form of address that summons to obedience and buoyancy. The 'canonists' make that claim formally; the 'contextualists' make the claim practically. Canonists and contextualists together stand distinct from old, liberal practice that refused such concreteness in the interest of an objective rationality. The long road since Karl Barth in 1919 has now largely repositioned interpretation away from modernist self-confidence and toward sub-communities who boldly enact testimony in the presence of hegemony. They do so in the conviction that this distinct testimony is a word of life even to the larger culture whose own pretensions cannot yield life.

Bibliography

Barth, K. (1968) *The Epistle to the Romans*. Oxford: Oxford University Press.

Barth, K. (1928) *The Word of God and the Word of Man*. London: Hodder & Stoughton.

Brueggemann, W. (1993) *Texts under Negotiation: the Bible and post-modern imagination*. Minneapolis, MN: Fortress Press.

Carroll, R. P. (1991) *Wolf in the Sheepfold: the Bible as a problem for Christianity*. London: SCM Press.

Childs, B. S. (1970) *Biblical Theology in Crisis*. Philadelphia: Westminster Press.

Childs, B. S. (1979) *Introduction to the Old Testament as Scripture*. Philadelphia: Westminster Press.

Childs, B. S. (1984) *The New Testament as Canon: an introduction*. London: SCM Press.

Childs, B. S. (1992) *Biblical Theology of the Old and New Testaments: theological reflection on the Christian Bible*. London: SCM Press.

Clements, R. E. (1996) *Old Testament Prophecy: from oracle to canon*. Louisville, KY: Westminster John Knox Press.

Dube, Musa W. (1999) Building a feminist sociological model of liberation: women in the Apocryphal Acts and the African independent churches. *Journal of Constructive Theology* 5, 87–115.

Dube, Musa W. (2002) Villagising, globalising and biblical studies, in J. S. Ukpong et al. (eds), *Reading the Bible in the Global Village: Cape Town*. Atlanta, GA: Society for the Study of Biblical Literature.

Fowl, S. E. (1998) *Engaging Scripture: a model for theological interpretation*. Oxford: Blackwell.

Green, Garrett (1989) *Imagining God: theology and religious imagination*. New York: Harper & Row.

Kearney, R. (1988) *The Wake of Imagination: ideas of creativity in Western culture*. London: Hutchinson.

Levenson, J. D. (1993) *The Hebrew Bible, the Old Testament and Historical Criticism: Jesus and Christians in biblical studies*. Louisville, KY: Westminster John Knox Press.

Lindbeck, G. A. (1984) *The Nature of Doctrine: religion and theology in a post-liberal age*. Philadelphia: Westminster Press.

Ochs, P. (2002) Talmudic scholarship as textual reasoning: Halivni's pragmatic historiography, in P. Ochs and N. Levene (eds), *Textual Reasoning: Jewish philosophy and textual study at the end of the twentieth century*. Grand Rapids, MI: Eerdmans.

Perdue, L. G. (1994) *The Collapse of History: reconstructing Old Testament history*. Minneapolis: Fortress Press.

Pinn, A. B. (2003) *Terror and Triumph: the nature of Black religion*. Minneapolis, MN: Fortress Press.

Ricoeur, Paul (1986) *Lectures on Ideology and Utopia*. New York: Columbia University Press.

Sanders, J. A. (1972) *Torah and Canon*. Philadelphia: Fortress Press.

Sugirtharajah, R. S. (2002) *Post-colonial Criticism and Biblical Interpretation*. Oxford: Oxford University Press.

Tamez, Elsa (2002) A star illuminates the darkness, in W. Dietrich and U. Luz (eds), *The Bible in a World Context*. Grand Rapids, MI: Eerdmans.

Thompson, T. L. (1974) *The Historicity of the Patristic Narratives: the quest for the historical Abraham*. Berlin: de Gruyter.

von Rad, Gerhard (1962) *Old Testament Theology* vol 1. New York: Harper.

Van Seters, John (1975) *Abraham in History and Tradition*. New Haven, CT: Yale University Press.

Wallace, M. I. 1995) *The Second Naivete: Barth, Ricoeur and the new Yale theology*. Studies in American Biblical Hermeneutics 6. Macon, GA: Mercer University Press.

Wimbush, V. L. (1997) Rhetorics of resistance: a colloquy on early Christianity as rhetorical formation. *Semeia* 79.

Wright, G. E. (1952) *God Who Acts: biblical theology as recital*. London: SCM Press.

CHAPTER 10:

Contextual and advocacy readings of the Bible

ZOË BENNETT AND CHRISTOPHER ROWLAND

Introduction

The nineteenth-century German philosopher G. W. F. Hegel writes of a type of theologian who resembles the counting house clerks, keeping 'the ledgers and accounts of other people's wealth, a wealth that passes through their hands without their retaining any of it, clerks who act only for others without acquiring any assets of their own'. In the twentieth century there have been great movements of Christian people who have refused to go on counting out other people's wealth and have put down stakes for the acquisition of assets of their own in the study of the Bible. Among these are the movements associated with liberation theology. The expression 'liberation theology' itself was initially associated with the rise in Latin American countries, starting with the conference of Roman Catholic Bishops in Medellin in 1968, of a theology grounded in the experiences of the poor and oppressed, which self-consciously embraced God's 'preferential option for the poor' and which challenged the hidden vested interests of other theologies supported by church or state. Liberation theology is explicitly 'contextual' – arising from, coloured by, and answerable to a context. As such the presuppositions of its biblical exegesis are laid open and acknowledged. It is also an 'advocacy' theology; its proponents, whether professional theologians or not, are explicitly committed to the well-being of people who have been oppressed, and this commitment is seen as deriving from a gospel imperative.

Either as specific forms of liberation theology, or as associated movements, a whole host of contextual, advocacy theologies have grown since the 1960s. Among these are Black theology, post-colonial theology, feminist theology and many more locally oriented theologies such as Dalit, Minjung and Palestinian liberation theologies. It is characteristic of this way of doing theology that we are not 'counting out other people's money' in an alienated fashion, but that through our own imagination, commitment, vision and spirit current political realities and everyday life are brought into real critical engagement with the Bible and with the Christian tradition. As the section on liberation theology below makes clear, such concerns and ways of reading the Bible are not only a recent phenomenon. It is, however, only since the mid-twentieth century that this has been consciously and explicitly thematised as 'liberationist'. Here we have taken two important and rather different members from this 'family' of theologies, liberation theology and feminist theology, to explore each of their approaches to reading the Bible. We take them as significant examples, not in any way claiming that they exhaust the field of contextual and advocacy theologies.

Power and ideology in the text and its use

The liberation movement in theology is significantly concerned with power. It is about a reversal of power and control in respect of the reading, interpretation and application of the Scriptures. It is about a reversal of power and control in the pastoral practices of the churches – as we live with one another and as we live in and towards the world. Hence a further aptness of Hegel's counting-house-clerk image. The liberationist educationalist Paulo Freire famously uses the image of 'banking' to describe the kind of educational practices imposed by oppressors on oppressed communities. This is education as the imposition, and the processing and internalising, of alien 'goods'. Instead education should be a process of 'conscientisation' and 'humanisation', coming to a truer understanding of the realities of power relations in the community and of what it might mean to live a fully human life of flourishing and of justice. Learning and searching for truth in the context of reading the Bible is subject to these same dynamics. The context and perspective of the reading community, of teachers and interpreters, and of the Bible itself must be taken seriously, as must the hidden agendas, the vested interests, and the consequent masked ideological distortions. The questions of power and of 'in whose interests?' must always be asked.

There is a complex dynamic of suspicion and trust operating when a community or individual reads the Bible in this way, seeking to remain true both to faithful Christian belief and living, and also to the realities of sinful distortion in religious texts and practices. Attentiveness to the ways of God in Jesus Christ through reading the Bible doesn't always sit easily with the suspicion fuelled by theoretical understanding of the workings of ideology or by practical experience of oppression from those who claim the Bible as justification for their acts and attitudes. Some forms of liberation theology are mainly concerned to expose false readings and 'abuse' of the text by oppressors, while still regarding the Bible itself as 'benign'. Other approaches, such as feminist theology, are more suspicious that the oppressor is embedded within the text itself. The actual text of the Bible carries both liberative and oppressive messages and claims. The Bible itself is part of the problem; exposing 'the Word in the words', as Barth would have it, avoids the most critical and difficult questions. This is the position many feminist interpreters feel forced to face.

All these issues have direct and urgent bearing on pastoral practice. Tackling the Bible is a critical moment in pastoral theology. The Bible shapes the lives of Christians and of others in many ways well beyond the explicitly Christian community. The Bible is a double-edged sword. It has been the source of emancipation and flourishing; and it has been the cause of oppression and suffering. The particular contribution of this chapter to the exploration of the Bible in pastoral practice is to ask the questions about biblical interpretation that are central to liberation and feminist theologies and to those theologies which are kin to them. Such questions are: whose voices are heard? Whose interests are served? Where and how do we understand the workings of the Spirit of Life in our lives, in our text and in their interconnectedness? These are questions of pastoral practice, concerning the building up of individuals and of communities into places of prophetic justice and of flourishing within the love of God.

In discussing liberationist readings of Scripture it is usual to start with twentieth-century examples, particularly from Latin America and other parts of the two-thirds world. The kinds of readings found in the Basic Ecclesial Communities in the late twentieth century are no innovation, however, and have a long tradition in Christianity, examples of which will complement the discussion of liberation theology from Brazil. We will start, therefore, by examining sixteenth-century Anabaptism, before moving to Brazilian grass-roots reading of Scripture. A perspective on all of this will be offered from the work of William Blake who particularly wished to enable ordinary people to use the Bible without the constraints of their ecclesiastical masters.

An early Anabaptist testimony

> 'What do you understand about St. John's Apocalypse?' the friar asked the chandler. 'At what university did you study? At the loom, I suppose? For I understand that you were nothing but a poor weaver and chandler before you went around preaching and rebaptizing ... I have attended the university of Louvain, and for long studied divinity, and yet I do not understand anything at all about St John's Apocalypse. This is a fact.' To which Jacob answered: 'Therefore Christ thanked his heavenly Father that he had revealed and made it known to babes and hid it from the wise of this world, as it is written in Matt. 11:25.' 'Exactly!' the friar replied, 'God has revealed it to the weavers at the loom, to the cobblers on the bench, and to bellow-menders, lantern tinkers, scissors grinders, brass makers, thatchers and all sorts of riff-raff, and poor, filthy and

lousy beggars. And to us ecclesiastics who have studied from our youth, night and day, God has concealed it.'

This extract comes from *The Martyrs Mirror* (Van Braght, 775), a collection of Anabaptist testimonies, and offers evidence of a different tradition of Christian discipleship which was formally outlawed in England at the end of the sixteenth century. There is evidence of an approach to the interpretation of Scripture that contrasts with Reformers like Luther and Calvin. Whether because they could not rely on a permanent leadership because of persecution, or because of a latent anticlericalism or out of a sincere conviction, there is much evidence to suggest that the whole congregation was involved in the interpretation of Scripture. Three theological convictions undergird the hermeneutic community, the centrality and continuity of the Church in God's purposes and the belief that the gathered church was the main locus of the Spirit's work. Although this model was not always practised, and the exigencies of persecution and the struggle for survival brought about a less participative practice, there is sufficient evidence to suggest that their practice provides a challenge to the assumption that ordinary readers or hearers of Scripture do not possess adequate hermeneutical competence. Undergirding it all is the conviction that ordinary believers can be informed by the Spirit.

This represents a rather different approach from what we find in Calvin's *Institutes* (3.1–13), where we have a picture of the learned pastor functioning as a teacher to guide his pupils into the ways of truth and guard them against false teaching. One might want to say that Calvin is the more realistic in his approach, more open to the ease with which the truth of God can be corrupted. But the early Anabaptist teachers were as aware of this as any. For all that, however, they hung on to the conviction that wisdom was given to ordinary Christians to find in the Scriptures things which might be hidden from the wise and learned. This need at all times to be subject to the discerning critique of the congregation was one of the gifts of the Spirit.

Reading the Bible in a Basic Ecclesial Community, São Paulo, Brazil

Another striking example of modern grassroots reading of Scripture is found in an account of a Bible study in a Basic Ecclesial Community offered by James Pitt when he went to a Bible study group on the periphery of São Paulo. The women present were all poor without much formal education. Most were migrants and could easily identify with a poor family on the move whose baby had been born in a stable. After an hour's discussion the catechist put the question: why did Jesus choose to be born poor and humble? 'Maybe', said one woman, 'it was to show these rich people that we are important too.'

There was a recognition of the possibility that God may be giving a clear statement about their humanity. Another young woman said, 'I think we still haven't got the right answer to the first question. I think that God chose his son to be born like us so that we can realise that we are important. It is not just to show the bosses. It's to show us too.' In response to what he had observed James Pitt commented,

> I saw what it means to say that the Gospel has the power to set people free, that the good news to the poor is a message of liberation … these women [were] fired by a sudden consciousness of their own worth, of their identification with Jesus Christ … they went on to discuss what they should be doing about the high food prices, about how a particular chain of shops had cornered the market and was overcharging, and how they themselves would link up with catechists' groups and basic church communities across the sector to organise a protest. (8–9)

Among such grassroots groups the Bible has become a catalyst for the exploration of pressing contemporary issues relevant to the community and offers a language so that the voice of the voiceless may be heard, releasing new thought and action related to the circumstances of everyday commitments. In the Basic Ecclesial Communities there is an immediacy in the way in which the text is used because resonances are found with the experience set out in the stories of biblical characters. The Bible offers a means by which the present difficulties can be shown to be surmountable in the life of faith and community commitment. To enable the poor to read the Bible has involved a programme of education of the contents of the biblical material, so that it can be a resource for thousands who are illiterate. In such programmes full recognition is taken of the value of the experience of life. It can be a form of Bible study that goes straight to the text with no concern to ask questions about its original historical context.

In this kind of Bible study the experience of poverty and oppression (often termed 'life' or 'reality') is as important a text as the text of Scripture itself. It represents another text to be studied alongside that contained between the covers of the Bible. God's word is to be found in the dialectic between Scripture and the continuing story to be discerned in the contemporary world, particularly among those people with whom God has chosen to be identified. This kind of scriptural interpretation, democratic and participative, unpredictable in its effects, is one of the main reasons why the base communities and their supporters have come under such suspicion. It has often been remarked that what was so problematic about the liberation theology of Leonardo Boff was not its Marxism but its indebtedness to radical Protestantism – the kind of thing, in fact, that one finds in the beginnings of Anabaptism in the sixteenth century.

William Blake: liberating Scripture for ordinary people

Here is a familiar set of words:

And did those feet in ancient time
Walk upon England's mountains green:
And was the holy Lamb of God
On England's pleasant pastures seen!

And did the Countenance Divine
Shine forth upon our clouded hills?
And was Jerusalem builded here,
Among these dark Satanic Mills?

Bring me my Bow of burning gold;
Bring me my Arrows of desire:
Bring me my spear: O Clouds unfold:
Bring me my chariot of fire!

I will not cease from Mental Fight,
Nor shall my Sword sleep in my hand:
Till we have built Jerusalem
In England's green & pleasant Land.

'Would that all the Lord's people were Prophets.' (Numbers 11.29)

In the immediately preceding context of what we now know as 'Jerusalem' are indications of what Blake considered to be some of the major obstacles to the use of Scripture. Chief among these was rote learning and the dulling effects of memory as opposed to imagination. Blake protests at the way in which the writings of classical antiquity are given prominence over those of the Bible . The effects of reading the Bible in the light of such texts is to quench the spirit of imagination. Blake wants to lead a movement of protest. He writes, 'We do not want either Greek or Roman models if we are but just & true to our own Imaginations, those Worlds of Eternity in which we shall live for ever in Jesus our Lord.'

This famous passage brings together several of the themes which we have touched on already. First and foremost it is written by a man without any formal education, whose wisdom is that of the streets, of popular culture, and the conventional arts of the apprentice. Second, we can see some of the recurring themes of Blake's writing: his campaign against an education based solely on memory rather than inspiration, and his conviction that the domination of classical culture had quenched the vitality of biblical inspiration. Third, the allusions to the Scriptures give a distinctive flavour of his interpretation. The New Jerusalem is not something remote or far off but a possibility, something that may be built in England's green and pleasant land. There is also no disjunction between human activity and divine activity; nothing here about 'leaving it all to God', for the simple reason that God is involved through the imaginative and creative work of the artist. Elijah's chariot is not just part of past history or even future expectation but something which can be the inspiration of the poet as a new Elijah comes on the scene condemning the idolatries of Ahab and Jezebel and offering an alternative to the Baalism of a contemporary culture which according to Blake had led to the capitulation of Christianity to a religion of virtues, rules and the acceptance of war and violence. The spirit and power of Elijah were ever available for those who would exercise their imagination and contemplative thought. Prophecy likewise is not just a thing of the past. It is the vocation of all people. The vision of the New Jerusalem is one that is open to all and the task of building belongs to all.

Blake understood better than any one the enormous difficulty in exploring the meaning of the Bible, what he called the 'Great Code of Art'. Simply putting the Bible in the hands of people did not deal with the stumbling blocks that stood in the way of understanding. It was not lack of learning that could be rectified by the experts so much as the way in which the cultural values of society had so permeated the consciousness and lifestyle of ordinary people that nothing less than a 'mental fight' was required to enable the 'disinfecting' of values and practices that contradicted the way of the Lamb. Blake the poet and artist knew that mere argument was insufficient, not least because it was the dominance of theology by the god of the philosophers which had in his view overwhelmed the wisdom of the Scriptures. To set that wisdom free required of the interpreter techniques that would enable the dominant and all-pervasive ideology to be challenged and to be flushed out of the system. The interpreter's role, then, was more than about technique and intellectual stimulation, telling people what the text meant and adjudicating between true and false opinions. Blake indeed would have none of the idea that there was a master of hermeneutics to be consulted; he even refused to offer an authoritative key to his own works. As the Bible was gateway to wisdom, it was up to all to make use of the gateway and enter and enjoy the garden of God in their own way and in their own time. It was the interpreter's job to provide the means of finding and getting through the gate of perception and imagination.

Blake was no naive populist with a slogan that the wisdom of the ordinary people must be right. He was emphatic that, to use the language of another era, 'false consciousness' was widespread among the population, rich and poor alike, in the way in which the potential of each and every person created in God's image was being stunted in its growth. At the heart of Blake's hermeneutic is the goal enunciated in the final stanza of 'The Divine Image':

> And all must love the human form,
> In heathen, turk or jew.
> Where Mercy, Love & Pity dwell,
> There God is dwelling too.

At the Reformation writers like Erasmus and Tyndale both stressed the importance of ordinary people reading the Bible. They viewed this text as one that was transparent because in a profound way it spoke to and informed people whether or not they had spent years studying it. In the Basic Ecclesial Communities the Bible has often been the means of enabling literacy. Through it people were taught to read, and that matches the way in which the Bible functioned in the early modern period in Britain. It was the tool of the education of ordinary people, enabling a Bunyan or a Blake to read, write and, as important, to reflect on the world in a way which enabled readers to glimpse something of the way of God. It is that aspect of literacy that concerns us here. The reading of Scripture in community is a way in which we can become more theologically literate in the strict sense of the word: having that ability to see and communicate things with a perspective that is attentive to the ways of God in Jesus Christ. That is something learnt as the result of the practical wisdom of the shared practice, and debate about practice, which comes as part of life in a Christian community. This will not always be plain sailing. Blake reminds us that merely reading the Bible will guarantee nothing. We face not only difficulties; we are also confronted by our own resistance to bits of the text and deep divisions between us as to what we are to make of different parts of it. How we go about sorting out those problems in a spirit that replicates and incarnates that of Christ is the issue, not how sophisticated our biblical interpretation is.

Expertise and understanding

In Latin American liberation theology there has been an ongoing issue about the role of expert Scripture scholars. Gerald West describes the careful and subtle way in which he, as an academic, was part of the process of biblical interpretation. The primary thing he got people to do was to keep coming back to what the text actually says. He describes his role as a facilitator, as an enabler of forms of criticism that would require him to provide resources on the kind of situation, community and society that produced the text. The familiar resources of modern academic biblical study were not used as a 'way in' to the text, however. Rather, the Bible study started with the life interests of the participants. He argues that the task of biblical scholars is not to do the reading for ordinary readers, nor simply to accept uncritically their readings. Rather it is to read the Bible with ordinary readers. In so doing one has to be as aware as one can be of one's own interests and to discern and engage with the power relations implicit in the reading process (1999).

This is a minimalist interpretative method, which tends to leave the possibilities in the text to be exploited by the interpreters themselves. The method is well summarised by William Blake when he was asked by an enquirer to offer a detailed guide to his own works. He describes the Bible as a gateway which draws in the reader and which requires not explanation but stimulation:

> You say that I want somebody to Elucidate my Ideas. But you ought to know that What is Grand is necessarily obscure to Weak men. That which can be made Explicit to the Idiot is not worth my care. The wisest of the Ancients consider'd what is not too Explicit as the fittest for Instruction, because it rouzes the faculties to act ... Why is the Bible more Entertaining & Instructive than any other book? Is it not because they [sic] are addressed to the Imagination, which is Spiritual Sensation & but mediately to the Understanding or Reason? (Letter to Trusler)

There is a continuing need to provide those basic tools to 'allow the faculties to act'. Scholars like Erasmus and Tyndale realised that there is a constant need to enable biblical literacy by the provision of the tools to be provided for the exploration to take place. One of these is going to be the assessment of the various manuscripts of the Bible; another is translation; a third is the provision of the circumstances in which text and experience can be explored – the testing of those explorations in the light of the Gospel; a fourth is the careful reflection which helps challenge lazy, self-indulgent, or superficial reflection; and a fifth is the use of historical imagination to aid understanding and reflection on the text. Various reconstructions of Christian origins, for example, have enabled the Pauline epistles to come alive just as the historical reconstruction of the context of prophetic oracles has done. Much of this is in one sense merely an exposition of what church should be about as the formation, and maintenance, of a literate theological community in which all God's people can contribute from the benefits of the Spirit: texts; translations; parameters for interpretation in which the different understandings and misunderstandings down the centuries can inform and guide contemporary readings; and exegetical grammar. Ancient Jewish and Christian interpreters contented themselves with offering exegetical guidelines as a way of enabling interpretation of the Scripture to take place rather than doing the job for people which most commentaries tend to do.

Blake recognises that the Bible was part of the problem as well as being a key to the solution posed by the ills of his day. His creative and innovative use of Scripture will offend our more literalistic temperament. But his plea that we recognise the dangers of a pedantic literalism ending up in an ungracious, oppressive religion is as much a challenge today as it was two hundred years ago. It is a way of interpreting the whole of life, body, soul and spirit. Blake made no neat distinction between the political and the spiritual. God was to be found in surprising persons, places and things:

> To see a World in a Grain of Sand
> And Heaven in a Wild Flower,
> Hold Infinity in the palm of your hand
> And Eternity in an hour.
> ...
> The Beggar's Rags fluttering in Air,
> Does to Rags the Heavens tear.
> ('Auguries of Innocence')

Interpreters like Blake challenge us to think about our use of Scripture, our tendency to caution lest we may be taken into paths that are both unfamiliar and uncomfortable.

What all these examples stress is that the Bible has been, and still can be, a key that can function to enable a creative understanding of God and the world as people's own experience is brought alongside the biblical passages. There is little or no attempt to find out the meaning of the passage and then apply it to a modern situation. Rather there is a creative interplay between the modern situation and the biblical text in which one plays off the other to throw new light on both.

Feminist biblical interpretation

A tradition of reading Scripture that is both democratic and participative is a good place to start a consideration of the issues and priorities in feminist biblical interpretation. Several of the themes noted in our discussion of liberation theology are directly applicable to feminist practices of reading the Bible, for example the politics of Bible interpretation, the significance of the Christian community, and the relationship between the Bible and life.

Politically speaking, the emphasis on the role of the uneducated, or rather of those not having had a traditional academic theological education, and the role of the socially and economically powerless, is echoed in feminist approaches to biblical interpretation where the experiences and views of women in such categories are taken with the utmost seriousness. The more the cultural and/or the religious background has traditionally kept women silent and excluded, the more striking is this emphasis. Kwok Pui-lan, writing of Asian feminist interpretations of the Bible, examines the recovery of the memory of women in the Bible to serve as role models in male-dominated churches:

> For example, a group of Asian women found that Naomi and Ruth were extraordinarily confident and courageous women, who participated actively in shaping their own destiny. In sharp contrast, the images of women conveyed from the pulpits are often gentle, submissive and obedient. (52)

This shows one cultural context; a quite different one is illustrated by an experienced woman in a Cambridge class who declared that after teaching RE to A level all her life she could just tolerate not being allowed to lead the Bible study in her church, but when the man leading came to ask to borrow her notes that was the last straw. In such contexts women's raised voices are effectively per se voices of political protest, challenging the dominant ideology of the churches.

The communal dimension of biblical interpretation, and the connection of this to liturgy and preaching, are important for Christian feminist theologians. Shared practices in the 'formation, and maintenance, of a literate theological community in which all God's people can contribute from the benefits of the Spirit' are a high priority. Here, very clearly, the pastoral practice of the churches will enable or disable the participation of the whole community – whether that be in home groups, Bible study meetings, pastoral visiting or the planning and the conducting of worship and preaching. Feminist approaches will always bring the 'gender question' to these issues, asking who has power to make decisions, to speak in public, to give an opinion that is taken seriously, or literally to handle the Bible.

Finally, feminist interpreters of the Bible are centrally interested in the connections between the Scriptures and our contemporary lives. They share with other liberation theologians a concern to use real life as an interpretative key to the Bible, indeed specifically the lives and struggles for justice of the poor and despised. Within this shared concern, however, can be identified two areas where feminist interpretation has difficulties and priorities not shared by liberation interpretation more generally. These arise from the specific experiences of women and the specific nature of the biblical text.

The Bible as the problem

The Bible was written in a patriarchal culture, and has been interpreted predominantly in patriarchal cultures until and including today. This coincidence of cultures has a mutually reinforcing effect. As a result women seeking to read the Bible in the light of recognising and resisting the patriarchal nature of society (a basic definition of what it is to be a feminist, which is more inclusive than many would imagine) find that the Bible itself may be more of a problem than other liberation approaches find it to be. For a start, women's experiences and voices are not nearly as easy to find as men's in the Bible, and when they are found they may be as worrying as they are helpful. Second, the actual view of women that prima facie has divine legitimation in the Bible, is in itself problematic. I shall take the second of these issues first.

At the end of a course, for ordinands and others training for Christian ministry, on the theology of Rosemary Radford Ruether, a feminist theologian, the group spent a day together writing a liturgy expressing what we had learned. After a while one woman said, 'We need a Bible reading in this service.' Another young woman responded, 'I would find that very difficult. The Bible has been used to damage me and downgrade my ministry so often; in this space where I have felt safe I don't want the Bible.' This incident reveals the depths of damage that are concealed under 'normal' Christian lives. It indicated a use of the Bible to legitimate the dominance of men in the ecclesial and domestic spheres and also to legitimate an estimation of the character, calling and abilities of women, which was experienced as undervaluing to the point of destructiveness.

A seminar group was discussing the interpretation of the texts in the New Testament about wives being submissive to their husbands (Eph. 5:21–33; Col. 3:18–19; 1 Pet. 3:1–6). The group was reluctant to accept that otherwise apparently 'normal' Christian men might deliberately use such texts to justify their own violence against their wives – until one of the members told us that her husband had done so for years. These examples of women's experiences are in no way isolated, and the connections between a biblical faith and domination and violence are well documented, both in academic research, in church studies and in contemporary literature. The father who rules his family by fear in Barbara Kingsolver's *The Poisonwood Bible* is a good example.

The Bible is a double-edged sword. It has without doubt been a source of hope and emancipation for women, as the Mexican theologian Elsa Tamez expresses:

> The tendency of some First World radical feminists to reject the Bible is … an exaggerated reaction. I think that by assigning too much importance to these peripheral texts, many leave aside the central message, which is profoundly liberating. From my point of view, it is precisely the gospel's spirit of justice and freedom that neutralizes antifemale texts. (176)

The Bible has, however, fuelled and underpinned abusive interpretations that have caused degradation and damage to women. 'Women as well as men have internalised scripture's misogynist teachings as the Word of God' (Schüssler Fiorenza, 1). 'Misogynist teachings' refers to such things as the legitimation of the male as the dominant partner in marriage and in social leadership, the prescription of women's speech, clothing and demeanour, and the stereotyping of 'woman' as sexual temptress.

The problem lies deep and has a complex set of tentacles that interlock. It is not only a question of the way in which women are portrayed, or even the acceptance of patriarchally constructed relationships between men and women; it is at a much deeper level an issue of the kind of God portrayed in the Bible, and the nature of the God who endorses and authorises the Bible. The problem stretches right back into our Christology and our doctrine of God. First there is the fact that the images and language for God, and the actions ascribed to God, are predominantly male in character. The male, and stereotypically masculine attitudes, capacities and actions are thus more highly valued and regarded as 'godlike'. Second, it is this God whose omnipotence authorises and guarantees the sacred text. Third, it is this God whose authorised interpreters are so often male, the justification for which is both biblical and also based on the very nature of God in Christ. There is a vicious circle here whose roots are ideological and whose grip on the Church in most of its life is tenacious and impossible to eradicate.

Women's experience – authority, violence and identity

Specific to feminist biblical interpretation is the question of women's experience. Liberation theology privileges the voices of those who are not being heard, of the oppressed. This in itself is based on an understanding of God's 'bias to the poor', as seen and expressed in the Bible. Rosemary Radford Ruether expresses this as the 'prophetic principle', seen most clearly in the Old Testament prophets and the life of Jesus, in which religion that supports the oppressive status quo is challenged by God's message of justice and flourishing for the oppressed. This she sees as being directly in correlation with the critical principle of feminist theology, which is the promotion of the full humanity of women.

Such a privileging of the experience of women gives rise to some concern among those for whom it is important to 'sit under the authority of the Bible'. What do we make, for example, of Marjorie Procter-Smith's contention that in feminist liturgical proclamation 'This commitment to women takes precedence over commitment to scriptural texts, recognizing that many scriptural texts have been and continue to be used to inhibit women's emancipation'? (314).

While some feminist biblical interpretation sits firmly with the ethos of liberation theology, committed to the biblical story of God's redemption, other voices within the discipline find that women's experience raises radical question marks over that story itself. Still others are interested in the Bible as a literary text or as a political and strategic religious document rather than as sacred and redemptive scripture.

It is in itself problematic to speak of privileging the experience of women as an interpretive key, since we must first ask, which women and which experience? There are different and contradictory voices within feminist theology. Two outstanding examples are the implicit racism of much early white North American feminist theology, and the anti-Judaism latent in interpretations that uncritically exalt the liberative practice of Jesus by contrast with the Judaism of his time. The question of the 'authority' of the text in relation to women's experience is further nuanced by the question of which 'women's experience' is brought to bear on the text. Numbers 12:1–16 may be understood quite differently depending on whether one highlights the gender question in relation to Miriam's role, or the 'race' and colour question in relation to Miriam and the Cushite woman, and the leprosy *white* as snow.

One particular feature of women's concrete lived experience which must be faced in relation to the biblical text, is the experience of violence.

> One of the most urgent challenges to emerge from the Decade of Churches in Solidarity with Women was expressed with courage and clarity by women from every corner of the globe. There is a global epidemic of physical, sexual, psychological, racial and cultural violence against women. It happens everywhere, including churches of all traditions and communions. (WCC 2001, 51)

Such violence is often justified by the perpetrators and those who collude in it on theological and biblical grounds. It was in 1984 that Phyllis Trible first published her book *Texts of Terror*. Her title has become a classic description of those passages in the Bible where the violence, and often sexual, abuse of women is portrayed. Trible's examples are the abuse of Lot's daughters, the murder of Jephthah's daughter, the rape of Tamar and the dismemberment of the unnamed woman in Judges 19. From the violent sexual and anti-female imagery of Hosea 2 and Ezekiel 16 to the injunctions to female submission in 1 Timothy 2 and 1 Peter 3, the Bible underwrites male dominance and suspicion of female sexuality. Such dominance and suspicion is the very stuff that fuels violence against women.

Given this, Carole Fontaine's question whether the Bible is abusive is neither frivolous nor faithless. It is a serious question, which those concerned for the faithful pastoral practice of the churches must address. Riet Bons-Storm writes:

> To acknowledge gender and sex in the pursuit of pastoral knowledge

> and practice means analysing the different meanings given to having a male or female body, and trying to find out what it means for a person to live faithfully as a sexual and embodied human being. (36)

Feminist pastoral theology addresses itself centrally to this question, of what it means to be a woman made in the image of God, and crucially to these two questions. First, how may the Bible be 'read, marked and inwardly digested' in such a way as to find out what it means to live faithfully in a female body? Second, what has the Bible to offer in the shaping of such faithful living that will bring wholeness and flourishing rather than damage and diminishment?

The liturgical, devotional and educational reading of the Bible is a means of shaping the lives of the faithful. This gives the Bible, and its authorised and respected interpreters within the community, immense power in shaping faithful identity. Feminist biblical interpretation asks questions about what kind of identities women in Christian communities are forming as they engage with the Bible as it is mediated to them. Forms of democratic and participative Bible interpretation are best placed to allow a helpful engagement between the text and the experience of women. Here also the theme which emerged from Blake's work – imagination – is vitally important.

The feminist biblical scholarship which engages with confessional theology and the practices of the churches can provide the means for women to find themselves in the text, and for both women and men to hear submerged voices in the text. The work of Elisabeth Schüssler Fiorenza has been seminal in both these respects. She has highlighted through historical and textual scholarship the extent to which women's voices and experiences are submerged in our biblical text. In her later work she has shown how we can creatively and imaginatively listen to some of those submerged voices. In so doing we can enter into the text ourselves as women, finding our own identity in dialogue with the story of God's life-giving love and liberation in the Bible.

> Years of pent-up emotion spilled from me in a torrent, unchecked. As I wept my tears of confession, I remembered all the wrong I had done. As I wept tears of anger and resentment, I remembered all the wrongs that had been done to me, and to women like me. As I wept tears of grief I remembered losses; my lost life, my lost identity and lost voice. (Kath Saltwell, quoted in Bennett Moore, 58)

Conclusion: reading the Bible pastorally

Interpretation of the Bible is a central issue in the pastoral practice of the churches. Our examination of liberation and feminist approaches has uncovered several themes familiar to pastoral theologians. In recent years pastoral theologians have explored the interweaving of the stories of our lives and the narratives of the Scriptures as a way to understand the role of the Bible in a postmodern context, and also the interpretation of such stories and their interweaving as a way to understand the role of the pastor. Identity is a paramount issue here: the identity of all God's people, male and female, slave and free, of whatever educational or cultural background.

In this the text of life is 'read" along with the text of the Scriptures, as was most clearly seen in the interpretations of the Base Ecclesial Communities. Pastoral theology has since the work of Anton Boisen in the 1930s appropriated the commitment to read not only the written texts of Bible, tradition and theology, but also the 'living human documents'. As a more communal and less individualistic paradigm has emerged within pastoral theology, the image of the 'living human web', as suggested by the feminist pastoral theologian Bonnie Miller-McLemore, may seem more appropriate. This emphasis has emerged strongly in our discussion of the communal dimensions of liberation and feminist interpretation of the Scriptures. The building of the 'New Jerusalem' as the task of all God's people arises from and is fed by such approaches to the Bible.

The 'practical wisdom of shared practice and the debate about practice' does not only open up human practices, perspectives and commitments, but also opens up the creative understanding of God, and enables us to see the kind of God portrayed in our written and our living documents. Practice in respect of the reading of the Scriptures contributes to the task of pastoral theology as a theologically disclosive discipline.

The family of liberationist and advocacy theologies, in their interpretation and use of the Bible, thus contribute substantially to the specific tasks of contemporary pastoral theology. The wealth of the Bible is the wealth of all God's people, and the counting out of it, and the weighing up of it, are essential elements of that reflection on practice which is also the task of all God's people. Liberation theologies offer methods and invite commitments that drive that task forward.

Bibliography

Bennett Moore Z. (2002) *Introducing Feminist Perspectives in Pastoral Theology*. Sheffield: Sheffield Academic Press.

Bons-Storm, R. (1996) *The Incredible Woman: listening to women's silences in pastoral care and counseling*. Nashville, TN: Abingdon Press.

Fiorenza, E. Schüssler (ed.) (1994) *Searching the Scriptures: a feminist introduction*. London: SCM Press.

Kwok, Pui-lan (2000) *Introducing Asian Feminist Theology*. Sheffield: Sheffield Academic Press.

Pitt, J. (1978) *Good News for All*. London: CAFOD.

Procter-Smith, M. (1993) Feminist interpretation and liturgical proclamation, in E.

Schüssler Fiorenza (ed.), *Searching the Scriptures: a feminist introduction*. London: SCM Press, 313–25.

Tamez, E. (1988) Women's rereading of the Bible, in V. Fabella and M. A. Oduyoye (eds), *With Passion and Compassion*. Maryknoll, NY: Orbis Books.

Van Braght, T. J. (1987) *The Martyrs Mirror*. Scottdale, PA: Herald Press.

WCC Network of Theological Research and Teaching: Decade to Overcome Violence 2001–2010 (2001) Overcoming violence against women. *Ministerial Formation* 93. Geneva: WCC Publications.

West, G. (1999) *The Academy of the Poor: towards a dialogical reading of the Bible*. Sheffield: Sheffield Academic Press.

PART III: The Bible and Pastoral Theology and Practice

This third section is somewhat more disparate than the previous two. Each chapter starts from a moment, tradition or theory within pastoral practice, and asks how the Bible should inform that practice, reflecting our recognition that such practice is multifaceted.

Herbert Anderson offers an account of how pastoral theologians have sought to understand the different ways in which the Bible has been used over the past decades, before revisiting a proposal that (post)modern understandings of narrative might offer a way of connecting text and practice. If the Bible is understood in fundamentally narrative terms, following on from indications offered in Part II, and human personhood is seen as an interweaving of many different narratives, then ways of applying the Bible to the care of human persons can be developed. He also notes the importance of cultural context, taking illustrations from examples such as Black theology. In this he links into the discussions set out by Bennett and Rowland and Couture.

John Colwell describes the Church as an ethical community, and asks how the Scriptures should shape that community. He offers perceptive criticisms of several current models of deriving ethical precepts from biblical texts, rejecting the attempts to find rules or principles or resources for reflection on experience/practice. In place of all of these, he again reaches for the concept of narrative: Scripture tells the story that grounds and guides the life of the Church, and so living within the Church is an indwelling (through the Holy Spirit, sacramentally mediated) of the story of the Bible.

David Lyall and Michael Quicke address the linked realities of worship and preaching. Both are careful to address the (disputed) relationship between these public events and the exercise of pastoral care. Lyall looks at the opportunities given in the 'occasional offices' (baptisms, weddings and funerals) where the relationship is perhaps more transparent, before offering some helpful reflection on the pastoral function of the Eucharist. Quicke offers a robust defence of the centrality of preaching to the pastoral task, informed by the 'new homiletics' that has so energised the study of preaching in American seminaries in the last few years, which can be seen as having affinities to some of the more recent approaches to biblical interpretation.

Derek Tidball and Philip Endean address two major strands of Christian spirituality: evangelical and Ignatian, and ask how the Bible functions within them. A particular attitude towards the Bible is obviously central for evangelicalism, rooted as it is in a particular strand of Protestantism, although Tidball helpfully points out the range of different positions that are, in practice, found. With particular reference to J. C. Ryle, but also to the wider discussion, he explores both the theological basis for evangelical belief in the centrality of the Bible for spiritual growth, and also the practical spiritual exercises that are traditionally recommended. Endean chooses to approach contemporary Catholic spirituality through a classically representative figure, St Ignatius Loyola, whose advice on praying with the gospels has been so influential, advice that has taken on a greater importance at a time of spiritual enquiry and renewed interest in contemplation and retreats. Ignatius offers an imaginative, open-ended way of encountering the biblical narratives and being changed by them, a way that can have profound pastoral consequences, as Endean illustrates.

Finally in this section, there is material relating to the artistic interpretation of the Bible, and how that might affect pastoral practice. Pamela Couture, again moving out of the Western context, movingly describes hearing Scripture interpreted through song in the Democratic Republic of Congo, and explores how that music functions pastorally, especially in terms of community building, overcoming political and cultural barriers and personal acceptance. Gail Ricciuti offers a broader discussion of the visual arts, exploring in anecdote and looking at key ideas of how Bible and art can intersect to provide pastoral help and resource for Christian people by engaging the emotions and imagination.

The overall impression is that there is growing exploration going on in practical theology about the use of the Bible as a resource to inform pastoral practice and as to how to engage with the themes and text of the Bible. There are clear signs that some of the new approaches to biblical interpretation are being welcomed and are actively drawn on in the quest to establish pastoral practice on more adequate theological foundations. However, in the ever-changing kaleidoscope of the contemporary situation it is unlikely that any one pattern will emerge as dominant. Rather, we are likely to find ourselves in a rich mixture of usages shaped by traditional and cultural differences, yet responding to the demands of living in very different circumstances. But this surely does not mean anything goes. There is a need to pay attention to the requirement of authenticity and truthfulness towards both the faith and the Scripture and to the present circumstances. Christian pastoral practice will always be explorative as well as hopeful and liberating. Practical theology is a mediating discipline whose task it is to support and encourage theologically practitioners in their day-to-day activity and to interpret the experience of those engaged in pastoral care as a resource for theological reflection and insight. This is not an easy position to be in; and from the point of view of this project obviously demands a great deal more careful and detailed enquiry both to tease out further the fundamental issues and to sustain the ongoing exploration that seems to be the inevitable consequence.

Perhaps the next task, therefore, is to move the discussion decisively more towards stimulating and evaluating actual practice, to work at a much more concrete level and to take greater note of how the Bible actually works with people as they seek to live faithfully. At the more formal level ways could be sought to bring together small groups of biblical scholars, pastoral practitioners and theologians over a significant period to engage with those 'at the coal face' in a particular context, who are struggling to let the Bible speak. Much could be learned from the experience of the 'base communities' of Latin America or the spontaneous folk spirituality of Africa. Such enquiries would have to be written up, so as to be accessible to a wider audience and contribute to the networks already exploring avenues of Christian experience and service that happen piecemeal across a wide range of pastorally relevant areas, such as pastoral care, worship and preaching, community and social involvement and spirituality.

CHAPTER 11:
The Bible and pastoral care

HERBERT ANDERSON

The goals and modes of pastoral care have varied over the centuries according to the demands of the culture or the needs of the situation, but the aim has been the same: to respond to human pain and struggle with understanding, compassion and grace. Sometimes, however, listening in the care of souls was the prelude to admonition, comfort, advice or judgement drawn from the Bible or other teachings of the Christian Church. The modern practice of pastoral care, partly to avoid such didactic or moralistic patterns of ministry, has generally promoted supportive listening but relied more on psychological language than Scripture for interpreting human situations. As a result, the divine narrative is often overlooked in pastoral conversations.

When it has been part of pastoral care, the use of the Bible has varied widely depending on divergent views of scriptural interpretation or authority and differing approaches to care. Even if one could settle these differences, it is a difficult linkage to make, not only because of the secularity of modern societies but because the complexities of life today seem far removed from the biblical world view. The lingering influence of the historical-critical method, by cautioning against any use of the Bible that would distort its original meaning and intent, also contributes to the absence of biblical references in pastoral care. The aim in this chapter is to identify and examine the connections that have been made between the Bible and pastoral care and propose some new directions for this crucial linkage in the care of souls.

Connecting the Bible and pastoral care: a conundrum

My context for writing this essay has been as Canon for Pastoral Care at St Mark's Episcopal Cathedral in Seattle, Washington, in the most unchurched region in the United States. People who worship at the cathedral are often unfamiliar with the Bible and reluctant to give it more authority than the Koran or the poetry of W. H. Auden or the spiritual writings of Henri Nouwen. One parishioner, for example, described a 'quiet meditative time' on the island of Maui studying *The Gospel of Mary*, Milton's *Paradise Lost*, and the *Bhagavadgita.* For many people I have met at the cathedral, the Bible is simply a sacred story that kindles the 'God within'. Sacred stories are like that: tales of ultimate concern that reveal and nurture our relationship to the divine (Simpkinson and Simpkinson 1993). In that context, the use of the Bible in pastoral care is limited because biblical images or stories have little prior meaning or authority.

If some churches have found the Bible less and less relevant for pastoral care, more conservative approaches to the Bible have made it authoritative both as a spiritual resource and as the norm for methods of care and counselling. Jay E. Adams (1977) and Lawrence Crabb Jr (1977) expanded the authority of the Bible and absolutised biblical claims in what has become known as 'biblical or Christian counselling'. Recently, a minister who introduced himself as a 'biblical counsellor' told me that when he counsels couples, his first question, before anything else is said, is 'will you obey God's Word?' If they do not agree to such blanket obedience to the Bible without content, the counselling ends before it began. Biblical counselling is problematic because it disregards both the complexity of the Bible and the freedom of the human spirit. In *Caring for Souls: counseling under the authority of Scripture* (2001), Shields and Bredfeldt present a more moderate alternative to previous claims of biblical counsellors. 'The Bible is completely true and reliable as our standard of truth' (40). The Bible remains absolute authority for salvation even though it is not the only source of truth or the only resource for methods in pastoral care.

Between these two alternatives, there are a myriad of ways to link the Bible and pastoral care. Many still regard the Bible as a resource for faith and life without absolutising its authority. Others will use a biblical story or theme in order to symbolise a modern human dilemma without critical attention to its origins in the biblical text. Still others hold that biblical themes and stories remain authoritative for Christian living and retain the power to disclose an alternative vision of life for people unfamiliar with the Bible and uncertain of its authority. Despite differences in interpretation and use, the Bible continues to be regarded generally as a living Word that discloses the character and will of God.

We face a conundrum in reconnecting the Bible and pastoral care. On the one hand, use of the Bible in pastoral conversation is one way to reclaim the roots of pastoral care in the Christian tradition. New approaches to the interpretation of Scripture and new strategies for care increase the possibility of reclaiming biblical language and images in the work of pastoral care.

However, the context for implementing a new interaction between Scripture and pastoral care is increasingly secular and the people seeking care are more and more unfamiliar with biblical content and reluctant to ascribe authority to ancient texts from faraway places and times. In order to understand the origins of this conundrum more clearly, a brief historical review is necessary.

The early efforts to connect the Bible and pastoral care

When Wayne Oates wrote *The Bible in Pastoral Care* (1953), he could assume that people to whom a pastor ministered had a positive attitude toward the Bible and some familiarity with its stories or themes. The Bible, Oates wrote, is a 'handbook of church and personal discipline, a treasury of ideals of human thought, feeling and conduct under God' (29). With this authoritative claim in view, it was relatively easy for Oates to use the Bible in a pastoral way for counsel, challenge, consolation and spiritual sustenance for 'the quiet needs of every day'. This understanding of the relevance of the Bible was supported by biblical theologians of the time who sought to discover anew the relevance of the Bible as a guide to the will of God and a reminder of the availability of divine grace for daily living (McNeil 1952).

Carroll Wise took a more thematic approach than Oates in *Psychiatry and the Bible* (1956). He believed that the Bible, properly used, could have beneficial effect in the alleviating of emotional distress. Earlier, in *The Art of Ministering to the Sick* (1936 [1960]), Richard C. Cabot and Russell L. Dicks had proposed using biblical passages in a similar way to suggest a new perspective for hospital patients who were afraid or suffering. While the pastoral care movement had begun to challenge the Church to think in new ways about the practice of ministry, the approach retained traditional views regarding the revelation and authority of Scripture.

Several things can be said about the Bible and pastoral care from writings more than half a century ago that remain critical issues for our time.

It was assumed that the Bible was authoritative in faith and life with positive, symbolic meaning for most recipients of pastoral care. Whether the Bible is regarded as an authority by the care receiver is a key factor in determining the effectiveness and even appropriateness of its use in pastoral care. One pastor described her use of the Bible this way: 'I share a particular scripture with people when I think it might be helpful to them, but also because I think it might be good for them to hear God's voice through the scripture.' It is easier to use the Bible as a source of consolation or assurance as well as instruction when one believes that reading the Bible is a way to hear a word from God.

The needs of the person receiving care should determine not only the mode of care but also the way the Bible is used. Although that perspective gave significant authority to psychological interpretations of a pastoral situation, it was a necessary corrective to the tendency to use of texts in pastoral care without regard to context. Certain texts, Donald Capps contends, are more 'appropriate for the grieving, other texts fit the birth of a child, still others are helpful for persons facing a difficult life decision, and so forth' (1981, 51). In order to insure that the biblical texts used are relevant and will be received positively, we still need to listen very carefully both to Scripture and to the human situation. Relevance is still linked to authority.

The use of the Bible should be consistent with good counseling principles. Seward Hiltner articulated that maxim in his early book *Pastoral Counseling* (1949). Reference to Scripture, he insisted, did not justify moralising with biblical legalisms. However, it is also appropriate and necessary to criticise liberal churches for muffling the voice of Scripture through excessive caution or benign neglect. If the Bible is regarded as a book of laws or mandates for holy and just living, then it will be used to direct towards the good life. If, however, the Bible is a framework for understanding the human struggle, then it may be the 'royal road' to the deeper levels of people seeking care, as Wayne Oates once observed (1953).

The use of the Bible adds a third voice to a pastoral conversation. Heije Faber and Ebel van der Schoot give only passing attention to the Bible as a distinctive resource for pastoral care in *The Art of Pastoral Conversation* (1965). They do suggest, however, that reading the Bible in a pastoral conversation diminishes the asymmetry of the relationship because both the helper and the one seeking help are on common ground, listening for a word from God. Even though the biblical reading has been chosen by the pastoral person, a new authority is introduced into the conversation to which both submit. Both participate in the same listening attitude to what God has to say. 'As a consequence the pastor who has explicitly given a place to the word of the Bible does something which will distract attention away from his own person, will prevent too strong a dependency upon him, and will explicitly refer to God' (210). This 'leveling before the Word' is particularly beneficial when the one seeking care has invested the caregiver with inordinate authority. The benefit of this use of Scripture as a pastoral intervention still depends for its effectiveness on a willingness to acknowledge the disclosure power of the Bible.

Early efforts to link the Bible and pastoral care should not be faulted for failing to take seriously the complexity of Scripture. We know now more clearly that the significance of the Bible is neither self-evident nor self-interpreting. Nor are there clear principles for using the Bible in pastoral care. Reference to the Bible requires human interpretation that will be inevitably personal and therefore must be provisional. Pastoral situations also require interpretation. The realisation that we are always interpreting situations and texts in forming an individual or communal narrative makes the task of connecting the Bible and pastoral care today both much more complex and infinitely easier. It is more difficult because we must be attentive to layers and layers of pre-understandings that influence any interpretive act. Linking the Bible and pastoral care is easier because there is new freedom to use narrative frameworks to connect our stories with the Christian story. Three pastoral theologians have explored the problems and possibilities of reconnecting the Bible and pastoral care: Donald Capps, Stephen Pattison and Charles Gerkin.

Three perspectives on linking the Bible and pastoral care

Donald Capps

No one has written more about the Bible and pastoral care or counselling than Donald Capps. His assessment of the literature emphasises the role of the Bible as a spiritual resource for pastoral care. In *Biblical Approaches to Pastoral Counseling* (1981), he proposed that the psalms be used in grief counselling, proverbs in pre-marital counselling and parables in marriage counselling. 'While these three biblical forms favor different types of metaphors, what unites them is their use of metaphors to deal with our sense of disorientation' (208). Understood this way, the Bible may be a resource for individuals and families whose lives are destabilised by unsettling transitions or radical change.

Capps identifies four principles that are constant in every effort to connect the pastoral care and the Bible. The first three principles of relevance, sensitivity and consistency regard therapeutic strategies as normative for how the Bible is used. A fourth principle proposes that whatever use is made of the Bible in pastoral care and counselling, it should be informed by the counsellor's awareness that biblical texts have the power to change attitudes, behaviour and perceptions (12–13).

For Capps, adding the principle of biblical power to effect change also redefines his principle of consistency. 'It is not that the Bible is conformed to therapeutic goals, but that the use of psychological theories and methods is to be consistent with the disclosive power of the Bible' (13). The 'disclosive role of the text' does not diminish the importance of listening carefully to the human story in the practice of pastoral care. Instead, it adds new criteria for evaluating therapeutic theories and techniques used in pastoral care: they should be determined by the disclosive power of the biblical texts used.

Stephen Pattison

Without acknowledging that scriptural texts have disclosive power, Stephen Pattison develops this point of view further in *A Critique of Pastoral Care* (2000). The historical-critical method, he argues, became a major division in the use of the Bible for pastoral care. Modern biblical criticism dealt a lethal blow to the traditional 'Scripture principle' that the Bible was inspired by God and uniquely authoritative for Christian living. Because the Bible is the work of human hands, its authority is limited and its applicability in pastoral situations is curtailed.

The insights of biblical criticism, especially those concerning the difficulties of interpretation, indicate that it is very difficult to relate the Bible to any modern situation without either subordinating the texts to the interests of the situation or, conversely, trying to make the latter fit one's own version of the meaning of the text. The former is danger for liberals, the latter for biblicists (Pattison, 114).

With these cautions in mind about relating the Bible to present pastoral situations, Pattison identifies five main approaches to using (or perhaps more accurately, misusing, in the case of the *biblicist* approach) Scripture in pastoral care. Whether the approach is *tokenistic* or *suggestive* or *informative*, Pattison contends, the Bible is neither a handbook for pastoral care nor can individual passages be used as a 'spiritual bromide in every pastoral situation' (129) or an 'analgesia for needy individuals' (130).

Although he acknowledges that the *thematic* approach is least likely to distort either the Bible or the pastoral situation, Pattison is nonetheless critical of William Oglesby's *Biblical Themes for Pastoral Care* (1980) because it misuses biblical texts by taking them out of context and applying them to pastoral situations in a piecemeal fashion. Pattison sets the bar high for using Scripture in a manner consistent with the historical-critical method. And he is correct in insisting that 'the biblical writings do not form a handbook of personal pastoral care, nor can individual passages of them be used as a spiritual bromide in every pastoral situation' (129).

Pattison's rigorous criticisms sounded a cautious alarm, however, and perhaps indirectly contributed to the silence of Scripture in pastoral situations today. His intent is to correct the misuse of the Bible, particularly in the practice of pastoral care, but his criticisms are so extensive that they are unnecessarily restricting or inhibiting. Pattison's critical contributions are themselves limited by the limits of the historical-critical method for interpreting the Bible.

Charles Gerkin

The work of Charles Gerkin (1984, 1986) was a major influence in establishing 'pastoral interpretation' as the framework for linking Scripture with pastoral events or relationships. The pastoral hermeneutical effort is directed towards bringing hidden or unintelligible elements of a situation to awareness so that a fitting response may be made. Gerkin summarised the hermeneutical perspective in this way:

> The hermeneutical perspective has become for me a way of seeing the life

> of the self or, in more Christian terms, the life of the soul. That life is first and fundamentally a life of interpretation of experience. (1984, 34)

The Bible is not simply a spiritual resource according to preset therapeutic strategies, or the authoritative guide that shapes pastoral action. Rather, the focus of pastoral interpretation is on a dynamic process of reciprocal influence in which the presumptions of the pastoral interpreter of both Scripture and the human situation are examined. Imagination is one dimension of the interpretation of both persons and text because it invites images of meaning and reality beyond observable experience and beyond a singular reading of the text or the situation. New perspectives in biblical interpretation have created freedom to move beyond both an overly simplistic equation between the biblical world and ours and an overly cautious distancing of Scripture from the present situation. The final aim of interpretation is to fashion liberating narratives of human life and life in God.

The narrative perspective and pastoral care

- The narrative approach reflects three interrelated assumptions about the nature of reality;
- reality is socially constructed over time and in time;
- reality is constituted through language and metaphorical speech;
- these socially constituted realities are organised and maintained through narrative.

People make sense of their lives through stories they fashion and cultural narratives into which they are born. Although the story of my life has included experiences and possibilities I did not imagine in my youth, in another sense I am never very far from my Swedish Lutheran roots in the Midwest of the United States.

Narrative has become a significant framework for understanding situations of pastoral care. If we are defined by our stories, then caring for people means listening for stories, not for historical facts or psychological symptoms. Stories are the content of pastoral conversation. When we listen carefully to people, we discover that they often live with competing stories, with no overarching way of stitching their stories together into a coherent whole and little understanding of the connection between daily events and larger narratives of life and faith. The first pastoral task is still to hear the story as fully and completely as possible. We must know their stories in order to help people reframe them.

The liberating promise of the narrative perspective is that if our lives are socially constructed, they may also be reconstructed. We are never fully trapped in the narratives we construct. It is always possible to narrate our lives in another way. Consequently, storytelling is an act of hope, and even defiance, because it carries within it the power to change. Although she does not make specific reference to the Bible, Christie Cozad Neuger is clear that a major part of the work of pastoral counselling from a narrative perspective is 'to help people generate new language and new interpretive lenses and thus create new realities' (2001, 232). If the aim of pastoral care and counselling is understood as helping people refashion their life story 'through the lens' of God's story, then the Bible is inextricably linked to the care of souls.

Besides finding our place in the divine narrative, we also want to discover God's presence in the human saga. One of the reasons why biblical stories are treasured is because of their timeless ability to narrate God's presence in the midst of human events. The Scriptures are full of stories about the presence of God in ordinary moments of sleeping or eating or fishing or meeting with friends. Such storytelling reveals the interrelated webs that constitute the fabric of our lives and locates us in the larger drama of God's journey with God's people. Adding a biblical framework to the lens through which we see another's story is an authentic reappropriation of the Christian heritage of pastoral care.

The Bible: our stories and God's stories

The Bible is first of all a book about stories of God and faith in God. The Bible tells the story of God in narrative form. The biblical narrative is the account of a creating, covenanting, redeeming, and sustaining God whose character is love. God is hidden and revealed, present and absent, powerful and vulnerable in the divine narrative. The language of biblical stories is metaphorical because it is the only way for humans to speak about the mystery of God. At the same time, the divine narrative is about the human struggle to live in the story of God.

The Bible is a book of human stories about unbridled passion, remarkable births, sibling rivalry, military heroics, political intrigue, and the complex dynamics of family living. As a remarkably honest collection of stories of the human struggle, the Bible is a book of observation as well as revelation. It is a script that reveals God's relentless love for the world and at the same time observes with ruthless honesty the human struggle to live faithfully in that love. Stephen Pattison acknowledged this human dimension to the biblical story: 'While the biblical writings do not give a literal historical record, they do give a profoundly truthful and eternally relevant account of aspects of the human condition' (111).

As such, the Bible is a literary resource for validating human experience today even when it is not regarded as divine authority. That is the point of empathy in pastoral care. When we are able to mirror back to someone their story, we not only let them know it has been heard: we confirm or validate that their experience is real. And that experience of validation is a word of grace. When people feel stuck or trapped in a negative narrative, the task of pastoral care is to create a framework in which they might think about their story in new and liberating ways.

Our stories and God's stories are inextricably linked together. When we are fully attentive to the stories of God, we are also in the midst of the human story – valuing our own past, pushed by the power of story, strangely aware of the One whom we dare to call God. Weaving the human and the divine enables us to hear our own stories retold with clarity and new possibility. And when we hear our own stories retold in relation to a larger and deeper narrative, our lives are transformed in the telling.

In *Mighty Stories, Dangerous Rituals: Weaving Together the Human and the Divine* (Anderson and Foley 1998), my colleague and I explored the relationship between narrative and ritual, worship and pastoral care. While the book is clear about the importance of reweaving human and divine stories, it did not explore how that work is done in the practice of pastoral care. What methods need to be fostered in the practice of pastoral care that will facilitate forming a transforming narrative? What situations lend themselves most readily to linking human and divine stories? How will reweaving a new life narrative liberate people from old confining stories, strengthen their sense of belonging, or free people to live more responsibly in the world? The aim of pastoral care, we argued, is

> to assist people in weaving the stories of their lives and God's stories as mediated through the community into a transformative narrative that will liberate them from confining narratives, confirm their sense of belonging, and strengthen them to live responsibly in the world. (48)

People discover new purpose and freedom when they begin to see their story in a larger narrative. Each of us has stories to tell that allow the divine narrative to unfold, and all human stories are potential windows to the story of God. The remainder of this chapter picks up this task.

Pastoral strategies for fostering a transforming narrative

Some methods or strategies of care are implicit in a narrative perspective. There are also therapeutic strategies informing the work of pastoral care today that encourage our weaving the human and divine stories together.

The caregiver is always an interpreter. When we listen, we interpret, whether we intend to or not. Every response to another's story is interpretation. The inevitability of interpretation in all human activity means that the neutrality of the caregiver is unachievable. The question is not whether our own perspective will intrude on a pastoral conversation but how it will and when. What some family therapists have referred to as 'the use of self' encourages the responsible, and always tentative, utilisation of a caregiver's own experience and interpretation in a pastoral moment.

Behind the narrative approach to Scripture is the presumption that truth is more than one. There is, therefore, more than one way of understanding any particular situation. *Saying the other side is sometimes a necessary pastoral strategy* in order to be sure that the whole story is told. By 'saying the other side' I mean something like inviting individuals and family members to examine what they believe and think how to interpret an event from a different, and maybe even contradictory perspective. 'Saying the other side' is necessary so that the silent voices are heard and the marginalised ones are included and no one idea or individual dominates. 'Saying the other side' is a way to avoid absolutising. In the face of fear and uncertainty and so much senseless suffering and flux, there is the human tendency to look for absolutes. Telling a biblical story or parable is one gentle way of inviting people to see another side to their story.

Edward Wimberly has written about the use of the Bible in pastoral counselling from an African American perspective with people who are largely familiar with Bible stories (1994). Wimberly is clear how biblical stories and characters had shaped his perception of reality and he uses biblical stories in a similar way. This is an important book if for no other reason than it proposes unapologetically to use biblical stories to reshape a person's view of reality. Here is how Wimberly states his use of the Bible in pastoral counselling:

> I am interested in how the Scriptures work to set us free from negative personal, marriage, and family mythologies and how this liberating activity can be blocked. My faith perspective leads me to proclaim that there is an objective reality behind the liberating work of Bible stories. (72)

The Bible is a spiritual resource that facilitates growth as well as consoles in the midst of a crisis. Although Wimberly may be correct in insisting that his approach works with people who are unfamiliar with the Bible, it is less likely to be an effective method for those who do not regard the Bible as an authority in faith and life. Regarding the Bible as an authoritative resource for life as well as faith is finally more important than knowing the biblical narrative in helping people live in a new narrative.

Being a pastoral person is liminal work. The power of the Bible, as Walter Brueggemann has observed, is that it is a primal antidote to technique and trivialisation. In order to evade ambiguity, we are tempted to 'thin the Bible and make it one-dimensional … [reducing] what is urgent and immense to what is exhaustible trivia' (Brueggemann, Placher and Blount 2002, 26). The paradox of pastoral care is this: we are familiar with the messy stuff of life and at the same time we are *theotokos* or bearers of God. In order to mediate between the all-embracing, ever-elusive mystery of the Divine and the ordinary stuff of human life, we need to be in habitual contact with the mystery of God while standing in the midst of human pain and struggle. In that sense, pastoral care is liminal work. The Bible is a dependable road to the divine mysteries. That is why it is so important for us to learn the art of weaving human and divine stories. Double listening and bimodal thinking are at the centre of the care of souls.

Pastoral care in a narrative mode must balance the mythic and the parabolic in life. Attending to biblical parables and to the parabolic in life has frequently been explored in writings about the Bible and pastoral care (Gerkin 1984; Capps 1981, 1990; Anderson and Foley). Parables subvert. Myths iron out the contradictions of our lives. Parables seek change by undermining the comfortable myths by which we seek to order chaos and unpredictability. The double function of myth is this: the resolution of a particular contradiction or set of contradictions and, more importantly, the creation of a belief in the permanent possibility of reconciliation. Parable, on the other hand, is not about mediation, but about contradiction. Parables show the fault lines beneath the worlds we build for ourselves. If the stories we create are to be authentic reflections of the lives we live, we need room for ambiguity and vulnerability. Parabolic narratives show the seams and edges of the myths we fashion. Myth may give stability to our story, but parables are agents of change. The paradox of the Christian story is that Christ achieves mythic reconciliation in a parabolic mode.

Weaving together human and divine stories

There are three situations in human life in which weaving together human and divine stories occurs naturally, even for those who have little familiarity with it and who do not regard the Bible as a source of authority for faithful living: the birth and baptism of an infant; marriage preparation; and death. While each pastoral moment is unique, the stories we fashion at these significant life-cycle moments have common themes that may connect with the larger human story through the biblical narrative. The ministry of pastoral care is particularly welcomed at these life-cycle events. They are occasions for telling and retelling the stories of our lives.

Birth. Each child is born into a web of stories, myths and legends. The naming process often adds new expectations carried in story for the life of the child. Inviting families at the moment of preparation for the baptism of a child to tell family birth stories may begin a process of retelling the significance of those stories from a wider perspective that might include the divine narrative.

Marriage. A marriage is a wedding of stories at many levels. The couple has a story of courtship. They may each have a life story of living alone that precedes the formation of this union. And each partner in a marriage brings a legacy of stories that carry values and rules and role expectations from their families of origin. Couples who are unfamiliar with the biblical narrative and for whom the Bible has little authority are nonetheless quite willing to explore Scripture in search of images or stories around which they might together form their new narrative.

Death. The work that someone who is dying has to do is to tell the story of a life, in so far as that is possible, so that the biography that is told after their death will be able to reflect the intentions of the dying. When we tell the stories of our lives in relation to the divine narrative, we invite people to identify purpose and meaning they might not otherwise have identified. We also make it possible for them to contribute their own perspective on their life for those who must fashion the biography of a life (Anderson and Foley, 57–122).

The task of weaving together human and divine stories without violating the integrity of the biblical narrative or the human story is seldom easy. Nonetheless, it is possible to connect biblical stories and our stories without violating the integrity of either. In *Jacob's Shadow: Christian Perspectives on Masculinity* (Anderson 2002), an effort to connect the male dilemma of today with the biblical narrative, a special resonance was found with Jacob's flawed humanity. The structure of this story provides a useful framework for understanding the costliness of deception and the agony of fear. The biblical character of Jacob is a man for our time because men can see themselves readily in his ambiguity.

> Jacob is a man for our time precisely because we can see ourselves in his ambiguity, we are comforted by his flawed humanity, and yet we are inspired by his persistent faithfulness … What I have learned from the Jacob story is that the journey to faithfulness in God is a bumpy road full of struggle and unexpected change. (5)

The Bible continues to be a spiritual resource but in this new way. When we weave together human and divine stories, our stories of God reflect at their deepest levels very human experiences of being overlooked or unacknowledged. If it is true that the need for recognition is a dominant force driving human beings, then there is some urgency to acknowledge human stories in the divine narrative and the divine narrative in human stories.

The Bible and pastoral care: the promise and the burden

New perspectives on interpreting the Bible and new approaches to pastoral care promise new possibilities for connecting the Bible and pastoral care in authentic ways. At the same time, there is a new awareness that pastoral care is ideally situated to recover the vital connection between the Bible and the moral dilemmas of our time. That is the burden. The work of pastoral care is frequently the context in which insights from the divine narrative intersect with the human story. We need transcending images that will enable us to lament in the face of pervasive irrational suffering. In cultures preoccupied with *technē,* the wisdom tradition provides an alternative vision of reality. The Bible is, however, more than a resource in pastoral care. There are common themes among the stories of God that provide thematic resources for rethinking the practice of pastoral care.

In his book *Integrity of Pastoral Care* (2001) David Lyall uses the term 'biblical care' to describe an approach to pastoral care grounded in biblical principles of covenant, community and the celebration of diversity. Lyall takes a similar thematic approach when he considers pastoral care in light of the Christ-event. The incarnation, he argues, implies that the 'communication of Christian truth is relational and not prepositional' (96). Pastoral care that is informed by the biblical narrative will embody the central themes of the Christ-event: incarnation, crucifixion, resurrection, and hope that endures in the Spirit of God.

What makes the incarnation a relevant theme for pastoral care is that the self-emptying of God is paradigmatic of the caregiver's emptying in order to make room for the other. Christ did not count equality with God something to hang on to, 'but emptied himself, taking the form of a servant being born in the likeness of humankind' (Phil. 2:5ff.). Effective pastoral care depends first of all on the ability to set aside personal needs and desires in order to make room for the life of the other. This emptying makes possible a kind of embodiment that ends with empathic understanding. In this way, the incarnation is the central paradigm for pastoral care. The incarnation, crucifixion, resurrection and ascension of Jesus not only shape the world view of pastoral caregivers: they also inform the structures of care.

The self-emptying of the caregiver is prelude to integrating human and divine stories. That integration does not depend on the correspondence between the person's story and the biblical story but on what is evoked within the caregiver. We hear the biblical story in the other's story when we listen with the disposition of wonder. When we listen with wonder, the recipient of pastoral care becomes the subject who incarnates for us the Gospel of God in surprising and vital ways. All care, it might be said, whether human or divine, moves from emptying to embodying and so to empathy (Anderson 1981).

The Bible will continue to be a spiritual resource for people who regard it as an authority for faith and life. Two recent books explore how the Bible may address the spiritual needs of people unfamiliar with its content and uncertain of authority. Daniel Schipani, in *The Way of Wisdom in Pastoral Counseling* (2003), proposes that 'wisdom in the light of God provides the guiding principle to reclaim and strengthen the theological and epistemological principles of pastoral counseling' (7–8). Even though his approach is more thematic and theological than biblical, I mention it here because 'wisdom in the light of God's reign' adds an emphasis on a vision of justice and moral agency to conversation about the Bible and pastoral care or counselling.

Rachel's Cry, subtitled *Prayer of Lament and the Recovery of Hope*, by pastoral theologian Kathleen D. Billman and systematic theologian Daniel L. Migliore (1999), is a compelling invitation to recover the prayer of lament as a way to hope in a time of irrational suffering and deepening despair. The question they ask is this: what guidance does the Bible and the theological tradition give us regarding the inclusion of lament as well as praise and thanksgiving in the practice of Christian living?

By the prayer of lament, Billman and Migliore mean the unsettling biblical tradition that includes expressions of complaint, anger, grief, despair and protest to God. They are most often, but not exclusively, found in the Psalms. While these prayers often make us uncomfortable, they are clearly an important part of the biblical tradition of prayer. Contrary to what we may assume, the Bible makes room in the life of faith for daring complaint to God rather than declaring such prayer off limits (6). This book is distinctive in its approach to lament in the Bible and in pastoral ministry in that, like Rachel's first cry of lament, the prayer of lament is addressed to the public spheres where injustice leads to unnecessary suffering. The recovery of lament is a critical alternative to apathy in our time. Unless we learn to lament, we are powerless in the face of so much irrational suffering in the world. We are empowered when we lament. It is something we can do when we feel powerless.

The structure of lament has implications for many aspects of the ministry of care and for the link between the Bible and pastoral care. The structure of lament is an alternation between resistance and relinquishment, between protesting against injustice and trusting in the mystery of God. Resistance without relinquishment ends in bitterness and relinquishment without resistance leads to quiet powerlessness in the face of evil. The language of lament gives voice to mute pain and creates communities of the suffering ones. The recovery of the language and structure of lament may be the most important aspect of connecting the Bible and pastoral care for our time. Recovering the rich biblical tradition of lament is necessary in order to live without apathy or the eclipse of hope in a time of pervasive irrational suffering.

A concluding postscript about words

Authentic expression of faith in God and care for others requires words. There is sighing in the presence of God too deep for words and there are human situations demanding care that render us mute, without words adequate to speak the depth or horror of human suffering. Most of the time we need words to validate the human story and convey our empathy. When we preach, we pay attention to the words we speak in order to render the hearts of the listeners pliable to a word from God. The work of pastoral care is the same. The gift of the parish ministries of care is that the preached word may become a resource for a moment of care. The words we use in response to another's story are ordinary holy words that are windows both to the divine and to the deeply human.

We are rightly cautious about making the pastoral care moment a bully pulpit or an occasion for admonishing. Good care is not individualised homiletics. Nor is it a moment for formulaic speech or unfamiliar images that do not resonate in modern ears. We have already noted that biblical images and stories are no longer common parlance in secular societies. Nonetheless, biblical language remains disclosive speech, opening us to words that invite us to see differently. In this sense, evocative biblical images and stories are as much a part of the tools of pastoral care as good listening skills and accurate empathy.

The care of souls has always sought to listen carefully to human stories and regard them seriously – even when they take us to the edge of being human. Because of the influence of the psychological paradigm, the language that has been used to describe the human one has included metaphors like psyche or self or person and more recently spirit, but seldom soul. Taking seriously our biblical roots and the disclosive power of biblical language may help to recover soul as the most comprehensive metaphor for the human one before God and from the earth. Soul (Hebrew *nephesh*) is the metaphor that reminds us most clearly that we come from God and yet we are from the earth as well. Soul is immersed in the world of human stories through intimacy, community, suffering and death. And yet the soul longs for God. Soul is the metaphor for the human one that most clearly embodies the liminal work of pastoral care between the human story of struggle and joy and the mystery that is God.

We often say about a moment of pastoral care that we have stood on holy ground, when we have been allowed to experience the depth of another's pain or been invited into the intimacy of very private fear or struggles of faith. It is also possible to think about such times as entering into the arena of

God-speak. Our words need to mirror God's blazing Word that is determined to melt frozen hearts or render our lives susceptible to the infectious love of God. Edward Foley has used the image of God as a 'wide-eyed insomniac pacing the night and scheming how to get us back'. In that sense, we are all open to being transformed. Standing on the 'holy ground' of a pastoral moment may be a dangerous thing precisely because both the recipient of care and the caregiver are vulnerable to God's relentless pursuit. The pastoral person might never be the same even if the one seeking care does not change. Experiences of authentic faith and good pastoral care are both moments when unexpected change is possible.

The biblical script insists that the world is not without God. We are very much aware that the darkness is real because of what we hear in listening care. What we all need is light enough to live boldly and faithfully in darkness we do not and cannot control. The Bible is a lamp, light enough to help us live in that darkness. Passionate, evocative words that startle and provoke us are more likely to pry open our hearts to the holy One who broods over us and longs for our love. The Bible is a resource of words that offers evocative images of hope and a transcending vision of God's relentless love that sustains as we care for one another in the darkness. In these times, we would do well to use what is entrusted to us in this book.

Bibliography

Adams, J. E. (1977) *The Use of Scriptures in Counseling*. Philadelphia: Presbyterian & Reformed.

Anderson, Herbert (1981) Incarnation and pastoral care, in *Pastoral Psychology* 32.4, 239–49.

Anderson, Herbert (2002) *Jacob's Shadow: Christian perspectives on masculinity*. Louisville, KY: Bridge Resources.

Anderson, Herbert and Foley, Edward (1998) *Mighty Stories, Dangerous Rituals: weaving together the human and the divine*. San Francisco: Jossey-Bass.

Billman, K. D. and Migliore, D. L. (1999) *Rachel's Cry: prayer of lament and rebirth of hope*. Cleveland, OH: United Church Press.

Brueggemann, W., Placher, W. C. and Blount, B. K. (2002) *Struggling with Scripture*. Louisville, KY: Westminster John Knox Press.

Cabot, R. C. and Dicks, R. L. (1960) *The Art of Ministering to the Sick*. New York: Macmillan.

Campbell, A. V. (1981) *Rediscovery of Pastoral Care*. London: Darton, Longman & Todd.

Capps, D. (1981) *Biblical Approaches to Pastoral Counseling*. Philadelphia: Westminster Press.

Capps, D. (1984) *Pastoral Care and Hermeneutics*. Philadelphia: Fortress Press.

Capps, D. (1990) *Reframing: a new method in pastoral care*. Minneapolis, MN: Fortress Press.

Capps, D. (1998) *Living Stories: pastoral counseling in congregational context*. Minneapolis, MN: Fortress Press.

Challis, W. (1997) *The Word of Life: using the Bible in pastoral care*. London: Marshall Pickering.

Crabb, L. J. Jr (1977) *Effective Biblical Counseling: a model for helping caring Christians become capable counselors*. Grand Rapids, MI: Zondervan.

Faber, H. and van der Schoot, E. (1965) *The Art of Pastoral Conversation*. New York: Abingdon Press.
Gerkin, C. V. (1984) *The Living Human Document: re-visioning pastoral counseling in a hermeneutical mode*. Nashville, TN: Abingdon Press.
Gerkin, C. V. (1986) *Widening the Horizons: pastoral responses to a fragmented society*. Philadelphia: Westminster Press.
Hiltner, S. (1949) *Pastoral Counselling*. New York: Abingdon-Cokesbury.
Hurding, R. F. (1992) *The Bible and Counselling*. London: Hodder & Stoughton.
Lyall, D. (2001) *The Integrity of Pastoral Care*. London: SPCK.
McNeil, J. T. (1952) *A History of the Cure of Souls*. London: SCM Press.
Neuger, C. C. (2001) *Counselling Women: a narrative pastoral approach*. Minneapolis, MN: Fortress Press.
Oates, W. E. (1953) *The Bible in Pastoral Care*. Philadelphia: Westminster Press.
Oglesby, W. B. Jr (1980) *Biblical Themes for Pastoral Care*. Nashville, TN: Abingdon Press.
Pattison, S. (2000) *A Critique of Pastoral Care*. London: SCM Press.
Schipani, D. S. (2003) *The Way of Wisdom in Pastoral Counseling*. Elkart, IN: Institute for Mennonite Studies.
Simpkinson, C. and Simpkinson, A. (eds) (1993) *Sacred Stories: a celebration of the power of stories to transform and heal*. New York: HarperCollins.
Shields, H. and Bredfeldt, G. (2001) *Caring for Souls: counseling under the authority of Scripture*. Chicago: Moody.
Wimberly, E. P. (1994) *Using Scripture in Pastoral Counseling*. Nashville, TN: Abingdon Press.
Wise, C. A. (1956) *Psychiatry and the Bible*. New York: Harper.

CHAPTER 12:

The Church as ethical community

JOHN COLWELL

Introduction

Amongst Protestants, if not amongst Catholics, Thomas Aquinas is rarely remembered as a 'practical' theologian. Yet his *Summa contra Gentiles* was probably intended as a handbook for Christian preachers working amongst Muslims in Spain, and his *Summa Theologica* claims 'to treat of whatever belongs to the Christian religion in such a way as may tend to the instruction of beginners' (*ST* xix). Moreover, the major part of this massive theological effort is devoted to an account of Christian virtue. Like Karl Barth's *Church Dogmatics*, it simply fails to acknowledge a distinction between doctrine and ethics, between what we are invited to believe and what we are invited to be (or to become). For Thomas the goal of human life is not merely, as it was for Aristotle, a temporal flourishing within society (*polis*) but an eternal vision of God: all human life is to be ordered to this goal; all virtues are to be ordered to the supreme theological virtue of love (*caritas*) which itself is also a passion. And inasmuch as Thomas gives space to a discussion of law, issues of what we ought to do, he does so within this overarching discussion of virtue, issues of what we ought to be. In recent years, and especially through the work of Alasdair MacIntyre, Jean Porter and Stanley Hauerwas, there has been something of a renaissance of virtue ethics amongst Christian moral theologians, though this has barely touched the life of the Church, at least in any conscious sense.

The Bible as a book of rules

Overwhelmingly in the churches known to me (and, I suspect, in churches not known to me so intimately) the Bible is 'used' practically and ethically as a compendium of rules, as a prescriptive and proscriptive blueprint for pastoral practice and moral behaviour, and this more often than not in a most uninformed and unreflective manner. I employ the word 'used' deliberately since the underlying assumption is that Scripture is a source book at our disposal rather than a means of God's grace through which we are formed and moulded; the notion is of us doing something with Scripture rather than of God, through Scripture, doing something with us.

One of the great ironies of theological movements is the rapidity with which they become, following Max Weber (1964), 'routinised', that is, developing structures and cultural norms that can in some cases produce a moralism or even a legalism. So it can be argued that the zealous fidelity of the Hasidim gives way to the Pharisees' apparent preoccupation with the minutiae of observance; the virtue ethic of Thomas Aquinas gives way to the natural law ethic of nineteenth-century Thomism; the pneumatological concerns of John Calvin and the best of the Puritans gives way to the harsh rigours of later Calvinism. For John Calvin, like Thomas before him, Scripture is given to shape us. The knowledge of God is transformative; the 'law' of God is engraved ultimately on human hearts rather than on tablets of stone. Yet Calvin's introduction of a 'third use' of the law as a means of guiding us in obeying God perhaps inevitably occluded his application of such guidance to those 'in whose hearts the Spirit of God already lives and reigns' (Calvin, *Institutes* II. vii. 12). Calvin quite properly (and perhaps in contrast to Luther) comprehends law as a means of grace rather than its contrary. Calvin is eager to identify the unity of the Old and the New. Yet his assumptions tend to obscure the provisionality and contextual rootedness of rules, and his attempt to distinguish between moral law and cultic law is inconsistent and ultimately unconvincing. And if such flaws are overlooked by Calvin they are certainly overlooked popularly in most contemporary pastoral and ethical uses of Scripture. A rule-based ethic is simple. A rule-based ethic, therefore, will always be attractive. But, as Thomas and Calvin realised, a rule-based ethic will always prove inadequate; merely doing the right thing and avoiding the wrong thing will never be sufficient to render a person godly.

But a quest for absolutes, indeed for biblical absolutes, persists – and it persists through a stubborn (and sometimes dogmatic) refusal to acknowledge the contextual rootedness of all rules. Even the Decalogue, with its commands not to kill, not to steal, not to commit adultery, is contextually rooted: the command not to kill, in reality, is a command not to murder, which implies notions of legitimate and illegitimate killing, which notions manifestly are contextually rooted; the command not to steal is transgressed by every Christian who has a bank account, a pension policy, an insurance policy or a mortgage, since stealing in context includes every form of usury; the command not to commit adultery is contextually rooted inasmuch as adultery within Old Testament society was a sin against God and against a husband but never a sin against a wife (it is in this respect at least that Jesus radically redefines this law in Matt. 19:9). And beyond the Decalogue the matter is compounded. On what valid basis might we disapprove of same-sex sexual relationships while eating shellfish and rare beef and while wearing clothes made of two different types of material? Moreover, Scripture is understandably silent on issues of nuclear power, genetic engineering, and countless other ethical dilemmas confronting the contemporary Church; and the attempt to press texts of Scripture into the service of such dilemmas is both artificial and disingenuous. Certainly there are rules within the narrative of Scripture but Scripture is not given to the Church as a book of rules and to use it as such is to misuse it.

The Bible as a source of principles

An honest acknowledgement of the contextual rootedness of biblical rules commonly issues in an attempt to identify principles or organising themes underlying those rules, which can then be interpreted and reapplied as a means of responding to contemporary questions. The attempt itself, of course, relies upon the critical tools of historical method: if the principles underlying Old Testament law are to be discerned, those laws must first be comprehended thoroughly within their own original context. While such an approach could be considered more 'enlightened', and while it certainly has potential for greater consistency and less self-deception, this reinterpretative strategy remains flawed and inadequate, a delusory advance.

In the first place it really is not possible for contemporary commentators to discern with any degree of certainty the principles and intentions underlying the laws of the Old Testament. The assured conclusions of historical criticism are really not quite as 'assured' as we all once assumed. We simply do not have sufficient information concerning original context to facilitate this interpretative method. More often than not we simply cannot discern the prin-ciples underlying these community rules: the food and purification laws of the Old Testament appear entirely arbitrary. Moreover, at a popular level, even the prerequisite attempt at critical distance is often half-hearted. Too often the food and purification laws of the Old Testament are referred to in Christian preaching carelessly and anachronistically as rules of hygiene. Too often we attempt to read back into an Old Testament context contemporary concerns for human dignity, proportionate justice and environmental responsibility.

In the second place, and perhaps more seriously, notions of justice, prudence, temperance, are as contextually rooted as the rules through which such notions are applied. Here the devastating critique offered by Alasdair MacIntyre (1985, 1988) is decisive; both with respect to his modernistic target and also with respect to the alternative. Having repudiated notions of universal justice, MacIntyre appears to propose a notion of universally compelling virtue. Even if we can identify notions of justice underlying

Old Testament law, such notions of justice appear radically discontinuous with contemporary notions of justice (which themselves, of course, are socially constructed). While wanting to affirm an underlying continuity between the Old Testament and the New Testament, between the early Church and the contemporary churches, a problematic discontinuity must also be acknowledged. Even if we could with certainty discern the principles underlying Old Testament law, such principles would similarly prove contextually rooted.

And even if we could discern such underlying principles, and transpose such principles to a contemporary context without hermeneutical naivety, the outcome would yet prove pastorally and ethically inadequate. We may have identified means to aid a decision-making process but we will have fallen short of a means to personal transformation. That such an outcome is, in fact, inadequate may seem surprising. We have grown accustomed to the dilemma-based ethics characteristic of modernist utilitarianism; to the assumption that ethics has to do with decision-making; but herein lies the ultimate inadequacy of all rule-based ethics. 'The moral life does not consist just in making one right decision after another; it is the progressive attempt to widen and clarify our vision of reality' (Hauerwas 1981a, 44).

Merely to do right things and to avoid wrong things, even supposing that we can identify appropriate means for discerning the right and the wrong, will not of itself issue in a morally good person. We rightly expect good people to do right things, just as good trees produce good fruit (Matt. 7:16ff.), but the latter is an outcome of the former, not the former of the latter. Our lives are identified through continuity of character rather than through a series of discrete responses to dilemmas, and the purpose of Scripture within the Church, or rather, God's purpose through Scripture within the Church, is to shape us as people, to bring us into conformity with Christ.

The Bible as a resource for pastoral and ethical reflection

During recent years, models for theological reflection have proliferated, though, for all their variety, they have in common the commitment to begin the reflective cycle with praxis, with a particular situation or anecdote that can be submitted to analysis. Concerns thus identified are then brought into engagement with Scripture and the Christian tradition issuing in a renewal of praxis. We have then a form of hermeneutical spiral. All of which may at first sight appear a helpful means of considering pastoral and ethical issues, but it ultimately fails for precisely the same reasons as the uses of Scripture already rehearsed: the pastoral and ethical goal, after all, is not that we should find ways of responding to problems but that we should be shaped as faithful men and women.

For all of the attractiveness and utility of beginning with the presenting problem this, in reality, is simply not where we ever begin. Life is not a series of discrete responses to dilemmas. Nor do we encounter such dilemmas as if we were blank sheets of paper: we encounter dilemmas as the people we are, with our baggage of presuppositions and prejudices, as those who have been shaped by communities with their distinctive traditions and stories. Our perception from the beginning is slanted; our retelling of the dilemma in anecdotal form already says as much about who we are as it says about the presenting problem. Moreover, the issues I identify as inherent within any particular dilemma, together with those aspects of the Christian tradition and those stories from Scripture that I utilise as means of responding to that dilemma, may serve as much to reinforce my assumptions as it may serve to challenge them. Once again it is a case of me doing something with Scripture rather than God doing something with me through Scripture.

In fairness, a number of friends and colleagues who espouse this method express considerable concern regarding the effectiveness with which Scripture and the Christian tradition are engaged. The method assumes a degree of biblical and theological competence and, where such is lacking, engagement with Scripture and tradition can prove piecemeal and naive. But I am suggesting that the problem is more fundamental – a misconstruing of the starting point rather than a misappropriation of the method; a misconstruing of the nature and function of Scripture within the Church rather than merely a misapplication of Scripture. The properly theological question is not that of how Scripture and the Christian tradition might aid me. Rather it is that of how I, as someone being shaped within the Church through its traditions and scriptural stories, respond to this particular dilemma in a manner that is coherent and consistent, trustful and faithful. The Bible functions properly within the Church as a means through which we are shaped and formed as a people who can live trustfully, faithfully, lovingly, hopefully, thankfully and worshipfully.

The Bible as transformative narrative

Overwhelmingly Scripture takes narrative form. It simply isn't a series of propositions and rules. It is a series of stories. The propositions and rules occurring in Scripture are rooted in and explicated by the narratives in which they occur. We know what 'love' signifies here inasmuch as God 'loved us and sent his Son as an atoning sacrifice for our sins' (1 John 4:10): the significance of the proposition is identified within the story. And it is by means of these stories that the character of God, and the character of those who respond to God, is rendered to us.

Stories form our values and moral sensibilities in more indirect and com-

> plex ways, teaching us how to see the world, what to fear, and what to hope for; stories offer us nuanced models of behavior both wise and foolish, courageous and cowardly, faithful and faithless. (Hays, 73)

Supremely and ultimately the Word takes flesh and dwells amongst us, and thereby, through the witness of Scripture, true God and true humanity are narrated. And neither God, nor God's invitation to humankind in Christ, can be reduced to a series of propositions and rules.

> At that time Jesus went through the cornfields on the Sabbath. His disciples were hungry and began to pick some ears of corn and eat them. When the Pharisees saw this, they said to him, 'Look! Your disciples are doing what is unlawful on the Sabbath.'
>
> He answered, '... If you had known what these words mean, "I desire mercy, not sacrifice," you would not have condemned the innocent. For the Son of Man is Lord of the Sabbath.' (Matt. 12:1ff. NIV)

This is one of two linked stories (Matt. 12:1–14; cf. Mark 2:23—3:6) about the challenge to Jesus by the Pharisees over the meaning of the Sabbath laws. According to Jesus' comments as we have them, one of the issues is that there is a deeper principle informing the Law than the observance of regulations. Two attitudes seem at variance: to defend one's integrity by ensuring right conduct; or to live out of an inner integrity. Whatever way the Pharisees may have argued, Jesus clearly here and elsewhere assumes the latter (see Matt. 7:17–18; Mark 12:28–34 and parallels). We do not become good people merely by being preoccupied with doing the right thing (or avoiding the wrong thing). We become good people by being shaped in the likeness of the one revealed through Scripture's story, by becoming living narratives of divine mercy, divine faithfulness. As Aristotle, Thomas Aquinas and John Calvin all acknowledge, law is useful for encouraging virtue and discouraging vice; but law alone cannot produce virtuous people. We are shaped as virtuous people through our indwelling, that is by our being embedded in and finding our truth, within virtuous communities; we are shaped as holy people through our indwelling of holy communities; we are made holy people through the indwelling of the Holy Spirit; theological virtue is an outcome of grace, not law. And Scripture therefore, like the community of the Church itself, is a means of this grace, a means through which we are shaped and transformed. And since this is the case, since Scripture functions within the Church sacramentally (if not as itself a sacrament), since Scripture is a means of grace, it functions within the Church as an outcome of promise. Whether we realise it or not, whether we acknowledge it our not, we are being shaped by the Spirit through the reading and hearing of Scripture. Even when we persist in misconstruing its purpose and function, its instrumental and spiritual functions endure. We may persist in using Scripture as a book of rules, as a source of principles, or as a resource for reflection, but even then the transforming instrumental function of Scripture may yet be fulfilled – it is a matter of promise.

The hearing of Scripture within the Church

For the majority of Christians throughout the greater part of the Church's history Scripture has been 'heard' rather than 'read'. In part this was an outcome of common illiteracy, but primarily it was simply an outcome of non-availability: before the advent of the printing press copies of the Scriptures were rare and precious. In this respect, of course, the current common availability of Scripture might be disadvantageous. The availability of Scripture as an object of personal study fuels the notion that this is Scripture's proper nature and function, as a resource of propositional truth and prescriptive rules. Conversely, a liturgical context for the hearing of Scripture promotes the recognition that the hearing of Scripture is itself a sacramental event, a means of grace through which something happens beyond the mere imparting of information. And, notwithstanding the hopes of evangelical clergy, one suspects that it remains the case that Scripture is more commonly 'heard' than 'read'. Admittedly, in some Free Church settings the place of Scripture within worship has been drastically reduced to a single (and often short) passage of Scripture read as a prefix to the sermon. But in more liturgical settings the traditional reading of a psalm, an Old Testament lesson, a passage from an epistle and a passage from a gospel is preserved. Even in more 'charismatic' and 'open' forms of worship, the reading of Scripture often is accorded prominence, albeit informally.

This priority for the hearing of Scripture, as distinct to the reading or study of Scripture, further clarifies the dynamic of the event in which this text – or any text – is appropriated. The Bible as a physical object too easily beguiles us into thinking of this text – or any text – as an object at our disposal and available to our scrutiny. But a text only exists as text in the event of reading and hearing. In this sense a text 'occurs', it never simply 'is'. All this is well-rehearsed (though continually contested) post-structuralist literary theory. But when applied to Scripture this radical literary theory acquires distinct significance. Any event of reading or hearing is inevitably interpretative and creative, but for Scripture to be read or heard as Scripture implies a distinctive instance of this dynamic. For Scripture to be read or heard as Scripture implies the expectation that this event will be divinely creative, interpreting the readers and hearers every bit as much as the readers and hearers interpret the text. Scripture comes to us in the context of the Church's liturgy, not as a dead letter on an ageing page but as the vehicle for a living word, as the means of divine address.

> For the word of God is living and active. Sharper than any double-edged sword, it penetrates even to dividing soul and spirit, joints and marrow; it judges the thoughts and attitudes of the heart. Nothing in all creation is hidden from God's sight. Everything is uncovered and laid bare before the eyes of him to whom we must give account. (Heb. 4:12f.)

When Scripture is read or heard we are addressed directly and immediately. While in one sense the Bible constitutes a series of ancient texts addressing ancient peoples, within the context of the Church's liturgy and pastoral discipline it constitutes an ancient text through which we, its contemporary hearers, are addressed. Just as the writer of the Letter to the Hebrews takes a psalm as a lens through which to view an ancient story of Israel's rebellion and, by means of such, recasts both psalm and story as a means of immediate divine address to his hearers, so whenever Scripture is read or heard as Scripture this immediate and direct divine address should be anticipated.

The directness and livingness of this address can, of course, be enhanced by contemporary translations, which sometimes, by their mere freshness and unfamiliarity, are arresting and engaging. Similarly, 'dramatic' readings of Scripture, or dramatic representations of Scripture, can capture imagination and can emphasise the narrative form of the text – though drama can blunt the directness of Scripture's address as readily as it can represent it. Most commonly, though, the livingness and directness of Scripture's address is represented in the sermon. Sadly the sermon can too easily become an occasion for shallow moralising or for reducing the text of Scripture again to a compendium of rules or principles for daily living; too easily the sermon can provide the occasion for law to displace grace, for the prescriptive to displace the descriptive and transformative, for the letter to displace the Spirit. The sermon, rather, should be the means through which the contemporaneity of the text becomes explicit, the means through which the livingness of the text recurs. Of course there is place here for explanation, for the imparting of information concerning the background to the text and its (possible) original hearers. But the genre of the sermon is properly proclamation rather than mere education, a rendering of the text rather than a mere explanation of the text. The sermon, like the text, is sacramental, a means of grace, an instrument through which the Holy Spirit promises to accomplish something creative and transformative. The sermon, then, represents the address of the text to the hearers and, at the same time, draws the hearers into the living address of the text.

And what is true of the reading and hearing of Scripture corporately, within the liturgy, is similarly true of the reading and hearing of Scripture more personally and pastorally. To read a psalm in a hospice, by the bedside of one who is dying, is surely most plainly of all where Scripture is 'used' sacramentally, as a means of grace, as a means of assurance, comfort and consolation. And this is surely true whenever Scripture is read and heard in a pastoral context: as a means through which the hearer may be challenged, rebuked, comforted, consoled, encouraged. Scripture is read as a means of spiritual formation, as a means of transformation. The issue is not just that of how Scripture narrates this story but also of how Scripture narrates my life.

The indwelling of Scripture by the Church

All of which, of course, implies a severe qualification of the critical distance characteristic of sound historical method. In fact 'critical distance', in some respects at least, is a vice rather than a virtue if Scripture is to be used pastorally and ethically. Paul Ricoeur speaks of a 'second naivety', of an approach to Scripture which, though fully aware of historical context and historical distance, nonetheless permits and expects Scripture to be heard as a living and transforming word. Indeed, entirely contrary to attempts at critical distance, Ricoeur speaks of our being drawn into the world of the text, of its story becoming our story, of the text interpreting our lives, rather than the other way around. Scripture, therefore, is to be read and heard imaginatively, in a manner that enables and promotes an indwelling of its story by those who read and hear it. Certainly this is not to dispute the appropriateness of historical study; but the Church does not maintain critical distance from Scripture – the Church comes to Scripture in faith, trust and expectation. Commonly the reading of Scripture and the preaching of the sermon are followed by the reciting of the creed. Having heard Scripture the Church affirms its faith. By reciting the creed the Church identifies itself as the Church, as continuous with the community of God's people through the centuries who have heard Scripture with faith and responded to Scripture with faithfulness. In response to that which has been heard through Scripture the Church reaffirms its trust in the one who therein is narrated. And in response to that which has been heard in Scripture the Church reaffirms its commitment to faithfulness. To recite the creed is not merely an affirmation of belief but is more foundationally an affirmation of trust and a commitment to faithfulness: this God is the creator and sustainer of all things; this Jesus is risen, ascended, and coming again as judge; this Spirit is the Lord and giver of life; this Church is one, holy, catholic and apostolic.

> The task of Christian ethics is to help us see how our convictions *are* in themselves a morality. We do not first believe certain things about God, Jesus, and the church, and subsequently derive ethical implications from these beliefs. Rather our convictions embody our morality: our beliefs are our actions. We Christians ought not to search for the 'behavioral implications' of our beliefs. Our moral life is not comprised of beliefs plus

> decisions; our moral life is the process in which our convictions form our character to be truthful. (Hauerwas 1984, 16)

Indeed, when Scripture is read and heard in the context of the Church's liturgy, the entire event of worship, prayer and confession functions as a means through which the congregation indwells the Christian story. Prayer and confession draw us into the presence of the one narrated through Scripture. Hymns and songs – or at least the best of them – either function as further credal commitments or as explicit means through which we enter the story narrated in Scripture. To sing of Christ's birth, life and ministry is to enter into those events. To sing of his agonising in Gethsemane is to participate in that struggle. To sing of the cross, most clearly of all, is to be drawn into Christ's passion and to know again that it was for us that he suffered. To sing of Christ's resurrection is to share in the Easter joy of the first disciples.

Definitively and ultimately, however, we enter into the narrative of Scripture sacramentally, through baptism and through our participation in the Lord's Supper. Through the means of baptism, as the apostle Paul so graphically puts it, we are buried with Christ and raised with him, we participate in his death and resurrection, his story becomes our story (Rom. 6:3ff.). Baptism, therefore, is not merely an affirmation of personal faith; it is a commitment of life; it is an identification of this story as our story; it is a confession of Christ as definitive of our humanity. And as we gather at Communion we are gathering with the first disciples in the upper room, we are gathering again at the foot of the cross, we are gathering together with all the saints in every generation who have gathered in this manner, we are gathering in anticipation of our ultimate participation in God through the Son and the Spirit. The Eucharist supremely is the means through which we participate in the Christian story, the story as narrated through Scripture, but the story also as narrated through the living history of the Church. The sacraments of the Church, then, are not mere remembrances, they are means through which we indwell the story of Scripture, means through which this story becomes our story, through which Scripture interprets our lives – means, therefore, through which we are shaped and formed.

The living of Scripture's story by the Church

And we are so shaped and formed, consciously or unconsciously. This is not an issue of effort (or, at least, not effort alone) but primarily of promise. Men and women who hear Scripture and who are drawn into the story of Scripture worshipfully, imaginatively and sacramentally, are shaped by that story of Scripture as a matter of divine promise. A transformed and transforming people is an inevitable consequence of indwelling Scripture's story: inevitable since God does what he promises; because the Holy Spirit's presence and action through the hearing of Scripture and through the sacraments of the Church is a reality. Here then is a rather different hermeneutical spiral: not a critical reflection on praxis that issues in renewed praxis, but rather a transformative indwelling of Scripture's story that issues in an ever more truthful hearing of Scripture's story. Truly to hear the narrative of Scripture is to be drawn into the narrative of Scripture and formed by that hearing and indwelling; and to be so formed by that hearing and indwelling is to be enabled to hear and indwell that narrative of Scripture more truthfully and faithfully (Stone 2003, 462f.). That which is at issue here is not the identification of criteria, drawn from Scripture and the Christian tradition, but the formation of a virtuous community that has developed habits and practices that enable it to live faithfully and coherently through life's decisions and dilemmas. A virtuous community will act virtuously – and this virtuous community that is the Church is shaped as such through its virtuous indwelling of this virtuous story rendered through Scripture. Moreover, only such a virtuous community, that is shaped through its indwelling of Scripture, will be able to hear Scripture and indwell Scripture truthfully, faithfully and virtuously. Here is a hermeneutical spiral, but it is of a rather different nature from those that recently have come to characterise pastoral theology: it is one that seeks to indwell Scripture in the hope of transformation. And since this is a hermeneutical spiral, the community of the Church itself is rendered the interpretative key to a truthful hearing and indwelling of the story. The living narrative which is the Church cannot be truthfully comprehended without reference to the story rendered through Scripture; and the story rendered through Scripture cannot be truthfully comprehended without reference to the living narrative of that story which is the Church. The Church, thus shaped through its hearing and indwelling of Scripture's story, itself becomes, like Scripture and the sacraments, a means of grace, a living sacrament, a rendering of divine promise.

All of which may sound hopelessly idealistic. Just where is this Church so shaped by its indwelling of Scripture that it too becomes a living telling of the Christian story? Unless such questions can be answered positively this entire strategy of receiving Scripture as a transforming narrative, as a means of grace, collapses. We might just as well continue using Scripture as a compendium of rules, principles and helpful moral tips. Of course one could respond that it is precisely this continuing use of Scripture as a compendium of rules, principles and helpful moral tips that undermines that sustained indwelling of Scripture. If Scripture is effectively to be heard within the Church (and through the Church) there is need for renewal of Scripture's place within the Church's liturgy, sacramental worship and pastoral practice.

But the Church itself, like the Father, the Son and the Spirit, is an article of the Church's faith, and notwithstanding every attempt within the Church to use Scripture, Scripture is yet read, heard and indwelt sacramentally. And precisely because this dynamic is sacramental, rooted in divine promise, it is effective despite our very best means to undermine it. The Church exists within the world as a witness to this Christian story; and precisely in its failures and frailties it witnesses to the mercy and grace that are at issue in that story. Moreover, local churches exist within society as means of forgiveness, healing and security, as communities that are transforming because they are themselves being transformed. And we celebrate the lives of the saints, those who have lived and are living still who have indwelt this story and themselves become fresh means of its retelling and its effectiveness. Only the gospel story as narrated in Scripture makes sense of the lives of Julian of Norwich, of Francis Xavier, of John Wesley, of William Carey, of Mother Teresa – and through the witness of such lives the story that shaped them is accessed. God keeps his promises.

Bibliography

Aristotle (1955) *Ethics*. Harmondsworth: Penguin.

Austin, J. L. (1976) *How To Do Things with Words*. Oxford: Oxford University Press.

Bartholomew, C., Greene, C. and Möller, K. (eds) (2001) *After Pentecost: language and biblical interpretation*. Carlisle: Paternoster Press.

Briggs, Richard (2001) *Words in action: speech act theory and biblical interpretation: toward a hermeneutic of self-involvement*. Edinburgh: T&T Clark.

Calvin, John (1960) *Institutes of the Christian Religion*. Philadelphia: Westminster Press.

Colwell, John E. (2001) *Living the Christian Story: the distinctiveness of Christian ethics*. Edinburgh: T&T Clark.

Gunton, Colin E. (2000) The Church as a school of virtue? human formation in trinitarian framework, in M. Thiessen and S. Wells (eds), *Faithfulness and Fortitude: in conversation with the theological ethics of Stanley Hauerwas*. Edinburgh: T&T Clark, 211–31.

Gustafson, J. M. (1968) *Christ and the Moral Life*. Chicago: University of Chicago Press.

Hauerwas, Stanley (1981a) *Vision and Virtue: essays in Christian ethical reflection*. Notre Dame, IN: University of Notre Dame Press.

Hauerwas, Stanley (1981b) *A Community of Character: toward a constructive Christian social ethic*. Notre Dame, IN: University of Notre Dame Press.

Hauerwas, Stanley (1984) *The Peacable Kingdom: a primer in Christian ethics*. London: SCM Press.

Hauerwas, Stanley (1993) *Unleashing the Scripture: freeing the Bible from captivity to America*. Nashville, TN: Abingdon Press.

Hauerwas, Stanley (1994) *Character and the Christian Life: a study in theological ethics*. Notre Dame, IN: University of Notre Dame Press.

Hauerwas, Stanley (1995) *In Good Company: the Church as polis*. Notre Dame, IN: University of Notre Dame Press.

Hauerwas, Stanley (1998) *Sanctify Them in the Truth: holiness exemplified*. Edinburgh: T&T Clark.

Hauerwas, Stanley and Willimon, W. H. (1989) *Resident Aliens: life in the Christian colony*. Nashville, TN: Abingdon Press.

Hays, R. B. (1996) *The Moral Vision of the New Testament: a contemporary introduction to New Testament ethics*. Edinburgh: T&T Clark.

Kevan, E. F. (1964) *The Grace of Law: a study in Puritan theology*. London: Carey Kingsgate.

MacIntyre, Alasdair (1985) *After Virtue: a study in moral theory*. London: Duckworth.

MacIntyre, Alasdair (1988) *Whose Justice? Which Rationality?* London: Duckworth.
Matzko, D. M. (1998) The performance of the good: ritual action and the moral life. *Pro Ecclesia* VII, 199–215.
McClendon, J. W. Jr (1986) *Systematic Theology: ethics*. Nashville, TN: Abingdon Press.
Milbank, John (1990) *Theology and Social Theory*. Oxford: Blackwell.
Porter, Jean (1990) *The Recovery of Virtue: the relevance of Aquinas for Christian ethics.* London: SPCK.
Ricoeur, Paul (1992) *Oneself as Another*. Chicago: University of Chicago Press.
Stone, Lance (2003) Word and sacrament as paradigmatic for pastoral theology: in search of a definition via Brueggemann, Hauerwas and Ricoeur. *Scottish Journal of Theology* 56.4, 444–63.
Thomas Aquinas (1981) *Summa Theologica* (Library of Christian Classics). Philadelphia: Westminster Press.
Wadell, P. J. (1992) *The Primacy of Love: an introduction to the ethics of Thomas Aquinas.* Mahwah, NJ: Paulist Press.
Weber, Max (1964) *The Theory of Social and Economic Organization.* ET, New York: Free Press.

CHAPTER 13:

The Bible, worship and pastoral care

DAVID LYALL

The interrelationships between the Bible, worship and pastoral care are far from simple and wide because the three terms 'Bible', 'worship' and 'pastoral care' each in themselves carry huge reservoirs of meaning. 'Worship' and 'pastoral care' encompass great diversities of practice and all three have their own history and literature and ways of being understood by different individuals and faith communities. Indeed there is a complex history of interaction between each of the pairs of these three entities. Further, any exploration of their mutual relationship will inevitably have an idiosyncratic quality shaped by the experience and understanding of the writer. First, therefore, some content will be given to my own perspective on each of these terms. Then, consideration will be given to some of the ways in which the Bible, worship and pastoral care relate to one another. Finally, an attempt will be made to explore three areas where this interrelationship is of great significance namely the occasional offices, preaching and eucharistic worship.

Bible

The reality of contemporary church life is that while the Bible has a central place, there are radically different ways in which the Bible is interpreted. These differences lead to the kind of angst that manifests itself when the Church must address such contemporary pastoral issues as homosexuality. At its most basic, there is a tension, not always creative, between those who take the Bible literally and those who (merely?) take it seriously. On the one hand there are those who consider the Bible to be the unchanging word(s) of God, eternally relevant independently of culture; on the other hand there are those who believe that the Bible is human witness to divine action in history, uniquely in the events surrounding the event of Jesus Christ, and that the diverse collection of writings which we know as 'the Bible' can only be fully understood in the light of its cultural contexts, and its relevance for the Church appropriated in the light of contemporary knowledge. In a recent essay, Edward Farley distinguishes between 'preaching the Bible and preaching the Gospel'. 'The former paradigm requires us to think of the Bible as a collection of passages each of which necessarily contains a preaching word or truth about God' (75). Farley sees this as a failed paradigm because, he argues, there is no reason to assume that any small piece of the Bible wrenched from its context necessarily contains the word of God. We certainly would not treat any other work of great literature in this fashion whether it be the *Iliad* or *King Lear.* In contrast, Farley affirms the need to 'proclaim Gospel'.

> What is Gospel? It is, of course good tidings. The Christian gospel is good tidings about 'salvation through Jesus'. And to attest to that is always to bring it in relation to the concrete, cultural, political and individual situations in which the preaching takes place. Minimally, we have as content of Gospel a radical version of human social, historical and individual sin and a paradigm of redemption. If this is the case, Gospel is not simply a clear and given content. It is the mystery of God's salvific working. Thus we can never master it, exhaust it, or directly or literally comprehend it. Rather we continue to struggle to fathom its reality. Gospel is not simply given all at once like a gift-wrapped package. It is something to be proclaimed, but the summons to proclaim it is a summons to struggle with the mystery of God's salvific action and how that transforms the world. To proclaim Gospel then is to enter the world of Gospel, struggling with questions of suffering, evil, idolatry, hope and freedom. (85)

The understanding of the Bible which lies at the heart of this paper follows closely that of Farley with its broader concept of 'Gospel' as the good news surrounding the whole event of Jesus Christ.

Worship

My assumption here is that a full understanding of worship requires some consideration of the nature of ritual, indeed that one cannot have the former without the latter. Even those Christian traditions which would vehemently defend their non-ritualistic integrity have their own rituals or habitual practices, whether it be the way in which the Bible is placed (or not) in the pulpit on a Sunday, or the way in which the offering is uplifted (or not), or the particular way in which baptisms, weddings and funerals are normally conducted.

It has to be recognised that worship and ritual can be understood from more than one perspective. Liturgical specialists will interpret the worship of the Church from historical and theological perspectives. Psychologists of religion will bring another perspective to bear. These different perspectives need not be mutually exclusive; rather they help us to view what is going on in greater depth. To give only one example, drawing upon the pioneering work of Bruce Reed (1978), Wesley Carr has demonstrated the roles of dependency and regression in worship particularly in relation to funerals.

> The term 'regression' sounds pejorative and is only used with hesitation. But at best it describes the process of such worship ... Human development consists in progression from childhood and dependence upon parents to adult acknowledgement of interdependence between responsible people, and not, as some think, to independence from others. As mature adults human beings live in an oscillation between these two states of dependence and autonomy. Regression to dependence, therefore, is not a reversion to infantile behaviour, but an aspect of adult life which requires affirmation and recognition. Worship and ritual have their place in this scheme. They provide specific occasions of and opportunity for controlled regression ... In order to facilitate this regression and the move back towards recovery of responsibility and autonomy, a containing environment is created. Liturgy performs this function, both through the way in which it is conducted and with its unfamiliar richness of ideas and images. Impressions and conveyed ideas, especially at a funeral, are more important than meanings. (Carr, 117)

The manner in which worship is conducted is as important as the words used. Worship will sometimes act as a container of feelings of grief or anxiety, allowing these to be expressed in a healthy creative manner. To be aware of the psychosocial dimensions of worship is not to detract from more traditional theological understandings but rather to deepen and fill out such understandings.

Pastoral care

'Pastoral care' is also understood in different ways, which I have explored elsewhere, suggesting the following definition:

> Pastoral care involves the establishment of a relationship or relationships whose purpose may encompass support in a time of trouble and/or a deeper understanding of oneself, others and/or God. Pastoral care will have at its heart the affirmation of meaning and the worth of persons and

> will endeavour to strengthen their ability to respond creatively to whatever life brings. (Lyall, 12)

I also suggested that pastoral care is located within the community of faith; is sensitive to the uniqueness of the spiritual journey of each human being; has a freedom (but not a compulsion) to draw upon the traditional resources of the community of faith such as prayer, the Bible and the sacraments; takes seriously the social and political context of ministry, seeing the purpose of that ministry as being not simply adjustment to circumstances on the part of individuals but the transformation of society. Having given some substance to my understanding of the Bible, worship and pastoral care, I now turn to exploration of how worship relates both to the Bible and to pastoral care.

The Bible and worship

Here there is an obvious relationship because we cannot worship – or at least we cannot engage in public worship – without some reference to the Bible. Some would argue that the climax of Reformed worship is the preaching of the Word, that worship in this tradition has as its central focus the sermon, the preached word being an exposition of the written word bearing witness to the incarnate Word. But this is no longer an insight limited to the Reformed tradition, if indeed it ever was. Right across the ecumenical spectrum, increasing use is being made of common lectionaries so that these lectionaries control the theme and the content of each act of worship. Further, the language of prayer, whether from service books or extempore, draws deeply upon the conceptual framework and language of the Bible. And the praise of the Church is replete with biblical imagery. This is especially so in those churches which draw deeply upon the psalms whether in prose or metrical form. Thus, as far as the normal Sunday worship of the people of God is concerned, the relationship between the Bible and worship is, at least at one level, self-evident.

Worship and pastoral care

If the relationship between worship and the Bible seems obvious and close, the same cannot be said about the relationship between worship and pastoral care. Indeed there is evidence of long-standing misunderstanding, if not mutual antipathy, between those whose main interest is in liturgy and those whose main interest lies in pastoral care. The criticism which each group makes of the other perhaps lies in the realm of caricature; but, of course, most caricatures usually contain an element of truth. In her book *Ritual and Pastoral Care* Elaine Ramshaw summarises the mutual accusations which have divided pastoral carers (especially counsellors) from the so-called 'specialist ritualists'.

> The counsellors too often feel that ritual lacks warmth and empathy; that its fixed forms are too insensitive to 'where the patient is'; that it staunches the flow of feelings; that it 'generalizes' the client's feelings; that it tends to reduce pastoral ministry to the magical.
>
> In return, the ritualists have attacked counselling as an anaesthetic or palliative which attempts to treat symptoms in isolation from the total situation, sidestepping confrontation with the deeper issues raised by personal crisis. The counsellor isolates the individual from community support and cuts him or her off from the stabilising anchor of ritual. (14)

Ramshaw summarises the arguments as follows:

> We all know too well the truths that give rise to these counter-accusations. Ritual can indeed be formalist, distancing, insensitive to the specificity or pace of the individual's needs, intent on enforcing a procrustean pattern. Equally sadly, even ' pastoral' counselling can be privatised, narrowly focussed on the needs of the moment, insufficiently grounded in the depths of the tradition, tone-deaf to mystery. (14)

So there is the contrast in its starkest expression. On the one hand there are the liturgists whose interest is mainly archaeological, trying to uncover and re-create worship as it once was, allegedly with little concern for pastoral relevance; on the other hand, there are the counsellors, supposedly value-free, trying hard not to impose their own beliefs, yet sometimes taking on quite uncritically the philosophical presuppositions as well as the techniques of the secular therapies, and unwilling to countenance any contribution to psychic or spiritual health to be found through participation in the worship of the Church.

But it need not be like this. Walter Brueggemann, who has contributed significantly to a biblical theology of pastoral care, in an essay on 'The Transformative Power of the Pastoral Office' (1991), argues that 'pastoral care is essentially a liturgical enterprise.' How does he arrive at this conclusion? Brueggemann recognises the need that existed for pastoral care to be set free from authoritarian religion. Now, he argues, the boot is on the other foot. While secular theory functioned for a while in emancipating ways, now that same theory, pushed to extremes, is seductive and destructive. He asserts that the counsellor's goal for her client is autonomy but argues that for the client the attainment of autonomy cannot in fact yield health because it eventually leads to an uncritical social conformity. The outcome, he believes is 'a kind of privatised well-being, devoid of community, unrelated to public reality. In the end such privatised well-being is no well-being at all.' Further, argues Brueggemann, pastoral care informed by biblical faith, in comparison with counselling, is committed to a very different understanding of what it means to be human. If the aim of counselling is adjustment, fitting comfortably into society, that of pastoral care is transformation. The task of pastoral care is to feed the imagination in such a way that people see life and its possibilities differently. He argues, 'Not only is the substance of this imagination crucial, but so is where and in what ways it is practiced and made available among us. This alternative imagination is shaped, mediated and made available primarily through the practice of liturgy' (176). It is for this reason, therefore, that 'pastoral care is essentially a liturgical enterprise' and that 'it should be possible to set as a requirement for personal or individual conversation, disciplined participation in a liturgical activity of the pastoral care community.'

He is arguing that worship itself is – or should be – a source of pastoral care; that worship provides a new way of understanding reality, and a new set of symbols around which people can reorganise their lives. Would that it were so! At any rate he presents us with a very different understanding of the relationship between worship and pastoral care, not one of conflict but one in which worship and pastoral care are complementary, the pastoral relationship finding its context in a liturgical context which challenges accepted conventional values and makes possible new ways of seeing things.

The occasional offices

We turn now to a consideration of those acts of worship most intimately associated with critical moments of transition in the lives of individuals and families. These are what some denominations refer to as 'the occasional offices'. They, most usually, are baptisms associated with new beginnings, weddings celebrating deep commitments and funerals marking inevitable endings. There is a subtle difference in nuance between the adverb 'occasionally' and the noun 'occasion'. Events that happen 'occasionally' happen 'as and when'. There is a serendipitous, hit-or-miss, feel to the word. Yet an event described as an 'occasion' has a very different feel to it. Occasions are often described as 'important' or 'great' and are carefully planned. In speaking of the 'occasional offices' this double nuance is integral to what is going on. For those most directly involved, those who might be described as recipients, both are important. We are (normally) only baptised once; if we marry more than once then it will not happen more than very occasionally; and we will (certainly) not have more than one funeral.

For ministers, whose involvement in the occasional offices may be much more frequent than implied by the word, these liturgical acts can easily elide into an indistinguishable blur of baptisms, weddings and funerals except for those uniquely remembered for some personal involvement or idiosyncratic feature. Yet there remains the obligation upon those who conduct these rituals to capture the uniqueness of the occasion for those involved and to use the service in such a way as to personalise each new liturgical event with pastoral sensitivity. It must never be forgotten that at the heart of every baptism, wedding and funeral there are a number of utterly unique personal stories. A baptism is a significant moment in the life of the baptised, albeit an unrecognised one in the case of an infant. For the parents, however, the birth of a baby, especially a first child, marks a significant development in the life of the couple and the baptism may mark for them a conscious renewal of their commitment to one another and to this new family they are bringing into being. Grandparents, too, will see this event as part of another chapter in their story begun so many years before. Weddings also involve people and their stories, not only the past histories of the two individuals involved, but the stories of the wider families (and sometimes previous marriages) in which they have been nurtured (and sometimes not). As far as funerals are concerned, Anderson and Foley (1998) believe that 'the great mystery of grief and sorrow that attend it requires rituals of storytelling and remembering' (viii).

In their book *Mighty Stories, Dangerous Rituals: weaving together the human and the divine,* they explore the relationship between pastoral care and ritual, their main thesis being that 'the public worship of organized religions is regarded as a particularly privileged place in which the divine–human relationship is rehearsed and realized.' Nevertheless, this does not happen automatically.

> Despite all its potential for facilitating the encounter between the human and the divine and thereby enabling believers to engage with God in the active co-authorship of their life stories, public worship often fails. Rather than the awesome or mystical arena in which the human and the divine meet, it is frequently experienced as boring and irrelevant. While there are many complex factors that contribute to this situation, one reason for this failure is a paradox; public worship, especially Christian worship, does not adequately mediate divine presence because it is inattentive to the human story. (42)

So where do the human story and the divine story interact in the occasional offices? It is surely too much to expect (though not impossible) that the liturgy alone will mediate grace. Indeed their very brevity (and sometimes their liturgical formalism) can make this difficult if not impossible. What is unique about the occasional offices compared with regular Sunday worship is that every baptism, wedding or funeral is normally the focus of quite intentional pastoral ministry related to the life change marked by the ritual. Ministers visit the parents of new babies in their own homes and learn something of their life together; couples about to be married are involved in pre-marital preparation of varying degrees of intensity; and every funeral must be the celebration of an individual life, whose story will probably have been told again and again in the days before the committal. It is the pastoral care offered in the preparation for the occasional offices which catalyses the mediation of grace in the offices themselves. For it is good pastoral care rooted in the Christian narrative which mediates grace, which 'proclaims Gospel', to use Farley's expression. But if liturgy alone may not mediate grace, neither may the pastoral relationship alone. For Brueggemann, the liturgy of the pastoral community exists to evoke within the imagination alternative ways of seeing reality. 'The purpose of such a liturgy would be to make available the grand themes of biblical faith, such as the metaphors friend of God, servant of God, child of God as the stuff out of which new self and new community may emerge' (177). When the individual stories which emerge in the pastoral relationship are offered to God in the context of a liturgy in which Gospel is proclaimed, then there exists the possibility of a genuine divine–human encounter through the occasional offices.

Sometimes issues are raised when the baptisms, weddings or funerals are requested for people who do not share the same faith perspective as the officiating minister or chaplain. How far can you go as a Christian minister in creating a service for someone who does not profess faith? There will be different responses to the situation. Some will offer only a service rooted in the Christian tradition; others will sit down with those requesting the service and try to work out something which maintains mutual integrity. We find an example of this in the work of Ewan Kelly, who has worked as chaplain in a large maternity unit. He describes his attempts to work with families in constructing meaningful rituals in situations of perinatal death. These rituals were designed both with theological integrity and a sensitivity to the faith/beliefs (or lack of them) on the part of those involved (2002). I suspect that this latter approach is not totally alien to Bruggemann's argument. To co-construct a ritual with parents who have lost a child a minister must listen to their story with deep seriousness; the very fact that a minister is prepared to do so may in itself 'proclaim Gospel'.

Preaching the word as pastoral care

Can preaching be pastoral? Is it possible for sermons to be constructed primarily to bring healing to broken hearts and peace to troubled minds? To those who preach, it might seem strange that these questions are even being asked. Yet to those who seldom hear sermons, and to those who regularly 'sit under' preachers of a certain style, the questions may not seem out of place. The words 'sermon' and 'preaching' do not have positive connotations in popular parlance! What, therefore, is the relationship between pastoral care and the proclamation of the Gospel? One view is that of Eduard Thurneysen

(1962) for whom pastoral care is essentially a proclamation of the word of God to the individual. The individual is a sinner under judgement and grace and the word is primarily one of forgiveness. For Thurneysen, then, pastoral care is a form of preaching. But is the opposite true? Can preaching become a vehicle of pastoral care? I do not wish to argue that pastoral care is the sole function of preaching. The history of the Church's proclamation is far too rich and diverse to make such a claim and a stress upon the need for preaching to have a pastoral dimension must not lead to a silencing of the Church's prophetic voice. With this qualification, how may a pastoral dimension be expressed in preaching?

The pastoral dimension may be expressed through preaching which embodies acceptance and availability. It is not difficult to identify ways in which preaching might be a barrier to pastoral care. Pastoral relationships are not readily established by preachers who by their words and their demeanour in the pulpit come across as cold and judgemental. On the other hand, preachers who demonstrate a pastoral heart, both in their handling of the biblical material and in their attitude to contemporary social issues, come across as human beings who are compassionate towards the frailty of others as well as being in touch with their own vulnerability. By their words and demeanour in the pulpit they create the conditions which encourage others to approach them with their sometimes unspeakable burdens. It is when preaching itself communicates the 'core conditions' necessary for therapy, that is, acceptance, empathy and integrity, that ministers make themselves available pastorally.

Preaching may create opportunities for pastoral care incidentally, almost by accident, as we can observe in the following story from a colleague in ministry:

> It was a terrible sermon. One of these efforts which was 'untimely born', and better not to have been born at all. Poor structure. Lack of focus. Theologically ragged. And the preacher was tired. The congregation was in single figures and made up of complete strangers to me. It had the feeling of being a waste of everybody's time! Somewhere in the middle of this sermon was the story of a man who had left church in a fury during the reading of the parable of the Prodigal Son. It was his 40th birthday. All his life he had been upstaged by a brother who had left home and wasted his life. The whole family lived in a state of constant anxiety over the waster, while the decent 'stay at home' brother was taken for granted. Arriving in church on his birthday to hear the Prodigal Son being celebrated was just too much to hear. He left in a rage but it was the beginning of a new honesty. At the end of the service, a lady asked to speak to me. From beginning to end the sermon had described her life, especially the man's reaction to the Prodigal Son. The outcome was a

> long discussion about sibling rivalries, family tensions and the recovery of faith in God. A poor sermon strangely used by God to help a woman reshape her life.

In this incident the normal preaching of the word of God on central themes of the Gospel triggered recognition and response. The preacher was unknown to the individuals, but the preaching carried over into personal conversation that proved pastorally healing. This story illustrates well the recurring mystery of preaching where people ask 'how did you know?' There are few preachers who will not be able to identify with this experience.

Preaching may attempt to have a pastoral dimension intentionally. I suspect, though, that when we set out to preach pastoral sermons in a vacuum, when we set out to preach *about* pastoral issues, the sermons fail to achieve all that we might have hoped for. We may communicate information, we may convey something of our attitudes and our availability (valuable though these may be) but we fail to move people. Perhaps good pastoral sermons are those preached in direct response to a given situation. One of the best, theologically and pastorally, was that preached in Lockerbie Parish Church by James Whyte, then Moderator of the General Assembly of the Church of Scotland, just days after the air disaster. In that sermon, he recognised the need for justice but not for retaliation. He identified the suffering of the innocent at the hands of evil men and in conclusion he asked:

> Where was God in all of that? Can anyone doubt that he was right there in the midst of it? If here in the midst of evil we find goodness, if here in the midst of darkness we find light, if here in the midst of desolation we find ourselves strangely comforted, can we doubt that our lives are touched by the God of all comfort, the God whose consolation never fails? It is the experience of humankind, that when we walk through the valley of the shadow, we are not helped by smooth words spoken from a safe distance, but by those who have known the darkness and are prepared to share it with us, and hold us till we see the light. This is the way the comfort of God touches us and holds us. For it is as we share the suffering that we share the comfort. 'Our hope for you is unshaken,' says Paul, 'for we know that if you share in our sufferings, you will also share in our comfort.' (95)

In the days which followed I met no one who did not find that sermon anything other than 'right' and deeply moving.

Eucharistic worship as pastoral care

Within the Reformed tradition, very little has been written about the pastoral dimension of the sacraments with the notable exception of Ralph Underwood's *Pastoral Care and the Means of Grace* (1993). There is of course a different emphasis within the Anglican, Roman Catholic and Orthodox traditions. While the Reformed churches regard only Baptism and Holy Communion as sacraments instituted by Jesus, churches in the catholic tradition recognise seven of which Confession and the Sacrament of the Sick have an obvious and direct pastoral relevance. And while the Eucharist has a central and normative place in Anglican and Catholic worship, in the Reformed and Free churches the ministry of the word is dominant with less frequent celebrations of communion. Anglican and Roman Catholic patients expect to be offered communion by their hospital chaplains, as an aid to recovery; Presbyterians may think they are being offered the last rites.

Despite its relative infrequency of celebration, Reformed churches in the tradition of Calvin and Knox have a 'high' theology of the sacraments. This is in some contrast to the Zwinglian emphasis for which the service was thought of as more like a commemoration of the death of Christ. There is, in my view, a correlation between a high view of the Eucharist and its pastoral significance, as I think can be demonstrated by an exploration of certain themes central to an understanding of the Eucharist. These are (a) real presence; (b) Eucharistic sacrifice and (c) eschatological hope.

Real presence

This is a phrase the interpretation of which has led to much controversy. There is however much that is held in common, not the least of which is an awareness of the 'spiritual presence' of Christ in the sacrament. No one can claim that the Westminster Confession of Faith is a document with Romanist leanings, but even that Confession says that those who come to this table in faith 'not carnally but spiritually receive and feed upon Christ crucified and all his benefits'; it also speaks of Christ being 'spiritually present to the faith of believers'. This has been a consistent theme in Reformed sacramental theology. In the sixteenth century, John Knox's successor as minister of St Giles in Edinburgh was a Robert Bruce, who in a sermon on the Lord's Supper posed the question, 'What do we get in the sacrament that we do not get in the preaching of the word?' His answer was 'Nothing, but we get a better grasp of it' (84).

Second, experience teaches that the grace of the real presence of Christ is communicated not only in the arena of public worship. It can also happen in more intimate celebrations. A parish minister recounts the following incident.

> I was visiting a home to give communion to a man who was very ill,

> indeed on the point of death. He had one son, mentally handicapped and the mother said to this son 'Now, Drew, this is not for you.' I asked 'Why not?' The mother said 'But he has never joined the church!' to which I replied 'He is baptised. He is one of God's children'. 'You mean he can take communion?' 'Of course' I said, and her eyes filled with tears as that little family gathered round that bedside table of the Lord.

Of course there are enough questions raised by this story to occupy the attention of the systematic theologians for long enough. Significantly, however, the minister involved in the above incident later suggested to me that 'something needs to be written on the changing face of pastoral theology, or rather how pastoral concern changes theology.' Precisely! What this parish minister was articulating was the realisation that his own pastoral theology was being forged in the furnace of pastoral experience. While the tradition of the Church is an indispensable factor in formulating our theology, for working ministers their 'owned' theology as opposed to the theology which they learned in college is generated out of the continual interaction between the tradition and their pastoral practice. The interaction, the 'mutually critical correlation', is important. Pastoral practice driven totally by the tradition leads to arid theology and irrelevant practice. Pastoral practice driven entirely by a pragmatic response to the situation leads to the non-engagement of a disembodied theology and an unprincipled practice. For the minister and family involved in the above episode, the real presence of Christ was not just a theological concept. It was the lived experience of 'holy communion' of that family with the Lord.

There is a third way in which the idea of 'real presence' is directly related to the experience of grace and that is through an analogical relationship with pastoral care. On reflection I realise that I have experienced grace most directly in human relationships. It has happened among family and friends; and it has happened in more particular relationships of pastoral care and counselling. All of these relationships were characterised by the fact that another person was 'really present' to me, enabling me to hear words spoken that I normally could not hear, words both of confrontation and affirmation, of judgement and of grace. It should not surprise us that we find such strong parallels between this sacrament and pastoral care. In the sacrament, word and sign are intimately related. And in pastoral care? Is there not the same kind of relationship between the words which are spoken and the quality of the relationship in which they are spoken? Is there not a sense in which the caring relationship itself has a sacramental quality, that pastoral care can be a parable of the Gospel, pointing beyond itself to the grace of a caring God? Is it not within the context of that relationship that words can be spoken and heard and their deeper personal meaning grasped? Does it not confirm for us that the communication of Christian truth is not propositional but relational?

'The Word became flesh and dwelt among us, full of grace and truth' (John 1:14).

Eucharistic sacrifice

I now turn to another phrase that in the past has divided Christians. But properly interpreted, I believe that these words, 'eucharistic sacrifice' or 'eucharistic offering' illuminate what is going on at the heart of ministry. Again I want to steer clear of past controversies and simply point out that the words are present either explicitly or implicitly in most communion rites. The emphasis is not upon any sacrifice which a priest makes upon the altar but upon the sacrifice which we ourselves make as we approach the table. In the Anglican *Alternative Service Book 1980* we find the words, echoing Romans 12:1 and Hebrews 13:15: 'Accept through him, our great high priest, this our sacrifice of thanks and praise'; and in the most recent Church of Scotland *Book of Common Order*, there is at the heart of the great communion prayer these words:

> Most gracious God,
> accept this our sacrifice
> of praise and thanksgiving
> and receive the offering of ourselves
> which now we make,
> our thoughts and words, desires and deeds.

But what does it mean to make an 'offering of ourselves'? What content ought pastoral carers give to the phrase 'thoughts and words, desires and deeds'? Is it not that along with the whole people of God, we offer all that is best in us as a response to the Gospel: time, talents, skills and training. These constitute our eucharistic offering, our thank offering. But we need to be clear that they are a response to the Gospel, gifts offered in freedom and not out of inner compulsive needs. Those who have studied Frank Lake's dynamic life cycle (1966) do not need to be reminded of the dynamics of grace and the dynamics of works. Whether in our own personal counselling or in supervision or in spiritual direction we need to become aware of our own pathology so that the offering of care which we make as part of our reasonable service is truly a free response to the grace which we have already received and not a neurotic attempt to answer our own deepest needs.

But there is a truth that is deeper than this, for our eucharistic offering consists of more than our gifts and skills. In our pastoral care, as in our worship, our eucharistic offering must consist also in the offering of our weakness and vulnerability. I suspect that for most people who find themselves in pastoral ministry, ordained or lay, there is an element of surprise. Many people come into pastoral ministry not because of their strengths but from a point of weakness. Having gone through a difficult time in their own lives, they have found themselves accompanied through the valley of shadows and cared for, and in being cared for themselves, they have experienced healing, grown in self-awareness and to their own surprise found themselves accompanying others on their journey. For many carers, the transition from being wounded to becoming healer is part of the journey. Brokenness and vulnerability are part of our eucharistic offering. But this should not surprise us. 'This is my body', said Jesus, 'broken for you' (1 Cor. 11:24). The mystery of grace is that healing flows from the cross. Some of the most moving services which I have had the privilege of leading have been communion services in the hospital chapel. For those who were regular communicants in their own churches, for those who had not been to communion for a long time and even for those with no prior experience of sacramental worship, the dominical words about a broken body and blood shed 'for them' touched a deep and healing chord within them at that moment of their own physical vulnerability.

Eschatological hope

The early Church was most vividly and intensely aware of living 'between the times', in the time between the events surrounding Jesus' first coming and the expected time of his second coming. Both the memory of his first coming and the hope of his second coming, the eschatological hope, were very real. For them communion belonged to the 'time between the times', both as memory and as hope, both as a remembrance of mighty acts which had already taken place, and as a promise, a foretaste of what was yet to be. For us, as the events surrounding the first coming have receded into history, so also has any awareness of a second coming become less central to our beliefs. What are the implications for pastoral care of these words 'you proclaim the Lord's death until he comes' (1 Cor. 11:26)?

It is easy to forget that when the early Church celebrated the sacrament, it was indeed a celebration. And it was a celebration because it was based on a twofold memory. It was certainly based upon the events which took place 'on the night on which he was betrayed' (1 Cor. 11:26), events related to betrayal and crucifixion and death. This must not be forgotten, though I have to say that I believe my own Presbyterian tradition has overdone this aspect somewhat. But each celebration of the sacrament by the early Church must have been infused with another set of memories; of a breakfast on the beach when the risen Lord said 'Come and have breakfast' (John 21:12), and of that other occasion when on the road to Emmaus, the risen Lord made himself known to them in the breaking of bread (Luke 24:28–35). So from the beginning, the celebration of Holy Communion embraced an awareness not only of the death of Christ but also of the experience of resurrection and with that experience, a foretaste of the ultimate triumph of God. 'As often as you eat this bread and drink the cup, you proclaim the Lord's death until he comes ...' (1 Cor.11:26). What then can we make of these words? Can I suggest that we interpret these words as an invitation, not certainly as an invitation to predict future events but rather as an invitation to invoke present imagination. When creeds and credal statements are interpreted literally, the result is usually disagreement and frustration; but when creeds and credal statements are interpreted imaginatively, the result can be a fresh awareness of the transforming power of the Gospel.

An understanding of what we are about as we approach the table can work a comparable transformation of what we are about in our ministry of pastoral care. For if our understanding of the sacrament is shaped by both memory and hope, if we remember not only the reality of the darkness of the cross but also reality of the light of the resurrection, then we shall also bring a different perspective to our ministry, a ministry which can give us strength not only to accompany others through the dark places of the human journey but also to bring to bear the transforming light of the Gospel. As we approach the holy table, as we partake, as we nurture within our hearts the thought that as often as we do this, we proclaim the Lord's death until he comes, is it possible that deep with us there can be stirred such an evocation of the imagination that our ministry is undergirded by the kind of hope which is central to that care and counselling which we call pastoral?

Of course we must be careful when we use the language of hope in pastoral ministry. There are practitioners, both secular and pastoral, who offer a hope that is too easy, like Bonhoeffer's cheap grace. There is, however, something deeper than that. I want to take seriously what Donald Capps says in his book *Agents of Hope* when he argues that while for other caring professionals hope is a by-product of their work, for pastoral carers hope is at the very core of their activity. Hope is central to pastoral ministry because hope is integral to the Gospel. What does this mean in practice? In his *Ethics,* Bonhoeffer makes a distinction between things which belong to the Penultimate, and those things which belong to the Ultimate. To the Penultimate belongs all our human activity, all our decision-making, all our successes and all our failures; to the Ultimate belongs only one thing, the justifying, saving Word of God. *Bonhoeffer 1945,* an imaginative and moving reconstruction of the martyr's last days in prison, was performed at the Edinburgh Festival Fringe in 1996. As the play draws to its conclusion, we hear coming over the loudspeaker system the infamous words that summoned Bonhoeffer to his execution. 'Pastor Bonhoeffer, come with us.' But with profound insight into the thought of Bonhoeffer, the writer does not end the play with these words. The play ends with Bonhoeffer on his knees, praying in the words of Psalm 150.

> Praise the Lord!
> Praise God in his sanctuary;
> praise him in his mighty firmament!

Praise him for his mighty deeds;
praise him according to his exceeding greatness! ...
(RSV)

The final words addressed to Bonhoeffer become the Penultimate words of the play. The word of condemnation is only the penultimate word. The final word is the Word of God, the word of grace.

Is there not here a word for our ministry of pastoral care? To the Penultimate belong all our human words, all that we have to offer, our training and our skills, our good intentions and our mixed motives. Yet in pastoral care, we offer that care in another context, the context of the Ultimate. In our pastoral care, with our imagination transformed by words of resurrection and hope. We know that beyond our words – and beyond our silence – there is another word. We offer our pastoral care imaginatively aware of the possibility of new beginnings. We sit with the depressed, believing that there is no human darkness into which a glimmer of light cannot break through, that the last word is not of despair but of hope. We stand by the remorseful in the conviction that there is no human folly that cannot be forgiven, that the final word is not of judgement but of grace. We support the bereaved, believing that there is no human grief that cannot in some measure be consoled, that the last word is not of death but of life.

Bibliography

Anderson, H. and Foley, E. (1998) *Mighty Stories, Dangerous Rituals*. San Francisco: Jossey-Bass.

Bonhoeffer, D. (1955) *Ethics*. London: SCM Press.

Bruce, R. (1958) *The Mystery of the Lord's Supper 1589*. Cambridge: James Clarke.

Brueggemann, W. (1991) *Interpretation and Obedience: from faithful reading to faithful living*. Philadelphia: Fortress Press.

Capps, D. (1995) *Agents of Hope*. Minneapolis: Fortress Press.

Carr, W. (1985) *Brief Encounters: pastoral ministry through the occasional offices*. London: SPCK.

Farley, E. (2003) *Practicing Gospel: unconventional thoughts on the Church's ministry*. Louisville, KY: Westminster John Knox Press.

Kelly, E. (2002) *Marking Life and Death: co-constructing welcoming and funeral rituals for babies dying in utero or shortly after birth*. Edinburgh: Contact Pastoral Monograph No. 12.

Lake, F. (1966) *Clinical Theology*. London: Darton, Longman & Todd.

Lyall, D. (2001) *The Integrity of Pastoral Care*. London: SPCK.

Ramshaw, E. (1987) *Ritual and Pastoral Care*. Philadelphia: Fortress Press.

Reed, B. (1978) *The Dynamics of Religion*. London: Darton, Longman & Todd.

Thurneysen, E. (1962) *A Theology of Pastoral Care*. Richmond VA: John Knox Press.

Underwood, R. L. (1993) *Pastoral Care and the Means of Grace*. Minneapolis: Fortress Press.

Whyte, J. A. (1993) *Laughter and Tears*. Edinburgh: St Andrew Press.

CHAPTER 14:

The Scriptures in preaching

MICHAEL QUICKE

Most books on Christian preaching presume the Bible to be foundational for their task. They urge the need to exegete its text, to interpret it for hearers and then to design material for communication. However, pastoral practice begins elsewhere with the needs of individual hearers or a group and the Bible is used reactively to these needs. Put bluntly, there seems to be contrast between the modes of preaching and pastoral care with regard to the use of the Bible. Though it may be the same person who stands in the pulpit on Sundays and counsels people on Mondays, too often preaching appears to operate by utterly contrary principles from those of pastoral practice. Preaching requires talking, a proclamation of the biblical text, as one person stands in front of others (often elevated in a pulpit) and calls for a response with blanket claims and general applications. It is public declamation at a distance. However, in pastoral practice one person sits with another, listens and shares an experiential word with broken reeds. It is close and private, using Scripture personally and sensitively. Nowhere are the tensions over using the Bible in pastoral practice more public than in preaching. Not only does the gap between biblical scholarship on one hand and practical application for everyday living on the other have to be bridged, but also pastoral practice itself deepens tension between the acts of preaching and pastoring. Most preacher/pastors will recognise the tension between these roles (Killinger, 71). This can lead to charges and counter charges about use and abuse of the Bible. Traditional preachers condemn any preaching that sounds too much like counselling and uses Scripture as a therapeutic resource. In contrast, others retort that preaching Bible texts in traditional format is remote and disconnected as it majors in prescriptive truisms. Frederick Buechner once commented about preachers: 'There is precious little in most of their preaching to suggest that they have rejoiced and suffered with the rest of mankind' (Dykstra, 4). This chapter will probe this tension between preaching, teaching and pastoring with regard to the use of the Bible. In particular it will examine some perspectives on 'pastoral preaching' that will provide a framework for considering important issues in this debate.

Three perspectives

Dykstra (2001) offers three contradictory perspectives on pastoral preaching. The first perspective regards pastoral preaching as *nearly impossible,* unkindly calling 'pastoral preaching' an oxymoron, holding that the gospel imperatives of preaching contradict directly the pastoral aim of struggling to meet people where they are. This obviously overstates the tension in absurdly negative tones. However strong the rivalry between these two aspects of a minister's calling, few would agree to their divorce. I shall argue that out of this inevitable tension have emerged creative results in new homiletical developments that show a rich diversity in use of the Bible.

A second view sees the relationship as *virtually inevitable* since most preaching is de facto in pastoral situations and preachers should be alert to the life situations of members of their congregations. This stance is most easily identified with H. E. Fosdick who defined his sermons as 'personal counselling on a group scale' (Killinger, 54). If the first perspective wildly overstates the tension this understates it, as it oversimplifies the self-understanding necessary of preacher and pastor – about themselves, their relationship with Scripture and with their listeners. Fosdick had a gifted, unusual (and controversial) ministry that has been rarely duplicated. However, for lesser mortals, this perspective emphasises the person of the preacher. It necessarily exposes links between psychotherapy and preaching and brings to the fore the ways hearers collaborate with preachers over the use of Scripture.

A third perspective is limited to content and sees pastoral preaching as *primarily topical* because it focuses on pastoral topics such as grief, addiction, divorce and sexuality. While this view confines pastoral preaching to subject boxes and disingenuously misses the wider debate, it highlights the need for preaching to address vital life issues. Use of the Bible for pastoral topics also needs attention.

While these perspectives contradict each other, together they raise different issues that are germane to the whole subject of Bible, pastoral care and proclamation. The rest of this chapter will examine some of these implications: first, how creative tensions in the use of the Bible have led to new preaching forms; second, some personal sensitivities required when using the Bible in pastoral preaching and some issues of collaboration; third, some specific pastoral topics that need to be preached when the Bible is used in pastoral practice.

Creative tension – new homiletics

Nichols in his classic *The Restoring Word* (1987) likens the contrast between proclamation and pastoral communication to the distinction between prophet and priest. He identifies three main differences: first, in terms of their kinds of language, prophetic preaching stresses biblical and theological language about God's mighty acts and calls for a response, often with a transcendental dimension, whereas the priest stays more in the human experiential domain. Second, they direct their messages differently – the prophet directs attention outwardly to change and service of a world in need, while the priest focuses on an inner direction, on the interior lives of listeners. Third, they have different views on the nature of their hearers. The prophet addresses people as a corporate entity with wider community concerns in contrast to the priest who more typically focuses on the individual (55–60).

Though Nichols believes that this distinction is false (and attempts to resolve it, as we shall see later), he points out its dire consequences as certain practices have often been sadly separated and professionalised in the church's story. *Kērygma* (proclamation) has become identified exclusively with preaching; *didachē* (teaching) with catechesis and education; and *therapeia* (care and nurture) with pastoral counselling. Indeed, larger church fellowships sometimes boast specialist staff in each of these areas who are likely to use the Bible in different ways: preaching, which heralds its gospel claims; teaching, which educates believers in Christian principles; care and nurture, which uses Scripture pragmatically in response to others' needs. Is proclamation destined to be separated from *didachē* and therapy?

I contend that preaching, by broadening its use of the Bible, should be involved in all three practices in the Church and that there is growing evidence of such increasingly diverse forms. No longer can preaching be regarded as a single category of proclamation, as some monolithic entity in contrast to pastoral care. In the latter part of the twentieth century new kinds of preaching have emerged, partly forged out of this tension between preaching and pastoral care. Today's preaching landscape offers a wide range of images and models, which show different possibilities for preachers to express the diversity of *kērygma, didachē* and *therapeia.*

Current preacher models

Building on the work of Thomas Long (1989), various contemporary preacher images have emerged: teacher, herald, pastor, narrative preacher (Quicke, 97–108). Until the mid twentieth century, the first two held sway.

The *teacher* preacher gives priority to teaching the ideas of Scripture. C. H. Dodd (1964) claimed that there was a technical distinction between the verbs *Kērygma* (public proclamation to the non-Christian world) and *didachē* (ethical instruction within the church). However, New Testament evidence shows these words are used far more interchangeably than might expected if a significant distinction was intended (Matt. 4:23; Luke 4:15, 16; Acts 28:31). In practice teaching and preaching belong closely together. Teacher preachers have a high view of Scripture and are concerned to communicate the ideas of the text as sermon ideas. An opening thesis is followed by a series of points or sub-theses, each of which is explained, illustrated and applied to listeners. Its style is at home in the classroom as well as in the pulpit with its linear logic and coherence making it a safe and efficient method of preaching. Its pattern of exegesis, exposition and application forms the bread-and-butter method of preaching. Some preachers, popularly described as 'left-brained' (Babin 1991), are strongly drawn to this form, which is sometimes typified as 'three heads and nine tails' (Craddock 1971).

The *herald* model gives priority to proclaiming God's word in Scripture and is strongly identified with declamatory styles of the nineteenth and early twentieth century. This model of preaching most typifies Nichols' 'prophet' stereotype as it authoritatively declares God's truth. Herald preachers give priority to proclaiming God's word in Scripture with a high view of Scripture and of God's presence in the preaching act. Long describes its dynamic: 'The primary movement of preaching is *from* God *through* the herald *to* the hearers' (Long, 28). Herald preachers see connections occurring through 'word-events' convinced that words both *say* and *do*. For Long, its main weakness relates to its secondary concern for the hearers. Indeed, such can be the 'emphasis on the purity and integrity of the message, [it] can give the impression of preaching as an anonymous message dropped into a box' (30). When pastoral issues are mentioned they are likely to take the form of illustrations about how a biblical truth applies to the hearers.

Teacher and herald preaching, traditional preaching, held the ground until the 1950s when a third kind of preaching model emerged. Long calls this *pastor preaching* – 'a whole ground-shift in the understanding of the preacher's responsibility' (31). 'The pastoral preacher must know more than a set of messages; the pastoral preacher must also know people and how they listen to messages' (31). This kind of preaching has a reverse dynamic – it moves *from* hearers back *to* Scriptures. Pastor preachers begin with hearers' needs, or even personal concerns, which then motivate appropriate sermons. The pastor preacher is concerned for what happens inside the hearer. Long also argues that such preaching 'contains a more historically based understanding of the scripture as the record of the interaction of the gospel with the concrete realities of human situations' (33). The Bible is about real lives then and now and is peculiarly suited to pastoral preaching. Of course, Long also notes weaknesses in the pastor image. It can focus on individuals and their needs rather than on communities and their strengths. It can 'overwork the notion of relevance' since Scripture points beyond to bigger complex truths in

God's kingdom. Further, it runs the risk of reducing profound scriptural truths to human sized, needs-based messages.

The description 'pastor preaching' is highly significant. While traditional preaching often contained short inductive movements, when a preacher moved from the hearers' particulars back towards the text, this phenomenon of 'pastor preaching' describes a thoroughly inductive style. What accounted for the appearance of this 'reverse dynamic' preaching? It appears to have two primary causes: the impact of pastoral care on the pulpit as preachers increasingly recognised the significance of listeners' needs, alongside an increasing dissatisfaction with traditional preaching (Craddock 1971, 1985).

In the1920s the pastoral care movement gained momentum in churches and pastoral psychology was seen as an aid to preaching. Later, in the 1950s, the term 'life-situation preaching' emerged. Charles Kemp uses this description in *Life-situation Preaching* (1956) to describe many practitioners such as Bushnell, Brooks and Fosdick. Though some argue that in this preaching there was 'often facile use of psychological answers to problems that may be as much theological as psychological in nature' (Willimon), others are more positive. Commenting on their role, Oates surprisingly claims: 'We can accurately say that the modern pastoral care movement had its beginnings in the pulpits of this country before it took root in hospital visitation of the sick' (450). Though this claim needs more research, undeniably preaching did take some pastoral initiative, particularly in the work of Fosdick.

Against this background Fred Craddock made a devastating critique of the form of traditional preaching in *As One without Authority* (1971). He condemned its deductive form which announces each point before it is developed, often has a weak relationship between the points, has a hortatory tone, and can lose momentum (51–76). All Bible texts are in danger of being forced into deductive packages of 'three heads and nine tails'. Craddock's book is regarded as the beginning of a revolution in homiletics that has since favoured the inductive sermon form over against the deductive. Increasing interest in forms of preaching has, however, led to a further category.

The fourth image is *narrative preaching*, which gives high priority to plotting sermons in narrative sequence so that they are both faithful to Scripture and relevant to hearers' listening patterns. Its inner dynamic has two equal movements flowing from opposite directions. One flows from hearing Scripture as God's story and the other from listening to the hearers' own story. Like herald preaching, Scripture's message must be told, yet like pastor preaching, hearers have a strong influence too.

The strength of narrative preaching lies in the attention it gives to Scripture's narrative, literary form. It fits in well with current biblical studies and a fresh appreciation of the role of story. Story has re-emerged as a potent vehicle to convey truth at many levels, cerebral and emotional, involving people holistically. Some have made connections between the value of story in preaching and in therapy. Kevin Bradt, in *Story as a Way of Knowing* (1997), uses the term 'storying' to describe the act of co-creation in storytelling by both teller and listeners. As a preacher he is concerned to see storying as a way of knowing and to emphasise the role of narrative in psychotherapy (108–17).

Some have argued that the whole shape of the sermon should be like a narrative with 'plotted moves' leading hearers through a series of responses. One of the most famous forms is Eugene Lowry's loop, which contains a sharp reversal within its five stages (1975). The first stage, 'oops!', upsets the equilibrium of the hearers so that they want to get into the sermon. He invites preachers to look for 'trouble' in the text that gives them an 'itch' which they convey to their hearers. Second, the 'ugh!' stage analyses the reason there is a problem and spends time on diagnosis. This is the most lengthy and critical part of the sermon. Lowry gives an illustration of diagnosing the problem of oppression and bigotry. When you ask, 'Why would people want to put others down?' the quick answer is pride and arrogance. However, further reflection exposes a mix of motives such as insecurity, and may lead to a conclusion: 'Self is the base line underneath the oppressive personality' (43). This leads to the 'aha!' stage, which discloses the clue to resolution. It brings the sermon to the one 'jigsaw piece' that brings the entire puzzle into focus. Listeners are surprised. This stage pulls the rug out from under them, though first it needed to be laid at the 'oops!' and 'ugh!' stages. The 'aha!' moment marks a radical discontinuity between the Gospel and worldly wisdom. The Gospel declares the last thing that they would expect to hear. His loop having gone downward through 'oops!' and 'ugh!' suddenly reverses upward at the 'aha!' to cross over in a new direction. Fourth, now on a fresh course, the 'whee!' stage expresses a new experience of the Gospel as it fleshes out good news for human life. After the induction process of the earlier stages, there is a deductive proclamation of the Gospel. Finally, 'yeah!' anticipates the consequences. The main climax of preaching is at the 'whee!' stage, but this last part asks, 'What shall we say to this?' because hearers are now in a new situation.

This loop movement may take various forms: 'running the story', which follows the actual flow of a biblical story; 'delaying the story' brings the biblical text into the sermon sequence later in order to resolve a perceived problem; 'suspending the story' begins with the text but suspends its action because of other issues along the way; 'alternating the story' divides the storyline into different sorts of material, interspersing the text with contemporary references (Lowry 1989).

Narrative preaching also has weaknesses. Long notes that not everyone has the same 'eureka' moments and a schema like Lowry's cannot do justice to every aspect of the Gospel. The more regularly it is used, the more predictable and contrived it may become (Long, 95). However, it clearly marks both an engagement with the text and also with the hearers that gives room for considerable pastoral sensitivity. Barbara Brown Taylor preaches a Lowry loop sermon on Luke 15:1–7 (the lost sheep parable), in which she raises questions about Jesus' method of pastoral care. She describes the Pharisees' anger because Jesus is treating sinners like special cases,

> which is as good as condoning their behavior and thereby robs them of their motivation to do better … All they have to do is wander off from the flock, pursuing their own whims, and the good shepherd will go off after them. It is not only bad shepherding; it is bad pastoral care. It is bad theology … What about the good people? What about us? (150)

This 'oops!' and 'ugh!' leads to an 'aha!' about discovering the radical nature of Jesus' pastoral care that focuses less on 'good people' than seeking and rejoicing with the lost.

The arrival of pastor preaching and narrative preaching has transformed the preaching landscape, making for a range of options set before biblical preachers (Quicke). The different types pursue diverse routes through biblical content, use of text and sermon form. Traditional types of preaching – teacher and herald – use Scripture in textual (one or two verses) or expository (at least one paragraph of Scripture) ways. With the advent of 'pastor' and 'narrative' preaching there are new possibilities using the text both in textual and expository form as well as topically or thematically drawing on the Scriptures.

Three sermon forms summarise these outcomes: 'mainly deductive' encapsulates design forms used by teacher and herald though it may contain strong inductive elements; 'mainly inductive' begins with listeners' needs or sees 'trouble' in the text that hearers readily relate to in a process which 'corresponds to the way people ordinarily experience reality and to the way life's problem-solving activity goes on naturally and casually' (Craddock in Long 1989, 98); 'Plotted moves' obviously includes Lowry's loop. Other sermon types also fall into this category including David Buttrick's phenomenological move sermons 'which comprise a series of moves to form faith in the consciousness of hearers' (1987) and Henry Mitchell's analysis of 'black preaching' with its 'flow in consciousness' leading to behavioural change (1990).

These four preaching models live in creative tension with each other and represent some of the conflict noted earlier between prophet and priest. No one form can claim to possess the monopoly of biblical preaching. This is partly because of the nature of the Bible itself. Teacher preachers react to ideas and propositions in Scripture that can be taught deductively by outlines. Narrative preachers respond to narratives in Scripture than can be preached inductively by stories. But, of course, Scripture does not present either/or choices. It contains ideas and stories, words and images. It provides preachers with a rich variety of propositions and representations, deductive and inductive approaches. It comprises a fertile diversity of genres that enable preachers to explore a range of preaching options. 'Scripture's diversity of genres legitimates all four models of preachers' (Quicke, 106). Over a period of time, the same preacher may therefore find himself or herself identifying with each of these styles depending on their text and their situation. Which of these four models is deployed depends greatly on the pastoral gifting and situation of preachers. Maybe some preachers are predisposed to the 'teaching' form because they are more left-brained with more cerebral congregations. However, preachers who are involved 'holistically' in the lives of individuals and community are more likely to employ pastor and narrative styles. It is vital to challenge all preachers to develop skills beyond their 'comfort zones'. Congregations contain a wide variety of people and needs – cerebral and less so. Biblical good news should be shared in diverse ways. The Church lives within the tension of proclamation and pastoral care. It needs preachers who represent the ministries of both prophet and priest.

Pastoral preaching – personal sensitivity to Scripture

The person of the preacher combines both roles of preaching and pastoring. Though Brooks deemed the two parts of a preacher's work to be in rivalry he insisted that in practice they are one. 'The preacher, who is not a pastor, grows remote. The pastor, who is not a preacher, grows petty ... you cannot really be one unless you also are the other'(Killinger, 71). For Killinger the public act of preaching belongs to the private act of pastoral care. Pastoral care for the hearers means that a preacher can only approach the Bible with a focus on people 'as the objects of God's love and redemptive activity ... it not only makes sermons more human, it makes them more responsive to the particular thoughts and reactions of specific persons in the congregation' (60, 61). A sensitive pastor 'is less likely to make sweeping generalized, universal judgments about the human condition' (Willimon, 363). Their relationship with their hearers is affected by the quality of empathy in their preaching and sermons may act as pre-counselling, preparing the way for hearers to seek further help.

Preacher/pastors also need to be aware of how much of themselves is involved in their use of Scripture. Traditional preaching in the forms of 'teacher' and 'herald' focused on the message at the expense of the messenger. Indeed some of its advocates warned against speaking in the first person and opposed using personal stories. In contrast, 'pastor' and 'narrative preacher' models inevitably involve the personhood of preachers and their relationships with their listeners. A preacher's character, integrity and listening skills are intimately involved especially with regard to use of the Bible. We need to see how closely linked are the roles of preacher and pastor and how some preachers have developed models of collaboration with hearers.

Preaching as pastoral communication

Earlier, we noted how Nichols contrasts prophet and priest by three main differences: use of language, direction of message and view of the hearers. In *The Restoring Word: preaching as pastoral communication* (1987) he argues that this distinction is false since prophet and priest have a dialectical relationship – 'it is not a "conflict" to be "resolved" but a dynamic interaction to be sustained' (60). For example, 'therapeutic communication' (the language of effective counselling) and 'religious communication' (the sermon) interact. Basing his analysis on the three areas of supposed difference above, he sees therapy's language as 'optimally self-involving, ambiguous and intense'. In preaching these are 'translated into ... ethical authority, transformational power and a sense of transcendence' (61). In pastoral communication God-talk cannot be separated from theological interpretation and experiential description. Proclaiming God's mighty acts, which calls for a response, requires the 'immediacy of our own often broken existence', and also engages the need to 'take and discharge ethical authority' (63). Self-involvement, therefore, involves ethical authority. Similarly 'ambiguity' comes from the tension of living between the past and the future, yet being caught up in the transformational power of God. Third, 'intensity' sums up the process of finding the most significant locus of response ('let anyone with ears to hear, listen'), committing hearers to examine their limited conditions of life and perhaps transcend them. Therapy and preaching may therefore function similarly. As a therapist gives permission for some things, reframes issues and teaches communication, so a preacher blesses, prophesies and teaches. Such preaching has a 'healing motion', from nurture to responsibility. Nurture on its own may lead to narcissism and responsibility to a 'works righteousness', but together they are good news (65). No wonder that, for Nichols, pastoral preaching 'is as much as anything a posture, a sensitivity, an attitude' (18). He warns how preaching without a pastoral sensitivity and attitude may inflict grave damage.

Inevitably, Nichols sees this dialectic most clearly focused in the person of the preacher, 'using the self as a communicative tool' (111–26). 'The preaching that is most faithful to gospel, most life-giving, and most vital to its hearers is forged on the anvil of the preacher's own self-investment and self-utilization in the preaching process' (114). He also recognises the dangers of illegitimate self-investment and self-utilisation in the sermon process. For example, when choosing a text and focus he pleads for genuine 'self-assessment' rather than self-justification. Self-assessment recognises that current personal issues inevitably influence choice and *may* serve as a point of entry but he asks hard questions about 'what we are engrossed with but do not know we are engrossed with' (115). As a safeguard, he recommends writing a pastoral log-book to help keep note of ideas and events, 'but also of the kind of investment and feeling we find ourselves having in them' (116). He further warns about the dangers of self-absorption, self-displacement and self-display. He uses a list of characteristics of the 'helper in a helping relationship' to describe the preacher's most appropriate use of self with questions like: 'Can I be in some way which will be perceived by others as trustworthy, consistent? Can I be expressive enough that what I am will be communicated unambiguously?'

More specifically, Dykstra has applied insights from therapy to the preaching task and particularly the use of Scripture. His book is evocatively titled: *Discovering a Sermon: personal pastoral preaching* (2001) and is perhaps the most rigorous analysis of sermon preparation by a counsellor. He sums up sermon preparation as 'discovery' – 'distinctively marked by the pastor's personal willingness to pursue enticing leads peculiar to every biblical text or human circumstance ... contingent not on giftedness for speaking but on intensity of attention and love' (6).

In particular he draws on the work of British psychoanalyst Donald Winnicott (known for his work on 'object relationship theory') to express the relationship of a preacher to Scripture. He compares the preacher's role in the earliest stage of sermon preparation to Winnicott's observations of how a toddler, secure on its mother's lap, can reach out for an object on a nearby table. The preacher is like the infant on its mother's lap (which represents the Church and its traditions), with God in place of the analyst and any particular text like an object on the table. Vitality comes from the preacher's 'discovering a specific biblical text on his or her own terms amid the watchful – and tempering – presence of God and the church' (16). For a toddler there is, at first, an 'illusioning' of 'omnipotence' as he or she seems able to do what they like with the object. Dykstra applies this to the need for pastors to experience a sense of 'omnipotence' with the text. He describes his experience of spending two hours on his own, without turning to commentaries or other helps, to bring 'the full range of my love and hate, my naiveté and suspicion, my faith and doubt, my sexuality and soul, and my knowledge and ignorance to the text under scrutiny' (22).

For a deep relationship with a text, a preacher has to develop a capacity to be alone – what Dykstra calls 'a ministry of absence' in which preachers are emotionally mature enough to experience 'playfulness, honesty, confidence and courage'. He encourages 'uncensored daydreaming' around the particular biblical text and then 'free association'. For Dykstra curiosity is essential as is the apparent 'capacity to waste time' as preachers spend one or two hours' reflection on unresolved problems in their personal lives. He describes how the Holy Spirit draws attention to moments of everyday life and incarnates the text into the preacher's own experience and helps the preacher to encounter the stranger within himself or herself. Only after this time of preparation should preachers turn to commentaries. The last stage of sermon preparation depends upon personal breakthroughs that 'emerge from placing on a collision course whatever may be the preacher's current preoccupation or desire with whatever may be the assigned or selected biblical text of the day' (106). As he puts it, 'Radically the edges of *any* story of interest to the preacher can be productively engaged at the edges of *any* biblical text' (107).

Dykstra shows great confidence (perhaps too much!) in the integrity of preachers when they allow themselves to live with a text and relate it to their life experiences. In a sermon entitled 'The Unreality of God', based on Mark 2:1–12, he frames its structure around a personal story about the breaking and renewing of a valuable Steuben vase (59–65). He asks honestly, 'Why this story?' He describes how it mysteriously came into his mind and then 'from the outset of my preparation I intuitively sought to factor in the story of the vase and likely read the biblical narrative all along through that particular lens' (68). The broken vase became the symbol for the paralysed man on his mat in Mark 2. Traditional preachers would criticise his 'exegesis of contemporary life' (66) at the expense of biblical exegesis, and would sound out more loudly Nichols' earlier warnings about the dangers of self-absorption, self-displacement and self-display. Yet Dykstra's description of how a preacher handles a text, his naming of the work of the Holy Spirit in the personal reflections of a preacher, and his awareness of pastoral issues, has much to teach traditional preachers. His challenge that ministers need to read beyond what parishioners are reading, to 'see something – some subtlety, some singularity, some mystery – that others overlook' (43), cannot be lightly dismissed.

Another important aspect of pastoral preaching concerns the role of hearers in the preaching process. John McClure, in *The Round-table Pulpit* (1995), contrasts 'sovereign preaching', which is hierarchical, putting the congregation into a position of dependence and submission, with 'collaborative preaching' in which preacher and hearer work together. He argues for a 'round-table pulpit' where members of the congregation participate. He has developed a long-term pattern that involves groups of ten people, men and women of various ages, interests and backgrounds, who collaborate with the preacher as they engage with the biblical text and one another. He describes five dynamics to describe the group's response to the text in sermon preparation: topic-setting, interpretation, empowerment, coming to terms and practice. Such a group context allows strong pastoral interaction. He gives examples of members reflecting on their own experiences of grief and enabling connections to be made with Scripture that others may never have considered. Issues of maintaining confidentiality are emphasised. McClure concludes from his own experience: 'over the course of time, collaborative preaching empowers members of a congregation to become interpreters of biblical faith and partners in the mission of the church' (108).

Others have similarly stressed the need to collaborate. Leonora Tubbs Tisdale (1997) offers the image of the preacher as 'dancer' extending a hand to partners in Scripture, congregation and church doctrine with the need to 'exegete the congregation'. Christine Smith (1989) uses a model of 'weaving the sermon' to describe the 'web of human relatedness' within the preacher's community. Whenever a preacher uses the Bible in dialogue with the hearers there is inevitably a deepening corporate experience.

Pastoral topics

The third perspective defines pastoral preaching by its content, when a sermon's subject focuses on a pastoral concern for individuals or community. Nichols comments how it strikes him as 'poor homiletical stewardship to let the whole area of mental health and human relationships remain a *tacit* dimension of our preaching' (18) or not even be mentioned at all. Issues such as depression, relationship breakdown or sexual relationships should not be left to television talk shows or popular magazines. However, in the recent phenomenon of much popular preaching in 'seeker service' contexts, preachers have increasingly used the Bible to address topics of human need and relationships. For example, Rick Warren, a pioneer of seeker services at Saddleback Community Church, California, states: 'Each week I begin with a need, hurt or interest and then move to what God has to say about it in His Word … I will use many verses from many passages that speak to the topic. I call this kind of preaching 'verse-with-verse' exposition' (1996). Preaching on pastoral topics is a vital part of a preacher's responsibility today.

Many preachers are peculiarly vulnerable when considering pastoral topics. This is partly because most literature on pastoral issues is complex and fails to mention preaching (Nichols, 157) and partly because Bible commentaries rarely give adequate detail about contemporary pastoral implications. Preachers are therefore left to make the connections between Scripture and pastoral topics themselves. The dangers are obvious. On one hand, complex pastoral issues can be oversimplified and, on the other hand, the Bible can be trivialised in its application or at worst misappropriated.

For example, 'depression' can be addressed as though it is a single category of illness without attention to its complexity. Nichols warns against overusing the word 'depression' and explains some important distinctions, such as between reactive or endogenous, and between transient or chronic. He suggests that preachers need to read about the subject in order to recognise its wide range of manifestations and causes that include: loss, helplessness, delayed grieving, anger turned inward, exaggerated hopes and aspirations, and holidays (158–63). He challenges preachers not to preach 'ought' sermons, but to help people make a distinction between sadness and depression, and to ensure proper account is taken of real anger, sin and death in the world. His sermon: 'The city of sadness' (Ps. 137:1–6; Heb. 11:1, 13–16; Rev. 21:2–4) develops a theme that 'a sense of sadness can be a form of love' (192–205). Here is no simplistic message.

To safeguard against pastoral oversimplification, a preacher needs to be aware of the literature and to listen to the experiences of the congregation. Leonora Tubbs Tisdale, in a sermon on forgiveness, deliberately deepens the issue (Elliott, 118–28). She confesses her difficulty with Luke 6:27: 'Love your enemies, do good to those who hate you.' She declares that 'forgiveness, in a biblical understanding does not always mean a resumption of former relations, a return to things as they were' (121). She quotes David Augsburger where he says that forgiveness understood as returning can be dangerous – 'a restitution of an old order, a backward movement, a regression to the previous situation with the old injustices that motivated the original action or injury' (122). Such analysis realistically probes at the complicated dynamics of forgiveness while dealing with the biblical text.

Other preachers have focused on particular pastoral subjects. Kathy Black, for example, specialises in a 'healing homiletic' (1996). She condemns the Church for long neglecting those with disability and gives rules for preachers. Jerrien Gunnick focuses on *Preaching for Recovery in a Strife-torn Church* (1989). He illustrates how one preacher in a divided church preached on 'anger (Eph. 4:26, 31), grief (a sense of loss), servanthood (Matt. 23:11–12), humility (Phil. 2:1–8), foot washing (John 13:14–15) and several topics from 1 Corinthians. These sermons helped to change the behavior of the affected people' (74). H. Beecher Hicks takes a similar theme in *Preaching through a Storm* (1987).

On the other hand, preachers can be vulnerable by trivialising the Bible's application to some contemporary need. Of course there are points of direct pastoral connection. Oates highlights the Bible's relevance to dealing with conflict situations (Matt. 18:15–20) and the ministry of widows (Acts 6:1–6; 1 Tim. 5:3–16; James 1:27 (453). David H. C. Read's sermon 'Access for the Disabled' comes directly from 2 Samuel 9, David's care for Mephibosheth (105–12). However some uses of the Bible seem highly inappropriate. The testing of Abraham (Gen. 22) is not primarily about how fathers should deal with teenagers; Psalm 23 is not about stress management; nor the David and Goliath story (1 Sam. 21) about overcoming debt. Nothing reveals who a preacher is more than the way he or she uses Scripture for preaching and teaching a pastoral topic.

The different preaching images – teacher, herald, pastor and narrative preacher – when a pastoral topic becomes the focus, will deal with Scripture in different ways with contrasting outcomes. For example, consider how different preachers use the Bible on the issue of marriage and divorce. Any congregation is likely to comprise hearers who have been divorced, children of divorcees, couples contemplating divorce and others who want an unambiguous 'hard line'. The tape *Preaching Today* 240 (2003) contrasts two approaches. Greg Lafferty in 'Passion for God's Covenant' uses Malachi 2:10–16 to condemn 'the breaking of faith ... divorce'. His stance is that of the herald preacher who has God's truth to declare. The flow of his sermon moves through expository use of text into a mainly deductive sermon form. He begins with distressing statistics about the devastating results of divorce and says that he intends 'going after the honour of marital faithfulness ... the whole world depends on marital faithfulness.' To those who are divorced he says: 'I ask you to bear the pain of the next twenty or twenty five minutes redemptively ... If you stick it out you can know that some people here will be prevented the mountain of grief you've suffered because you've been divorced.' His sermon has three points each beginning 'Marital faithfulness represents a passion – for God's covenant, for God's community and for God's children.' At his conclusion he has a word of grace from Malachi: 'Even if you've experienced divorce, God will not divorce you.'

In contrast Bob Russell focuses on those who are divorced. He demonstrates the pastor-preacher style in 'Wisdom for the Divorced'. The flow of his sermon moves through topical use of text into a mainly deductive sermon form. From concern for those who have been divorced or are going through a divorce he draws out six points to help them. He says that 'the church should hold high the ideal of marriage but acknowledge complexities' and encourages hearers to takes these steps: reconcile if possible (Deut. 24:1); repent if you're guilty (Ps. 34:18); accept it if it's over (Phil. 3:14); allow time for healing (Isa. 40:31); forgive your ex-partner (Rom. 12:19); extend yourself to the church (John 13:1–17); walk straight (Eph. 5.3). Few of the texts he refers to directly relate to the issue of divorce, but he arranges them in his pastoral theme so that 'the divorced can find God's peace and joy for their future'.

In a much more complex sermon, Dykstra (114–26) exhibits narrative preaching. The flow of his sermon moves through textual use of the Bible into a 'plotted moves' sermon form. Preaching from Mark 10:1–12, and the following verses 13–16 (the blessing of little children), he emphasises Jesus' behaviour. Instead of a topical sermon on divorce he questions the text's dynamics and context. Jesus is resolute about divorce but he seems even more opposed to the insinuations of the Pharisees. They ask about divorce, Jesus speaks of what God desires for marriage. 'Yes, you can get away with divorce, but what you can get away with is often so much less than what you could actually have, than what God intends for God's beloved' (116). Dykstra widens the theme beyond the immediate topic of divorce, to challenge all who are trying to get by with so much less than they could actually have. Puncturing smugness among those not divorced, he says: 'I think we should be grateful for divorced persons in our midst, for they know far better than most ... that Jesus is right, who know in their own flesh and blood that divorce is the last thing God intends for human beings to suffer ...[and] that divorce can be what finally sets them free to experience anew the extravagant mercy of God' (117–18). As he interweaves stories, he challenges hearers about measuring their lives by what they can get away with rather than what God offers.

Though the Bible teaches directly on marriage and divorce, treatment of other pastoral issues may need to rely implicitly on principles of Christian ethics embodied in the New Testament. David Read pleads for consistent preaching of the Bible as an 'intensely human book'. Commenting about contemporary questions like stress, anxiety, grief or terminal illness he states: 'The root values and emotions to be found in all such situations are already to be found in the Bible.' Modern questions such as sex determination, abortion, cloning, AIDs, concern the very nature of human beings 'and are untouched by the advance of science and technology' (63). The great biblical themes of creation, fall and redemption 'refer to the human condition and underlie any sermon that attempts to bring a biblical perspective to the confusions and anxieties of those who come to worship today' (64). Indeed, Read argues that preachers should not be over-anxious about dealing with individual pastoral needs every time they use the Bible. 'Someone in real trouble will look for signs that the preacher is speaking from living experience in today's world, has tested beliefs in the crucible of suffering and is speaking of a living God and not a dead dogma' (43).

Conclusion: preaching remains central to pastoral practice

This chapter has argued that different kinds of preachers can use the text by both textual-expository and topical modes in order to develop contrasting preaching forms and that the newer models of pastor preaching and narrative preaching have particular relevance for the pastoral use of the Bible. It has stressed the pastoral quality of a preacher's personal involvement with the Bible using insights of therapy, as well as emphasising how hearers can be involved in collaboration. It has also shown how preaching on pastoral topics is a significant part of a preacher's responsibility and how different kinds of preachers may use the Bible.

At the heart of Christian community lie word and sacrament. Vital though pastoral care is for the health of individuals and community, its context is God's gracious work in Jesus Christ. The communication of biblical good news is essential. As Willimon comments: 'Without the weekly demands of the preaching office, the pastor's care easily degenerates into mere care with little else to inform or to form that care than the latest psychotherapeutic trends ... preaching is pastoral care's criterion for fidelity' (363). Today, opportunities in new kinds of biblical preaching, with greater insights into a preacher's relationship with Scripture's text, invite preachers into fresh ways of using the Bible in pastoral practice.

Bibliography

Babin, P. (1991) *The New Era in Religious Communication*. Minneapolis: Fortress Press.

Black, K. (1996) *A Healing Homiletic*. Nashville, TN: Abingdon Press.

Bradt, Kevin M. (1997) *Story as a Way of Knowing*. Kansas City: Sheed & Ward.

Buttrick, D. (1987) *Homiletics: moves and structures*. Philadelphia: Fortress Press.

Craddock, F. B. (1971) *As One without Authority*. Nashville, TN: Abingdon Press.

Craddock, F. B. (1985) *Preaching*. Nashville, TN: Abingdon Press.

Dodd, C. H. (1964) *The Apostolic Preaching and Its Development*. New York: Harper.

Dykstra, R. C. (2001) *Discovering a Sermon: personal pastoral preaching*. St Louis: Chalice.

Elliott, M. B. (2000) *Creative Styles of Preaching*. Louisville, KY: Westminster John Knox Press.

Gunnick, Jerrien (1989) *Preaching for Recovery in a Strife-torn Church*. Grand Rapids, MI: Zondervan.

Hicks, H. Beecher (1987) *Preaching through the Storm*. Grand Rapids, MI: Zondervan.

Kemp, C. (1963) *Life-situation Preaching*. St Louis: Bethany.

Killinger, John (1969) *The Centrality of Preaching in the Total Task of the Ministry*. Waco: Word.

Lafferty, G. (2003) Passion for God's covenant, in *Preaching Today* tape 240. Carol Stream, IL: Christianity Today International.

Linn, Edmund Holt (1966) *Preaching as Counseling: the unique method of Harry Emerson Fosdick*. Valley Forge, PA: Judson Press.

Long, T. G. (1989) *The Witness of Preaching*. Louisville, KY: Westminster John Knox Press.

Lowry, E. (1975) *The Homiletical Plot*. Atlanta, GA: John Knox Press.

Lowry, E. (1989) *How to Preach a Parable*. Nashville, TN: Abingdon Press.

Mitchell, H. H. (1990) *Celebration and Experience in Preaching*. Nashville, TN: Abingdon Press.

McClure, J. S. (1995) *The Round-table Pulpit*. Nashville, TN: Abingdon Press.

Nichols, J. R. (1987) *The Restoring Word: preaching as pastoral communication*. San Francisco: Harper & Row.

Oates, Wayne (1992) Preaching and pastoral care, in M. Duduit (ed.), *Handbook of Contemporary Preaching*. Nashville, TN: Broadman.

Quicke, Michael J. (2003) *360 Degree Preaching: hearing, seeing and living the word*. Grand Rapids, MI: Baker.

Read, D. H. C. (1988) *Preaching about the Needs of Real People*. Philadelphia: Westminster Press.

Russell, B. (2003) Wisdom for the divorced, in *Preaching Today* tape 240. Carol Stream, IL: Christianity Today International.

Smith, C. M. (1989) *Weaving the Sermon*. Louisville, KY: Westminster John Knox Press.

Taylor, B. B. (1993) *A Preacher's Life*. Cambridge, MA: Cowley Publications.

Thomas, F. A. (1997) *They Like to Never Quit Praisin' God*. Cleveland, OH: United Church Press.

Tisdale, L. T. *Preaching as Local Theology and Folk Art*. Minneapolis: Fortress Press.

Warren, R. (1996) Preaching to the unchurched. *Preaching* 12.2.4.

Willimon, H. W. (1995) Pastoral care and preaching, in H. W. Willimon and R. Lischer (eds), *Concise Encyclopedia of Preaching*. Louisville, KY: Westminster John Knox Press.

CHAPTER 15:
The Bible in evangelical spirituality

DEREK TIDBALL

Who are the evangelicals?

Evangelicalism is marked both by diversity and unity. Those within the movement are fond, therefore, of describing it as a mosaic, a kaleidoscope, an extended family or a tree with various branches. Historically Evangelicalism traces its roots back to the Protestant Reformation and owes much to Puritanism with its emphasis on the word of God and the message of grace. As a modern movement, however, it seems to have come into a self-conscious existence through the Evangelical Awakening of the eighteenth century associated with Jonathan Edwards, George Whitefield and John Wesley. Reacting to the sterility of a church that had sold out to rationalism, formalism and deism, they urged the necessity of conversion so that people could experience the grace of God that flowed from the cross of Christ. To them, genuine religion was a 'felt' religion and issued in a life of devotion, moral transformation and missionary activity. Whilst Edwards and Whitefield and their followers drew from the wells of Reformed theology, Wesley's circle introduced a holiness perspective that drew from the wells of German Pietism. The holiness strand taught, in various forms, that believers in Christ could experience a 'deeper life', 'a second blessing' or Wesley's somewhat confusing concept of 'perfect love'. The 'Reformed stream' flows today through many Presbyterian, Anglican and independent evangelical church channels. The 'holiness' stream also finds expression in many independent mission halls; in the various branches of Methodism; the 'Keswick' movement, highly influential in the late nineteenth and early twentieth centuries; the classical Pentecostal movement that came into being in the early twentieth century; and in the charismatic movement which blossomed from the mid-1960s.

What is it, given these diverse expressions of the faith, that enables us to speak of Evangelical*ism*, as if it were a coherent movement? David

Bebbington (2–17) has argued that Evangelicalism is marked by four distinctive characteristics. Central to their outworking of the Christian faith is:

1 A belief in the need for conversion. People are estranged from God because of sin and need to be reconciled to him through 'justification by faith'. Great effort is expended in persuading people to turn in repentance towards Christ and receive his salvation. Conversion is a gateway into a new life that exhibits signs of a growing, yet assured, relation with God.
2 Activism. Converted people have a concern to develop their understanding of the faith, to bring the Gospel to others, to exhibit the characteristics of a holy life and engage in energetic missionary activity and good works. It has also led to the growth of a complicated network of parachurch organisations engaged in specialised missionary, educational, social, pastoral, publishing or other support work.
3 A high view of the Bible. They demonstrate a devotion to the Bible, have a high view of its authority and inspiration, and regard it as a vital instrument of spiritual growth.
4 A stress on the atonement. The theological framework adopted by Evangelicalism puts the cross at the centre. While having an important place for other doctrines, such as creation or incarnation, and other events, such as resurrection or Pentecost, it is the doctrine of atonement and the event of Good Friday that is 'the fulcrum' of their theology.

Others have delineated the nature of Evangelicalism in different, but not contradictory, ways. Robert Johnston states, 'Evangelicals are those who believe the gospel to be experienced personally, defined biblically and communicated passionately' (Dayton and Johnston, 261). Stanley Grenz has recently articulated its original features as those of 'convertive piety' and 'experimental piety'. Early evangelicals, he explains, 'cherished the Bible' long before a 'cognitive-doctrinal' element emerged which crystallised and formalised the principle of the centrality and trustworthiness of the Bible (40–52, 84). Understandably, no one has sought to characterise Evangelicalism without highlighting the prominence the movement gives to the Bible. To this we might add that it tends to be a popular movement. Although its history has spawned some excellent thinkers and strategic church leaders, it is inclined to be a religion of the grass roots, to be enmeshed in popular culture, and is even often culturally despised. Its strength and energy is often derived from being in opposition to the religious establishment, or at least in being a movement of outsiders who are distanced from the mainline of church and culture (Smith, 1998). From an evangelical standpoint, therefore, the Bible is not the book for scholars or official teachers of the Church alone, but for all disciples of Christ; to be read and understood and, if necessary, self-taught, as well as obeyed by all.

Evangelical attitudes to the Bible

All evangelicals, then, maintain the centrality of the Bible and exhibit a devotion to it, believing it to be a reliable revelation both from and of God. But they approach and handle the Bible in different ways in practice. It is Fundamentalism rather than Evangelicalism that adopts a woodenly literalist approach to the Bible (Tidball, 17–18; Edwards and Stott, 89–95) and, eschewing all biblical scholarship, espouses extreme views, such as arguing that where science and the Bible disagree it must be science that has got it wrong.

Evangelicalism proper ranges from those who stress the complete accuracy of the Bible in all things (the usual term is 'inerrancy') and are cautious, even sceptical, about the value of modern scholarship, but even so adopt hermeneutical devices to avoid a wooden literalism, to those who are happily at home in using the tools of post-Enlightenment scholarship to unlock its meaning. Many evangelical scholars are thoroughly conversant with the tools of historical criticism and subsequent schools of biblical scholarship. Equally, many are also now welcoming the more postmodern approach of a scholar like Walter Brueggemann (1993), even if dissenting from his formal theology of the Bible, because it overcomes some of the aridity of earlier scholarly rationalism and releases the Bible's meaning (Hart 1997). While not letting go of the importance of truth being expressed in propositions, there is now a greater appreciation of narrative and the place of imagination (McGrath, 107–12). Others are grappling even more adventurously with the implications of postmodern literary approaches in their handling of the Bible (Tomlinson 1995). The implications of the latter for an evangelical commitment to the Bible are currently unclear but lively debate is engaged. John Stott may be taken as expressing the representative evangelical approach in the debate with David Edwards, where, while he recognises that evangelicals differ, he robustly expounds the core evangelical belief that 'the Bible is God's word through human words' and therefore is 'trustworthy' (102). This leads him to conclude, 'I think I would characterise Evangelicals as those who, because they identify Scripture as God's word, are deeply concerned to submit to its authority in their lives ...' (104).

Realism compels one to observe, however, that there is a distinction to be made between the work of evangelical scholars and leaders and the use of the Bible at a more popular level. There, pre-Enlightenment attitudes and pious illuminism (by which one's predetermined inner convictions are read into Scripture, rather than Scripture being wisely interpreted and its meaning being read out of the text) often reigns.

A charismatic use of the Bible owes much to Evangelicalism. Recent articles in the *Journal of Pentecostal Theology* (Archer; Baker; Ellington; Johns and Johns) have debated the distinctive approach of charismatic evangelicals to the Bible, which gives greater credence to the role of the Holy Spirit as interpreter than they perceive some older schemes allow. For them, reading Scripture is about 'a sacred encounter with God' in the context of the covenanted community for the Church (Johns, 118f.; Ellington, 17). It is a more dynamic experience of meeting the living God through a reading of his personal, inspired, yet objective, word. It involves the emotions as well as the mind. Yet, all this is, at most, only a difference of degree from older evangelical approaches to the Bible. However, the Bible is taken at face value 'without any concern for the historical distance' between its original setting and the contemporary Church. 'The Holy Scriptures for early Pentecostals were not viewed as a past "static deposit of truth" but as the present "primary source book for living Pentecostal life"' (Archer, 66). At a popular level this leads to raiding the Bible to find support for one's experience or to reading the Bible without any recourse to formal methods of study and learning, leaving one with an immediacy of God speaking and, perhaps, illuminism.

What is spiritual development?

Paul's desire was to proclaim Christ, 'admonishing and teaching everyone with all wisdom, so that we may present everyone perfect in Christ' (Col. 1:28). Equally we might summarise the evangelical attitude to spiritual development by reference to Philippians 3:10: 'I want to know Christ and the power of his resurrection and the fellowship of his sufferings, becoming like him in death ...' Spiritual development is focused on Christ. It is to know the trinitarian God personally and with a developing intimacy, and to allow that relationship to impact all one's life and relationships. Christ is the only route through which the Father can be known (John 14:6). Consequently, spiritual development is about one's growing relationship with Christ, made effective through his Spirit, becoming Christ-like in character. It is progressively 'to be conformed to the likeness of his Son' (Rom. 8:29 NIV). This entails carefully obeying Christ's teaching, and identifying, in all of life's ambiguous experience, with the paradox of his self-giving on the cross and the fullness of his resurrection life. It strives for a purity of life in every dimension – inward and outward, social, sexual, economic, conversational as well as religious.

All this will have implications for one's participation in the Church, for one's emotional and social well-being, for one's wholeness and integration, even for one's health and freedom to function in society. There will be strong implications for one's humanness and role within the created world, for it means that the believer 'is being renewed in knowledge in the image of its Creator' (Col. 3:10). The process of renewal means that Christians accept more and more the role and responsibilities within the world God had intended for the human race before its fall. Spiritual development is not primarily defined in terms of personal or emotional development – the psycho-social dimension – as others (Jacobs, 2–4) might define it. It is about the spiritual core of our being.

How does one develop spiritually?

A classic statement may be found in Bishop J. C. Ryle's *Practical Religion* (1878) where he speaks of the Bible as '*the chief means by which men are built up and stablished in the faith*, after their conversion' (italics his, 81). It is not the only means. Other chapters dealing with prayer, the Communion, works of charity and so on, surround his chapter on the Bible. Today there is a greater appreciation among evangelicals than ever before of other traditions of spiritual formation, yet in the evangelical spiritual mindset, the Bible remains 'prominent and foundational'. It is not 'dominant', as David Gillett, whose carefully chosen words we have just used, points out. What is in 'the dominant position belongs to the grace of God and the power of the cross for a sure salvation and a life of holiness' (136). But the Bible assumes a position of real importance in the evangelical scheme.

Why should this be so? Ryle begins by referring to two texts, neither of which is an exhortation in its original setting, but he transforms them into such. We are to search the Scriptures (John 5:29) and answer the enquiry of Christ, addressed to one of the religious teachers of his own day, as to how he read the law (Luke 10:26). But the main platform is the Bible's own claim that the Scriptures 'are able to make you wise for salvation' (2 Tim. 3:15; Stott, 12–17). Ryle neither wastes time proving the inspiration of the Bible nor justifying it as the perfect 'Word of God'; a term frequently used by evangelicals which stresses the intimate relationship between Christ as the incarnate Word of God and the Bible as the written word of God. 'The Book itself,' he claims, 'is the best witness to its own inspiration' (71). It is unique among the literature of the world.

Given this, he sets out its role as providing the knowledge that people need to know God and that will prove eternally, as distinct from merely temporarily, useful; including God's plan of salvation, an account of the work and person of Christ Jesus, examples of good people worth following and examples of bad people to serve as warnings, promises to be believed, hopes to be held on to, and light to live by. Historically, both in the Church and the world, Ryle claims, the Bible has had a wonderful effect on humanity, turning the world upside down. There is no book to compare with it in teaching everything people need to know both for initial salvation and for ongoing spiritual growth, doing its work as the Holy Spirit brings home particular texts to people's hearts and consciences.

> In this way the Bible has worked moral miracles by thousands. It has made drunkards become sober, – unchaste people become pure, – thieves

> become honest, – violent-tempered people become meek. It has wholly altered the course of men's lives. It has caused old things to pass away and made their ways new. It has taught worldly people to seek first the kingdom of God. It has taught lovers of pleasure to become lovers of God. It has taught the stream of men's affections to run upwards instead of running downwards. It has made men think of heaven, instead of always thinking of earth, and live by faith, instead of living by sight. All this it has done in every part of the world. All this it is doing still.
>
> (Ryle, 80–81)

The way its message is conveyed varies. It happens through the Bible being read or by it being preached. It can happen in company but even a solitary individual, however isolated, can be transformed if he or she has a will and the ability to read the Bible. Ryle admits that some find the Bible difficult. But difficulty ought not, he says, discourage us from persisting, any more than we permit children to give up their education because it proves demanding for them initially. He also recognises that it is possible to read the Bible without benefit. To profit from it, people need to read the Bible with humility, faith, a spiritual thirst and accompanied by 'earnest prayer' (83). Sermons, opinions and ministers are to be weighed by their adherence to the Bible's teaching. It is also to be a guide to behaviour. A person 'must make the Bible his rule of conduct. He must make its leading principles the compass by which he steers his course through life' (86). It is the means by which God sustains and nourishes believers on their journey, right to the end, bringing comfort to them in the last moments before death. Those who are truly 'born again' love the Bible. In fact, in an exaggerated fashion, Ryle posits that a person's attitude to the Bible can be used like a thermometer, measuring their spiritual health. He refers to Psalm 1:2 with its assertion that those who are 'blessed' are those whose 'delight is in the law of the Lord'. He holds Job up as an example: 'I have treasured the words of his mouth more than my daily bread' (Job 23:12 NIV). He cites the example of Jesus himself, who showed a reverence for fulfilling the Scripture and, as the risen Christ, gave an understanding of the Scriptures to the disciples on the road to Emmaus (Luke 24:45). He takes his stand with the Psalmist in declaring 'Oh, how I love your law!' (Ps. 119:97).

A wider perspective

Ryle's view would be echoed by evangelicals down to our own time, as James Gordon's major study of evangelical spirituality demonstrates. John Newton called for a 'continuous exposure of heart to scripture' (Gordon, 88). Alexander Whyte agreed that one should 'saturate the soul with Scripture' (247). Campbell Morgan urged that in view of the Bible's importance,

Christians should 'spare no effort to establish the meaning of Scripture' (269). It was 'bread to be broken, shared and assimilated' (270). In comparing the spirituality modelled and taught by C. H. Spurgeon and R. W. Dale, Gordon concludes:

> The attitude of reverent submission before the biblical text, exemplified so differently by Spurgeon and Dale, has been characteristic of Evangelical spirituality. Differences of interpretation abound, but there has been virtual unanimity in the conviction that the Bible is God's word, revealed truth, sharp, two-edged, piercing to the deepest recesses of mind and heart. (315)

David Gillett rebuts the charge that evangelicals worship the Bible and engage in bibliolatry. Nor is it a burden to carry. The Bible is there not as an end in itself but to lead us to Christ (John 5:39–40). The Bible is held in high esteem because 'there is that deep affection and excitement for the Word of God that echoes emotions seen long ago in the psalmist' (129). Psalm 119 speaks of the delight the Psalmist experiences when studying and keeping God's statutes and how they are the subject of his longing and the object of his meditation all day (and, when sleepless, all night) long. He values them more than gold and finds them as sweet as the taste of honey. The role of God's word in the life of the Christian are brought into focus in Psalm 119.

First, it provides guidance as to how to live wisely, to distinguish right from wrong and to grow in holiness. 'How can the young keep their way pure? By living according to your word' (119:9) has been frequently quoted as providing a key insight into spiritual development. The same is true of v. 105, 'Your word is a lamp to my feet and a light to my path.' Other verses repeat the same thought. The Bible is a handbook for living.

Second, when it becomes a deep part of one's thinking it provides strength against temptation and prevents one from falling into sin. 'I have hidden your word in my heart; that I might not sin against you' (Ps. 119:11, 113).

Third, the Bible provides sustenance during the weary and difficult days of pilgrimage. A recurring sub-theme of the psalm is the way in which the Psalmist is conscious of being attacked by his enemies (Ps. 119:28, 50, 116, 156). These are just a few of the verses that highlight God's compassion and ability, both in the general drift of life and in particular circumstances, to defend his people and keep them safe.

Fourth, the evangelical experience of obeying Scripture is that to do so is anything but restricting. It does not keep people unnecessarily dependent and craven before God, as Marxists would have it, but is genuinely liberating. Living according to God's word is the true path to freedom and real human autonomy. 'I run in the path of your commands, for you have set my heart free' (Ps. 119:32, 35, 45).

Fifth, freedom arises because those who delight in God's law have been set free from slavery to worthless idols and the ill-conceived icons of the age. Living according to God's will sets a true and worthy agenda for life and releases one from the deceptive and valueless ambitions of human wisdom. 'Turn my eyes away from worthless things; preserve my life according to your word' (v. 37). This is what one might expect if God truly is the creator since he is more likely to understand better than his created subjects do, at least unaided, the best way for them to be at home in his creation (Ps. 119:73, 90–93, 134).

Sixth, the psalm presents God's law as standing over against the Psalmist, leading him to change direction, correct his course in life and to live according to God's way. It thus points out sin and serves as an agent of change and a catalyst of holiness (Ps. 119:5–6, 25–26, 36) though, to some extent, the theme is more implicit than explicit. Evangelicals would often turn to Hebrews to point out that the Bible plays a role in pointing out what is wrong in our lives, which usually proves to be the first step in seeking to correct it.

> For the word of God is living and active. Sharper than any double-edged sword, it penetrates even to dividing soul and spirit, joints and marrow; it judges the thoughts and attitudes of the heart. Nothing in all creation is hidden from God's sight. Everything is uncovered and laid bare before the eyes of him to whom we must give account. (Heb. 4:12–13)

The heartbeat of the psalm is strong and positive. God's words are 'trustworthy' (v. 86); 'eternal' (v. 89); marked by boundless perfection (v. 96); awesome (v. 120); 'wonderful' (v. 129); 'right' (v. 137) and 'true' (v. 160). No wonder the Psalmist takes delight in them, loves them, and seeks not to stray from them but rather to build them into the very fabric of his life. This attitude to Scripture is a far cry from contemporary attitudes, which see the Bible as problematic. We shall see later how evangelicals are able to adopt such an attitude in the face of the obvious struggles others have with it.

Spiritual development: a practical review

It is not surprising that books designed to help Christians with their spiritual growth all stress the importance of the regular use of the Bible, whether one looks at R. A. Torrey (1906), Godfrey Robinson and Stephen Winward (1954), Michael Green (1973), David Watson (1975 & 1981), Leroy Eims (1976), John White (1977), Donald Whitney (1991) or the recent Alpha material (Nicky Gumbel, 1993). The basic approach is one of regular, preferably daily reading, of a portion of the Bible. The purpose of doing so is not the acquisition of head knowledge but of a living encounter with the God who spoke and continues to speak by means of his Spirit through the Bible

(Gillett, 136). Evangelicals are wise enough to point out that this is not a magic formula for spiritual growth. The mere ritual of reading part of the Bible without engaging with it with one's mind and heart will accomplish nothing. The Bible needs to be read with faith (Heb. 4:2). It also needs to be read systematically, rather than randomly or haphazardly. This avoids the danger of misinterpreting its message by reading things out of context and checks a pious but ill-founded descent into proof-texting.

To reading, Christians need to add study. Understanding the Bible more deeply through learning about the historical and social setting of the books, the theological perspective and motivation of particular writers, the place they occupy in the sweep of God's salvation history is considered of the utmost importance. To this end, evangelicals have constantly produced a wealth of material to aid Bible understanding: from daily and devotional reading notes, survey books and popular commentaries to many serious works of biblical scholarship.

A key element in study is the discipline of meditation. Meditation is currently promoted widely as an aid to spirituality, not least among those who are disposed to an Eastern religious outlook, a therapeutic stance or New Age spirituality. But evangelicals have long advocated it, although meaning something rather different than many do. It is not the mystical meditation that centres down to a self-emptying but an active reflection on the teaching of the Bible and the Lord of whom it speaks. Simon Chan quotes the Puritan Richard Greenham as writing, 'to read and not to meditate is unfruitful; to meditate and not to read is dangerous; to read and meditate without prayer is hurtful' (Chan, 158). He himself calls for a spiritual reading of the Bible that goes beyond the explicating of the meaning of the text and its application for life and 'calls us to God' (159). Meditation is, he says, 'the main link between theology and praxis. It is the way to make truth come alive as it courses from mind to heart to daily living. Seen in this way, meditation plays a critical role in forging the integration of heart and mind in the spiritual life' (167).

No better statement concerning an evangelical understanding of meditation has been penned than that by J. I. Packer in his book *Knowing God*:

> How can we turn our knowledge *about* God into knowledge *of* God? The rule for doing this is demanding but simple. It is that we turn each truth that we learn *about* God into a matter of meditation *before* God, leading to prayer and praise *to* God …
>
> Meditation is the activity of calling to mind, and thinking over, and dwelling on, and applying to oneself, the various things one knows about the works and ways and purposes and promises of God. It is the activity of holy thought, consciously performed in the presence of God, under the eye of God, by the help of God, as a means of communion with

> God. Its purpose is to clear one's mental and spiritual vision of God, and to let the truth make its full and proper impact on one's mind and heart. (18–19)

Another step that is frequently commended is that of memorising the Bible. It may be true to say that this spiritual discipline is not as widely practised now as once it was. The cacophony of Bible versions, many of which lack the poetic quality of older translations that served as an aid to the memory, together with an aversion to rote learning in our culture, has made it less agreeable than it was to earlier generations. Nonetheless, the justification for it is worth recalling. It was never practised to be used like a magic spell to ward off temptation, protect one from harm or provide instant guidance. Rather, memorising was a means of letting the Bible's words become a deep part of one's being, of sinking into one's mind and becoming the default mechanism by which one thought and acted. It was a way of emulating the Psalmist: 'I have hidden your word in my heart that I might not sin against you' (Ps. 119.11 NIV). Many would testify to the positive benefits of confidently knowing verses of Scripture so that they may be brought to bear on a variety of situations instantly, rather than having to search around for something that might be appropriate. Of course, the approach is subject to abuse and can lead to superficial application and to pastoral insensitivity when cheaply applied either to oneself or to others. Even so, the benefits are seen to outweigh the liabilities. And while 'proof-texting' is to be avoided, who can deny that within the sweep of Scripture there are not key 'sound bites' that aptly state a biblical truth in a few well-chosen words?

The final step in an evangelical use of the Bible is that of obedience. Their reverence for Scripture means that evangelicals desire to sit in submission to it rather than stand as critics or authorities over it. John Stott writes of 'their *a priori* resolve to believe and obey whatever Scripture may be shown to teach' (Edwards and Stott, 104). The qualification 'whatever (it) may be shown to teach' is important. It avoids the naive literalism that leads to the stoning of rebellious children, the refusal to wear clothes of mixed fabrics, the patriarchal subjection of women and the abusive use of violence. The use of common-sense hermeneutics which interpret these issues in context and disclose the intention that lay behind them so that their significance can be applied in fresh ways today, is sufficient to avoid the charge so often falsely mounted against an evangelical misuse of the Bible. But the qualification should not be permitted to obscure the main point: that devotion to the God who has revealed himself through Christ as recorded in the Bible and so obedience to his revealed will is the chief end of reading the Scripture. In 2 Timothy 3:16 Scripture is spoken of as inspired and 'useful for teaching, rebuking, correcting and training in righteousness ...'. The dimensions of our obedience are twofold. It is obedience to truth, to what one is to believe as

Christian orthodoxy. It is obedience to lifestyle, to how one is to behave as Christian orthopraxy; v. 17 adds, 'so that God's servant may be thoroughly equipped for every good work'. Evangelicals believe that the Bible is a sufficient tool when used by the Holy Spirit, our contemporary and dynamic teacher (John 16:12–15), as the medium of God's instruction to produce all that is needed for spiritual maturity, that is, for knowing God and serving him in his world. 'As Luther put it, we read Scripture not simply to learn the commands of God but to encounter the God who commands, and to be transformed as a result' (McGrath, 102).

The context of spiritual growth

It should not be thought that these practical steps are steps to be taken by the individual believer alone. Because of Evangelicalism's roots in the Enlightenment and its insistence on the personal nature of faith, evangelicals have sometimes suffered from an unhealthy individualism. But, as Gillett explains, 'there exists a threefold chord within evangelical spirituality that provides the necessary strength for understanding and obeying the Word of God' (157). It consists of the individual practice of personal devotion; the corporate study of the Bible in small groups and the exposition of Scripture through preaching in the church. Each is a channel through which the Christian might grow and each is necessary as a balance to the others. Individuals operating alone might well develop some distorted or misguided ideas. Yet without the individual reading and study of God's word we often lack personal knowledge of it and conviction about it. The small group gives scope for the sharing of experience as the Bible is studied and applied to our lives and it provides the corrective balances that individuals need, overcoming shallow individualism (McGrath, 96). Furthermore, groups can supplement the preaching of the Church and provide a more beneficial learning environment for some. But they also need complementing for they are not automatically worthwhile and can degenerate into a sophisticated sharing of ignorance unless well managed by instructed and gifted leaders. Hence, there is also need for the ministry of preaching which has been so prominent in evangelical tradition. Preaching is to be judged by its ability to take, explain and apply a part of the Bible, with a transforming effect, to the contemporary situation of the listeners.

The practical work of spiritual development, then, may be undertaken both as individuals and in company with other Christians and preferably in both spheres simultaneously. In the pressure of modern living these personal spiritual disciplines may be less regularly or intensely exercised than once they were. Concessions to the demands of 'life in the fast lane' have undoubtedly been made. Yet, they remain central to evangelical spirituality, and are still widely practised and often creatively so. In our own time advantage has been taken of modern technology through the use of CDs or the Internet and this is especially true in comparison with other wings of the Church.

Problems with the evangelical approach to Scripture

Evangelicals would defend their position on Scripture both by reference to their formal doctrine of the Bible as God's inspired and reliable revelation and also by claiming that they represent the mainstream position of historic Christianity. Nonetheless a number of particular problems with their position might be raised and briefly responded to on the basis of the previous discussion.

Does it not lead to a spirituality that is book-centred, legalistic and even idolatrous rather than a life-centred relationship with a contemporary and living God? Any spiritual discipline can degenerate into empty and meaningless ritual. But no spiritual discipline should be dismissed because it is subject to abuse or distortion. At the heart of the evangelical practice of what was traditionally called 'the Quiet Time' was an understanding that life is busy and people are demanding. If we are to know God then we need intentionally to set aside time and space to nurture our relationship with him through both listening to him and speaking to him. Of course he can be encountered through other people and in the hurly-burly of life. But if we want the relationship with God to mature then, as with any human relationship, it needs to be cultivated personally to afford both focus and intimacy. The practice of Bible reading is a means, not an end in itself. Evangelicals do not stop with the Bible but with the Christ of whom the Bible speaks. The Bible is read, studied, reflected on, memorised and obeyed in order that we might know him. When Christians come to reading God's word aware of the amazing grace he has poured into their lives, they will read with an appetite to know God better. Grace not law, relationship not ritual, gratitude not duty dominates.

Does an evangelical approach to the Bible reduce it to fragments and titbits of advice that, because they are taken out of context, can be positively misleading? An old evangelical practice was that of the 'promise box'. Each day a little scroll containing a verse of Scripture would be drawn out of a box at random to provide the enquirer with guidance or assurance for the day. In a similar way the Gideon Bibles, placed in schools, hotels and hospitals, contain a list of verses to consult, which address a variety of different needs. It is easy to call such practices into question as they do not respect 'the original purpose and integrity of scripture' which was not originally designed to provide individuals with a personal emotional fillip (Pattison, 129–30). But such criticisms might be justified if this was the exclusive or predominant use of the Bible by evangelicals. And one cannot help but feel that the criticism often comes from the intellectually superior who fail to understand the dynamics of popular religion and the way in which God, in his gracious condescension, does communicate through all sorts of imperfect channels with his people. People will look for daily guidance and reassurance in all sorts of directions. Better that they look to the Bible than elsewhere.

Is the evangelical faith in the Bible misplaced? To many the Bible seems a violent book and their reading of it leads them to believe that the God of whom it speaks advocates genocide, permits the abuse or subjugation of women, enshrines corporal and capital punishment in his law, advocates an eye for an eye and a tooth for a tooth, does nothing to remove the injustice of slavery, and lives by a very illiberal agenda riddled with exclusion. This is a serious challenge, not to be dismissed lightly. It contrasts strongly with the positive attitude to the Bible found among evangelicals. The fact is that while some at the more fundamentalist end of the spectrum will use the Bible to justify authoritarian and oppressive attitudes, this is not how the vast majority of evangelicals approach it. Because they believe that revelation is a process that reaches its fulfilment in Christ, they are able to take many of these issues as belonging to an earlier age and to have been overtaken by the example and teaching of Christ. He epitomises the reverse of many of the positions claimed above. He absorbs violence, preaches non-retaliation and love for one's neighbour, exhibits great respect for women, and embraces the marginalised, 'unclean' and insignificant. It should be said he does so in perfect harmony with the God who is primarily shown to be a God of compassion and grace and to abound in love and faithfulness and maintain love for thousands (Exod. 34:6). Christ's example is exactly what one would expect of the Son of a God who is 'a father to the fatherless [and] a defender of widows', who puts the lonely in families and releases prisoners into joyful liberty (Ps. 68:5).

Furthermore, evangelicals are able to nuance their understanding of biblical doctrine and ethics, by putting it through the grid of creation, fall, redemption and consummation. So, for example, many will see that the subjugation of women, so amply testified to in the Old Testament, is not part of God's creation plan (Gen. 1:27), but is a result of the fall (Gen. 3:16), and is being overturned in the Church through the redemptive work of Christ (as seen, for example, in the ministry of Jesus, Acts 2:17; Gal. 3:28), and that creation will be fully restored one day at the consummation of all things when all people, men and women alike, enter into their full liberty as children of God (Rom. 8:19–21). Those commands that appear oppressive to wives (Eph. 5:22; Col. 3:18; 1 Pet. 3:1–6) are only so if they are read selectively, ignoring the context where husbands are enjoined to imitate the self-giving love of Christ (Eph. 5:25–33; Col. 3:19; 1 Pet. 3:7). The full text removes any possibility of the Bible being used to justify the oppression of a marriage partner.

It would be foolish to pretend such an approach settles all issues easily, as recent debates about the role of women in church leadership or sexuality show. But wherever the Bible's teaching is less than plain, evangelicals will want to engage in serious discussion with the text and with others until greater clarity is reached.

Respected academic research demonstrates, moreover, that the popular picture of evangelicals as conservative, bigoted and intolerant people who seek to create a 'pure' society by overturning the multi-faith and pluralist society in which they live, needs demythologising (Smith 2000, 193–6). Evangelicals cope reasonably well with the tensions and ambivalences thrown up by their negotiating between the ideals they see in the Bible and the complex realities that surround them. The overwhelming experience of evangelicals is that the Bible is a life-giving, life-enhancing and life-developing book whose wisdom is keenly sought and whose teaching is liberating.

Does the Bible not require hermeneutical skills beyond the ability of uninstructed laity? Basic hermeneutical skills are taught, at least implicitly, in most evangelical churches where people gain an understanding of the need to consider the genre of the passage they are reading, where it comes in the unfolding plan of God, how to read it in context and relate it to other parts of Scripture, and make the connection between the Bible's own time and our own. But the evangelical insists, too, that the Holy Spirit is guide and interpreter. The disciple who is open to his direction is, therefore, not engaging in an exercise akin to the reading of any other book. Whatever the similarities between the Bible and other literature, and they are many, the Bible is different. In reading it people are engaging with the living God himself.

Does the evangelical use of the Bible betray a naivety as to how different people will both use and hear the Bible? For some, indeed, the Bible will be used as a weapon to justify their position and status. Others will read or hear it as authoritarian and oppressive, because of the way in which it has been used in their experience. The Bible certainly can prove damaging and condemning in the lives of many and used to bolster the unwarranted authority of a pastor or preacher (Pattison, 132). The same, of course, is true of any teaching, especially political correctness, which pretends to tolerance while disguising a vigorous intolerance of all those who dissent. The point is that any communication needs to be sensitive not only to what is said but to why it is being said and what is heard. Pastoral wisdom requires that pastors do not use the Bible as a sledgehammer or steamroller but to help those they lead explore a way forward in their journey of knowing God. Aware of their own weaknesses (Gal. 6:1–5), they use the Bible for the building up of those to whom they minister whether they directly quote from it, simply make allusion to it, or merely allow their conversation to be informed by it. Christians who are only familiar with the Bible being used in an authoritarian manner may well need the help of gentle interpreters to guide them to those parts of the Bible which will lead to growth and confidence in God, to hear his loving, forgiving and accepting voice, and to discourage them from being drawn, as a moth is drawn to a bright light, to the negative aspects of its message. If approached correctly and interpreted rightly within the supportive fellowship of God's people this will be the means of life and growth even for the most timid, crushed and fearful of individuals.

Conclusion

In an evangelical world view, the Bible plays a vital role in enabling Christians to grow to maturity in Christ. Evangelicals reflect with sadness on 'the strange silence of the Bible in the church' (Smart). They refuse to accept that contemporary scholarship that has done so much to illuminate the Bible's message has simultaneously destroyed the possibility of our using the Bible or denuded it of authority. It has certainly made the task more difficult. It has certainly made people aware of the different voices within the Bible and the various ways in which the writers have socially constructed their message. Faced with an overwhelming amount of scholarship, it has made people hesitant to read and interpret the Bible for themselves. But the Bible disappears from a Christian's radar screen at their peril. For it to be lost to the consciousness of the Church and the believer condemns us to live stunted Christian lives and leaves us unsatisfied, with the result that we will look elsewhere in the (false) hope of cultivating our full spiritual potential. But this need not be the scenario. We need not be intimidated. For the Bible remains God's living and active word to us. And, as James Smart affirms in the concluding chapter of his book, we might yet be astonished at the possible impact when people open themselves 'to the full range of divine and human reality that meets them in the Scripture' (Smart, 169). And while nothing exempts us from taking the hermeneutical task seriously, we might also discover that 'a preacher with an atrocious hermeneutic who really cares what is happening in the lives of his people may let Scripture have its voice, while another who is more concerned about the intellectual respectability of his discourse than about the coming of God into the midst of his people's life, may produce only a silence' (Smart, 172). If spiritual development is to take place, evangelicals believe the Bible must find its voice again in the Church and the life of the individual disciple of Christ.

Bibliography

Archer, Kenneth J. (1996) Pentecostal hermeneutics: retrospect and prospect. *Journal of Pentecostal Theology* 8, 63–81.

Baker, Robert O. (1995) Pentecostal Bible reading: towards a model of reading for the formation of Christian affections. *Journal of Pentecostal Theology* 7, 34–48.

Bebbington, David (1989) *Evangelicalism in Modern Britain: a history from the 1730s to the 1980s*. London: Unwin Hyman.

Brueggemann, Walter (1993) *The Bible and Postmodern Imagination*. London: SCM Press.

Chan, Simon (1998) *Spiritual Theology*. Downers Grove, IL: InterVarsity Press.

Dayton, Donald W. and Johnston, Robert K. (eds) (1991) *The Variety of American Evangelicalism*. Downers Grove, IL: InterVarsity Press.

Edwards, David L. with Stott, John (1988) *Essentials: a liberal-evangelical dialogue*. London: Hodder & Stoughton.

Ellington, Scott A. (1996) Pentecostalism and the authority of Scripture. *Journal of Pentecostal Theology* 9, 16–28.

Eims, LeRoy (1976) *What Every Christian Should Know about Growing*. Wheaton, IL: Victor Books.

Gillett, David K. (1993) *Trust and Obey: explorations in evangelical spirituality*. London: Darton, Longman & Todd.

Gordon, James M. (1991) *Evangelical Spirituality: from the Wesleys to John Stott*. London: SPCK.

Green, Michael (1973) *New Life, New Lifestyle*. London: Hodder & Stoughton.

Grenz, Stanley J. (2000) *Renewing the Centre: evangelical theology in a post-theological era*. Grand Rapids, MI: Baker Academic.

Gumbel, Nicky (1993) *Questions of Life: a practical introduction to the Christian life*. Eastbourne: Kingsway.

Hart, Trevor (1997) Response to Brueggemann's 'The Bible and postmodern imagination', in A. N. S. Lane (ed.), *Interpreting the Bible: historical and theological studies in honour of David F. Wright*. Leicester: Apollos.

Jacobs, Michael (1988) *Towards the Fullness of Christ: pastoral care and Christian maturity*. London: Darton, Longman & Todd.

Johns, J., Johns, D. and Bridges, C. (1992) Yielding to the Spirit: a Pentecostal approach to group Bible study. *Journal of Pentecostal Theology* 1, 109–34.

McGrath, Alister E. (1996) *A Passion for Truth: the intellectual coherence of evangelicalism*. Leicester: Apollos.

Packer, J. I. (1973) *Knowing God*. London: Hodder & Stoughton.

Pattison, Stephen (2000) *A Critique of Pastoral Care*. London: SCM Press.

Robinson, Godfrey and Winward, Stephen (1954) *The Way: a practical guide to the Christian life*. London: Scripture Union and CSSM.

Ryle, J. C. (1878) *Practical Religion*. London: James Clarke.

Smart, J. D. (1971) *The Strange Silence of the Bible in the Church: a study in hermeneutics*. London: SCM Press.

Smith, Christian (1998) *American Evangelicalism: embattled and thriving*. Chicago: University of Chicago Press.

Smith, Christian (2000) *Christian America? what evangelicals really want*. Berkeley, CA: University of California Press.

Stott, John R. W. (1972) *Understanding the Bible*. London: Scripture Union.

Tidball, Derek J. (1994) *Who Are the Evangelicals? tracing the roots of today's movements*. London: Marshall Pickering.

Torrey, R. A. (1906) *How to Succeed in the Christian Life*. London: James Nisbet.

Tomlinson, David (1995) *The Post-Evangelical*. London: Triangle.

Watson, David (1975) *Live a New Life*. Leicester: Inter-Varsity Press.

Watson, David (1981) *Discipleship*. London: Hodder & Stoughton.

White, John (1977) *The Fight: a practical handbook for Christian living*. Leicester: Inter-Varsity Press.

Whitney, Donald S. (1991) *Spiritual Disciplines of the Christian Life*. Colorado Springs: NavPress.

CHAPTER 16:

Ignatius Loyola, prayer and Scripture

PHILIP ENDEAN

A survey of how Roman Catholic spirituality uses the Bible is clearly out of the question in a short essay such as this. We have to focus on a representative example. Ignatius Loyola (1491–1556) lived at the dawn of modernity and at the beginning of the period where Catholic and Protestant Christianity split. His *Spiritual Exercises*, and the styles of mental prayer that grew from them, have been highly influential among Catholics since they were first published in 1548. In 1929, Pius XI wrote an encyclical commending retreats to Catholics the world over, and spoke of how the method of Ignatius' Exercises,

> ... adorned by the full and repeated approbation of the Holy See and honoured by the praises of men, distinguished for spiritual doctrine and sanctity, has borne abundant fruits of holiness during the space of well nigh four hundred years ... as a most wise and universal code of laws for the direction of souls in the way of salvation and perfection; an unexhausted fountain of most excellent and most solid piety.
>
> (Pius XI, n.16)

Since the Second Vatican Council, the range of people making the Exercises has broadened, and it now extends beyond Roman Catholics. The testimony is less florid but often equally enthusiastic. Thus an evangelical Anglican lay woman could describe the fruit of an Ignatian retreat:

> I found that making a retreat helped me to follow God's call and live out the gospel in my daily life ... What that first retreat gave me was a new vision of Jesus not only as central in my own personal life but also as central in the Church of which I am one part ... I am convinced as never before that prayer and service and witness in the world are not incompatible activities ... St Ignatius helped me understand better St

> Paul's 'in everything God works for good with those who love God, who are called according to God's purpose'. I know that this is true. Whatever the future may hold, a retreat gives me the confidence in God I need now in order to turn and face in the right direction. (Netherwood, 131)

Ignatius' text

Such enthusiastic testimony seems at first sight to be belied by the starkness of Ignatius' instructions for prayer on the New Testament. The general pattern is set out most fully in contemplations (nos 101–17 in the paragraph numbering standard in modern editions) on the annunciation and on the birth of Christ, both drawing on the Lukan narratives. Ignatius begins with three preambles, or preludes. The first is the reading of the story:

> The first Prelude is the narrative and it will be here how Our Lady went forth from Nazareth, about nine months with child, as can be piously meditated, seated on an ass, and accompanied by Joseph and a maid, taking an ox, to go to Bethlehem to pay the tribute which Caesar imposed on all those lands.

The second is referred to in the jargon as the 'composition of place', though Ignatius' phrase is 'composition, seeing the place', that is, setting oneself within the scene. So, in the case of Luke's account of Christ's birth:

> It will be here to see with the sight of the imagination the road from Nazareth to Bethlehem; considering the length and the breadth, and whether such road is level or through valleys or over hills; likewise looking at the place or cave of the Nativity, how large, how small, how low, how high, and how it was prepared.

The third 'prelude' is a prayer,

> ... for what I want: it will be to ask for knowledge of the Lord from inside, Who for me has become human that I may more love and follow Him.

After this prayer for knowledge, love, and dedication to service, there follow, typically, three main points: one focuses on how the scene appears visually, another on what the characters are saying, a third on what they are doing. After each point, you are expected to 'reflect and draw profit' – a phrase to which we shall return. Though the contemplation on Christ's birth is presented more fully than most, its second and third points are stark: the focus is named, and then simply the injunction to reflect. In the first point, Ignatius adds, most unusually and perhaps only by way of example, a detail of his own:

> … I making myself a poor creature and a wretch of an unworthy slave, looking at them and serving them in their needs, with all possible respect and reverence, as if I found myself present.

The prayer ends with a 'colloquy', an imaginative conversation, exemplified in the account of the annunciation:

> At the end a Colloquy is to be made, thinking what I ought to say to the Three Divine Persons, or to the Eternal Word incarnate, or to our Mother and Lady, asking according to what I feel in me, in order more to follow and imitate Our Lord, so lately incarnate.

Ignatius encourages us imaginatively to engage one of the figures in the scene, and to develop a conversation that might somehow lead us closer to the goal desired.

In a volume dedicated to the use of the Bible, there is a small point to be highlighted that in other contexts might be passed over. The phrase 'as may be piously meditated' in the first prelude of the nativity contemplation is a correction added in Ignatius' own hand. The original manuscript on which most modern texts of the Exercises are based is called the Autograph; not because Ignatius wrote it, but because he at least corrected it in a few places. This correction evinces a sensitivity to the biblical text. It is qualifying details not to be found in Luke: Joseph and Mary riding to Bethlehem on a donkey, and Mary being fully nine months pregnant. The qualification may indicate a recognition on Ignatius' part of the difference between the sacred text of the Bible and what subsequent tradition has added. In this connection, the verb he uses may also be significant: 'meditate'. In Ignatius' language, the sense of a higher, more concentrated form of prayer, a sense indicated by the word 'contemplation', is generally used when the prayer centres on the gospels themselves, as opposed to other sources. (In this regard Ignatius differs sharply from mainstream tendencies to construe 'contemplation' in terms of passivity – a point that has caused difficulties throughout the history of Ignatian interpretation.) When, therefore, Ignatius adds a detail that is not scriptural, he uses the less elevated term, 'meditate'. It is probably significant that such sensitivity – which is not consistent throughout Ignatius' text – comes *only* as a correction, in the 1540s, when biblical and university learning have come to influence the Ignatian movement profoundly.

The pastoral virtue of boringness

All this may seem, no doubt, very edifying. But it is hardly remarkable or unusual. Moreover, it appears so bald, so schematic. It also looks as though we are being put through a kind of mental gymnastics that we are not going to find congenial or prayerful. Why has this approach to biblical prayer been so influential and significant?

We can begin to answer that question by looking at some of the instructions which Ignatius gave for the retreat-guide only.

> … the person who gives to another the way and order in which to meditate or contemplate, ought to relate faithfully the events of such Contemplation or Meditation, going over the Points with only a short or summary development for if the person who is contemplating takes the true foundation which is the story, working on it and thinking about it on their own, and finds something which makes them understand or feel for the story a little more … (it is better) … than if the one who gives the Exercises had explained and expanded the meaning of the story a great deal – for it is not the knowing of much that contents and satisfies the soul, but the feeling and relish for things from inside. (Exx 2)

Here Ignatius tells the one giving the Exercises to be boring, and thereby also tells us why his own writing on biblical prayer is so low-key. The one giving the Exercises has to be reticent because what is meant to be happening is that the one receiving the Exercises should be discovering their own truth. Ignatius' process is not primarily a matter of passing on information, of biblical catechesis. Rather, he is trying to create the conditions in which they can discover, in the way and at the pace that is right both for them and for God, what God is saying to them.

In other contexts, persuasive rhetoric may be in order: fund-raising, teaching, a certain form of preaching. But persuasive rhetoric imposes itself, often unconsciously, and therefore all the more powerful; it suggests that my style of being Christian, of understanding and responding to the Gospel, should be normative for you. Ignatius, in perhaps the most famous and significant of his instructions to the retreat-giver, at once acknowledges the place of such communication in Christian ministry, and insists that it has at most a minor place in the Exercises.

> The one who is giving the Exercises ought not to influence the one who is receiving them more to poverty or to a promise than to their opposites, nor more to one state or way of life than to another. For though, outside the Exercises, we can lawfully and with merit influence every one who is probably fit to choose continence, virginity, the religious life and all

> manner of evangelical perfection, still in the Spiritual Exercises, when seeking the Divine Will, it is more fitting and much better, that the Creator and Lord Himself should communicate Himself to His devout soul, inflaming it with His love and praise, and disposing it for the way in which it will be better able to serve Him in future. So, the one who is giving the Exercises should not turn or incline to one side or the other, but standing in the centre like a balance, leave the Creator to act immediately with the creature, and the creature with its Creator and Lord. (Exx 15)

It is because Ignatius is convinced that the Spirit can communicate through the biblical text directly with the individual that he encourages the minister to hold back. The Bible is prersented in a low-key, muted way, so that the interest and the excitement can come from what happens in the one who hears and reads the story, and not simply be manufactured by the teller. All the exercitant needs is a foundation.

Other features of Ignatius' language reinforce the point. Modern Ignatian jargon speaks of 'the director of the Exercises' – both as a result of later cultural developments within the Ignatian movement and as a matter of linguistic convenience. The overtone is one of a fixed syllabus, studied under firm leadership. Ignatius' own language is more tentative and suggestive. In place of a director, Ignatius speaks of 'the one who gives to another'. The process is courteous and respectful; both personalities are involved. A gift is something entrusted to the freedom of the other; a freedom that will make use of the gifts in ways that are perhaps not foreseen by the giver, ways that may disappoint, ways that may be breathtakingly surprising. Moreover, Ignatius is surprisingly uninsistent on his fixed programme: the first of his notes at the beginning suggests that he is giving only a selection of ways for helping the soul, that can and should be supplemented, while in the second he describes what is given as 'the way and ordering of meditating and contemplating'. 'Way and order': what we hand on is not a finished body of truth, but a set of resources for engaging in an activity, for finding truth. The text gives no more – and no less – than a framework for helping people make their own meaning under God's guidance. As Ignatius put the matter in a commentary on the text:

> ... one should not linger very much with them unless it is necessary, nor expand so much on what is being said that the other gets to the point of not wanting to know more, or think that they cannot make the effort required to find something more to say – but one should give them some opportunity and structure so that they have the ability to find it, because it seems that this is normally helpful. (1996b, 4:15)

Reflecting, drawing profit, and making colloquies

These notes – in English Ignatian jargon 'annotations' – bring out how much the individual hearer or reader contributes to the meaning of the Exercises, and thus suggest that the activities designated as 'reflect and draw profit' are central to the process. The English word 'reflect' has two senses: a person may reflect on any number of matters, while a mirror can reflect the light that shines on it. Modern Spanish distinguishes these two senses by using different words: *reflexionar* and *reflejar*. It seems likely that the Spanish of Ignatius' day, like modern English, had only the one word, though Ignatius spells it in a variety of ways: *refletir*. Moreover, Ignatius' usage seems to denote a complex reality that involves both sets of connotations.

The other place where Ignatius uses the word comes towards the end of the Exercises. Ignatius asks us to consider different ways in which God is good to us: God creating us, God forgiving us and saving us, God giving us a whole range of personal gifts. He then continues:

> And with this to reflect within myself, considering very rightly and justly what I must for my part offer and give to His Divine Majesty, that is, all things that are mine and myself with them … (Exx 234)

In that context comes the prayer of Ignatius sometimes reprinted in prayer books:

> Take, Lord, and receive all my liberty, my memory, my intellect, and all my will – all that I have and possess. You gave it to me: to you, Lord, I return it! All is yours, dispose of it according to all your will. Give me your love and grace – this is enough for me.

The process involves reflecting in both modern English senses: first, we think about the goodness of God, we reflect *on* who God is; second, we do something likewise, and in that sense reflect God by responding to God in kind. Something similar happened at the very beginning of Ignatius' own converted life, when he was on his sickbed in Loyola after the battle at Pamplona. He has been reading books, and then the text (for some reason written in the third person) says:

> … while reading the lives of Our Lord and the saints, he would stop to think, reasoning with himself: 'How would it be, if I did this which St Francis did, and this which St Dominic did?' And thus he used to think over many things which he was finding good, always proposing to himself difficult and laborious things. (1996a, 7)

Ignatius has much maturing to do at this point, and much to learn. It must also be admitted that he does not directly use the word 'reflect' here. But the dynamic is there already: you read, you think about the story, and you respond by doing something that is not exactly the same, but is nevertheless similar, nevertheless a kind of response or continuation. By using the word 'reflect' in his instructions for gospel prayer in general, Ignatius is suggesting that this prayer implies a dynamic of pondering the story we are told about, and then responding to it, reflecting it, for ourselves. He is encouraging us to get to know the gospel 'from inside', to become participants in it, and to follow Jesus, its central character, wherever he may be leading us. (Literal and standard translations, unconsciously influenced by Enlightenment preferences for interiority, speak of 'interior knowledge' – and thereby introduce associations surely foreign to Ignatius' mind.) The process is then taken up into the *colloquy* at the end of the prayer, the imaginative conversation that Ignatius encourages us to hold at the end with any one of the characters in the scene, 'asking according to what I feel in me'. That last phrase indicates that the colloquy, which has traditionally been taken as the heart of the whole Ignatian process, will be utterly personal and unpredictable.

We possess an early version of about half of the *Exercises*, probably written by one of the first ten Jesuits, Jean Codure, who died in 1541. Whereas Ignatius' own texts are terse, Codure's is rhetorical, and seems to present what Codure imagined a retreat-giver might actually say. Codure's interpretation of the colloquy at the end of the contemplation is suggestive:

> And here you should set out what you want, not in order to teach God – who knows what you desire before you come to prayer – but in order to inflame your own mind with a greater desire of this gift as you name it and explain it verbally.
>
> (Exx MHSJ, 576: see in bibliography Ignatius 1996c)

For Codure, Ignatian prayer enables the Scripture to awaken our desires. We do not need to tell God about these, because God knows them already – but we do need to become aware of those desires, and perhaps to begin to live our lives in a way that is in tune with what we really want rather than with what convention and duty have made us.

Importantly, too, the impression of remorseless thoroughness in Ignatius' method disappears as we come to appreciate the importance of the retreatant's response. Another of Ignatius' instructions is particularly important in this context:

> ... in the Point in which I find what I want, there I will rest, without being anxious to pass on, until I content myself. (Exx 76)

There is no question of having to cover all the ground. When we have begun to learn something, when our imagination has somehow been caught and our heart stirred, we should break off. Ignatius is schematic, not because he wants to exercise, exhaustively and exhaustingly, every possible use of the imagination. The intention behind the text's comprehensiveness, rather, is to leave scope for each person to find the detail that they need, and then take the process further from there. When we come back to prayer, when we do what the jargon calls a 'repetition' of this kind of exercise, we do not simply do it again – we do not repeat in the standard English sense of the word. We do something closer to the root Latin sense of the word; *repetitio* in Latin means seeking again or asking, petitioning again – we start at the points where we found what we desired, and move forward from there (Exx 62).

Varieties and discernment

The most appropriate response at this point would probably be for the reader to break off and try some version of this sort of prayer, and to compare their own responses with that of others. Only so can one come to appreciate fully how this style of biblical prayer can engage us at levels of which we would normally not be aware, and the sheer variety of ways in which this can happen. Here, we can give simply one example, from Gerard W. Hughes's *God of Surprises*, regarding a gospel contemplation centred on the marriage feast at Cana.

Most conventional meditations on the marriage feast at Cana in the Catholic tradition focus on the relationship between Jesus and Mary; others, more aware of the symbolic dynamics of John's gospel, may take the transformation of water into wine as a sign of how Jesus transforms Jewish tradition and inaugurates the new age, with wine as a symbol of the messianic banquet. But Gerard Hughes tells the story of Fred, an earnest and pious young man, engaged in every possible kind of good work, who thus inevitably arrived at a retreat house to make a retreat. Fred had a vivid imagination and had seen tables heaped with food set out beneath a blue sky. The guests were dancing, and it was a scene of great merriment. 'Did you see Christ?' asked the retreat-giver. 'Yes,' Fred said, 'Christ was sitting upright on a straight-backed chair, clothed in a white robe, a staff in his hand, a crown of thorns on his head, looking disapproving' (Hughes 1985, 36). This was no doubt a strange and rather disturbing experience, but also, in the end, a liberating one. Fred would have at the conscious level certainly believed that God had sent Jesus into the world so that we could have life, and have it to the full. But in his unconscious something much more demonic was at work: here was a young man who simply could not enjoy himself because he was driven by a false sense of piety. With help he was able to recognise that he was suffering from what Frank Lake called the 'hardening of the oughteries'. He began to recognise that he was being driven by a pious caricature, and that life in the Spirit of Jesus involved his learning to relax and to enjoy life.

Quite apart from what this story says about how personal temperament and need determine what Ignatian biblical prayer amounts to, and hence about its radical pluralism, it also shows us that not all of these ways are necessarily constructive. Suppose Fred had come to another sort of retreat-giver, who was even more driven and hung up on duty than he was. The result, surely, could have been disastrous. Fred could have been reinforced in the destructive way he was living his life, and all the more destructive because it could masquerade as being religious. Perhaps, too, some of us do need a prayer experience where Christ comes into our life-world looking disapproving because there is indeed something there for him to disapprove of. The general point is that just because something happens in prayer, it does not mean that it directly indicates how the Spirit of God is at work in our lives. This kind of prayer may get us in touch with movements and desires within us that we might otherwise not know of – but when they do surface, then further testing and sifting needs to be done. When Ignatius talks about how to take a decision on the basis of this sort of prayer, his language is very suggestive. He talks about our making a decision 'when enough light and knowledge is received by experience of consolations and desolations, and by the experience of the discernment of various spirits' (Exx 176). It can only happen when you have had several experiences of this kind, and only by a kind of comparative testing that involves the negative as well as the positive. In that connection, the role of the one who gives the Exercises, or of some kind of spiritual guide in the course of everyday life, may be crucially helpful.

Wider horizons

The principal task has been simply to explain one particularly influential way in which the Bible has been used within the Roman Catholic tradition. But it may be appropriate also to situate this approach to the biblical text more broadly – in terms of cultural history and of theology.

Ignatius lived in the sixteenth century, as Western Christendom began to be formally divided. In many ways, he and his movement represent a 'Counter-Reformation'. One of the issues at stake in the Reformation was, of course, the role and authority of the Bible in the Christian life. Whereas Protestantism has often taken the idea of 'Scripture alone' as a manifesto or slogan, Catholic Christianity has always wanted to see the text of Scripture within a wider context of tradition; and Ignatius' whole method, particularly with its openness to how the scriptural dynamic continues in the lives of Christ's followers here and now, and with its origins in paraphrases of the gospels rather than the biblical text itself, fits surely within that Catholic trend.

But there are other ways of considering early modern Christianity. There was a schism indeed, and if the schism shapes our perspective, then Catholicism appears as something which did not fundamentally change in the sixteenth century – it simply took on, rather belatedly, new energy in reaction to the Protestant threat. Equally, however, one can see the Reformation as a time of far-reaching change that affected Western culture as a whole, and therefore also Western Christianity. Ignatius and Luther encountered the biblical story in different forms, and developed their visions of Church along quite different lines. Nevertheless they are at one in being in the first generation of educated Christians for whom access to the printed book was easily possible. The invention of the printing press brought with it an expansion of possibilities for the human spirit; it made the experience of frequent reading possible, and thereby also significantly enriched the human consciousness that took in this new range of information. The reading of holy texts could become a central Christian practice, and the new sense of interiority this encouraged needed to be expressed and nurtured. Any discussion of the use of the Bible must pay heed to the technologies by which the Bible comes to us. Something radically new happened in Christianity with the invention of printing – something that is now so all-pervasive for us that we can hardly imagine that there was a medieval and early Christianity that lacked that technology. If that kind of observation shapes our thinking, then Ignatius and the great Protestant Reformers come to appear as complementary rather than conflicting figures. And we are left with an obvious question that at present we are still learning to answer: how the new possibilities of our own era might be working an equally far-reaching change in the way Christianity is being lived.

More theologically, and in a more straightforwardly Catholic vein, we need to recognise that Ignatius models for us a rich and helpful account of the word of God and of its workings among us. Ignatian prayer places us within the movement of the biblical text. We come to know the Christian mystery 'from inside'; we come to participate imaginatively in the events which the biblical text narrates. The work of the Holy Spirit that is the Word of God is not – if one follows Ignatius' logic – confined to the written text and to the events of the life of Christ. These represent only a beginning – a definitive and irrevocable beginning, a beginning which we must never forget, but equally a beginning which must be completed, perhaps in ways that we cannot now even dream of. Perhaps, too, Ignatius' sense that the Word of God continues to speak here and now, that the Spirit's work with the Bible is not yet finished, might help us move beyond the sense of paralysis that has crept into mainstream theology at the moment with the recognition how problematic it is to make any claims about what an old text meant in its original context, let alone claims that might ground a life commitment such as that of Christianity. Ignatius' method suggests that the Word of God works through the biblical text in interaction with the circumstances and temperaments of its readers. Within such a vision, the instabilities in our knowledge of the past, and the variety of possible reconstructions of the life and teaching of Jesus are no threat. Rather, they reflect the pluralism and variety that are inherent in the divine Word, a Word from which ever more of the Lord's light and truth can break forth.

Bibliography

Hughes, Gerard W. (1985) *God of Surprises*. London: Darton, Longman & Todd.

Ignatius Loyola (1996a) *Autobiography* [*Reminiscences*], *Diary*, and selected letters, in J. A. Munitiz and P. Endean (trans. and eds), *Personal Writings*. London: Penguin.

Ignatius Loyola (1996b) *Directories* (written also by followers), in M. E. Palmer (trans. and ed.), *On Giving the Spiritual Exercises: the early Jesuit manuscript Directories and the Official Directory of 1599*. St Louis: Institute of Jesuit Sources.

Ignatius Loyola (1996c) *Spiritual Exercises*, 'The Literal Version', in David L. Fleming (ed.), *Draw Me into Your Friendship: a literal translation and a contemporary reading of the Spiritual Exercises*. St Louis: Institute of Jesuit Sources. (Originals in MHSJ *Sancti Ignatii de Loyola Exercitia Spiritualia*, ed. José Calveras and Cándido de Dalmases. Rome, 1969).

Netherwood, Anne (1990) *The Voice of This Calling: an evangelical encounters the* Spiritual Exercises *of Saint Ignatius of Loyola*. London: SPCK.

Pius XI (1929) *Mens nostra*. http://www.vatican.va/holy_father/pius_xi/encyclicals/documents/hf_p-xi_enc_20121929_mens-nostra_en.html

CHAPTER 17:

Bible, music and pastoral theology

PAMELA COUTURE

We sat in the front of the newly built church, neatly painted and comfortable, a symbol of stability and hope for a future. In Kamina, in the southwestern Democratic Republic of the Congo (DRC), we had already visited the Centre des Enfants Malnutris (Centre for Malnourished Children), where, since 1982, children on the verge of slow death from starvation have been fed and comforted until they recovered or died. At the Centre des Enfants Abandonnes (Centre for Abandoned Children) we had already ladled beans, rice, meat and casava onto the plates of eight hundred orphaned children under ten years of age. Many of these children were displaced; they had been separated from their parents as they fled from the war that spread throughout much of the DRC after 1996. We had talked to widows, old and young, who otherwise had little means of support in Congolese society but through the Church's ingenuity had been employed to care for the children.

We had asked to talk with a few 'internally displaced people', refugees within the country who do not qualify for international aid. An announcement in Sunday services four hours earlier invited them to come to the church to tell their stories. Now we sat before a full church – two hundred elderly men and women, men and women in the prime of their lives, children and infants on their mothers' hips or in their fathers' arms. They came to tell us their sacred stories – how they fled from village fires and soldiers' bullets from ten other regions of the DRC, walking from seven hundred to a thousand kilometres to arrive in Kamina where they found the protection and care of their brothers and sisters in Christ. For the next two hours we heard their stories of being hungry, of needing clothing, of resisting solders, of watching their family members die, of protecting church property. When they finished I said, on behalf of the group, 'It has been difficult to listen. We would take away your pain if we could, but we are helpless to do so. In our country we say, "God bless you". It would be our privilege to shake your hands and offer God's blessing.' The Congolese moderator, Revd Kapongo, indicated that they should come forward a row at a time. As they began to form a line, he broke into a spontaneous song: 'Alleluia, Alleluia!' The singing rang, echoed, resounded, as the displaced people sang 'Alleluia!' over our melody 'God Bless You', like the rhythms that overlie one another in African drumming. And I thought, 'These people are alive because they can sing!'

This essay explores the intersection of the Bible, music and pastoral theology through the narrative of Congolese United Methodist singing, as we experienced it in August, 2003 in Kamina, DRC. The music we heard is biblically based, drawing on and interpreting passages in the gospels, Psalms, Pauline letters and Revelation. It is sung with Congolese melody, rhythm, and chord structure in the languages of *kiluba, urrund, bemba, swahili, lingal, tetela, shiluba* and *shona*. In what follows I will interpret the singing we heard in relationship to four functions: joining personal to corporate narratives; transforming emotions; crossing social and economic boundaries; and enacting non-market values. In these four ways music functions as pastoral care and pastoral theology.

Joining their stories to the stories of faith

Architects of twentieth-century pastoral care have long suggested that a primary pastoral function is helping people join their individual narratives to the narrative found in the faith story (Gerkin). In other words, how can I find in my personal story places that connect with the biblical faith, and how does the biblical faith help me understand my life? This meaning-making process is central to pastoral care. It also appears in many settings not generally associated with pastoral care. A recent example of this was reported in the base Christian communities of liberation theology, as in *Love in Practice: the Gospel in Solentename*, where Nicaraguan peasants interpreted the gospel through their life experiences and vice versa (Cardenal). Christian music has often served this function (Wilson-Dickson). For example, Wesleyan hymnody certainly sought to teach the faith and bring people into growth in Christian life and understanding, as studies of the *Collection of Hymns for the People Called Methodist* (1780) have shown (Wesley).

In the last two decades this meaning-making process in pastoral care has been aided by the development of narrative therapy, a counselling process developed in New Zealand in conjunction with the Maori people. In adapting the narrative therapy to pastoral care, writers have formulated the processes by which people create hope for their lives (Wimberly, Lester, Neuger, Kotze et al.). People hope when they are able to identify the core values and identities of their past lives, affirm them in the present, and use them to create a future story. They transform despair into hope when a story that is burdened by the trauma and suffering of the past is retold in a way that takes strength, courage, self-affirmation and meaning into the future.

As biblical songs were sung by these internally displaced people and their brothers and sisters in Christ who have embraced them in Kamina, the songs were literally breathed in and out in such a way that the songs fill the bodies of individuals and the community. The Congolese song fills a person's body so that dancing and clapping and waving arms is as necessary a part of the song as the rhythm, melody, words and musical accompaniment. The Kaminan biblical song creates the identity of a community that willingly takes into it – literally breathing in and out of the body as the body of Christ – the care of widows, orphans and displaced strangers. Like breathing, the care of internally displaced persons is sometimes taken for granted so that Kaminans and refugees are not distinct from one another. After one internally displaced pastor came forward to tell his story, my translator turned to me in surprise and said, 'I never knew he was displaced!' Like breathing, the care of a large internally displaced community sometimes becomes laboured. The exertion caused by emotional suffering and trauma and the scarcity of food, clothing, educational opportunities and income strain the whole community, requiring it to work to catch its breath.

When the people sing and dance together, the body rejoices and hope revives. In a particularly poignant moment that August, half a dozen internally displaced pastors and their wives were presented with bicycles, the primary mode of transportation in Kamina. They had missed the previous year's distribution as they had not yet emerged from the bush and were not known to be alive. One recipient, believed to be over eighty, had defied soldiers by guarding the precious tin roofs intended for new churches and homes – and had lived to tell about it! His struggles as a refugee were not over, nor was his trauma. After the church presented him with a bicycle, however, the music began and he was danced into the circle of presentees by two women half his age. The music filled his body; his legs began to dance; his wizened smile and sparkling eyes kept the beat. It was as if he was singing and dancing with Hannah:

> [The Lord] raises up the poor from the dust;
> he lifts the needy from the ash heap,
> to make them sit with princes
> and inherit a seat of honor.
> (1 Sam. 2:8 NRSV)

Transforming emotions

Hopelessness leads to death; hope bears the fruit of compassion, gratitude and welcome. Singing is a survival strategy for these Congolese Christians because singing transforms the hopelessness that leads to death into the hope that gives life. Singing does so by transforming the emotions. What are emotions? *Affect* refers to bodily changes that occur in response to stimuli, with or without awareness; *feeling* refers to the awareness of affect; *emotion* is a complex mixture of personal memories and associations that are connected to feelings and affect (Rose). Singing in such a way that one's whole body is engaged is dialysis for the soul; it reprocesses the raw emotions of suffering and trauma, giving them form and strength, often creating delight and joy. Singing, playing instruments, and dancing *is* African therapy. This therapy is not only the joining of the personal and the biblical narrative but the fact of the religious experience that is rendered in musical expression itself.

Suzanne Langer, a prominent philosopher of aesthetics, suggests that music exists alongside language as an alternative expression of emotional life. Music is not secondary to language, but a process, like language, by which raw emotion takes on form in order to make expression possible. Music in the presence of sacred ritual has particular transformative qualities. She argues that music in the presence of sacred ritual touches the whole cycle of human emotions – a cycle of life and strength, of humanity, of challenge and death. In religious ritual the outbursts that express our awareness of such emotions become formalised and habitualised. In a spontaneous moment religious ritual and music may express and *relieve* emotions, as I believe our impromptu ritual of blessing did for both the internally displaced persons and those of us who heard their stories. Music in the presence of repeated rituals, such as the distribution of bicycles, forms feeling into a habit, such as welcome and gratitude; the music and ritual then *demonstrate* feeling.

A further transformation occurs, according to Langer, when an act is not the compulsive demonstration of feeling but when it is used to create a feeling, to denote it and bring it to mind. We experienced this use of biblical song when our seven-person plane landed on the airstrip. The community – including, we learned later, the native Kaminans, religious leaders from other parts of DRC who had been attending a meeting and had awaited our arrival before departing, the orphans, widows and displaced persons, many of whom were also pastors and district superintendents – greeted us with song, dance and speeches. In this case the Bible-based words and music were designed to arouse feelings of welcome, gratitude and unity, through emotions associated with our common language – the biblical word. In this form, the musical act – performed by strangers for strangers to be welcomed – becomes a *symbol* of meaning; its expression is a *gesture* of the meaning of welcome that is expected to be associated with the act. Music, particularly in the presence of the sacred, formalises meaning in at least three ways: by catharsis, by demonstrating a felt emotion, and by creating a 'complex, permanent attitude' (Langer, 157ff.).

We use the Bible to communicate desired virtues and habits of character that the biblical story suggests: justice, compassion, gratitude and welcome have been mentioned in this story so far. It seems that in the context of a community such as Kamina, the sung biblical text exerts a power to enable the expression of emotion and to create attitudes that counter hopelessness and are consistent with the biblical message.

Joining narratives and transforming emotions are well-known functions of twentieth-century pastoral care. Now I will consider two functions that are emerging as important in the conditions of the twenty-first century: building community and enacting non-market values.

Crossing social and economic boundaries

A distinction of pastoral care in the United Kingdom has been its community focus. In recent years pastoral theologians in the United States have been thinking and writing about the relationship of pastoral care and the community, particularly the congregation. They have understood pastoral care to have a corporate function of building up the community, not just responding to intrapersonal or interpersonal crises (Marshall, Kornfeld, *Circuit Rider* (the United Methodist periodical for pastors)). For the most part, these analyses focus on the congregation as a place from which various people, ordained and lay, can respond to the suffering that arises within and outside the congregation. In Emmanuel Lartey's work the focus is slightly different. Lartey reinforces this idea when he says:

> Pastoral care is an expression of human concern through activities … Various helping activities such as counselling may offer such an expression but so are *celebrating, commemorating, rejoicing* and *reflecting*, as well as *mourning* or *being present* with people at different times of life. (5)

If much need of pastoral care arises in the midst of the isolation, fragmentation and destruction of communities – a statement that is differently accurate in the postmodern North Atlantic and the war-torn DRC – then the building up of communities is also an appropriate pastoral theology function. Biblical singing is an activity that helps to express, in a communal form, the mourning and the rejoicing that is shared in the community, and in so doing, helps to build its life. It does so, in part, when it bring people together who have different social and economic backgrounds.

Different musical forms, historically, have directly reflected the social and economic classes within which those forms arose in Northern Atlantic countries. For example, symphonic music arose from aristocratic classes, gospel music from slaves and their descendants, bluegrass from lower-class whites, etc. Some musical forms, such as jazz, developed within communities that were willing to cross established social and economic boundaries in order to make music together. Music that is performed may draw more homogeneous audiences, but participatory music tends to bring together people of different social and economic classes. Participatory music communities bring together persons of different social and economic backgrounds who otherwise would not meet or talk with one another, because they enjoy making music together. At music festivals where pickup groups play together, one learns a new friend's favourite tunes and style of playing long before one learns whether the new musical friend is a corporate manager or a person who lives on the verge of homelessness. In newly emerging orchestras of senior citizens it is irrelevant whether one was formerly a physician, a waitress, or a housewife.

In Kamina musical events also drew together people of different social and religious classes. In one case, the government commissioner (an official who functions as a county executive of a region the size of the state of New Jersey) visited our group to discuss the political and economic situation facing the DRC. He spoke to us of the widely held conviction that President Bill Clinton gave approval for the Ugandan invasion of the DRC in 1996. In this situation the United Methodist Bishop, Ntambo Ntanda Nkulu, had a distinctive strategy: to show government officials that people from the USA who come under church auspices can be trusted to help support Congolese efforts to build the DRC politically and economically. His specific hope is to offer an alternative to the suspicions of the USA that have been aroused by international relationships between the USA, Uganda and Rwanda. In the course of our conversation, Bishop Ntambo spoke of the farewell ceremony in which bikes and hoes would be distributed. The Commissioner asked that hoes be given to some of his people. The bishop agreed. The hoes were presented to the Commissioner by Bishop Ntambo, with assistance from guests from the USA, at the first farewell with the same rituals and in the context of the same biblical singing as the distribution of bicycles. It was deeply reminiscent of Isaiah 2:4:

> They shall beat their swords into ploughshares,
>   and their spears into pruning hooks;
> nation shall not lift sword against nation,
>   neither shall they learn war any more.
> (NRSV)

The conversation and the biblical music, which helps to form habits and attitudes, clearly aimed to provide alternative ways of thinking about the relationship between the DRC and the USA. This alternative offered a vision of transformed economic and political relationships.

In the week that followed the farewell ceremony a second group of Americans arrived in Kamina. The Commissioner invited the Bishop and the new group to a meal at his home – a symbolic action of reciprocity between the church and the government of the two nations. In a second farewell ceremony another kind of social interaction occurred. The Bishop invited a Roman Catholic group to sing. This group's Congolese conductor had Western training and introduced three kinds of music: African biblical songs, traditional African songs and dances, and songs from the European classical tradition. The European songs, sung in the style of a British boys' choir, stretched the Congolese audience into a different way of hearing, even as a rural congregation from the United Kingdom would have been stretched by the African traditional dances. The Bishop specifically quieted a small group that failed to show the kind of respect he expected to be shown by Christians formed by the biblical message.

In both of these events the distinction between performative and participatory music was blurred. The events occurred in the large backyard of the Bishop's house, and specific spaces around the perimeter had been set aside for different groups. Closest to the performers were wooden chairs for guests; behind and around to another side were plastic chairs for church members and others; other areas of lawn had been reserved for children and performers; each ensemble had its own place to sit. Some items were distinctly music or dance performed for the crowd. Traditional numbers called forth participation from the crowd, as some people offered performers money and occasionally children joined the performers in dance. On occasion a few children joined in the dance inappropriately and were chased back to the audience by the Bishop. After the presentation of farewell gifts, the dancers and others in the crowd 'danced' the guests and recipients into the dance, although the high-ranking officials – the Bishop, his wife, the commissioner and his wife – did not dance. Clearly, distinctions and boundaries were maintained, even as people danced to biblical songs. Music does not integrate persons together across social and economic in a seamless process. The music did serve, however, to set in place some of the foundation stones that had been prepared for building bridges across social and economic boundaries that have divided the DRC – rich and poor, low and high, church and state, Roman Catholic and Protestant, traditional Congolese and Western missionary. Appreciation grew, aided by the biblically sung message.

Practising non-market values

Pastoral care and counselling in the United States, and to an extent in countries influenced by the United States, has been shaped by market forces (Couture and Hester). Recent works in pastoral care have shown that economic globalisation and the anthropology and values inherent in the philosophy behind free-market economies continue to infuse the cultures of the United States, other Western industrialised countries, and the world in general (Poling; Louw). These values include a belief in efficiency, the pursuit of self-interest, the eudaemonistic assumption that seeking individual interest leads to the common good, and satisfaction with choices based on utilitarian thinking. These are dependent upon an understanding of time that considers time like money.

In a metaphor that the Congolese (who became miners under Belgian colonisation) would appreciate, for capitalist time is like a mineral to be mined, a scarce commodity that must be extracted from our lives. Time, like money, is hoarded. Paratelic time, or time that suspends goals for the sake of play, is rare (Couture). One of the Bishop's favourite ways of capturing this difference between Americans and Congolese is in his oft-repeated maxim, 'Americans keep time; Africans make time.' Economic understandings of time add to the stress and strain of life in industrialised countries. Efficiency and 'time is money' can eliminate time for deep psychological processing, spiritual connection and discernment, and both the pastoral and the care in modern living.

I have observed in the USA that participatory music groups are arising that help people fight back against this encroachment on time. Amateur participatory groups, from church choirs to bands and orchestras, do indeed have performance goals – but primarily the people who participate are amateurs in the best sense of the word. They make music together 'for the love of it' (Booth).

In Kamina I might have modified the Bishop's maxim by saying, 'Africans fill time.' In one sense of the word our hosts filled our time with a schedule that would make an employer happy; they were not about to leave any of our precious time not filled with an experience of Kamina. I wondered about the close scheduling, about the people we often kept waiting. Their time, I thought in my economic way, was as valuable as ours. Were we respecting their time? After a few days I realised that when an event was announced for 9:00, we were expected at 9:30 or 9:45. Why? For at least the first half hour people gathered – and sang (Saliers). No one waited impatiently; rather, where two or three had gathered, the singing began, continued, and heightened until the guests of honour arrived. No serious business was done without a little party first! In American Methodism we sometimes say that no gathering can take place without food. In Kamina biblical songs functioned as food, the essential nourishment that was shared by all the people. One of the guests from the USA commented, 'It sure was nice not to be rushed all the time.' Booth had been plagued for decades with questions: 'How can anyone defend a "useless" task like practicing the cello? … The questions I faced were precisely those that everyone might well ask about ways of spending time – or wasting it, or salvaging it' (7, 13). This question would never occur to the Methodists of Kamina. Both are necessary, a seamless web of time.

It's a mistake, however, to think that the Congolese believe that life lived exclusively in paratelic time is a life well lived. Rather, they know that it is the relationship between paratelic and telic time (or time with a purpose) and the movement between them that offers good care of self and community. They fill time with singing, but they are also very goal-oriented people. During our visit they wanted to be introduced to economic planning processes so that they could create plans for small businesses, community projects and grants. They had large farming operations already that grew the food for the centres for abandoned and malnourished children, and they wanted to improve their productive abilities. Building the economy of Kamina was something they needed, not only for the care of their own families, but for the care of those whose lives were dependent upon them. And they absorbed the instruction with great concentration. They were eager to balance the paratelic time in which they create community and culture with the telic time that recreates their political and economic society. As they find their balance, perhaps they will teach us how to strike ours. In the United States we tend to devalue paratelic time and deplete ourselves. We are, however, beginning to create time and space for self-care that for some is filled with participatory music.

Conclusion: Singing with the widows, the orphans and the internally displaced persons

The care and inclusion of internally displaced persons is a plumbline for the exercise of justice in the Hebrew Scriptures. In Exodus 20:2 in the preface to the Ten Commandments we read, 'I am the Lord your God who brought you out of the house of Egypt, out of the house of slavery.' In Exodus 22:21–22 widows, orphans and resident aliens are repeatedly identified as those who are most likely to be disenfranchised: 'You shall not wrong a stranger or oppress him, for you were strangers in the land of Egypt. You shall not afflict any widow or orphan.' In Deuteronomy 14:28–29 the idea is introduced of tithes that support priests and widows, orphans and resident aliens. In Deuteronomy 17:13–14 the whole community – those who are not in danger of disenfranchisement and those who are – are enjoined to worship and celebrate the Festival of the Weeks together. Here and in many other places, widows, orphans and resident aliens are a central part of Hebrew religious life. In the DRC the religious community did not need to be enjoined to be 'inclusive' – this wholeness of community embodied religious life together. When the community sang together, the blend of their voices offered no distinction between fed and educated Congolese and those whose food supply and educational system had been dramatically interrupted.

This is not a romantic vision. The care of hundreds of displaced families, widows and orphans in a community already impoverished by the effects of political and economic turmoil is an agapic – loving but wrenching – act. It is not as if rural Kamina is unaffected by modernisation. The war that has been waged by Uganda and Rwanda is largely over control of territory in the DRC that is rich with coltan, a mineral required by computers and cell phones. Mimicking the way the cold war created an arms trade and suffering from war throughout Africa, this war of the turn of the twentieth century creates poverty and suffering in the fight for mineral wealth desired first and foremost by wealthy nations and companies. Where the embodiment of biblical religion meets modernity in a rural town in the DRC, people are singing their faith as part of their survival strategy.

Bibliography

Booth, Wayne (1999) *For the Love of It: amateuring and its rivals*. Chicago, IL: University of Chicago Press.

Cardenal, E. (1977) *Love in Practice: the Gospel in Solentiname*. London: Search.

Couture, Pamela (2003) Time suspended: poverty meets grace, in A. Resner Jr, *Just Preaching: prophetic voices for economic justice*. St Louis, MO: Chalice.

Couture, Pamela D. and Hester, R. (1995) The future of pastoral care and counselling and the God of the market, in P. D. Couture and R. Hunter (eds), *Pastoral Care and Social Conflict*. Nashville, TN: Abingdon Press.

Gerkin, C. (1984) *The Living Human Document*. Nashville, TN: Abingdon Press.

Kornfield, M. Z. (1998) *Cultivating Wholeness: a guide to care and counselling in faith communities*. New York: Continuum.

Kotze, Dirk et al. (eds) (2002) *Ethical Ways of Being*. Pretoria: Ethics Alive.

Langer, Suzanne (1942) *Philosophy in a New Key*. Cambridge, MA: Harvard University Press.

Lartey, Emmanuel (1997) *In Living Colour: an intercultural approach to pastoral care and counselling*. London: Cassell.

Lester, A. D. (1995) *Hope in Pastoral Care and Counselling*. Louisville, KY: Westminster John Knox Press.

Louw, D. J. (2002) Pastoral hermeneutics and the challenge of a global economy: care to the living human web. *The Journal of Pastoral Care and Counselling* 56.4, 339–50.

Marshall, J. L. (1995) Pastoral care in a congregation with social stress, in P. D. Couture and R. Hunter (eds), *Pastoral Care and Social Conflict*. Nashville, TN: Abingdon Press.

Neuger, C. C. (2001) *Counselling Women: a narrative pastoral approach*. Minneapolis, MN: Fortress Press.

Poling, James (2002) *Render unto God: economic vulnerability, family violence and pastoral theology*. St Louis, MO: Chalice.

Rose, G. (1996) *Necessary Illusion: art as witness*. Madison, CT: International Universities Press.

Saliers, Don (1997) Singing our lives, in D. C. Bass (ed.), *Practicing our Faith: a way of life for searching people*. San Francisco: Jossey-Bass, 179–93.

Way, P. (guest ed.) (2001) How can the congregation act as a caring community? *Circuit Rider* 4.25 (July/August).

Wesley, John (1983) *The Works of John Wesley: a collection of hymns for the use of the people called Methodists* vol. 7. Oxford: Oxford University Press.

Wilson-Dickson, Andrew (1996) *The Story of Christian Music*. Minneapolis, MN: Fortress Press.

Wimberly, E. (1991) *African American Pastoral Care*. Nashville, TN: Abingdon Press.

CHAPTER 18:

The Bible and the arts

GAIL RICCIUTI

A group of adults is working in rapt contemplation, absorbed in the books covering a table in their midst. It is Thursday evening, and they have gathered, as they do every other week, for Bible study and sharing in one member's comfortable dining room. The study this night, however, is distinct from the usual words and discussion. To be sure, they will eventually arrive at words (and to their surprise, the conversation will have an unusually energetic flow); but for now, they prowl the glossy pages of these piled art books with silent fascination. The pastor, tonight's leader, has opened the evening with a provocative question: 'What is your "functional" understanding of Jesus Christ? That is, how does your personal Christology companion you in the midst of the daily stresses of being human?' Some of those present are bearing the 'sandwich' responsibility of parenting restless teenagers while providing care for ageing parents. Others are coping with diagnoses of cancer or other serious illness. Financial stress or job loss in a 'downsized' market dogs the heels of many, while one corporate manager is struggling with moral ambiguities in the workplace.

The christological question in itself could loom dauntingly large, but it is soon sized to fit every participant's theological ability. Instead of posing a heady discussion at the outset, the pastor asks these friends to wander through artistic representations of Jesus, both classic and contemporary, 'secular' as well as 'sacred', and to select the one or two that seem to leap out. 'What was it about a particular portrait, sculpted image, or painting that "grabbed" you in this way?' she will ask; and subsequently 'What do the characteristics of this image tell you about your own individual Christology? And how does *that* Jesus sustain you in the midst of trial, crisis or grief?' Their answers, working inductively from a piece of art to lived theology, will surprise the participants themselves. On this night they may also recognise in their own reflections a spiritual strength that for many of them has heretofore functioned only subconsciously but now, through the vehicle of art, skyrockets to articulate knowing.

An imaginative pastor has just brought together the Bible, art and pastoral care in a trinity whose interactivity is reminiscent of the *perichoresis* – the divine 'dance' – of trinitarian theological understanding. The scenario is but a single example, from a panoply of unlimited possibilities, of the synergy available for pastoral application at the junction of Scripture and art. Like tinder and spark, the Bible and the arts strike fire when juxtaposed in such a way that each becomes interpreter of the other: it is not overstating the case to say that they are two *essential* components of a rich pastoral practice. 'Training in perceptual skills is comparable to training in literacy,' says one artist (Milgrom, 5); and if that is so, then biblical literacy can well be seen as an outgrowth of practice in discerning the art in the biblical record, as well as recognising biblical truth in the guise of art. Further, it is in the practice of preaching that the Bible and the arts make most frequent and intimate contact.

The nature of art

If by 'arts' we were to mean primarily visual art, drama and music – the crafted, spoken, and sung – then in this sense, preaching itself is an art form. It builds the bridge between Scripture and life experience; it is a kind of pastoral glue or connective tissue that holds the 'feet' of the people's lives to the fire of divine revelation. However, a weakness in much contemporary Christian preaching is that it has failed to keep pace with the culture in which its hearers have their being. In a social environment saturated with imagery, form, sound and colour, preaching often fails to follow the Bible's own lead in using art as a tool of communication. More importantly, in the observation of Susanne Langer, 'More than anything else in experience, the arts mold our actual life of feeling … Artistic training is, therefore, the education of feeling' (401). The *education of feeling* constitutes the underground root of pastoral theology and practice, if members of the community of faith are to mature in receptiveness toward the movement of God in their lives.

However, great art goes beyond the education of feeling, beyond the articulation of what we cannot otherwise fully express. In her work on liturgy, Catherine Madsen points out that the poetics of liturgy is akin to the greatest art in its complexity and demand upon the participant. 'It need not spell out everything it means us to feel. It leaves something up to experience' (2). It does not do *all* the cognitive work for the one who beholds (or hears) it. 'Good' art also *destabilises* us in the same way that powerful liturgy or the authentic hearing of the word (or skilful therapy or pastoral counsel) does. Just as Scripture calls us to account, so art itself calls the Bible to account in human life. Jacob groans in wrestling with the angel, 'I will not let you go until you bless me.' There is a synergy at work here: the Bible evokes art and inspires artistic interpretation, which in turn *redescribes* its primary text.

It is intriguing that scholars of Christian aesthetic theory (most notably Calvin Seerveld) understand and define art in terms congruent with the self-understanding of practical theologians and pastoral care practitioners. Seerveld identifies the qualifying function or defining component of art as 'allusiveness'. No painting or sculpture, he observes, is merely a xeroxed copy of what meets the eye. 'Instead, the artist apprehends things visible and invisible, very complicated meanings, affairs we all know experientially like sin and love and meekness but could never duplicate in a mirror ...' (1980, 79). One might say it is a way of looking at a text (whether it be a Scripture passage or a human condition) 'slant', in the sense employed by Emily Dickinson:

> Tell all the Truth but tell it slant –
> Success in Circuit lies
> Too bright for our infirm Delight
> The Truth's superb surprise
>
> As Lightning to the Children eased
> With explanation kind
> The Truth must dazzle gradually
> Or every man be blind –
>
> (Poem 1129)

Scripture is often perceived by the casual church member as a judgemental rather than an illuminative document. Witness the appellation 'Bible-thumper' to refer to preachers, in popular parlance! But where an individual congregant or an entire congregation can experience this *slant* view of the biblical text, such defensiveness is derailed at the outset of theological inquiry.

> If the 'allusive mode' of creaturely reality is denied or neglected, or, if in reaction to the fastidious idolatry of aesthetes, one decides to live in aesthetic disobedience, the result is aesthetic closure to life. And a man or woman's life deprived of 'allusive' *shalom*, when school life or church life is unimaginatively dead, is a very sad, impoverished kind of closed-down creaturely existence. (Seerveld 1980,134–5)

Art, the Bible and pastoral practice at its best each share in this 'slant' allusive character of the *intuitive* and *imaginative*, the elements missing in any form of human life that is lived as less than human. The point is reiterated in the more recent work of John De Gruchy, written from a post-apartheid South African context, who notes 'the deep underlying relationship between theological conviction, aesthetics and ethics' (1).

This allusive realm of the visual arts is a medium distinct from the intellectual argument typical of much traditional preaching and pastoral counselling. The kinaesthetic arts (such as dance and drama), as well as music, are also accessed at different levels of consciousness. Those who employ argument as the main (and sometimes exclusive) tool of the pastoral craft make their own work much more difficult than it should be; because argument begs for self-defence or counter-argument. Immediately, the hearer's defences are raised. To use a visual metaphor, the incorporation of art, rather than argument, into pastoral practices, constitutes the difference between setting two adversaries on either side of a fence over which they argue face to face, or setting the two on the same side of the fence so that they contemplate together, with non-defensive interest, what may lie over on the other side – and thus become peers.

Art and the Bible

No matter how the perceived legitimacy of art has ebbed and flowed throughout church history, the Bible over all lays a richly artful foundation for faith and practice. The biblical story begins with the metaphor of a Creator's experimental crafting of earth and skies, filling them with what is 'pleasant to the sight' (Gen. 2:9). Although later writings, from the Deuteronomic reforms (seventh century BCE), banned sacred images from the Temple, the book of Exodus incorporates artistic vocation, artistic activity and spirit. When Moses put forth the call for the skilled to come forward and make the appointments of the holy place commanded by the Lord, the people's response included human artistry: 'All the skillful women spun with their hands, and brought what they had spun in blue and purple and crimson yarns and fine linen; all the women whose hearts moved them to use their skill spun the goats' hair' (Exod. 35:25–26 NRSV). It seems significant that the first biblical personage described as being full of the Holy Spirit is Bezalel, the craftsman who – along with his co-artisan Oholiab – became responsible for adorning the tabernacle. Exodus 35:31–33, 35 delineate the importance of this calling as strongly as any other biblical text:

> [The Lord] has filled [Bezalel] with divine spirit, with skill, intelligence, and knowledge in every kind of craft, to devise artistic designs, to work in gold, silver, and bronze, in cutting stones for setting, and in carving wood, in every kind of craft … He has filled [Bezalel and Oholiab] with skill to do every kind of work done by an artisan or by a designer or by an embroiderer in blue, purple, and crimson yarns, and in fine linen, or by a weaver – by any sort of artisan or skilled designer. (NRSV)

The parallelism of skill, intelligence and knowledge in craft with the fullness of divine spirit is strikingly clear: these artistic gifts come directly from God's hand, and thus are closely linked with the indwelling Presence. The four succeeding chapters comprise a rich description of Bezalel's work, with other artisans as supporting cast – a sensuously detailed description of the architecture and appointments of tabernacle, ark, court, lamp stand, altar and vestments. All of this is paradoxical, of course, in light of the commandment of Exodus 20:4 against the making of sculpted images of anything in heaven or on earth; but the distinction seems to centre on the second part of the commandment, forbidding the making and worshiping of *idols*: 'You shall not bow down to them or serve them.' It seems apparent that the God of Israel not only invites artistic co-creation by human beings, but also personally enjoys participation in the creative act and its results.

Again and again, we find biblical texts in which some form of art or artistry functions as communicative of God's voice and leading. God lushly creates *ex nihilo* at the genesis of the earth; sends graphic prophetic visions such as the mysterious and fearsome 'handwriting on the wall' of Daniel 5 (a 'divine' form of the ancient cave drawings?); inspires the Psalmist to extol 'the work of your fingers' (Ps. 8:3), handiwork proclaimed by the firmament (19:1); and speaks through vivid symbolic depictions in the eschatological writings of the New Testament canon (such as Revelation). Jesus himself teaches principally through the fascinating word-pictures of story – speaking in parables, metaphors, images, verbal paintings, twists of plot, using all the resources of the imagination. Indeed, 'without a parable he taught them nothing' (Matt. 13:34). In surveying the rich interweaving of art and artistry throughout the Bible, it is evident that such truth cannot be adequately conveyed except through the allusive quality of art.

The Church and the arts: a rocky relationship

Given the kinship between Scripture and the arts, and their relevance to pastoral practice, it is somehow surprising that Christian artists, like other artists (poets, composers, actors, choreographers), 'normally live hand-to-mouth as eccentric outcasts from many a Bible-believing communion' (Seerveld 2000, 41). In questioning how that state of affairs has come about, Seerveld rightly suggests that much is at stake for the community of faith that does not parallel its prayer list of missionaries with a prayer list of artists as well.

Although the first Christians had adopted and transformed pagan symbols to decorate the walls of the catacombs, church fathers like Clement of Alexandria did not approve of adornment of the sanctuary, or (as with Tertullian) tolerated only minimal, prescribed symbolism. Change came with Pope Gregory the Great (590–604), who regarded art in the Church positively and saw Byzantine art, with its gold mosaic backgrounds, as a potential teaching aid richly suggestive of the world beyond. While the sixteenth century saw the height of artistic creativity in the Roman Church, the leaders of the Protestant Reformation waged a fierce battle against iconography on the grounds that representational art detracted from the focus on salvation through faith alone revealed in the Word. This puritanical influence has perpetuated the suspicion of art within Protestant churches to the present day, a kind of dis-ease with aesthetic concerns. In his work on the imagination as a 'means of grace', Leland Ryken observes that Christians often distrust the arts, both because their theology is inadequate and because they misconceive the nature of art. Imagination itself has also been historically suspect in the Church since medieval times, when holistic perception, skill with spatial and visual patterns, and intuition – what is called 'right-brain thinking' today – was associated with the demonic. Such fears are readily understood in light of the nature of intuitive perception, which, because it is beyond conscious control, is ungovernable and thereby a potential threat to the 'powers-that-be'. Webster's *New Collegiate Dictionary* (1977) still includes, among several definitions of imagination, 'fanciful and empty assumption'. It is easy to strike fear into the heart of many a Christian by pointing out that the incorporation of the arts makes biblical preaching a 'sensuous' experience; since most of us have confused the meaning of the word with the connotation of 'sensual'. However, while 'sensual' implies indulgence of the physical appetites, the sensuous is that which possesses a strong sensory appeal through imagery aimed at the senses. For all our squeamishness about the concept, it is in fact the Bible's own approach to transmitting words of life. Perhaps, however, whatever modern reluctance remains in understanding art as an interpreter of Scripture (or at the least a worthy companion to Scripture) stems from a tendency to confuse art with kitsch, the 'backside' of art. Those who mistake the latter for the former inadvertently but rightly perceive the way pastoral care might be cheapened or rendered ineffective, counterproductive, or even damaging thereby.

A note about kitsch

Much that passes for 'biblical' art has been bad art (or kitsch), in that it lacks such allusiveness. 'Art' that attempts to oversimplify, wrap up all answers, and leave no suggestiveness or beckoning questions to entice the observer is as lacking in quality as the artless preaching that thrusts solutions at congregants rather than helping them to seek and discover emerging answers for themselves. Kitsch is the kind of art that 'specializes in shallow emotion' (Brand and Chaplin, 107). It is work in any of the arts that is pretentious, inferior, or in poor taste. The word itself comes from the German, meaning 'to put together sloppily' but is most often used to describe what oozes sentimentality. Kitsch fakes the affect of deep emotion, but without employing the rigorous artistic process by which those depths are genuinely accessed. It is said to depend upon 'immature sincerity' (Seerveld 2000, 145); it introverts or insulates one from the messiness of the real world, distancing us from the complications of community – thereby shrinking human experience rather than making it more expansive. It deals in cliché, never the grasp of a new or radically transformative insight. As Seerveld so vividly describes, kitsch 'wallows in self-congratulatory longing, superficially fulfilled, and therefore encourages one to be babyish' (1980, 63f.). It feeds our hunger for nostalgia.

Unfortunately, in these very ways it is a medium fit for those who would oversimplify the Bible or see the thrust of the biblical witness as shaped by dichotomy without complexity.

> The bane of the arts in preaching is using them simply to illustrate what we know – a misuse to be decried along with proof texting from the Bible. We are taking arts seriously in preaching if unexpected insights emerge in the sermon as a result of including the art form – insights that add to or alter what we originally intended to communicate before we engaged the art. (Adams, 20)

Clearly, in light of these definitions there is a certain kind of pastoral practice that is at heart kitsch-related: the sentimental 'comfort' easily offered in crises that defy cheap solutions, the encouragement of a childish dependency upon the practitioner (whether intentional or inadvertent), or the manipulation of emotions to lead in a direction predetermined by the counsellor. Through its very shallowness and sentimentalism, kitsch deadens feeling. As much as fine art has to do with biblical truth, those who seek to engage the conversation between art and the Bible should do so with caution, so as never to subvert the power of sacred text to awaken feeling, to trade a heart of flesh for a heart of stone (Ezek. 36:26).

The Bible and the visual arts in pastoral practice

The Jewish artist Jo Milgrom offers one excellent example of a deep intersection between art and scriptural inquiry with her 'Handmade Midrash Workshop' approach. Beginning with the inquiry whether 'marks on paper' interpreting biblical passages could be set up side by side with analytic verbal interpretation to yield a more integrated understanding of the text, Milgrom developed a technique that overcomes the 'poverty of symbols' bred of our science-oriented culture. Seeking to recover symbolic access to the process of the Bible itself, she invites seekers to respond to study of the biblical text by tearing and pasting paper or muslin in a method designed to set the interference of ego aside and 'allow fragments of fantasy to emerge into consciousness' (6). The simplicity of this 'hands-on creative art play' disarms natural inhibitions and frees the student to follow the unique trajectory of the text. The abstract shapes that ensue are always suggestive and often revelatory, reflecting the principle that 'Creative analogy makes the familiar strange in order to see it in a new way' (10). Once again, we hear the echo of Seerveld's defining characteristic of art as allusiveness: one [strange] thing leading to another [new] understanding. What Milgrom observes about this creative process also applies to the deeply artful design of the Bible itself: 'Handmade *midrash* is not art for art's sake; it is form for symbol's sake.'

A congregation that has cultivated an integration of the arts with their biblical understanding and ecclesial identity is the episcopal parish of St Gregory of Nyssa, Potrero Hill, San Francisco. Art is so pervasive of congregational life and spiritual nurture – including dance, iconography, architecture, folk art (vestments made of African cloth, Ethiopian processional standards, a Thai howdah used as a presider's chair) and music (ancient and modern, from Gregorian chant to Hebrew strains and Shaker rhythms) – that it is the natural vehicle for all that goes on pastorally in the church (Bush, 18). Drama pervades the order of worship. The gospel is symbolically carried through the congregation to be touched or kissed. Saints from every age, circle-dancing hand in hand, encompass the worship space in a life-sized mural of contemporary icons. The iconographer, a young African American artist, Mark Dukes, read the Bible for the first time while in art school; and he alludes to the powerful conjunction of Scripture and artistry in his own experience when he reflects upon his vocation to paint holy icons: 'I want to speak eloquently about things of a high order' (Barger, 5). From such creative diversity, visual symbolism and colour, St Gregory's also draws its sustaining stamina for mission.

Like the imaginative pastor at the art-covered dining table, pastoral practitioners who understand the organic (indeed, even inseparable) relationship between the two realms of Bible and art will be on a continual mission to find or create resources to facilitate the juxtaposition of fine art with biblical teaching. It is no small part of our vocation among the people to 'intrigue' them into the realm of God, feeding the hunger God has planted in all hearts for beauty, fascination, liveliness, colour, mystery, adventure, risk and surprise. Both Scripture and the arts are vehicles for all of those. Employing them to tell the Truth 'slant' is deeply integral to the calling to be a conduit for the Spirit to transform the community of faith, creating space for God to speak to contemporary life.

Bibliography

Adams, Doug (1978) Scripture, dance, and visual arts in the shape of preaching, in *Authority and Creativity in Preaching*, Papers of the Academy of Homiletics. Princeton, NJ, 20–8.

Ballard, P. and Couture, P. (eds) (2001) *Creativity, Imagination and Criticism: the expressive dimension in practical theology*. Cardiff: Cardiff Academic Press.

Barger, M. (2003) The light within: an interview with Mark Dukes. http://gods-friends.org/Vol16/No3/Light_Within.html (accessed 25/11/03).

Brand, H. and Chaplin, A. (1999) *Art and Soul: signposts for Christians in the arts*. Carlisle: Solway.

Brown, F. B. (2000) *Good Taste, Bad Taste, and Christian Taste: aesthetics in religious life*. New York: Oxford University Press.

Bush, T. (2002) Back to the future. *The Christian Century* Nov. 20–Dec. 3, 18–22.

De Gruchy, J. W. (2001) *Christianity, Art and Transformation: theological aesthetics in the struggle for justice*. Cambridge: Cambridge University Press.

Dickinson, Emily (1976) *The Complete Poems of Emily Dickinson*, ed. T. H. Johnson. Boston, MA: Little, Brown & Co.

Langer, Susanne (1953) *Feeling and Form*. New York: Scribner.

Madsen, Catherine (2003) Love songs to the dead: the liturgical voice as mentor and reminder. *Crosscurrents*. http://www.crosscurrents.org/madsen.htm (accessed 19/09/2003).

Milgrom, Jo (1992) *Handmade Midrash: workshops in visual theology*. Philadelphia: The Jewish Publication Society.

Ryken, Leland (2002) The imagination as a means of grace. *Communique: A Quarterly Digital Journal*. http://www.communiquejournal.org/q4/q4/_ryken.html (accessed 25/02/2002).

St Gregory of Nyssa Episcopal Church, San Francisco. http://www.saintgregorys.org (accessed 14/11/2003).

Seerveld, C. (1980) *Rainbows for the Fallen World: aesthetic life and artistic task*. Toronto: Tuppence.

Seerveld, C. (2000) *Bearing Fresh Olive Leaves: alternative steps in understanding art*. Toronto: Tuppence.

Index of Biblical References and Names

Because Scriptural passages are often indicated by allusion rather than explicit textual reference an index of names has been appended to the normal list of references, enabling the reader the better to trace the use of the biblical material in the discussion.

The Hebrew Scriptures or Old Testament

The New Testament

Biblical Names

Index of Names and Subjects